# Build Your Own Pentium® Pro Processor PC

## Aubrey Pilgrim

**McGraw-Hill**

New York  San Francisco  Washington, D.C.  Auckland  Bogotá
Caracas  Lisbon  London  Madrid  Mexico City  Milan
Montreal  New Delhi  San Juan  Singapore
Sydney  Tokyo  Toronto

**Library of Congress Cataloging-in-Publication Data**

Pilgrim, Aubrey.
    Build your own Pentium pro processor PC / Aubrey Pilgrim.
        p.   cm.
    Includes bibliographical references and index.
    ISBN 0-07-050187-4  (p).  — ISBN 0-07-050186-6  (h)
     1. Pentium (Microprocessor)  2.  Microcomputers—Design and
construction.   I.  Title.
    QA76.8.P46P53   1996
      621.39'16—dc20                   96-18005
                                              CIP

## McGraw-Hill

*A Division of The McGraw-Hill Companies*

1 2 3 4 5 6 7 8 9 0   DOC/DOC   9 0 1 0 9 8 7 6

ISBN  0-07-050187-4 (PBK)
       0-07-050186-6 (HC)

*The sponsoring editor for this book was Brad Schepp, the editing supervisor was Lori Flaherty, and the production supervisor was Pamela Pelton. It was set in ITCCentury Light by Jana Fisher through the services of Barry E. Brown (Broker—Editing, Design and Production).*

*Printed and bound by R.R. Donnelley & Sons Company.*

 This book is printed on recycled, acid-free paper containing a minimum of 50% recycled, de-inked fiber.

McGraw-Hill books are available at special quantity discounts to use as premiums and sales promotions, or for use in corporate training programs. For more information, please write to the Director of Special Sales, McGraw-Hill, 11 West 19th Street, New York, NY 10011. Or contact your local bookstore.

# Contents

# Acknowledgments

There are several people who helped make this book possible. First I want to thank Brad Schepp and all of the editors at McGraw-Hill.

Joanne Hasegawa of Intel was a great help in sending me photos and information about the Pentium Pro. I had a lot of difficulty in procuring a Pentium Pro motherboard when they were first available. Most of the motherboards were allocated to large corporations. Joanne put me in contact with ASUS Computers and Jeanette Hong. Jeanette arranged to ship me one of the first ASUS 200MHz Pentium Pro motherboards.

I especially want to thank Julie Di Bene of Micronics for arranging to send me a 150MHz Pentium Pro motherboard for testing and evaluating. She cut through lots of red tape at Micronics to make sure that I got a motherboard for this book. Julie also was responsible for the Micronics Pentium M54Li motherboard that I used for the Cyrix 6x86 system. I am very grateful for her help.

Kim Stowe of the Diamond Corporation was very helpful in providing me with a Stealth 64 Video Accelerator for testing and evaluating. That accelerator helps make the Pentium Pro a pleasure to operate.

To all of these good people, thank you very much for all your help.

# Introduction

Every day more and more ways are being found to use the computer. In most cases, the technology is making life simpler and better for all of us. However, quite often, computers are being used to take over and perform jobs that were once done by human beings. For example, most offices have replaced receptionists with telephone answering machines using voice recognition and voice emulation. Many large factories have installed robots to do jobs that humans once did. As each job is taken over by a computer, the displaced person must learn to do something else and compete for a new job or face unemployment. The competition for available jobs is becoming more of a problem every day.

## Build your own and join the revolution

So what is a person to do? You can join the computer revolution and learn all you can about them, or you can face the possibility of being a casualty. One of the better ways to learn about computers is to build your own. This book can help you learn about computers, and even save you a bit of money.

Thomas Alva Edison helped start the present day revolution when he recorded sound on his cylinder wax records. Of course, without any electronic means to amplify the sound, it was rather crude. The vacuum tube was developed a few years later, which put us in an evolution like nothing ever seen before in the history of the world. Soon we had amplified sound, radio, movies, and then TV. Today we have computers that can include all of those technologies and more.

The computer was originally developed to solve mathematical problems. (According to the American Heritage Dictionary, the word *compute* means to "determine by mathematics.") However, it now does much more than that. Besides being a fantastic mathematical problem solver, a computer can record and recall text, graphics, photos, and music. With a modem, it can allow you to communicate with anyone else anywhere in the world who has a computer and modem. It can output speech and recognize spoken commands. Computers are becoming smarter every day and becoming more adept at artificial intelligence. It's enough to give a person an inferiority complex to think that a piece of machinery might be smarter than he or she is.

We have truly become a jaded society. At the time of Thomas Edison, the sight of a bare ankle caused men to become very excited. Women wore high-top shoes and long dresses to deprive men of this scandalous and forbidden pleasure. Today we can go to the beach and see near or total nudity and scarcely an eyebrow will be raised.

We have also become jaded as far as computers are concerned. A few years ago, we were very excited if we could get our hands on a computer with 64K of memory and two floppy drives that could format and read 140K single-sided disks. Today, a 200MHz Pentium Pro computer with 128Mb of memory and a couple of 9GB hard disks hardly causes anyone to give it a second glance.

# Moore's Law

Of course not everyone needs or can afford a top-of-the-line Pentium Pro such as this, but they are available. Besides, at this time, a computer such as this is still rather expensive. If you can wait a couple of years, they might be no more expensive than what an obsolete and lowly 486 costs today. At this very moment, Intel is busily working on the next generation P7 chip. This chip will almost double the number of transistors and power of the Pentium Pro.

A few years ago, a man named Moore studied the microprocessor industry and noticed a very definite trend. He observed that the 286 had 125,000 transistors, more than three times the 29,000 in the XT. Very soon the 386 was introduced with 275,000 transistors, which more than doubled the 286. Then came the 486 with 1.2 million, then soon after the Pentium with 3.1 million, and now the Pentium Pro with 5.5 million. The new P7 will have over 10 million transistors.

The trend is that every 18 months or so the number of transistors and computing power more than doubles. This trend has become so predictable that it is now known as Moore's Law.

Intel said at one time they would eventually have microprocessors with 100 million transistors. According to Moore's Law, it will only take another three or four generations to reach that level, which should occur sometime within the next five or six years. What a fantastic era we are living in.

# Ease of assembly

Despite the extraordinary power of the Pentium Pro, anyone can assemble one. You don't have to be an engineer or electronic technician or know anything at all about electronics or computers. The components all plug together, so there is no need for any soldering. There is also no need for any electronic testing or tuning. The only tools that you will need are a couple of screwdrivers and perhaps a pair of long-nose pliers. Figure I-1 shows some of the tools that you might need. You might not need the wire strippers in the center. You probably won't need the filler for the blank slots on the back of your computer case. However, if you ever have to remove any of the plug-in chips, it makes a great tool for prying them up.

**Fig. I-1** Tools needed to assemble a Pentium Pro.

Except for the motherboard, the Pentium Pro will use the same basic components as all of the previous Industry Standard Architecture (ISA) or IBM compatible computers. The Pentium Pro is no more difficult to assemble than an old XT. In fact, a Pentium Pro is even easier to assemble because we now have *Plug and Play*. I have spent many hours in the past trying to install things such as modems, sound cards, and even something as simple as a mouse. Plug and Play will make it much easier.

## Do you really need a Pentium pro?

There are a lot of people like me who yearn to be the first to own anything that is new. It is called *technolust*. This character flaw has cost me a lot of money. Almost always, anything newly introduced will cost much more. I paid $4450 for my first 486 motherboard that operated at a blazing 25MHz. Today I can get a 486 motherboard that operates at 120MHz for less than $200. The 200MHz Pentium Pro motherboard that I used as a guide to write this book cost $2500. I am sure that, if I had waited for a while, it would probably cost about one-third that amount.

The point is that, if you don't need all of the power of a Pentium Pro at this time, you might be better off waiting for a while. There are still lots of things that you can do with a low-cost 486 or a Pentium. However, just because you might not need a Pentium Pro at this time, don't let that stop you from buying this book. Even if you don't build your own, this book can help you learn a lot about computers.

## Upgrading an older computer

If you have an older computer, you can easily upgrade it. Just pull out the old motherboard and replace it with a new Pentium Pro motherboard. If you are a bit short of money, replace your old motherboard with a low-cost Pentium clone such as those from Cyrix or AMD/NexGen.

Replacing the motherboard in an older system is very easy to do. You can re-use most of the components that you already have. A new motherboard can give you all of the advantages of a new powerful system and save you hundreds of dollars. You can find complete instructions in chapter 3.

Another alternative is to buy a Pentium motherboard and install a Cyrix 6x86 in it. I have seen some Pentium motherboards for sale at this time for less than $200. You can buy a Cyrix 6x86 P150 CPU for $469 and, for less than $700, have a motherboard with almost all of the computing power that you would get from an $1800 150MHz Pentium Pro motherboard. I'll have more to say about this alternative in chapter 3.

# Saving on software

Even if you don't build your own computer, you will need software. Software is every bit as necessary as the hardware. Just as you can't run an automobile without gasoline, you can't run a computer without software. Some software packages can be very expensive. The information in chapter 16 about Surplus Software can help you save hundreds of dollars.

# Overcoming obsolescence

Intel, IBM, Microsoft, General Motors, and all other manufacturers spend millions of dollars each year to develop newer and better models. You might not believe this, but Intel is not spending a lot of money developing the P7 just because they like you and want you to have the latest and best. The reason that they are pushing new products out the door, even before you get home with your latest purchase, is primarily to make obsolete the product that you just bought. They institute high-powered sales campaigns to convince you that you shouldn't be caught dead with the product that was the latest and greatest just yesterday. However, if you buy this new product, it will make you happy beyond belief. After all, if you are satisfied with yesterday's product, then you won't buy a new one.

Another major reason for the constant change is the competition. The competition is always trying to convince you that their product is much better than the other guy's. To stay in business, they must continually offer you something that the other guy doesn't give you.

A third major reason for change is because of technolust. There are many people in this world who must have the latest and greatest even if it means that the kids have to go without a $90 pair of sneakers. I hate to admit it, but I am one of those people who is frequently overcome with lust when I see a powerful new computer.

I am probably committing some kind of sin when I lust in my heart, but I don't care. Because I can't afford to buy some of the new technology stuff, I build my own.

Due to the major forces listed here, the companies must constantly revise, improve, and change their products. Just as surely as change is necessary and inevitable with a new baby, so it is with technology.

If you know what is inside your computer, you won't have to buy a new one every other day. You can just buy the necessary items that will be needed to upgrade and make it every bit as good or better than the latest ones. It is very easy to do. Anyone can do it. This book will show you how.

# How this book is organized

Chapter 1 will have an overall discussion of the major components in a Pentium Pro. Chapters 2 through 9 will discuss each of the major components in detail. Chapter 10 will have photos and detailed instructions on how to assemble a computer.

I suggest that you read each of the chapters before buying your components and starting the assembly. There are hundreds of different components that you can install in your computer to configure it any way that you want to. That is what makes a computer so fantastically versatile. If you are fairly new to computers, these chapters can help you decide what to buy.

If you decide to buy a fully assembled system, you probably will want certain components installed in it, depending on what you are going to use it for. This book can help you determine what to buy.

# The future

We are living in a digitized world. This world allows us to digitize data, photos, movies, sound, speech, music, and virtual reality. Once these objects are digitized, we can change them, compress them, add to them, or manipulate them in hundreds of ways. There are some people who might be unhappy with this digitized world. They might complain that it's not really real. These people had better learn to live with it. It is the vanguard of the future. The Pentium Pro will help make it happen.

# 1
# The powerful Pentium Pro

In this chapter, I will talk a bit about the phenomenal Pentium Pro and why you need one. I will also discuss some of the basics of how a computer works. Some of the most popular and successful books on the market today are those with "Dummy" in the title. I know that you are not dummies. I know that you probably already know how a computer operates, and I do not mean to insult your intelligence. So please feel free to skip the last part of this chapter if you are an old pro.

## Our digital world

One of the most important aspects of the computer is that it allows us to digitize so many things. We can digitize drawings, photos, movies, sound, speech, music, virtual reality, and many other things. Once these objects are digitized, we can compress them, add to them, delete portions, or manipulate them in hundreds of ways. Sometimes it might be difficult to determine reality from virtual reality. A good example was Forrest Gump having a conversation with LBJ who has been dead for several years.

A short time ago, we couldn't do many of the things that we take for granted today because we just didn't have the computer power. The powerful Pentium Pro is going to make it possible to digitize even more of our world.

## The phenomenal Pentium Pro

The 486 was able to perform an instruction in a single clock cycle, even though the clock frequency was faster than any PC ever before. The Pentium Pro has again raised the performance so that it can do several instructions in a single clock cycle, moving 32-bit chunks of data at 200 million times per second (200MHz). The lowly XT can process about 38 million bits per second; the Pentium Pro can process almost 13 billion bits per second.

During the boot up of a 200MHz system, you won't notice much speed difference than a 486. It will also be much the same if you are doing simple word processing or running an older DOS-type 16-bit program. However, it will really whiz when running things like large databases or doing number crunching.

# Ways that the speed is increased

When it comes to computers, speed is everything. The faster that it can process data, the more powerful and better the computer. At this time, the Pentium Pro is about the fastest all around computer that you can buy. (Digital Equipment Corp. has a faster RISC type system, but it is limited in what it can do. I'll have more to say about RISC later in this chapter.) Intel lists three ways to increase the speed of a CPU: add more transistors along with a cache, increase the clock speed or frequency, and increase the number of instructions executed per clock cycle.

The 486DX CPU has an 8K cache built in among its 1.2 million transistors. The Pentium and the Pentium Pro have two L1 8K caches. However, the Pentium Pro also has a close-coupled L2 cache in the same CPU enclosure.

The Pentium Pro also has superscalar technology. The term *superscalar* means that the CPU architecture consists of more than one execution unit or pipeline. The superscalar technology enables the Pentium Pro to process data simultaneously through different pipelines. A pipeline is an arrangement of registers within the CPU. They are also called *execution units*. Each register performs part of a task, then passes the results to the next register. The Pentium Pro can even execute parts of a task out of order.

The early CPUs required several clock cycles to execute a single instruction and the tasks had to be executed in order. The Pentium Pro has multiple parallel pipelines or data streams that allow it to move on to other instructions while waiting for another instruction to finish. So a Pentium Pro can process much more data than a 486 or Pentium in the same amount of time.

## The Pentium Pro cache

When a program is being processed, it is loaded into Random Access Memory (RAM). An electronic signal travels at just a bit slower than the speed of light, but it still takes a finite amount of time. The further it has to travel, the slower the response will be.

Quite often, a program will loop in and out of memory many times while processing data. If a nearby cache is provided, it can process the data much faster. The Pentium Pro has 5.5 million transistors in its CPU, which measures .691 × .691 inches. In among those 5.5 million transistors are two 8K Level 1 (L1) caches. A closely coupled chip in the same package has another 15.5 million transistors for a 256K of Level 2 (L2) cache or 31 million transistors for 512K of L2 cache.

Figure 1-1 shows a Pentium Pro CPU with its heat sink cover removed. The CPU is on the left and the L2 cache is on the right. The 486, Pentium, Cyrix, and AMD CPUs place the L2 cache on the motherboard, which is much less expensive; however, the added distance reduces the processing speed of the CPU.

There are several other undesirable factors such as capacitance, inductance, and resistance involved when moving data at a very high frequency over any long distance. The nearby closely coupled L2 cache of the Pentium Pro has a dual bus that can operate at the 200MHz frequency of the CPU or at ½, ⅓, or ¼ of CPU frequency.

**Fig. 1-1**
A Pentium Pro with the heat
sink cover removed to show the
CPU and the L2 cache. The CPU
is on the left, and the L2 cache
is on the right.

Note that there are more transistors in the L2 cache memory than in the CPU itself. Unlike DRAM, which requires just a single transistor for each bit, this memory
must be made up of fast transistors and requires more than seven transistors for
each bit. Memory will be discussed in more detail in chapter 4.

Figure 1-2 shows an ASUS 200MHz Pentium Pro motherboard and some of the
chips and sockets for chips and plug-in boards. There are three slot connectors for
16-bit Industry Standard Architect (ISA) type plug-in boards and four slots for 32-
bit Peripheral Component Interconnect (PCI) boards. The fourth PCI slot also has a
media bus extension for special multimedia boards. The four white slot connectors
at the lower right corner of the motherboard are for 60 nanosecond (ns) single in-
line memory modules (SIMM) of dynamic random access memory (DRAM) memory.

**Fig. 1-2** An ASUS 200MHz Pentium Pro motherboard.

Below the SIMM slots is the Dallas plug-in battery that provides voltage to the low-power Complementary Metal Oxide Semiconductor (CMOS) transistors in the Basic Input Output System (BIOS). The Dallas battery provides the power for these transistors when the computer is shut down. To the right of the Dallas battery is the AMI BIOS chip. The BIOS chip keeps the date, time, disk types, and boot up information by way of the CMOS transistors.

This AMI BIOS is plug-and-play and can automatically detect hard drives and plug-in boards manufactured to the plug and play specifications. This AMI BIOS looks very much like the older BIOS chips, but it contains flash memory that can be updated as necessary. In the past, when you needed to add a new feature or attribute to the BIOS, you had to buy a new chip. With the BIOS in flash memory, it can be updated with a floppy disk.

Above the PCI slots is the fan that sits over and cools the 200MHz Pentium Pro central processor unit (CPU). There are several other very large-scale integrated (VLSI) chips on the board, which includes the Intel Orion Chipset with input/output (I/O) subsystem. At the top-left part of the motherboard are several upright pins for Enhanced Integrated Disk Electronics (EIDE) controllers for hard disks. It has pins for floppy drive control, which include 360K, 1.2MB, 720K, 1.44MB, and 2.88MB. There are also upright pins for an enhanced parallel printer (EPP) connection. The EPP can allow high-speed external tape backup systems, CD-ROM drives, and other peripherals to be used. In addition, there are two sets of pins for high-speed universal asynchronous receiver/transmitters (UART) serial enhanced capability ports (ECP) for a high-speed modem, a mouse, plotters, printers, or other serial devices. Figure 1-3 is a diagram of the ASUS 200MHz motherboard.

## Faster memory

Most standard DRAM up until now has been 70ns to 80ns. The faster Pentiums and Pentium Pros require much faster DRAM to keep the CPU busy. Many Pentium and Pentium Pro motherboards are designed for a type of DRAM called Extended Data Output, or EDO DRAM. (Some use the even faster Burst EDO.) The EDO DRAM allows faster access and output than the standard DRAM. The motherboard must be designed and have special chipsets in order to use EDO memory. The ASUS 200MHz motherboard that I have does not support EDO, but it does support 60ns fast page mode and symmetric and asymmetric memory.

## Multiple CPUs

For mainframe-type of very heavy multiprocessing computing, two, and up to four, Pentium Pro CPUs can be installed in a symmetrical multiprocessor (SMP) environment to operate in parallel. A few years ago, Intel persuaded 486 motherboard manufacturers to add a second socket for a Pentium upgrade chip. They are now asking manufacturers to add a second Pentium Pro socket to the motherboards so that an additional Pentium Pro CPU can be added.

Intel is developing a special computer for the U.S. Department of Energy. It will have 9000 Pentium Pro processors working together. This will be the world's fastest supercomputer with a trillion operations per second. It will deliver 10 times the performance of today's fastest supercomputers. A computer like this is a little bit more than what the average small office or home office (SOHO) would need.

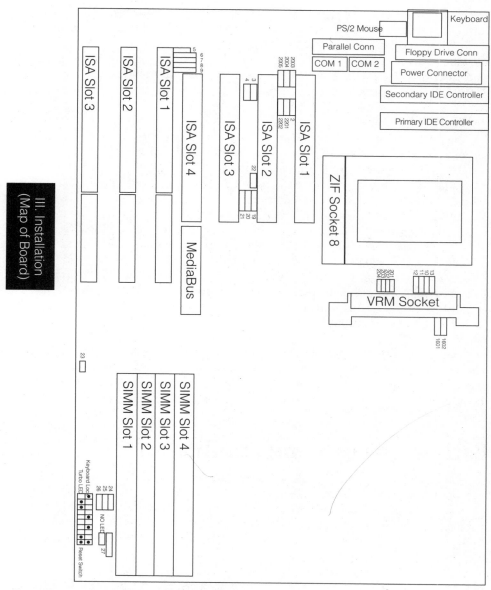

**Fig. 1-3** A drawing of the ASUS motherboard.

We thought that the original PC, which operated at 4.7MHz, was fast. How times have changed. At the present time, Intel has introduced Pentium Pros that operate at 150MHz, 166MHz, 180MHz, and 200MHz. It is expected that a 250MHz CPU will be introduced shortly. The Pentium Pro speed of 200MHz is only 31.6 times greater than the original 4.7MHz; however, because of design improvements, the 200MHz Pentium Pro processes data more than 300 times faster than the original PC.

## Benchmarks

One of the most important measures of a computer's performance is how fast it can process various forms of data. The performance is a function of the different parts of the computer and the type of program that it runs. In 1991, a software benchmark product was developed by the Standard Performance Evaluation Corp. (SPEC) called SPEC91. SPEC is a nonprofit group of computer vendors, system integrators, universities, research organizations, publishers, and consultants from around the world. SPEC91 was revised in 1992 to SPEC92 and to SPEC95 in 1995.

SPEC95 can compare the performance of various computer systems doing compute-intensive workloads. There are two parts of SPEC95: SPECint95 for measuring and comparing integer compute-intensive operations and SPECfp95 for measuring and comparing floating point performance. According to Intel, a 133MHz Pentium has a SPECint95 of 4.14 compared to a 200MHz Pentium Pro with a SPECint95 of 8.09. The 133MHz Pentium has a SPECfp95 of 3.12; a 200MHz Pentium Pro has a SPECfp95 of 6.75.

There are several other benchmarks that can be used to measure the performance of a computer. Norton Utilities has had a Systems Information (SYSINFO or SI) for years. It measured the speed of several of the computer's components against the original XT. The Norton SYSINFO has recently been redesigned as SI32 for 32-bit Windows 95.

# Early software compatibility

The old XT was an 8-bit machine, so the software and hardware developed for it was 8-bit. When the 16-bit 286 was introduced, lots of new 16-bit software and hardware was developed. However, to run all of the original 8-bit software and hardware, it remained downward compatible. When the 32-bit 386 was introduced, very little 32-bit software was developed. Even today, there is still a lot of 16-bit software and hardware on the market.

The Pentium Pro will be able to run all present and past software, but it is optimized to run 32-bit software. It has been criticized because it runs some of the older software a bit slow. There is finally some new 32-bit software on the market and a lot more is being developed. Many software companies are now recompiling and modifying the older software to make it run better and faster on the Pentium Pro.

# Future software compatibility

Software lags behind hardware developments. The 32-bit 386 was introduced in 1985. More than 10 years later, very little software had been developed to take full advantage of the 32-bit bus of the 386 and 486.

For example, the Pentium Pro's floating point operations are several times faster than the fastest 486. However, there are not many general business type applications that can take advantage of this fact. You can expect several new and improved packages very soon. Eventually all newly developed software will be 32-bit. Not too far in the future, we will have 64-bit hardware and software systems.

# The need for a Pentium Pro

If you do nothing but simple word processing, then the original PC or XT might be all that you would need. There are several million 286, 386, and 486 computers in offices and homes all over the world still going strong and doing what they were designed to do. Even if you are processing graphics, large spreadsheets, or large databases, you could probably get by with a low-cost 486. Many vendors are practically giving them away. I have seen motherboards with the AMD 120MHz 586 advertised for less than $200.

To give you an idea how prices have gone down, two years ago, I paid $1350 for a motherboard with a 60MHz Pentium. My two-year old Intel 60MHz Pentium cost almost seven times more than a motherboard with the 120MHz AMD chip. If you don't need the Pentium Pro at the moment and have more time than money, within a year or so, the Pentium Pro prices will be much more reasonable. Of course, by that time, Intel will have the P7 on the market. The P7 will have 10 million transistors, almost twice that of the Pentium Pro.

If you need a lot of power and speed right now, then you should consider the Pentium Pro. Data that might require an hour or more for an XT to process might take less than a few seconds for a Pentium Pro. It is ideal for many PC applications, such as CAD/CAM, manufacturing/process control, financial models, stock trading, desktop video conferencing, multimedia, 3-D design, scientific modeling, mathematics, medical research, database management, speech and handwriting recognition, and many others. It will also allow full-screen motion pictures to run. The Pentium Pro will be ideal for running the 32-bit Windows 95, Windows NT, and OS/2 applications.

A company might be paying an engineer $60 an hour to design and process critical data. If the engineer has to sit and wait for the computer to process the data, the company is wasting money. They are also wasting the engineer's time, which could be better spent doing productive work. In a situation such as this, a Pentium Pro would pay for itself in a short time.

In the past, many networks required a mainframe server. The Pentium Pro can be as powerful as some mainframes, yet it costs just a fraction of what a mainframe would cost. The Pentium Pro is ideal for use as a network server.

# Alternatives to the Pentium Pro

There are several alternatives to the Intel Pentium Pro. At one time, Intel owned all of the multi-billion dollar 80x86-type CPU market. Because they had no competition, they could do just about anything they wanted. They could charge any price that they wanted and release only whatever products they wanted to. They could leave a product on the market and milk it dry. They weren't necessarily motivated to make a lot of investments to improve the product. However, they are finally getting a bit of competition.

Intel still owns about 80% of the CPU market, but because their competitors are yapping at their heels, they have had to constantly introduce new and better CPUs. No longer can they introduce a CPU like the 486 and sit back and relax. Advanced Micro Devices (AMD), NexGen, and Cyrix introduced clones that were faster and less expensive than the Intel 486. Intel fought back by introducing the Pentium and waging a campaign to convince users that the 486 was dead. (That isn't necessarily so. The inexpensive 486 can still run many programs as well as the Pentium or Pentium Pro.)

The cloners answered with their own 586 CPUs. (The next generation chip should have been called the 586, but Intel could not patent these numbers, so they settled for the name Pentium, which they could patent.) Some models of the clone 586 chips were faster and more powerful than the equivalent Intel Pentium. In every case, the clones were less expensive.

There was still a lot of life left in the Pentium, but Intel was forced to keep a step ahead, so they introduced the Pentium Pro. AMD and NexGen have merged and will have introduced their Nx686 or K6 by the time you read this. The Cyrix 6x86 is on the market and available at this time. Cyrix does not have its own foundry to grow the silicon chips, so it has contracted with IBM and SGS Thompson to use their foundries. Part of the deal with these companies is that they can sell the Cyrix 6x86 on their own. Being in partnership with IBM and SGS Thompson gives Cyrix a lot of clout and ensures that they will be able to provide plenty of product.

The AMD K6 and the Cyrix 6x86 will be software compatible with the Pentium Pro, but not pin compatible. You will not be able to install a K6 or 6x86 in a motherboard designed for the Pentium Pro. However, the 6x86 is pin compatible with the Pentium and can be installed in some of those motherboards. Some of the clone CPUs might be faster than an equivalent Pentium Pro. At the present time, the clones do not have the enclosed close-coupled L2 cache; however, they might offer other benefits not available on the Pentium Pro. They will also be considerably less expensive. Figure 1-4 shows a Cyrix 6x86 with the cover removed.

**Fig. 1-4** A Cyrix 6x86 CPU.

As you might expect, Intel is working very hard to get their next generation, the P7, ready for market. Of course, AMD and Cyrix are also working on clones of the P7. Isn't competition great for us consumers?

## CISC versus RISC

Another alternative to the Pentium Pro are RISC systems. The original PC and all PCs up through the Pentium Pro are complex instruction set computers (CISC). This means that the CPU has a set of complex instructions built into it. Whenever it is asked to perform a task, it might have to sort through several hundred instructions to find the ones needed to accomplish the task. Having to sort through the instructions takes a finite amount of time that slows the CPU.

A reduced instruction set computer (RISC) might have to sort through less than half the number of instructions to perform a task. The DEC Company has developed the fastest RISC chips. Their Alpha 21164 operates at 400MHz. The IBM/Apple/Motorola PowerPC RISC chip has 2.8 million transistors and can perform 100 million instructions per second (MIPS).

The RISC computers can use most of the same hardware, such as plug-in boards and disk drives, that the CISC computers use, but they require special software. When I press an *A* on my CISC computer keyboard, a voltage signal is sent to the CPU and certain transistors are turned to process the *A* in the DRAM and to display an *A* on the monitor. If I were using a RISC computer, a different set of transistors is turned on to accomplish the same thing.

The software for CISC and RISC computers are like two different languages. Just like there are interpreters that can translate between two different languages, there is software that can translate between CISC and RISC. The interpreters are also called *emulators*. The Digital Equipment Company, and some others, are now adding chips to their systems that can emulate CISC software. However, the translation or emulation takes a finite amount of time and slows down the high speed of the RISC.

There are well over 100 million PCs in use that are based on the Intel 80x86 architecture. There are thousands and thousands of vendors competing for this PC market. The large number of vendors has made the market very competitive. This competition has made the computer industry about the only industry in the world where the prices continually go downward. The intense competition also causes the manufacturers to continue to develop new and improved products.

At the present time, DEC has little or no competition for its Alpha system. The IBM-Apple-Motorola PowerPC also is a lone product with no competition.

Ideally, to get the optimum speed from a RISC computer requires that native software be developed for RISC. However, there are millions more CISC computers than there are RISC. The software developers spend most of their resources developing for the largest market. At the present time, there are less than 1500 software titles available for the Digital RISC systems. Most of these are based on Microsoft's NT. There are literally tens of thousands of software packages based on the CISC x86 systems.

If a software developer has a choice of developing a program that can run on 100 million machines or use his time to develop a program that will only run on a very limited number, what system do you suppose he will choose? The same thing is true for the PC hardware designers and developers. They are all going to go with the greater opportunity for sales.

Another big factor working against RISC machines is that there is no standardization. RISC systems from different companies require different software. Even the PowerPCs produced by the coalition of IBM and Apple each requires different operating software. At this time, the Pentium Pro is the fastest and most powerful system that can run all existing PC software.

There is no doubt that the RISC systems have some advantages over the CISC systems. However, it is highly doubtful that the RISC systems will ever become as prevalent as the CISC systems. At least not for awhile. In the meantime, I would suggest that you stay with the Pentium Pro CISC systems.

There are several different RISC CPUs, and Intel has several Pentium Pro CPUs that operate at different frequencies. At the time of this writing, a comparable RISC CPU costs much less than what an Intel Pentium Pro CPU costs. However, as Intel manufactures more of Pentium Pro chips, the yield that they get from each batch will become greater and the costs will go down. Another reason for Intel to lower the prices on their CPUs is that they now have some competition from AMD/NexGen and Cyrix.

At this time, there are very few manufacturers of RISC motherboards for end users. IBM and a few other companies are manufacturing a limited number of RISC motherboards for original equipment manufacturers (OEMs). There are many more Pentium Pro motherboard manufacturers for OEMs and end users. The competition will keep the prices fairly reasonable.

As the CISC CPUs become more powerful and faster, many of them are adopting RISC internal operations. Many of the RISC CPUs are developed with some CISC operations. There is no law that says a CPU must be a pure CISC or RISC; the designers are taking a bit of the best of each to form a better CPU.

## Cost

Again, I don't like to mention prices because, by the time you read this, they will have changed. However, for comparison purposes, at the present time, prices for Pentium Pro CPU chips are:

- 150MHz is $974
- 180MHz is $1075
- 200MHz with a 256K L2 is $1325
- 200MHz with a 512K L2 is $1989

Prices quoted are for each in quantities of 1000. The Intel Pentium 120MHz is $357, and the Cyrix 5x86 120MHz is $159.

When the 486 and Pentium CPUs were first introduced, they were about as expensive as the current price of the Pentium Pro. Intel is having very good yields for their Pentium Pro. Because of the good yield and because of a bit of competition, within six months to two years, the cost of a Pentium Pro will be about half of the present cost listed earlier. If you can afford to wait, I guarantee that it will cost you less. However, just think of all the benefits that you might miss by waiting. Besides, by that time, the P7 will be out, and the Pentium Pro will be as obsolete as the Pentium is at this time.

# How computers work

You don't have to be an automotive engineer in order to drive a car; however, if you were going to build one from parts, you probably should know a little bit about an automobile. Though not absolutely necessary, you should know a little bit about computers before assembling one. Incidentally, if you bought the parts to assemble an automobile, it would cost about three times as much as it would to buy a car off the showroom floor. However, there is a whole lot of difference in the computer industry and the auto industry.

You can buy the components to assemble a computer for a lot less than what a dealer would charge for a complete system. The cost of almost everything imaginable is constantly going up except for the computer industry. At one time, I listed prices of parts in my books. However, by the time the book was published, the prices had completely changed. Even the ads that you see in computer magazines might have changed from the time the ads were made up and when the magazine was published. Isn't it great to be living in an era like this?

Here are some of the basics of how a computer operates that will help you select the components to build a Pentium Pro system.

Computers only work because of voltage and because we can control the voltage very accurately and route it to wherever we want it to go. We can control and route the voltage by means of several electronic components and devices, such as capacitors, resistors, coils, transformers, and transistors.

Electricity is the lifeblood of a computer. Under the control of the software and hardware, small voltage signals are sent to different areas of the computer to accomplish the various tasks.

All matter is made up of atoms. Atoms are made up of a nucleus that contain a given number of protons and neutrons and several electrons in orbits around the nucleus. The number of protons, neutrons, and electrons in the atom will depend on what the substance is. Ordinarily, the number of electrons in orbit around a nucleus balances the protons and neutrons in the nucleus. However, electrons can be displaced from the orbits of some substances. When this happens, there is an imbalance. Just as water will seek its own level, an atom that is imbalanced will try to regain its balance.

Italian Count Alessandro Volta (1745-1827) developed the first battery. We have improved batteries considerably since then, but they still use the same basic principle. We have also developed electric generators since then. We can use batteries and generators to create an imbalance of electrons.

Batteries and other electric sources have two electrodes: a positive and a negative (or ground). The negative pole will have an excess of electrons. If we provide a path with no resistance between the electrodes, the excess electrons will rush through the path at almost the speed of light to get to the positive pole.

If we place something, such as a light bulb, between the two poles, the bulb will light up. The reason the bulb lights up is because the bulb filaments are made of a material that offers a resistance to the flow of electrons. The resistance causes heat, and the bulb filaments will glow white hot, which gives off the light.

If we place a motor in the path between the electrodes, the flow of electrons through the coils of wire around the rotor will create a magnetic force, which will cause the rotor to spin.

Soon after the battery was developed, Georg Simon Ohm (1789-1854) discovered that there was a direct relationship between the amount of voltage, the resistance of the path, and the number of electrons passing through the path. Resistance (R) is equal to the voltage (E) divided by the current (I). This is known as *Ohm's Law.*

Using Ohm's Law, if we know any two values, we can determine the other one. Electrons moving through a circuit can be called *current*, which is measured in *amperes*. An ampere is a very large number of electrons that pass a given point in a given amount of time. It was named for French mathematician Andre Marie Ampere (1775-1836).

When presented with two or more resistive paths, the electricity obeys Ohm's Law exactly. Using Ohm's Law, circuits can be designed in thousands of ways to make electricity work for us by controlling and directing it to where we want it to go. We can control voltage with switches, transistors, resistors, capacitors, inductive coils, transformers, and various other electronic components.

The first and foremost reason that we have computers today is because we have transistors. The transistor effect was discovered by three scientists working in the Bell Labs in the late 1940s. The scientists—William Shockley, John Bardeen, and Walter Brattain—were awarded a Nobel prize in 1956. (I believe that the importance of the discovery and development of the transistor should rank right up there alongside the discovery of the wheel and fire.)

A very basic computer, the Electronic Numerical Integrator and Computer (ENIAC), was developed in the early 1940s. We had no transistors in those days, so the computer used thousands of vacuum tubes and cost millions of dollars. It took several large rooms to house one of these computers. It was used during World War II to calculate cannon trajectories. It took 30 to 40 hours for hand calculations for each trajectory, but the new computer could do it in 30 seconds. It could perform fewer functions than a present day $2 calculator. Computers now can do the same trajectory calculations in about 30 nanoseconds.

Technology made a quantum leap forward when the transistor was invented in the mid 1940s. So how do we get those transistors to work for us? We use software that instructs the computer to turn the transistors on and off to perform the various tasks. Although most software is something that is written, when it is typed into the computer from a keyboard, each time a key is depressed, it generates electrical pulses that turn the transistors on and off. When the software is loaded in from a disk, the magnetic flux of the disk is converted to electrical pulses that are identical to those created by the keyboard. The end result of all software applications, no matter how they are input to the computer, is to cause the generation of on and off voltages that control the transistors.

Ordinarily, the more complex the software and the more transistors available, the more work that a computer can accomplish.

The transistor can act as a switch. It has three basic elements: the collector, the base, and the emitter. Suppose the collector of this transistor is connected to the positive pole of a 6-volt battery and the emitter is connected to the negative pole. No voltage or electrons will pass through the transistor. However, if we connect a small voltage, as little as a millionth of a volt on the base of the transistor, it can act like a switch and allow electrons to flow through the transistor from the negative pole to the positive pole of the battery. So a very small voltage on the base of a transistor can cause it to switch a much larger voltage on or off.

The transistor can also act as an amplifier. If the small voltage signal on the base of the transistor goes up gradually, then goes down, the transistor can cause a large voltage to go up and down in an exact replica of the input signal. When a radio or TV station broadcasts its signal, it throws a high voltage out into the air. By the time it gets to your radio or TV, it might only be a millionth of a volt. Using transistors, this voltage can be amplified in an exact replica of the original voltage signal so that it is strong enough to power a loudspeaker or to drive a 25,000-volt electron gun in a TV set. The picture tube or cathode ray tube (CRT) of a TV or computer monitor is similar to a vacuum tube. Figure 1-5 is a diagram of an old fashioned vacuum tube circuit and a transistor circuit. The transistor circuit can be thousands of times smaller and use only a fraction of the energy needed for the vacuum tube. The radio and TV voltages vary up and down and are called *analog voltages*. Figure 1-6 is a diagram of square waves and analog sine waves.

Computers use thousands of transistors. The main chip, or brains of a computer, is the central processing unit (CPU). In addition to the CPU, there are several other chips and components on the motherboard with many more thousands of transistors.

The transistors in the CPU, those on the motherboard, and those on the various plug-in boards and peripherals all respond to signals or voltages that are fed to them from sources such as the keyboard, floppy disk drives, hard disk drives, modems, scanners, or any of several other input devices. The voltages used by computers are digital voltages that have two states: either off or on. If we have two switches or two transistors, we can have four different states as follows:

- #1 off and #2 off
- #1 on and #2 off
- #1 off and #2 on
- #1 on and #2 on

If we have four transistors, we can have 16 different states. If we double the amount of transistors to 8, which would be 2 to the power of 8 ($2^8$), we can have 256 different states. If we double the number to 16 ($2^{16}$) we can have 65,536 different states. The different number of states goes up by the power of 2 with each additional transistor or switch. With 32 transistors, 4,294,967,296 different signals can be produced.

Computers work with 1s and 0s, or *bits*. (Bit is a contraction of *B*inary dig*it*.) It takes eight bits to make one byte. It takes eight bits, or one byte, to represent one letter of the alphabet or a single number.

For certain digital states, we can assign a number or a letter of the alphabet. In our decimal system, we assign values to wherever the numeral happens to be. For example, in the number 321, the 3 is in the hundred place, the 2 is in the ten place, and the 1 is in the 1 place. In the digital system, each place also has a value, but it works a bit differently than the decimal system. The right column is 1, the next is 2, the next is 4, then 8, then 16, 32, 64, 128, 256, etc. Note that each new column

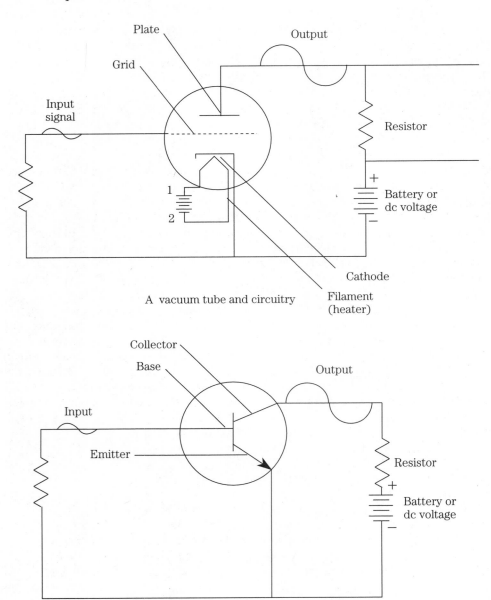

A vacuum tube and circuitry

A transistor and circuitry

**Fig. 1-5** Vacuum tube and transistor circuits.

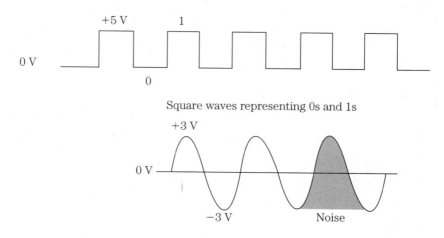

Square waves representing 0s and 1s

Analog voltage

**Fig. 1-6** Square waves and analog sine waves.

toward the left doubles. Here is what the output of four different switches, or transistors, would look like:

```
0000 = 0 = all off
0001 = 1 (the 1 place)
0010 = 2 (the 2 place)
0011 = 3 (the 2 place + 1)
0100 = 4 (the 4 place)
0101 = 5 (the 4 place + 1)
0110 = 6 (the 4 place + 2)
0111 = 7 (the 4 place + 2 +1)
1000 = 8 (the 8 place)
1001 = 9 (the 8 place + 1)
1010 = 10 (the 8 place + 2)
1011 = 11 (the 8 place + 2 + 1)
1100 = 12 (the 8 place + 4)
1101 = 13 (the 8 place + 4 + 1)
1110 = 14 (the 8 place + 4 + 2)
1111 = 15 (the 8 place + 4 + 2 + 1)
```

## The ASCII code

When teletypes were developed, they used the digital system to devise a code so that messages could be sent over telephone wires. This was called the American Standard Code for Information Interchange, or ASCII (pronounced *asskee*). The original code was 128 different characters, which included all of the characters found on a typewriter keyboard, including punctuation and spaces.

If the letter *A* was typed on a teletype keyboard, it would cause a voltage to be turned on and off to produce 100001, which is the equivalent to decimal 65, to be sent over the teletype wire. If a teletype machine in another city was connected to this teletype, the letter *A* would be typed out. If a *B* was typed, the signal 100020, or

66, would be produced. (The fourth place to the left is 16, the fifth is 32, and the sixth is 64, or $2^4$, $2^5$, and $2^6$, respectively.) This 128-character code worked very well for several years.

Later the ASCII code was extended by an additional 128 characters and symbols for a total of 256, or $2^8$. The extended ASCII code uses smiling faces, playing card symbols, Greek letters, and numerous other symbols. If you would like to see what some of these symbols look like, at the DOS prompt, use the command TYPE to type out any command that has an .EXE or .COM extension. For instance at the DOS prompt, type:

```
TYPE COMMAND.COM
```

## Software

If you type an A on a computer keyboard, like the teletype, it causes a digital voltage to be created equivalent to 1000001 or 65 decimal. This would cause certain transistors inside the computer to be turned on or off, and the *A* character would be displayed, stored, printed, or whatever the software told it to do.

## Inputs

The computer keyboard creates digital voltages for each key that is typed. However, there are other ways to input data to a computer. The floppy and hard disks have a magnetic coating very similar to the tape in a tape recorder. A small voltage is created when the data is read by the head. This voltage then is amplified and routed to wherever the software tells it to go.

We can also have inputs from such things as a mouse, a modem, a scanner, or a network. They all produce a digital voltage that is used by the software and hardware to accomplish a task.

## System clock

The computer has a real-time clock and calendar that keeps track of the date and the time. However, the computer also has a system clock that is much more precise than the real-time clock. Everything that a computer does is precisely timed. The timing is controlled by crystal oscillators.

The computer carries out each instruction in a certain number of clock cycles. On the early XT system, the clock operated at 4.75 million Hertz (MHz), or cycles, per second. Even so, it often took several clock cycles to perform a single instruction, moving 8 bits at a time. The Pentium Pro can operate as fast as 250MHz and process several instructions per cycle. The foregoing is rather simplified, but it might help you understand what is happening inside your computer.

# You can do it

In spite of the fact that the Pentium Pro is so powerful, it is basically assembled the same as the old XT. It is very simple to plug the components together. It does not require any soldering or electronic testing. You don't have to be an electronic engineer or technician to assemble a computer. It is even easier to assemble a Pentium

Pro than the earlier machines because most of the components today are manufactured to the Plug-and-Play specification. You can add hundreds of different components to your system and configure it to suit you.

## How much can you save?

I am asked that question many times. It is very difficult to answer. It will depend a lot on how well you shop and whether you insist on buying the brand name components or the less expensive clone components. In some cases, you might not be able to save very much, especially if you buy a system from a discount store or mail-order house. Many of them work on a very small margin.

Ordinarily, you should be able to save at least $200 or more on a system. It will take less than an hour to plug the components together once you have bought them all. You can save even more if you are upgrading an older system and can use most of your older components. So it is well worth the effort. Besides, no amount of money can equate the feeling of accomplishment that you get from building your own computer system.

Incidentally, this is a new age that we are living in. At one time, computers and electronics were considered to be the absolute domain of men, but no more. Many women have bought my previous books and have assembled their own computers. You might have thought I was going to say, "If a woman can do it, you can do it." However, I am not about to say something as sexist as that.

# 2
# Components needed for a computer

All personal computers, from the lowly XT up to the Pentium Pro, use the same basic components. This chapter will give a brief overview of the hardware components that are needed to assemble a computer. I will discuss each component in greater detail in separate following chapters. After all of the components have been discussed, chapter 10 will have photos and detailed instructions for the assembly of the components.

Unless you are an expert, I suggest that you read the rest of the book and find out more about the various components before you purchase them.

## Cost of components

A very big factor in the cost of a system is where you buy it. If you shop wisely, buy the components, and assemble them yourself, you can save from $200 and up to $500. To stay in business, a vendor must pay his employees, cover the cost of his overhead, and make a certain amount of profit. By doing it yourself, you can usually save the amount that the dealer would charge for his profit.

Not all dealers have the same prices or aim for the same profit margin. Some dealers have more overhead than others. If you check the ads from several different companies for equivalent systems, you will probably see that prices can vary from $100 and up to $500.

Another big factor in cost is brand name. The large brand name products nearly always cost more than the no-name brands. In many cases, the no-name product will work just as well.

Still another factor is how long the product has been on the market. If it is new, it will almost always cost more. If it has been on the market for a while, then there will likely be some competition, so the price will often be lower.

Whether the item is popular and in high demand is another price factor. If the item is in high demand, it might be available from several different vendors, each one vying for your dollar, so the competition might cause the price to be lower.

## Barebones systems

You might see advertisements for barebones systems at a very good price. A barebones system might be just a case, power supply, keyboard, and motherboard. You need more than that to do any computing. However, if you are short of money, you can buy such a system and add to it as you can afford it. Adding components to make a complete system or adding components for an upgrade is very simple.

You also might see a picture of an advertised complete system at a very good price; however, in small print, it might say that the monitor, keyboard, or both is not included. Quite often motherboards are advertised for very good prices; however, in small print, it might say "CPU sold separately." You have to read the ads carefully.

You should be subscribing to several of the computer magazines listed in chapter 17 so that you can learn about computers and learn what is available. The *Computer Shopper* is one of the better ones for ads. It usually has about 1000 large tabloid size pages each month. I check the ads, compare the prices, then usually order by mail. Decide what you want in your system, or if you are like me, how much you can afford, then order the components. If you live in a large city, such as the Los Angeles area, there are usually swap meets and computer shows every weekend. Several local vendors will meet in a large area, such as a football stadium or fairgrounds, set up tables and booths, and sell their wares. There is usually lots of competition, and you can get some very good bargains.

You should be aware that there are hundreds of vendors for computer components. A motherboard, or any component, from one vendor might be slightly different than one from another vendor. There are many ways to cut corners to save a few pennies. That is why you need to learn as much as you can about hardware. If you are fairly new in computing, please read the chapters about the main components before buying them.

There is no question that you can save money by doing it yourself. How much you save depends on how wisely you shop, how well you shop, and where you shop.

## Hardware components

The IBM compatible or industry standard architecture (ISA) personal computers (PCs) are open systems, which means that they allow you to add a large variety of different products to them. Computers are made up of several different hardware components, most of which just plug together. Some components are connected by cables, while others plug directly into slots on the motherboard.

There are hundreds of different computer components, boards, and devices available. Using these various components, you can configure your computer in hundreds of different ways. You can add the components to do almost anything that you could want to do with your computer. If you don't have the money at the moment, you can always add more components or upgrade the components later.

This versatility of PCs is one of the reasons for their great success; they can be utilized for so many different things. For example, if you intend to do a lot of communicating to access bulletin boards, the Internet, or online services, you could install a board with a fast modem and a fax. If you wanted to do desktop publishing (DTP), you would probably need to import photos, text, and graphics into your computer files. You could do this with a scanner and a plug-in board to drive it. There are thousands of different boards that are available for thousands of different applications.

### Essential hardware

There are a few hardware components that are absolutely necessary for a functioning computer. They are a motherboard, memory, floppy and hard disk drives and controllers, keyboard, monitor and adapter, case, and power supply.

### Optional hardware

Depending on what you are going to use your computer for, there are several components that are optional and might not be absolutely necessary for a functioning computer. You will probably want a printer, modem, fax, scanner, and mouse. For multimedia, a CD-ROM, a sound board and speakers, and several other special boards might be necessary.

It is very easy to assemble and customize a computer with any of the several hundred available components.

## Motherboards

Figure 1-2 in chapter 1 showed a motherboard, which is the largest and most critical component in your system. It sits on the floor of the standard desktop computer. It is a large board and usually has five to eight slotted connectors for receiving the various plug-in boards. It will have the all important CPU chip, memory chips, and several other chips needed to control and operate the computer. I will discuss motherboards in more detail in chapter 3.

### CPU

Besides the slots and other chips, the motherboard has the central processing unit (CPU) that determines the type of computer it will be. Your motherboard will have a Pentium Pro CPU. In Fig. 1-2, the CPU is beneath the square fan near the top rear area. Figure 1-1 showed an Intel Pentium Pro CPU with the cover removed. There are 5.5 million transistors in the CPU area on the left. A level 2 (L2) 256K cache is on the right with 15.5 million transistors. Some of Pentium Pro CPUs have a 512K L2 cache with 31 million transistors.

Leads from the CPU are connected to pins that fit in a zero insertion force (ZIF) socket on the motherboard. (See Fig. 2-1.) A ZIF socket has a lever that, when raised, loosens the sockets so that the CPU can be dropped in. When the lever is pressed down, it clamps the sockets around the pins of the CPU.

The CPUs are differentiated by the speed or frequency at which they operate. Of course, the higher the frequency, the faster the computer will be. The frequency or speed of the CPU should match that of the motherboard. Most Pentium Pro motherboards will have jumpers or switches that can be set to match the speed of the CPU that is chosen.

### Other chips

The motherboard will also have several other chips on it that controls such things as the input and output (I/O) of data, the memory chips, and timing. Everything that happens in a computer is based on precise timing, so it has very accurate oscillators and crystals to generate the timing signals. You can see several square chips on the

**Fig. 2-1** A ZIF socket.

motherboard in Fig. 1-2. These are very large scale integrated chips (VLSI) that combine many functions into a single chips. In the early days, each function required a separate chip. VLSI uses less space, is more reliable, and is generally faster.

The four white sockets in the bottom right are sockets for dynamic random access memory (DRAM). The DRAM comes on single inline memory modules (SIMMs).

### Buses

The motherboard might have from five to eight connector slots for plug-in boards. The motherboard in Fig. 1-2 has three ISA slots for 16-bit boards and four Peripheral Component Interconnect (PCI) slots. The connectors have pins on each side of the slot that contacts the edge connectors of a board when it is plugged in. Each pin on every connector makes connection to the same pin on all of the other connectors by way of the printed circuits on the motherboard. So an ISA board can be plugged into any open ISA slot; a PCI board can be plugged into any open PCI slot.

The printed circuits on the motherboard that connects all of the connector slot contacts, and certain other controller chips, is called the *bus*. There are different types of buses such as the industry standard architecture (ISA), which was originally called the IBM-compatible bus, and extended industry standard architecture (EISA). A very popular bus up to now has been the Video Electronics Standard Association (VESA) local bus. It is a very popular, low-cost 32-bit bus for memory, hard disk drives, and networks. However, the PCI bus is a bit faster and offers a few other benefits. Most of the faster Pentium Pros will use the ISA and PCI architecture. I will discuss buses in more detail in chapter 3.

### Plug-in boards

The slots for plug-in boards in a computer can be filled up very quickly. Here are just a few of the various boards that are available to plug into the motherboard slots: a monitor adapter board, an input/output (I/O) board to control the printer, a disk controller board, a CD-ROM interface board, a modem and fax board, a scanner interface board, a board for sound, a board for importing video, and a board for TV. I will briefly discuss these boards later.

This short list does not nearly cover all of the boards that can be installed in a PC. There are several billion dollars worth of hardware available for the PC. This is one of the reasons why the PC is so easy to configure and is so versatile.

### Memory

When you create a file or work on a file that has been stored on a disk, the file is copied into RAM. When you have completed work on the file, it is copied back to the hard disk, sent to a printer, or transmitted. My first Morrow CP/M computer only had 64K of RAM and two single-sided 140K floppy disks. It is difficult to work on most programs today without a minimum of 8MB of RAM and a 540MB hard disk.

There are several different types of memory, including as read-only memory (ROM), dynamic random access memory (DRAM), static random access memory (SRAM), Extended Data Output RAM (EDO), Synchronous DRAM (S-DRAM), video random access memory (VRAM), flash memory, cache memory, and several other new types of memory.

Memory is also rated by the speed or frequency at which it can operate, usually in the amount of time it takes to refresh it. This time is usually in billionths of a second or nanoseconds (ns).

I will discuss memory in more detail in chapter 4.

## Power supply and case

Some of the hard drives and other devices require 12 volts dc. The power supply takes the 110 volts ac from the power outlet and converts it to the low dc voltages that are needed. Most of the chips in a computer need about 5 volts dc to operate, some require +5 VDC, others –5 VDC. The Pentium Pro CPUs use 2.9 VDC. This voltage must be closely regulated and exact, so some motherboards have a special voltage regulator module. There are no high or dangerous voltages inside a computer except inside of the covered power supply.

The power supply usually comes with the case. Figure 2-2 shows a standard power supply and its connecting cables. Figure 2-3 shows an ATX type power supply. It is the same as the standard, except that it has a large molded connector for the motherboard connection. Unlike the standard motherboard power connector, this molded connector can only be plugged in properly. A small bag of screws and plastic standoffs will also be included with the case.

The power supplies are rated by the amount of wattage that they can deliver. You shouldn't even consider one less than 200 watts. That might sound like a lot, but

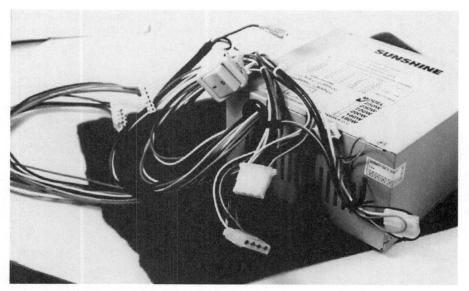

**Fig. 2-2** A standard power supply.

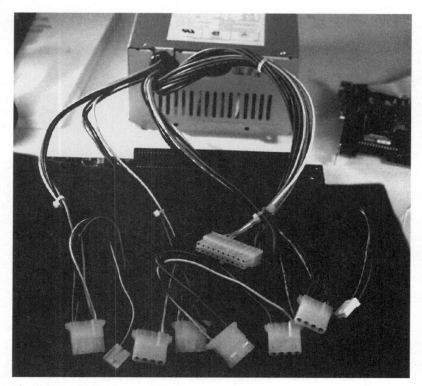

**Fig. 2-3** An ATX power supply.

that is only equivalent to the power used by two 100-watt light bulbs. If you are going to be installing two hard drives and a CD-ROM drive and filling up all the slots with plug-in boards, a 200 watt power supply might not be enough. You might need 250 or even 300 watts. It doesn't hurt to install a more powerful supply. Physically, no matter what wattage, all of them are usually about the same size.

## Power strip

You will have several devices that need to plug into a power outlet. Most wall plates only have two outlets. There are adapters that can fit over the outlet to increase the number to four or even six. You might be tempted to run extension cords to other outlets. However, it will make life a lot easier, and safer, if you buy a power strip that has about six outlets. Try to find one that is switchable and has a built-in fuse or circuit breaker.

I use a power panel that is about 15" square and has six individual lighted switches: one for the master input power, a switch for the computer, one for a monitor, one for printer, and two for auxiliary devices. I usually sit my monitor on this panel. This panel is very handy and is rather inexpensive at about $15.

Some of the more expensive ones have surge protection. Some also have sockets with surge protection for connecting a telephone line for a modem. If you are in an area where there are large heavy-duty electric motors, they might send very high voltage surges through the line. These surges could severely damage your system. There are different levels of quality surge protectors. Some are very inexpensive but might not offer much protection. Some of the UPS companies listed in the following section also sell good quality surge protectors.

## UPS

If you are working on data that is critical and you live in an area where there are a lot of electrical storms, power outages, or brownouts, you should install an uninterruptible power supply (UPS). As mentioned earlier, when you are working on a file, it is loaded into RAM. This memory is volatile; that is, if the power is interrupted, even for a brief fraction of a second, the RAM loses all of its memory. The data that is being worked on will disappear and be gone forever. A UPS can take over when the power is interrupted and keeps the computer running until it can be safely shut down.

If you live in an area where there are electrical storms, then by all means you should have a good lightning rod installed. If a severe electrical storm comes up, even with a good lightning rod, you should turn off your computer and unplug it. Just one good bolt can burn your system to a crisp.

Here are just a few companies who offer UPS devices:

| | |
|---|---|
| American Power Conversion | (800) 800-4272 |
| Best Power Technology | (800) 356-5794 |
| Deltec | (619) 291-4211 |
| International Power Technologies | (800) 944-0356 |
| Minuteman UPS | (800) 238-7272 |
| Tripp Lite | (312) 755-5400 |

Call these companies for brochures and information.

## Computer case or enclosure

Quite often the power supply comes with whatever case you order. There are several different types of cases: desktop, mini tower, medium tower, and large tower. The power supply usually comes with the case, but there are different types of power supplies and different wattages. If necessary, the power supply can be purchased separately. Power supplies do fail occasionally.

## Floppy disk drives

It would be very difficult to operate a computer without floppy drives. At one time, all software came on floppy disks. Now many of the larger packages come on CD-ROM. The 5.25" drives are practically obsolete; however, there is still a lot of older software on 5.25" disks around. It might be advisable to have both 5.25" and 3.5" drives. Most floppies are now integrated with both drives in a single unit that mounts in a single bay opening, such as the one shown in Fig. 5-2 in chapter 5. This is desirable, because most desktop cases only have four or five bays for mounting drives. I will discuss floppy drives in chapter 5.

## Hard disk drives

It would be almost impossible to do any kind of productive computing today without a hard disk. At one time, 10MB was large enough for most applications. Today you need a hard drive of at least 540MB, even better would be two drives with a capacity of 540MB or more. The most popular hard drives sold today are the enhanced integrated disk electronics (EIDE) and those that use the small computer systems interface (SCSI, pronounced *scuzzy*). I will discuss hard drives in detail in chapter 6.

## Drive interfaces

The floppy and hard drives usually connect with the computer bus through an adapter or interface board. These boards plug into one of the slots on the motherboard. Many manufacturers now integrate the controller interface chips on the motherboard. They then provide a set of pins so that the drive cables can be connected to these pins. This integration saves having to use one of the plug-in slots. The interfaces will be discussed in chapters 5 and 6.

## Backup

You never can know when disaster might strike. There are hundreds of ways that you could lose data that you might never be able to replace. If your data is worth anything at all, then you should have it backed up. I will discuss some of the several ways to backup your data in chapter 7.

## Monitor

There are a large number of different monitors available. They are categorized by such things as screen size, resolution, scan rates, and several other specifications. Monitors will be discussed in chapter 8.

## Display adapter

A monitor needs an adapter board to interface with the computer. The adapter plugs into one of the slots and drives the monitor. To a large extent, the adapter determines the resolution and many of the other monitor specifications. A good adapter board can cost more than a monitor.

There are a large number of different adapters on the market, at many different prices. Of course, the faster the scan, the better resolution, and the more colors the adapter can provide, the more expensive the board will be. I will have more to say about monitors and adapters in chapter 8.

## Input devices

There are several ways to get data into your computer. The following sections cover just a few. Input devices will be discussed in chapter 9.

### Keyboard

The keyboard is the most intimate contact that you have with your computer. It is a small computer in itself. Each key sends out a unique electrical signal that connects directly to the very inner bowels of the computer.

Because it is your most intimate contact, it is important that you get a keyboard that suits you. There are many different types, with different keys, different key locations, and a different touch required to activate the keys.

### Mice

A mouse is absolutely essential to computing today. A mouse can take control of the cursor and quickly move it to any area of the screen. The mouse first gained great popularity on the Macintosh. Instead of typing in commands, just use a mouse to point and click. It would be very difficult to run Windows type programs without a mouse.

There are several different types of mice and several different prices. For professional CAD type work, fine resolution is needed. For example, if the engineer is designing a product that has very precise measurements, then the movement of the mouse and cursor is critical. For simple point and click, the resolution is not a problem.

You can buy a simple point and click mouse for as little as $10. A high resolution one might cost up to $100 or more.

Mice are serial devices and are usually connected to one of the COM ports as an interface.

### Trackballs

Some systems use a trackball to control the cursor. A trackball's function and operation is very similar to that of a mouse. There are several different types. For some applications, a trackball might be better than a mouse, but it might be a bit more expensive than a mouse.

Most standalone trackballs are much more expensive than a mouse. Some can cost as much as $125, whereas a mouse can cost as little as $10.

### Scanners

A scanner can read text from a printed page and import it into a computer without having to type it in. A scanner can also import sketches, drawings, and photos into a computer file.

There are several different types of scanners, including handheld, flatbed, monochrome, and color. There are also different resolutions and, of course, different prices.

Most scanners are SCSI, so they need a SCSI adapter. There are some low-level scanners that can use the parallel or printer port to input data.

### Input/output boards

In the past, an input/output (I/O) board was usually needed to furnish the interface for the computer ports. Most motherboards now have the ports integrated onto the motherboard. A computer usually has four ports: two parallel ports and two serial ports. The parallel ports, LPT1 and LPT2, are used primarily for printers, but they can also be used for special hard disk drives and tape backup drives. The serial ports, COM1 and COM2, are used primarily for a mouse, a modem, a serial printer, or other serial devices, such as plotters.

## Communications

The computer is great for communication. You can send faxes, e-mail, log onto the Internet, or communicate with thousands of bulletin boards or other computers. Chapter 10 will discuss communications. The following section covers a few of the communication devices.

### Modems

Computers are great for communicating. With a modem, you can communicate over the telephone lines with any other computer that has a modem. There are also thousands of bulletin boards that have public domain software that is free for the cost of the telephone call. There are several national online services—such as Compuserve, Prodigy, Genie, and others—that offer mail services, online shopping, stock market quotations, and many other services.

There are two primary types of modems: internal ones on a board that plug into a slot and external ones that sit on the desk and plug into one of the COM ports. There are also different types according to the speed of transmission and certain other features.

### Fax boards and fax machines

A fax board will let you send or receive a fax with your computer. If a fax is received by a fax machine in a large office, it can be seen by several people. If it is received by your computer, it can assure privacy. It is convenient and can save time. Many fax boards are now integrated with modem boards.

A standalone fax machine can be left on 24 hours a day and use very little energy. Many of the newer machines are combinations that can fax, scan, copy, or print.

## Printers

It is almost essential that you have a printer for your computer. There are several types that are discussed in chapter 12.

## CD-ROM

The compact disc read-only memory (CD-ROM) disc can store up to 650MB of information. An entire encyclopedia can be stored on just a small portion of a small disc. For multimedia, a CD-ROM drive is essential.

Usually the CD-ROM drives are mounted in a bay, much like a floppy drive. However, there are external models that can be used if you don't have an open bay. The external models are more expensive, usually about $100 above the cost of an internal drive. Whether you opt for the internal or external model, they will require an interface plug-in board to control them.

The CD-ROM interface might be built into your sound board. On some, it is on the same Enhanced Integrated Disk Electronics (EIDE) board that controls your floppy and hard drives. Some other CD-ROM drives use a small system computer interface (SCSI) board. The SCSI board can control up to seven other SCSI devices, such as two CD-ROM drives, two hard disk drives, a scanner, and a tape drive. The single SCSI interface can save having to use one or more of the eight slots.

At one time, the CD-ROM recordable (CD-ROM-R) units were very expensive; however, they are now quite reasonable and can cost less than a high-capacity hard drive. They offer several advantages over other types of storage.

There are several different types of CD-ROM drives. I will discuss them in detail in chapter 13.

## Sound boards

You won't be able to take full advantage of the multimedia products unless you have a sound board. Like most other products, there are a large number of manufacturers of sound boards. There is a wide range of features on the many boards. Of course, there is also a wide range as to their cost. Many of the sound boards come bundled with other hardware and software, such as a microphone or an encyclopedia on a CD-ROM disc. Sound boards and music are discussed in detail in chapter 14.

## Loudspeakers

Your computer has a loudspeaker, but it won't allow you to take advantage of the sound benefits and utilities available to multimedia. The loudspeaker in most computers are very small and quite limited in frequency response. The original purpose of a small speaker in a computer was so that it could beep at the operator. The beep could alert the operator that the boot process had successfully completed or let the person know that it was time to insert a new floppy disk or do some other task. So you will need at least one loudspeaker for your sound board. Most people buy two of them for stereo sound. Most sound boards have a very limited output wattage, so many loudspeakers have a built-in amplifier. Some companies offer high-end, high fidelity speakers for computers. Of course they can also be high priced.

## Microphones

If you want to add sound to your files, you will need a microphone. A low-cost microphone will do fine unless you are planning to create some professional type high fidelity music.

I'll have more to say about speakers and microphones in chapter 14.

## Voice recognition

The voice of every person is different and every word spoken by each person is different. If a person's voice is recorded on a hard disk, it forms a distinct and unique pattern. Just as no two snowflakes are the same, no two voice patterns are the same.

Using a board, microphone, and the proper software, a person can "train" a computer to recognize certain words and commands and perform any of several tasks. The person could issue commands verbally rather than typing them in from the keyboard.

## Automated voice

If there are a limited number of words to be delivered, the words can be recorded, then each one accessed as needed by a computer. However, if a large variety of words are needed, then artificial voice might be utilized.

There are a little over 40 recognizable phonemes, or linguistic sounds, in the English language. These sounds can be digitized and installed on a fairly small chip. A computer program can then have these bits of sound assembled and linked together so that almost any word can be created and spoken.

## A board for TV

Boards have been developed that will let you view TV on your computer. These boards have all of the TV channels so that you can use your keyboard to select a channel. You can watch TV in a corner of the monitor while concurrently doing some other task.

## A board for videotape input

There are boards that will allow you to use a video tape recorder with your computer. With these boards, you can import a videotape, then use the computer to change or edit single frames.

## Other plug-in boards

There are many other specialized boards that can be plugged into your computer motherboard. Developers are working overtime to create newer and improved ones. Remember, however, you only have eight slots. Some computers have even fewer slots because they might not have some of the needed functions built into the motherboard.

It might be difficult to install eight different plug-in boards. A *port* is needed to govern and control the flow of data from serial devices into and out of serial the central processing unit (CPU). Serial devices process data one bit at a time in a continuous stream. Serial devices can be components such as modems, mice, serial printers, plotters, network interface cards (NIC), and several other plug-in boards and peripheral devices. The computer only has two serial ports: COM1 and COM2.

Before you plug in a board, check the documentation that you should have received with it. It will probably have some switches or jumpers that must be set to have it operate with the proper COM port and at the proper address. In some circumstances, two virtual ports, COM3 and COM4, might be able to share the two main ports. *Virtual* means that these ports are not physically present; however, if COM1 or COM2 is not in use at that time, COM3 or COM4 might be able to use their address.

You won't be able to use COM3 or COM4 in all cases. Some devices are rather selfish and ungenerous. Some of them grab hold of the COM port and will not share it at all.

# Compatibility

In the early days, compatibility was often a problem, but it causes very few problems today. I do a lot of my shopping at weekend computer swaps and through mail order. When I order by mail, I look through several computer magazines and decide which component is the better buy. I have few concerns about whether it will be compatible or not.

The Pentium Pro and the Pentium are much faster and more powerful than the 486. However, except for the motherboard, they all use the same basic components. In fact, they all use the same basic components as those found on the old antique, obsolete XT.

The detailed discussions of these major components in the following chapters will help you make a better and more informed choice when you purchase the components. If you are not an expert computer whiz, I suggest that you read those chapters before you buy your parts.

# Software

The most powerful computer would be worthless without software to control it. To a computer, software is like gasoline is to an automobile. However, the gasoline analogy doesn't tell the whole story. There is only one basic kind of gasoline. There are many thousands of software programs designed for thousands of different applications and functions.

Software can be more expensive than hardware. In chapter 16, I will tell you how you can buy surplus software and save hundreds of dollars on the essential software that you will need.

# 3

# The motherboard

The motherboard is one of the most important components in your computer. It is also the largest board in your computer system. Except for the motherboard, all the rest of the components in a computer can be the same. For example, a 286 and the most powerful Pentium Pro can both use the same type floppy drives, hard drives, keyboards, and plug-in boards. Even the RISC motherboards use the same basic type components.

The motherboard has the central processing unit (CPU) chip, such as an Intel Pentium Pro, an AMD/NexGen K6, or a Cyrix 6x86. The type of CPU on the motherboard determines the type of system. The primary difference in all personal computers is the motherboard with its CPU. The Pentium Pro motherboard looks very much like the 386 or 486 motherboards. Even the old original XT motherboard has a lot in common with the most powerful Pentium Pro.

Besides the CPU, the motherboard will have several other chips; five to eight slot connectors for plug-in boards; sockets or slots for memory chips; and upright pins for printer, mouse, and disk interface cable connections. I still have a 286 motherboard from my first 286 computer. It is the AT "standard" size or about one-third larger than the "baby" AT size of almost all motherboards today. Figure 3-1 shows my old 6MHz 286 board on the left and a Micronics 150MHz Pentium Pro on the right.

My old 286 motherboard has over 150 separate chips on it. Soon after the 286 came out, Adaptec and several other companies started integrating several chips into a single package. Most of the motherboards now have about 20 separate chips. With fewer chips, there is less chance of having solder problems, less chance of stray capacitance, less distance between the components, and much greater reliability. It also costs much less to manufacture a board with fewer chips.

Even with 150 separate chips on the old 286 motherboard, I still had to buy a separate board for the mouse and printer, a separate controller board for the floppy drives, and one for the hard drives. Motherboards now have sets of upright pins for most of those functions. All that is needed are cables from such peripheral components as the disk drives, mouse, printer, or CD-ROM.

**Fig. 3-1** An old 286 standard size motherboard on the left, and a Micronics 150MHz Pentium Pro on the right.

Figure 3-2 is a photo of a 150MHz Micronics M6Pi motherboard. There are a lot of components on this motherboard. The motherboard is 9" wide and 13" long. One of the little niceties that Micronics did was to put marks in inches from 1 to 13 along the sides of the board and from *A* to *I* in inches along the ends of the board. This is somewhat like a map, and with the coordinates, you can easily find any jumper or component on the board.

**Fig. 3-2** A Micronics Pentium Pro motherboard.

Figure 3-3 is a diagram of the Micronics motherboard, which shows the various chips and slots. Note that it has built-in connections for a parallel printer, floppy drives, a primary and secondary Enhanced Integrated Drive Electronic disk drives, and serial ports COM1 and COM2. The primary set of EIDE pins can be used for two IDE hard drives. The secondary set of EIDE pins can be used for IDE CD-ROM drives, tape backup drives, or other IDE devices.

The original IDE interface was usually on a plug-in board. This IDE interface wouldn't let you use a hard drive with more than 1024 cylinders and 63 sectors, or a maximum of 528MB. It also had a rather slow transfer rate 5.22Mb/second. The enhanced IDE supports a transfer rate of 15.5Mb/second. It can also support hard drives with up to several gigabytes capacity.

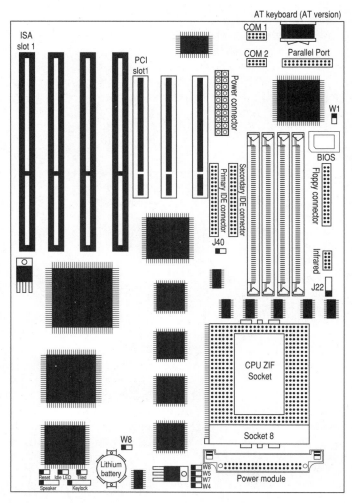

**Fig. 3-3** A diagram of the Micronics Pentium Pro motherboard.

The set of pins for the floppy drives can control two floppy disk drives. They can be any two drives, such as 360K, 1.2MB, 720K, 1.44MB, or 2.88MB. The parallel port connector is for the printer or other parallel device. It has Enhanced Parallel Port (EPP) and Expanded Capability Port (ECP). Parallel ports have eight lines and transmits one bit of data at a time on each line. Ordinarily a parallel port only transmits data out, but these ports can be used for output or input. The EPP and ECP ports can operate at the same speed as the ISA bus and can transfer data at up to 1Mb/second. These ports can be used not only for printers, but also for tape backup drives, external hard disks, CD-ROMs, small local area networks and several other new products.

The serial COM1 and COM2 ports has the 16550 Universal Asynchronous Receiver Transmitter (UART). This UART is much faster than the earlier 16450 chips. Computers handle data in 8-bit bytes, or one word; however, mice, modems, and several other peripherals are serial devices. They use data one bit at a time. For output, the serial ports change the standard 8-bit bytes into single bits for transmission. When receiving data, it changes the single bits back into 8-bit bytes.

The motherboard will have slot connectors, or an expansion bus, so that different boards can be plugged in. It will have a small battery, crystal oscillators, timing chips, memory chips, and several other chips that are necessary for the operation of the computer.

Table 3.1 shows some of the characteristics of a few of the CPUs. MIPS is an acronym for *millions of instructions per second*.

**Table 3-1.  The characteristics of a few of the CPUs.**

|  | XT | 286 | 386 | 486 | Pentium | P6 |
|---|---|---|---|---|---|---|
| Transistors | 29K | 134K | 275K | 1.2M | 3.1M | 5.5M |
| Frequency | 4.7–10 | 6–25 | 16–40 | 25–100 | 60–133 | 150–250 |
| MIPS | .75 | 2.66 | 11.4 | 54 | 112–150+ | 150–250 |
| Bits | 8 | 16 | 32 | 32 | 32 | 32 |
| Memory | 640K | 16MB | 4GB | 4GB | 4GB | 4GB |

When the 286 was introduced, it was a great leap forward. It operated at a blazing speed of 6MHz and had a 16-bit bus. The frequency of the 200MHz Pentium Pro is only 33.3 times faster than the 6MHz 286; however, because of the improved processing, it is actually about 300 times faster. We have truly come a long way since the early 1980s.

Though the Pentium Pro might be 300 times faster than the 286, it can still run all of the old programs. However, since the Pentium Pro was designed for 32 bit software, it might run some older 8- or 16-bit programs a bit slow.

Note that the 386, 486, and Pentium can address up to 4 gigabytes (GB) or 4,000,000,000 bytes of memory. (The prefix *giga-* means *billion*.) At the present time, I don't know of any vendor who makes a motherboard that would accept that much memory. Most Pentium Pro motherboards are designed to accept up to 128MB of RAM.

# CPU & voltage regulation

In the past, most CPUs operated off 5 volts dc (VDC). The Pentium Pro operates off 2.9 VDC. One reason for this is to reduce the amount of current in the chip, which in turn reduces the amount of heat generated. Heat is the enemy of semiconductors, which is why they have a small fan and a lot of heat sink material on the CPU. They managed to cram 5.5 million transistors into a space a bit less than .7" by .7".

To get this many transistors into such a small area meant that they had to reduce the connecting lines and distances between transistors to .6 microns (.6 millionths of an inch) in the CPU. A large voltage spike could jump across these very narrow lines and possibly ruin the CPU. To prevent this from happening, most of the Pentium Pros are now using a sophisticated voltage regulator module. The module plugs into a socket near the CPU. Figure 3-4 shows the module being plugged. Eventually, this module will be integrated on the motherboard.

**Fig. 3-4** A voltage regulator module for the 2.9 VDC of the CPU.

I hate to admit it, but I am not always as careful as I should be. In testing out the Pentium Pro motherboard from Micronics, I set it up on a bench. I installed all of the components and ran several tests. They all ran great until I reached across the setup to move a cable and just brushed across the voltage module with my hand. A ring on my finger just barely touched the terminals of a capacitor on the module and wiped it out. Without the module, the system would not work. Fortunately, it did not affect the CPU. Micronics replaced the unit without charge. I felt so ashamed that I would do such a stupid thing, I would have probably felt better if they had charged me.

As I point out in chapter 18, "Troubleshooting and Repairing Your PC," there are a thousand and one things that can go wrong. (Maybe I should have said a thousand and two things.)

# The effects of competition

Ordinarily, in the past, Intel would not introduce a newer, more powerful CPU until they had milked the current one for as much as possible. However, Intel introduced their Pentium Pro well before they had fully squeezed all they possibly could from the various Pentium versions. One reason that they did it was because Advanced Micro Devices (AMD), NexGen, and Cyrix were developing clones of the Pentium and Pentium Pro. They were nudged a bit more when AMD merged with NexGen to pool their resources. So, with AMD/NexGen and Cyrix yapping at their heels with clones of the Pentium and Pentium Pro, Intel released the Pentium Pro sooner than expected.

Intel is trying to stay ahead of the cloners. At this very moment, they are busy working on the next generation P7 and P8 CPUs. Eventually, the P7 and P8 will have a more complete name; however, at the time of this writing, that is all we have. Of course, AMD/NexGen and Cyrix are working on similar clones.

The competition is causing prices to fall like autumn leaves.

# The Pentium Pro versus RISC

The Pentium Pro has 5.5 million transistors in its CPU. Some of the reduced instruction set computers (RISC) CPUs might have only half that many transistors. The Pentium Pro can operate at 200MHz at the moment but is expected to operate at 250MHz soon. Some of the RISC machines can now operate at frequencies above 300MHz.

To a great extent, the cost of a computer closely correlates to the cost of the CPU. The IBM and Apple PowerPC RISC CPUs costs about one-fourth as much as a Pentium Pro CPU at this time. However, CPUs made by the Digital Equipment Corp. (DEC) and some of the other RISC companies are much more expensive than those made by Motorola for IBM and Apple.

The RISC machines require special software, so the overall cost to operate might be higher. All CPUs are different. Ordinarily, software is written for a specific type of CPU. Because the Intel and Motorola CPUs are different, an instruction written for the Intel 80x86 CPUs would turn on or off different transistors than those written for the Motorola 680xx CPUs. Programs that are written for the 80x86 and that written for the 680xx are like two foreign languages. They cannot understand the instructions unless they are written in their own language. That is why you can't take software that is written for the Macintosh and run it on a machine that has an Intel 80x86 CPU unless you use special software.

The RISC CPUs can only recognize instructions that are written in their own language. If you want to run a DOS program or a Macintosh program on a RISC machine, the program has to be revised or compiled to recognize the software instructions. A compiler can convert a high-level programming language into a machine-level language of 0s and 1s that the CPU can recognize. What makes it even more complicated is that RISC CPUs made by different companies are all different and each needs its own special software. There is no standardization for the RISC machines. Even the IBM PowerPCs and the Apple PowerPCs are not compatible at this time, although they are working on a compatible system that should be available soon.

There are some programs that can interpret and emulate the DOS and Macintosh programs so that they can be run on a RISC machine, but they will run a bit slower because it will take time to do this. Speed is the primary reason for RISC machines; therefore, if you have to use software to emulate programs, the advantage of RISC might be lost.

At this time, there are a few software companies who are developing native software for the Apple PowerPCs. IBM is also developing some software for their PowerPCs. However, it will be some time before there is anywhere near the amount of applications that are available for the industry standard architecture (ISA) machines. Also, at this time, there are very few manufacturers of RISC motherboards. A motherboard with a very high speed RISC CPU that is made by a company other than IBM, Apple, or Motorola can cost as much as $4000.

There are many Pentium motherboard manufacturers. The competition will keep the prices fairly reasonable. The Pentium Pro will be able to run all present software. Lots of new software that will take full advantage of the 32-bit bus is still being developed at this time.

One of the best uses of the RISC machines is for high-end workstations for engineering design, Computer Aided Design (CAD), and specialized research. Of course, special proprietary software is needed for projects of this type. When an engineer or scientist is using this specialized software, there might be times when he or she needs to do some plain old word processing or run some other simple DOS or Windows software. He or she might not be able to do this on a RISC machine, but it can be easily done on a Pentium Pro. The Pentium Pro, as a workstation, can do almost everything as well and as fast as most RISC machines.

Intel, AMD/NexGen, Cyrix, and others have realized that RISC technology does have several benefits. In their latest designs, these companies have incorporated and mixed many features of RISC technology in with CISC to give us the best of both worlds.

# Architecture

The architecture of the computer refers to the overall design and the components it uses. The architecture is also concerned with the type of bus that is used. The bus is the internal pathways over which data is sent from one part of the computer to another. The 8-bit systems use 8-bit parallel paths, 16-bit uses 16, 32-bit uses 32, and 64-bit uses 64. The flow of data over a bus is often compared to the flow of traffic on a highway. If there are only two lanes, the flow of traffic might be limited. Adding more lanes can vastly improve the flow of traffic.

## ISA

The industry standard architecture (ISA) is what was once known as the IBM-compatible standard. IBM more or less abandoned the standard when they introduced their micro channel architecture (MCA) in 1987. There were far more IBM-compatible clone computers in existence than computers manufactured by IBM. Because IBM was now directing most of its efforts toward the MCA, the clone makers took over the standard and changed the name.

An ISA computer can be anything from the oldest and slowest XT up to the newest and fastest Pentium. The old XT 8-bit bus, had 8 parallel lines connected to the same pins on all of the slot connectors for plug-in boards. When the 286 was being developed by IBM, it became apparent that an 8-bit bus was too slow and was clearly inadequate. So, they devised a 16-bit slot connector by adding a second 36-contact connector in front the original 62 contact connector. This was a brilliant innovation that allowed the use of 8-bit or 16-bit boards.

## Compatibility

There were about $5 billion worth of 8-bit hardware in existence at the time IBM introduced their 16-bit AT 286. The industry loved it because they could use either 8-bit or 16-bit plug-in boards.

This downward compatibility still exists even with the latest, fastest, and most powerful Pentium Pro. However, there is a price to pay for the compatibility. The CPU operates over a special memory bus to communicate with RAM at the CPU's rated frequency. However, the systems can only communicate with their plug-in boards and peripherals over a 16-bit bus. Even though the Pentium Pro can operate at up to 200MHz, to be able to run all of the previous software and hardware, the ISA bus is limited to a speed of about 10MHz and an I/O bus width of 16 parallel lines.

## MCA

When IBM decided that the 16-bit ISA system was inadequate, they designed the micro channel architecture (MCA) system. This architecture was a 32-bit bus system for plug-in cards and memory. However, it was incompatible with all of the 8-bit and 16-bit hardware. Only MCA boards could be used in the MCA system.

The wider MCA bus was a much faster and more powerful system. However, IBM also wanted to be downward compatible with the available software, even if they weren't compatible with the hardware. So the speed from the plug-in boards and peripherals was still limited to 8MHz to 10MHz.

It was a great idea, but ahead of its time. The MCA is now obsolete.

## EISA

A group of compatible or IBM-clone makers realized that IBM was right about needing a wider bus and more room for expansion and improvement. They devised the extended industry standard architecture (EISA). This standard specified a new connector with almost double the number of contacts and added several new improvements to the ISA standard. Unlike the IBM MCA system, the EISA system was downwardly compatible with all previous hardware. The billions of dollars worth of present boards could still be used with the EISA system, even the old 8-bit plug-in boards.

The standard contact on an ISA connector is .06" wide. There is a .04" space between each contact. The EISA board was designed with a second set of contacts immediately below the ISA contacts. A connecting trace was placed in the .04" space between the ISA contacts for the lower set of EISA contacts. The EISA plug-in slot on the motherboard has two sets of contacts to match ISA and EISA contacts on the plug-in boards. The EISA boards have cutouts on the boards to match bars across the lower EISA section of the slot connector. When an ISA board is plugged in, the bars prevent it from being inserted deep enough to contact the EISA contacts.

Like the MCA system, the EISA system provides a 32-bit bus. However, also like the MCA, they wanted to remain downward compatible with earlier software and hardware. Therefore, the communication between the plug-in boards was still limited to a speed of 8MHz to 10MHz.

Most Pentium Pro motherboards have not chosen to use the EISA system.

## The VESA local bus

The PC bus has long been a bottleneck. The 8-bit bus at 4.77MHz was okay for the XT. The 16-bit bus was a great technological improvement when the 286 was introduced. The 286 CPU communicated with its RAM over a 16-bit memory bus at the CPU operating speed. However, the input/output (I/O) bus speed of plug-in cards and peripherals was locked in at 8MHz to 10MHz.

When the 386 and 486 were introduced, they communicated with their RAM over a 32-bit memory bus at the speed of the CPU. However, like the 286, the I/O bus still operated on a 16-bit bus at 8MHz to 10MHz. Some peripherals, such as fast hard disks and monitors, were slowed down considerably.

The Video Electronics Standards Association (VESA) developed a set of specifications for a VESA local bus (VLB) that eliminated some of the bottlenecks.

The VLB specification added a second slot connector in line with the 16-bit slot connector. This solution is similar to that used to migrate from the 8-bit slot to the 16-bit. The VL bus added a second connector in line with the 16-bit connectors so that 8-bit, 16-bit, and VLB boards can be used in these slots.

The VLB portion of the connector uses 116 miniature contacts that are similar to the MCA connectors. The connector provides a 32-bit path from the plug-in boards and peripherals to the CPU. The VL bus is a direct extension of the CPU bus and runs at the same speed as the CPU. The VL bus increases the performance of a PC considerably, yet adds very little to the cost of the system.

The VL bus is not a perfect solution. The VL system only allows three connectors. They are ordinarily used for fast IDE hard disks, video adapters, and network interface cards (NICs).

The VL bus allows communication over the 32-bit lines at the same speed as the CPU. However, the other input/output (I/O) components in the system are still relegated to the 16-bit bus at 8MHz to 10MHz. Even the Pentium Pro has this same standard bus speed for non-VLB I/O components and peripherals to remain backward compatible.

The VL bus was quite popular for the 486 and Pentium motherboards, but it is not used in most of the Pentium Pros.

## The Intel PCI bus

Intel introduced their Peripheral Component Interconnect (PCI) local bus in July of 1992, a month before the VL bus was officially introduced. Integrating the PCI bus circuit on a motherboard involves special chips and is a bit more expensive than the VL bus. In addition, plug-in boards for the PCI bus are usually more expensive than VLB. So it took some time before PCI was widely accepted.

The VL bus connects directly to the CPU. The PCI bus is a bit different than the VL bus in that it is a separate standalone bus. Boards designed for the VL bus system are not standalone because the boards use both the 16-bit and the VL bus pins.

It can sometimes be very frustrating when adding a plug-in board. Often you have to set several dip switches or jumpers so that it does not conflict with the assigned interrupt request (IRQs), serial and parallel ports, and DMA channels of other plug-in boards.

The VL and PCI buses have an auto-configuration capability that will automatically configure an add-in board if the board meets the plug-and-play specifications. Eventually, all plug-in boards will conform to the plug-and-play specification. Of course, you will still have to do it the old fashioned way if you are installing boards that were designed before the plug-and-play specifications were adopted.

The PCI system can allow up to ten PCI connectors. However, for most practical purposes, the same three used in the VL system—hard disk, video, and network—will be all that is needed at this time.

The VLB and PCI bus can be used with ISA, EISA, MCA, and RISC motherboards. Many of the less expensive Pentium systems still use the VL bus because it is less costly to integrate, but most of the Pentium Pro motherboards will have the PCI bus.

## Built-in goodies

It is amazing how soon you can fill up all of the available slots on the motherboard. One way to get around having to use plug-in boards is to have many of the functions built-in on the motherboard. Most Pentium Pro motherboards now have several built-in functions. Refer back to Fig. 3-3. One of the arguments against built-in functions is that the built-in functions might become obsolete or defective. However, if necessary, the on-board utilities can usually be disabled and replaced with a plug-in board. The following sections cover some of the things that might be built in.

### EIDE interface

Most Pentium Pro motherboards now have the EIDE interface for hard disks and a floppy disk controller built-in on the motherboard. They have rows of pins protruding from the motherboard that will accept the ribbon cables from the drives. The EIDE is much faster than the older IDE and can control up to four devices, including some CD-ROM drives and tape backup drives. The newer motherboards now usually have two sets of EIDE pins.

### SCSI interface

Many of the Macintosh models have built-in SCSI interfaces. That is one of the reasons for their popularity. The PC industry has been lax in not following suit. SCSI is something that is essential, not only for multimedia, but for many PC applications. A few motherboard manufacturers are now including a built-in SCSI interface. One reason why it is not on the PC motherboard is because the SCSI specification has changed several times in the past and even more improvements are imminent.

### Serial ports

Many motherboards provide pins for two serial ports. Mice, modems, and many other devices need a serial port. Some multifunction boards provide them, but it is much simpler to have them built-in on the motherboard. A united serial bus (USB) specification is being readied and should be available by the time you read this. It will be much faster than the present serial bus and will allow several devices to be connected.

### Printer port

There are very few computers that are not tied to a printer of some sort. There are still a few printers that use the serial port, but most printers today use one of the two parallel ports: LPT1 or LPT2. Many of the motherboards now have a set of pins for LPT1. Otherwise you will need to buy a plug-in card such as a multifunction board.

Most of the Pentium Pros will have LPT1 built-in on the motherboard. It will also be an expanded capability port (ECP) and an enhanced parallel port (EPP). This means that the port can be utilized for input/ouput for devices such as scanners, tape backup systems, and peripherals other than a printer.

### Game ports

Many of the multifunction boards sold today have a game port for joysticks used with several of the games that are available. With the increased interest and popularity of multimedia, the game port has become almost mandatory. Some motherboards have a set of pins for a game port built-in.

### Infrared connectors

Many of the Pentium Pro motherboards have an infrared connector. There are now several components that operate off infrared signals, the same type of signal used with TV remote controls. Years ago, IBM used infrared for their PCjr keyboard. Several companies are again designing keyboards, mice, and laptop computers with infrared connectors. Even printer cables can be eliminated with an infrared link from the computer.

### Monitor adapter

Every computer needs a board or adapter to drive the monitor. Some motherboards have had built-in monitor adapters for some time. They are great for many applications. The main problem is that the developers keep making the adapters faster, with better resolution, with true colors, and more complex. If your adapter is built-in, then you are stuck with whatever resolution or functions that it provides. Most of the motherboards with built-in functions have jumpers or switches that will allow you to disable those functions so that a board can be plugged in to take over the built-in functions.

## Other motherboard chips

Besides the CPU and memory chips, there are several other chips and systems on the motherboard. The early PCs and the AT had a very large number of chips. I have a standard early 286 motherboard with 1MB of RAM in the dual in-line pin

(DIP) chips. This motherboard is about one-third larger than the "baby" AT size motherboards. The memory chips take up about one-fourth of the entire board. Altogether, this 286 board has over 150 separate chips on it.

The Chips and Technology Company, using very large scale integration (VLSI), combined several of motherboard chips into just a few chips. Other companies followed them so that today we have only a small number of chips on the motherboard.

The smaller number of chips means fewer solder connections, more reliability, more speed, less board real estate required, and less cost. The Pentium Pro motherboards are now about one-third smaller than the original standard 286. Instead of over 150 separate chips, the Pentium Pro motherboard may have only five or six large VLSI chips on them.

### ROM BIOS

You won't have to worry about read only memory (ROM). ROM is memory that cannot ordinarily be altered or changed. ROM comes with the motherboard. The principal use of ROM in PCs today is for the basic input/output system (BIOS).

The BIOS chip is second in importance only to the CPU. Every time you turn your computer on, the BIOS does a power on self test (POST). The BIOS checks all of the major components to make sure that they are operating properly. It also facilitates the transfer of data among peripherals. Many BIOS chips also have diagnostics and several utilities built-in. BIOS sounds a bit like BOSS, and that is its principal job.

The BIOS performs its important functions under the control of firmware programs. These programs are similar to software programs except that the ROM is actually made up of hundreds of transistors that are programmed to perform certain functions.

Most newer BIOS chips now use flash memory. Until recently, the ROM BIOS programs were usually burned into electrically programmable read only memory (EPROMs) chips. Special devices were used to input a software program into the ROM chip. As the program voltages pass through the chip, the transistors are turned on and off to match the input program. When a normal transistor has voltage applied to it, it will turn on or off as long as the voltage is present. The EPROM transistors are different from ordinary transistors. When the EPROM transistors are turned on or off, they remain in that condition.

Fairly large programs and text can be stored on a ROM chip. The ROM BIOS for an early XT could be programmed onto a 64K ROM chip. The 486 ROM BIOS uses a 512K. All of the text in the book you are holding in your hand can be stored in less than 512K. The Pentium Pro BIOS requires almost 1MB.

Most Pentium Pro motherboards now have a BIOS in a flash memory chip. Often, new developments and devices require that the BIOS be upgraded. In the past, to upgrade an older BIOS chip meant having to open the computer case, pry out the chip and replace it. It sounds simple, but it can cause problems. I worked in the electronic industry for over 30 years, but I once plugged in a BIOS chip backwards and ruined it. A replacement BIOS chip is rather expensive. The flash BIOS chips can be easily updated and upgraded by software from a floppy disk or even downloaded by modem through the telephone line.

### System configuration and CMOS

When you first turn your computer on, you have to input several pieces of information into the BIOS, such as the date, the time, and the type of drives installed. At one time, there were only 47 types of hard drives. Now there are hundreds. The hard drive type includes the number of heads, cylinders, and sectors and other information. The Pentium Pro motherboards now have a plug-and-play BIOS so that it can recognize and automatically configure most hard drives. (The BIOS can also automatically recognize and configure a plug-in board if it has been manufactured to the plug-and-play specifications.)

The configuration system also needs to be informed as to what kind of floppy drives you have. If you want to reset the time or date, you do it with the system setup.

The system configuration or setup information is stored in complementary metal oxide semiconductors (CMOS) as part of the BIOS. These CMOS transistors use very little power, so there is a small battery for CMOS mounted on the motherboard. This battery keeps the transistors turned on so that they retain the date and time and setup information even when the computer is turned off. The battery can last from three to five years. The batteries were soldered to the older motherboards, which made it very difficult to replace them. Most of the newer motherboards have a plug-in type Dallas battery, such as the one on the 200MHz ASUS motherboard. The 150MHz Micronics motherboard has a large round flat lithium battery, similar to camera batteries, that is easy to replace. This battery can be seen in the diagram in Fig. 3-3 and in Fig. 3-4.

The early PCs did not have the CMOS setup with the on-board battery. You had to input the time and date each time you turned on the computer. It is helpful if the time and date is correct because every time a file is created, DOS stamps the file with the time and date. This makes it very easy to determine which of two files is the later one. The time and date also makes backup a lot easier.

### Keyboard BIOS

The keyboard is a small computer in itself and has its own special BIOS chip on the motherboard. A scan code or signal is sent to the BIOS when a key is pressed and another signal is sent when the key is released. When two keys are pressed, it can detect which one was pressed first. It can also detect when a key is held down longer than normal and will start beeping at you. The last 20 keystrokes are stored in the keyboard memory and are continually flushed out and replaced by new keystrokes.

### Timing

A computer depends on precise timing. Several of the chips on a motherboard control the frequency and timing circuits. The timing is so critical that there are usually one or more crystals on the motherboard that oscillate at a precise frequency to control the timing circuits. In Fig. 3-5, the pen points to a small crystal. The round object below the pen is the battery for the CMOS transistors.

### Memory

The older PCs reserved about one-fourth of the motherboard area for memory chips. The early boards used 64K chips. (64K is 64,000 bytes.) It took nine chips to make 64K, and that is all that some of the motherboards had. Later they developed

**Fig. 3-5**
The pen points to a crystal that controls the operating frequency of the system. Above the pen are jumpers that can be set for different CPUs. The round object in the foreground is a lithium battery for the CMOS.

256K chips, and up to 640K was installed on some motherboards. Still later they developed single in-line memory modules (SIMMs) with 30 contacts with up to 4MB in a single module. Today we have 72-contact SIMMs with up to 128MB that allow us to install up to 512MB on a motherboard in less space than it took for the original 64K. The new dual in-line modules (DIMMs) have 168 pins and up to 128MB per module.

### DMA
The direct memory access (DMA) system allows some processing to take place without having to bother the CPU. For example, the disk drives can exchange data directly with the RAM without having to go through the CPU.

### IRQ
The interrupt request (IRQ) system is a very important part of the computer. It can cause the system to interrupt whatever it is doing and take care of the request. Without the interrupts, nothing would get done. Even if the computer is doing nothing, it must be interrupted and told to perform a task.

There are 16 IRQs, numbered from 0 to 15. Each input/output (I/O) device on the bus is given a unique IRQ number. Software can also perform interrupt requests. There is a priority system, and some interrupts take precedence over others.

Sixteen IRQs might seem like a large number, but it isn't nearly enough. Several of the interrupts are reserved or used by the system so that they are not available. It would have been wonderful if the Pentium had provided about twice as many, but no such luck.

If you want to see how your system is using IRQs, if you have DOS 6.0 or later, just type MSD (for Microsoft Diagnostics). This command will not only let you look at your IRQs, it will tell you about most of the other important elements in your computer.

## Expansion slots
Most of the older ISA motherboards had eight connector slots for plug-in boards. There are several billion dollars worth of boards that have been developed for the PC. You can plug one or more of these boards into a slot and expand the utility and function of your computer.

Quite often eight slots were not enough. We needed slots for such things as floppy and hard drive controllers, serial COM ports, a LPT1 printer port, a monitor adapter, network cards, and several other devices and peripherals. Many of those functions are now built-in on the Pentium Pro motherboards, so we don't need as many slots.

Most Pentium Pro motherboards will have three or four ISA slots and three or four PCI slots.

### The CPU frequency

Ordinarily, the CPU operates externally at the same frequency that it does internally. However, it can be very difficult and expensive to design a circuit that operates faster than 66MHz. The length of circuit traces can have losses due to unwanted capacitance, inductance, resistance, and radiation. However, it can be rather simple to have the CPU operate at twice or even three times as fast over the short circuits inside the CPU. The Pentium Pros operate externally at 60MHz or 66MHz and internally at 150MHz, 180MHz, or 200MHz. Eventually, they will operate internally at 250MHz.

## Alternatives to the Pentium Pro

If you don't have a pressing need for the Pentium Pro at the moment, you can save money on a new Pentium system. The prices have come way down. Some of them will do almost everything a Pentium Pro will do. Intel has increased the speed up to 200MHz on some of the Pentium CPUs. They have also introduced the special Pentium P55C chip that has Intel's multimedia extensions. This chip adds significant improvements to audio and video multimedia.

If you have an older Pentium, Intel has a couple of Pentium overdrives: a 150MHz to replace 75MHz or 90MHz and a 120/133MHz to replace 60MHz or 66MHz CPUs. It is very easy to upgrade to these CPUs. Just lift the lever on the ZIF socket, remove the old CPU and drop in the new one.

### The Cyrix 6x86

Some time ago, several companies came out with clones of the 386 and 486. Intel took them to court for copyright infringement, but they were told that they couldn't copyright a number. So, what should have been called the 586 became the Pentium, and the 686 is the Pentium Pro. Pentium and Pentium Pro are copyrighted names, so Cyrix and NexGen were happy to be able to call their clones 6x86 and Nx686.

### Building a Pentium Pro alternative

The AMD/NexGen Nx686 and the Cyrix 6x86 CPUs are not pin compatible with the Pentium Pro. For one thing, none of the clones will have extra pins for the L1 cache in the Pentium Pro CPU enclosure. However, the clones are pin compatible with many of the Pentium motherboards such as those made by Micronics and others.

There are not many Pentium Pro motherboards available. The ones that are available are rather expensive. There are lots of very reasonable Pentium motherboards available. You can buy a Pentium motherboard and put together a system that will give you most of the power of the Pentium Pro at a very reasonable price. An equivalent clone CPU will cost much less than the genuine Intel.

Here are some price figures at this time. They will be different by the time you read this. I bought a Cyrix 6x86 P120 for $279; an Intel Pentium 120MHz sells for $429. A Cyrix 6x86 P133 sells for $469; an Intel Pentium 133MHz sells for $569. The Cyrix P120 CPU actually operates at 100MHz, but it can outperform an Intel Pentium 120MHz by 30% to 40% in most tests.

They added a *P* to all of their CPUs to indicate the Intel Pentium equivalent. However, remember that the Cyrix 6x86 is a sixth generation CPU being compared to a Pentium, which is a fifth generation chip. However, the Cyrix does almost everything that a Pentium Pro will do and, in some cases, will do it better. The Cyrix CPUs can run all 16-bit and 32-bit software. The Pentium Pro will sometimes be rather slow in running 16-bit software.

Some of the early Pentium motherboards were designed for 5 volt CPU power. The later Pentium, Cyrix, and NexGen CPUs were designed for 3.3 VDC. The early 5 volt Pentium sockets are larger than the 3.3 volt sockets, so you can't install a 6x86 or Nx686 in one of those motherboards.

Another area where the Cyrix 6x86 might not be compatible with a Pentium motherboard is the motherboard frequency. Motherboards have a small crystal that determines the operating frequency. The CPU and motherboard should match. Many motherboards have jumpers that will let you configure it for several different frequencies. The Micronics P54Li motherboard in Fig. 3-6 has jumpers that allows CPUs with frequencies of 75MHz, 90MHz, 100MHz, 120MHz, and 133MHz.

**Fig. 3-6** A Micronics P54Li Pentium motherboard with a Cyrix 6x86 P120 CPU.

If you need Pentium Pro power at this time at a very reasonable cost, then you should consider assembling a Cyrix 6x86. It is assembled exactly the same as the Pentium Pro.

## Upgrading an older computer

If you have an older computer, you can easily upgrade it by installing a new Pentium, Cyrix, or Pentium Pro motherboard.

Many businesses with older computers can save a lot of money by just replacing the motherboard. An enterprising person could save these companies thousands of dollars by upgrading the older computers with new motherboards.

Upgrading with a new motherboard could also save a lot of time. If an older computer is scrapped, along with its hard disks, then backups must be made of all of the data. The data would then have to be re-installed on new hard disks. It would be much quicker and easier to re-use the old hard disks. If more space is needed, add a second hard disk.

A new motherboard will give you all of the advantages of a newer computer but will be much less expensive than buying a complete new system. This is one of the most cost effective ways to move up to a newer system. You should be able to use most of your old components because all PCs use the same basic components other than the motherboard.

However, except for the case, there probably isn't much you could use from an old XT. The XT keyboard looks just like the 286 and all later keyboards, and even has the same connector, but it is electronically different. Keyboards are relatively inexpensive and can cost from $10 to $50.

### Instructions for upgrading with a new motherboard

**Step 1: Know your CMOS setup** *Important!* You must be able to tell the CMOS setup on your new system what type of hard disk drive you have. If you do not furnish all of the proper information as to the type, the number of cylinders, the number of heads, and the number of sectors, you might not be able to access the data on your hard disk. The BIOS on the Pentium Pro is a Plug-and-Play, so it might be able to recognize your hard disk unless it has been formatted differently than factory specifications.

The BIOS on some of the older systems could not recognize any hard disk over 500MB without special drivers and other software. Because of this limitation, some people might have formatted a 540MB or greater disk as a 500MB. In a case like this, then you should input the number of cylinders, sectors, and heads to match how the disk was originally formatted.

If you don't have your system configuration written down somewhere, run your system CMOS setup to determine the data. Many of the older machines used several different methods to access the CMOS setup. If you have documentation, it should tell you how to access the setup mode. On most systems, you are given the opportunity to press something such as the Escape key and Del key while the system is booting up. On some systems, if you hold down a key of the keyboard while it is booting up, it will give you an error and tell you to press F1. This usually puts you into the setup mode. Run it and write down the type of drives, the number of cylinders, heads, sectors, landing zone, and any other information given. You might not need it, but you should stop and make a complete backup of your hard disk before you remove the old motherboard.

The next thing to do is to shut off the power and disconnect the power cord and the keyboard cable. You will probably have several other cables on the back of the PC. It is very easy to forget how and where things were plugged in. It might be a good idea to use a felt marking pen and put a distinctive mark across the cable connector and the board connector. When you get ready to plug the cables back into the new boards, all you have to do is line up the various marks on the cables and board connectors. This will assure that the cables are plugged back into the new system correctly.

**Step 2: Remove case cover**   Locate and remove the screws that hold the case or cover on. For most early systems, there were five screws on the back panel: one in each corner and one in the top center. For the tower cases, there are usually three screws on each side in the back. The four screws that hold the power supply in place should not be removed. Once the cover screws are removed, you can slide the cover off toward the front. For the tower cases, the cover slides off to the rear.

**Step 3: Make a diagram before disassembly**   Once the cover is removed, before doing anything else, take a piece of paper and make a rough drawing of where each board is plugged in and any cable that might be plugged into it. Then again use a felt marking pen to put a mark across each cable and connector in a way so that you can be sure to match the cable and connectors back up to the same board. For example, if you mark a slash on the cable connector and board near one end, it will be easy to match the two when you plug them back together.

Some cables can be plugged in backwards or upside down. You can prevent this if the connectors are marked. Note in particular how the two connectors from the power supply are plugged into the motherboard. Note that the four black wires are in the center. These two connectors must be connected to the new motherboard in the same way.

Some systems are using the newer ATX power supply and motherboard connector. This has a molded connector that can only be plugged in properly. Figure 3-7 shows the ATX power supply motherboard connector. Except for the connector, the ATX power supply is the same as the older standard. However, note that, because of the connector, this power supply could not be used with the old standard motherboard and neither could a standard power supply be used with an ATX motherboard. When ordering the case and motherboard, make sure that they are compatible, one way or the other.

The cables to be removed from the old motherboard might be ribbon cables from the floppy and hard drives to the controller. If at all possible, leave the cables connected to the boards and just pull the boards out of the motherboard slot. You shouldn't have to remove any of the disk drives. Leave the cables plugged into the drives if possible.

At the front of the motherboard, there will be several small wires for the front panel light emitting diodes (LEDs) and for the speaker. If these small wires and connectors are not marked, you might take some masking tape and put labels on them. Your new Pentium Pro motherboard will have similar pins for the connectors, but they might be in a different location.

**Fig. 3-7** The ATX power supply connector for the motherboard.

Once all of the boards are removed and all of the cables are disconnected, look for a screw near the front and in the center of the motherboard and another in the rear of the motherboard. When these screws are removed, pull the motherboard to the left then lift it out. You might have to jiggle it a bit. The motherboard has grooved plastic standoffs that slide into raised slots.

**Step 4: Set switches and jumpers** You should have received some documentation with your new motherboard. Set any switches or jumpers that are needed to configure the system. Install the memory chips. You might not be able to use the memory chips from your old motherboard if they are not fast enough or if they are 30 pins. (Several companies make adapters so that 30-pin memory can be used in 72-pin sockets. Call SIMMSaver at 1-800-636-7281, the Minden Group at 1-800-746-3973, or SIMMStack at 1-800-209-7126.)

The SIMMs are very easy to remove and install, just press the lever at the ends. To install, just drop in the slot at an angle and pull forward until the catches at the ends engage. The SIMMs have a notch on one end so that they can only be inserted properly. Make sure that they are completely seated, otherwise the computer might not boot up. I'll have more to say about memory in chapter 4.

**Step 5: Install the new motherboard** You might have to remove the white plastic standoffs from your old motherboard and use them on your new one. To remove the standoffs, use a pair of pliers and compress the portion of the standoff on the topside of the motherboard.

There might be extra mounting holes in the motherboard. Make sure that you have installed the plastic standoffs in the proper holes, then drop the motherboard into the slots and push it to the right until it locks in place. Replace the screws in the front and back of the motherboard.

Connect all of the front panel LED wires and the speaker wires. The motherboard should have some markings to indicate where each small connector should be plugged in. You might have to refer to your documentation for some wires. Your new motherboard might not use all of the front panel LED wires.

Next, connect the two power supply cables to the motherboard. (*Note! These connectors can be plugged in wrong. When connected properly, the four black wires will be in the center adjacent to each other.*) The power supply connector is usually in two separate cables with six wires in each cable. They are sometimes marked P8 and P9.

If you have an ATX power supply and motherboard, you will have a connector such as that shown in Fig. 3-7. This connector can only be plugged in properly.

**Step 6: Re-install boards**  Re-install all of your plug-in boards and reconnect any cables that were disconnected. Connect the monitor and keyboard. Plug in the power cord. Recheck all of your connections to make sure that everything is plugged in properly.

**Step 7: Turn on and boot-up**  Now, turn on the power. You should try the system before you put the cover back on. This way, if it doesn't work, it will be fairly easy to check all of the boards and cables to make sure they are installed correctly.

If you have reconnected everything right, the system should work. Run the setup routine to tell the CMOS and the BIOS the time, the date, and other information. You must input the exact numbers for cylinders, heads, and sectors for the type of hard disks that you have. Otherwise, you will not be able to access your hard drive.

**Step 8: Re-install cover**  If everything works okay, put the cover back on and congratulate yourself for saving a bundle.

### Do you need to upgrade?

In December 1993, I paid $1350 for a motherboard with an Intel 60MHz Pentium. I can buy a motherboard today with a Cyrix 5x86 120MHz CPU for about $200. At this time, the Cyrix 133MHz 6x86 CPU chip is priced at $450 each in lots of 1000. The Intel 150MHz CPU chip is priced at $974 each in lots of 1000. The ASUS motherboard with an Intel 200MHz CPU costs $2595 at this time.

Prices quoted are for comparison only and will be different by the time you read this. If you can afford to wait for awhile and don't really need a Pentium Pro at the moment, I suggest replacing the motherboard in your older computer with a low cost Pentium clone motherboard. For $200 to $600 you can have an upgrade that will do almost everything the Pentium Pro will do. In a year or so, the prices of the Pentium Pro will be a lot more reasonable.

# Which motherboard should you buy?

What you should buy will depend on how much you want to spend. If you can afford it, buy the fastest Pentium Pro or Pentium Pro clone.

Each company tries to differentiate their product from the others. So you will have several choices. Some companies might claim that their system runs certain tests a few microseconds faster than another. Because of this, they might charge a lot more money than one that is a fraction of a second slower. Which system you choose should depend on what you want to use your computer for, how much money you can afford to spend, and whether you can afford to spend a few extra microseconds waiting for your system to process data.

# Sources for motherboards

I do a lot of my buying and shopping by mail order. I look through computer magazines—such as the *Computer Shopper*, *Byte*, *PC World*, *PC Magazine*, and about 50 others—and compare prices and products. Several of the computer magazines have a section near the back where they list the products advertised for that month. The items are categorized and grouped by product type. The page number for each ad is listed, so it is easy to find what you are looking for. This is a great help when you consider that the *Computer Shopper* can have 1000 large tabloid sized pages.

If you live near a large city, there will probably be several computer dealers in your city. You can ask them about components. The local dealers might be a bit more expensive than mail order, but the local dealer might be able to help you if you have any problems, so the extra cost might be worth it.

Again, if you live in a large city, there will probably be computer swap meets every so often. Most of your local dealers will meet at a large auditorium or fairgrounds and set up booths to sell their wares. Most dealers usually offer very good prices and discounts at the swap meets. You can go from booth to booth and compare prices and products. I often go to swap meets even if I don't need anything. There is usually a large crowd and lots of excitement in the air. It's almost like a circus.

# 4
# Memory

Memory is one of the most critical elements of the computer. Computing as we know it would not be possible without memory. There have been some fantastic advances in computing in just a few short years. Much of that advancement is because of the new memory technologies. One of the first computers, the ENIAC, was built in the early 1940s. It used a very large number of diode vacuum tubes. The tubes could be wired so that they acted like switches that could be turned on or off. They required an enormous amount of energy and space. The tubes also burned out frequently. They usually had one person who did nothing but replace burned out tubes.

In the late 1950s and 1960s the computers used core memory. The cores were small iron donuts. Two coils of wire were wound around each core. When dc voltage was passed through the coils of wire, depending on whether the polarity was negative or positive, the core could be magnetized or demagnetized. The state of magnetization of the core could then represent a 1 or a 0. The cores had to be hand wound and required a lot of intensive labor, which made them very expensive. They were also very bulky, so the amount of memory on a computer was very limited. On the plus side, the cores used very little energy, and they did not burn out.

Later transistor memory and then DRAM was developed. The memory developments helped launch the computer revolution that has changed the world forever. The revolution is not over yet.

The PC uses two primary types of memory: ROM and RAM.

## ROM

Read only memory (ROM) is memory that cannot be altered or changed. Some early laptop and notebook computers had DOS stored in ROM. However, the principal use of ROM in PCs is for the basic input/output system (BIOS). It facilitates the transfer of data among peripherals. The BIOS contains routines that do a power on self test (POST) when you first turn the computer on. Depending on the vendor, the BIOS might also have plug-and-play, several diagnostic routines, and other utilities.

Earlier, the ROM programs were usually burned into electrically programmable read only memory (EPROMs) chips. Most BIOS chips for the Pentium Pro now use flash memory. Fairly large programs and text can be stored on a ROM chip. The ROM BIOS for an early XT could be programmed onto a 64K ROM chip. The 486 ROM BIOS uses a 512K chip. All of the text in the book that you are holding in your hand can be stored in less than 512K. The Pentium Pro BIOS requires even more ROM. If you refer back to Fig. 1-2, you can see the AMI BIOS chip in the lower-right portion of the motherboard.

The computer industry never stands still; it is constantly in a state of change. Often, these changes make it necessary to update or upgrade the BIOS. With the EPROM chip, the computer had to be opened up to remove and replace the BIOS. With the BIOS in flash memory, all that is necessary is to use software to update it.

# RAM

If we open a file from a hard disk or a floppy, the files and data are read from the disk and placed in random access memory (RAM). When we load in a program, be it a word processor, spreadsheet, database, or whatever, we will be working in the system RAM. If we are writing, programming, or creating another program, we will be working in RAM.

Actually it is dynamic RAM or DRAM. Random access means that we can find, address, change, or erase any single byte among several million bytes.

We can also randomly access any particular byte on a floppy or hard disk. We cannot randomly access data on a magnetic tape system. The data on the tape is stored sequentially. To find a particular byte, we would have to run the tape forward or backwards to the proper area.

Being able to randomly access the memory allows us to read and write to it immediately. It is somewhat like an electronic blackboard. Here we can manipulate the data, do calculations, enter more data, edit, search data bases, or do any of the thousands of things that software programs allow us to do. We can access and change the data in RAM very quickly.

RAM memory is an essential element of the computer. Of course, if you are working on a large file, you will need a lot of RAM. If you are using Windows and you don't have enough RAM, some portions of the file might be loaded onto a special area of the hard disk and used as a swap file.

## RAM volatility

An important difference in ROM and RAM is that RAM is *volatile*. That is, it disappears if the machine is rebooted or if you exit a program without saving it. If there is a power interruption to the computer, even for a brief instant, any data in RAM will be gone forever.

You should get in the habit of saving your files to disk frequently, especially if you live in an area where there are power failures due to storms or other reasons. Most word processors and some of the other programs can be set up to automatically save open files to disk at frequent intervals.

I hate to admit it, I have occasionally become distracted and shut the power off without saving my data. I am sure others have done it also. I am very thankful that my system usually had done an automatic backup so that I didn't lose too much data.

If you are working on critical data, you should also have an uninterruptible power supply (UPS). If there is a power outage or brownout, the UPS can take over and keep the computer running until you can save your data to disk and shut down.

## How RAM is addressed

Each byte of memory has a separate address. The cells in the memory bank could be analogous to the "pigeon holes" for the room keys of a large hotel. They would be arranged in rows and columns so that the pigeon holes would correspond to each room on each floor. If the hotel had 100 rooms, you could have 10 across and 10 down. It would be very simple to find any one of the 100 keys by counting across and then down to the particular room number. Memory addressing is a bit more complicated than the hotel pigeon holes, but with just 20 address lines (220) any individual byte out of one million bytes (1MB) can be quickly accessed. Actually 1MB, or 2 to the 20th power, would equal 1,048,576 bytes.

One byte is also called a *word*, so the old 8-bit XTs can only address one word at a time. The 16-bit 286 can address two words, the 32-bit 386, 486, Pentium, and Pentium Pro systems can address four words at a time.

## DRAMs

Dynamic RAM, or DRAM, is the most common type of memory used today. Each memory cell has a small etched transistor that is kept in its memory state, either on or off by an electrical charge on a very small capacitor.

Capacitors are similar to small rechargeable batteries. Units can be charged up with a voltage to represent 1s or left uncharged to represent 0s. However, those that are charged up immediately start to lose their charge. So they must be constantly "refreshed" with a new charge.

Steve Gibson, the developer of SpinRite, compared the memory cell capacitors to a small bucket that has a hole in the bottom. Those buckets, or cells, that represent 1s are filled with water, but they immediately start leaking out through the hole in the bottom. So they have to be constantly refilled. You don't have to worry about filling those buckets, or cells, that represent 0s.

A computer might spend 7% or more of its time just refreshing the DRAM chips. Also each time a cell is accessed, that small voltage in the capacitor flows through a transistor to turn it on. This drains the charge from the capacitor, so it must be refreshed before it can be accessed again. In our bucket of water comparison, when the cell is accessed, the bucket is turned upside down and emptied. So, if it represents a 1, it must be refilled immediately. Of course, it takes a finite amount of time to fill a bucket or to place a charge on a capacitor. If the memory cell has a speed of 60 nanosecond (ns), it might take 60ns, plus the time it takes to recycle, which might be 100ns or more, before that cell can again be accessed.

### Refreshment and wait states

The speed of the DRAM chips in your system should match your system CPU. You might be able to install slower chips, but your system would have to work with wait states. If the DRAM is too slow, a wait state will have to be inserted. A wait state causes the CPU and the rest of the system to sit and wait while the RAM is being accessed and then refreshed. Wait states could deprive your system of one of its greatest benefits: speed. Wait states are a terrible waste of time.

If the CPU is operating at a very high frequency, it might have to sit and wait one cycle, or *one wait state*, for the refresh cycle. The wait state might be only a millionth of a second or less, which might not seem like much time; however, if the computer is doing several million operations per second, it can add up.

It takes a finite amount of time to charge up the DRAM. Some DRAM chips can be charged up much faster than others. For example, the DRAM chips needed for an XT at 4.77MHz can take as much as 200 nanoseconds (ns) or billionths of a second to be refreshed. A Pentium Pro running at 200MHz needs chips that can be refreshed in 60ns or less time. Of course, the faster chips cost more. Even the fastest conventional DRAM must wait while it is being read or written to. It must also wait while it is being refreshed. So it requires two wait states.

### Interleaved memory

Most of the newer faster systems use interleaved memory to reduce the need for wait states. The memory is always installed in multiples of two. You can install two banks of 2MB, 4MB, 8MB, 16MB, 32MB, or 64MB of memory.

One half of the memory would be refreshed on one cycle, then the other half on the next cycle. If the CPU needed to access an address that was in the half already refreshed, it would be available immediately. If the needed address happened to be in the side being refreshed, it would have to wait. Interleaving does reduce the access time somewhat, but it isn't a perfect solution.

### Extended Data Out (EDO)

As the CPUs keep getting faster and faster, it is increasingly difficult to develop DRAM chips that can keep up. A new type of DRAM being manufactured by Micron Technology (208-368-4000) is called Extended Data Out (EDO). It operates about 10% faster than ordinary DRAM and is still fairly reasonable in cost.

Conventional DRAM requires two wait states for accessing and refreshment times. Due to its architecture, EDO only needs one wait state. EDO also uses a wider bandwidth during the address select so that there are fewer cache misses. The motherboard must be designed to accept the EDO DRAM.

An advanced type of EDO memory is *Burst EDO*. Its design and architecture requires zero wait states to read or write. BEDO DRAM will increase system efficiency by as much as 13% or more.

### Synchronous DRAM

Another type of memory is Synchronous DRAM (S-DRAM). Several companies are manufacturing it. It is very fast and comparatively inexpensive. Some believe that it will eventually displace standard DRAM chips and be the choice for the main memory.

Several other types of memory are being developed, such as Burst EDO, Rambus DRAM, fast Page Mode DRAM, hyperpage DRAM, and synchronous graphics RAM (SGRAM).

## SRAM

Static RAM is made up of actual transistors. It requires a single transistor for each bit. The transistors can be turned on to represent 1s or left off to represent 0s and will stay in that condition until they receive a change signal. They do not need to be refreshed, but they revert back to 0 when the computer is turned off or if the power is interrupted. They are very fast and can operate at speeds of 15ns or less.

The 486 and Pentium machines all have a level 2 (L2) cache on the motherboard made up of SRAM chips. However, the Pentium Pro has a 256K or 512K L2 cache in the same enclosure. It is very near to the CPU and is closely coupled, so there is no need for an external L2 on the motherboard. However, the 15.5 or 31 million transistors in the Pentium Pro cache do add to the cost of the CPU.

## The CPU and the RAM bus

The CPU is the brains of the computer. Almost everything that happens in a computer must travel over a bus path and go through the CPU. The CPU and computer bus could be compared to your brain and the nerves in your body.

You will probably have several plug-in boards and peripheral components in your computer. The Pentium Pro usually has three or four ISA slots and three or four PCI slots. The boards plugged into the ISA slots will communicate with the CPU over a 16-bit bus at about 10MHz. This slow speed is so that the system will still be compatible with the early hardware and software. The boards in the PCI slots will be able to communicate at the CPU external frequency. The CPU will move data back and forth to the RAM at the CPU external frequency on its own 32-bit special memory bus.

The early CPUs had a single external and internal frequency. However, newer systems operate at faster and ever higher frequencies. If the frequency is very high, say above 66MHz, the signals can be very difficult to control. The least amount of stray capacitance, inductance, or resistance in a circuit can play havoc with the signal and cause all sorts of errors. However, within a small confined area, such as the CPU, high frequencies can be tolerated. So Intel developed their DX2 CPUs, then later the DX4s. These CPUs go back and forth to the RAM at a fairly leisurely pace of 33MHz or so; however, once the data is inside the CPU, it can be processed at two or three times the speed that it took to move it to the CPU. The Pentium Pro can process data internally at 150MHz, 180MHz, or 200MHz, but externally it operates with a crystal controlled frequency of 60MHz or 66.667MHz.

## Cache memory

A cache system can speed up computer operations quite a lot. When running an application program, the CPU often loops in and out of certain areas and uses portions of the same memory over and over. A cache system is usually made up of very fast memory chips, such as SRAM, that can store the often-used data so that it is quickly accessible to the CPU.

The data that is moved back and forth between the CPU and RAM is comprised of electrical on and off voltages. The electrons move at almost the speed of light. Still it takes a finite amount of time to move a large amount of data. It takes even more time to access the RAM, find the data that is needed, then move it back to the CPU.

The computer might be slowed down considerably if it has to search the entire memory each time it has to fetch some data. If data that is often used is stored in a cache, it can be accessed by the CPU very quickly. A good cache can greatly increase the processing speed.

### Level 1 and level 2 caches

The 486 CPU has an 8K built-in cache among its 1.2 million transistors; the Pentium Pro has two 8K built-in caches among its 5.5 million transistors. The built-in cache is called a *level 1 cache*, or *L1*. Because it does not have to travel outside the CPU, it operates at the same internal speed as the CPU. Many of the CPUs operate externally two to three times slower than the internal speed.

The 486 and Pentium CPUs also used a *level 2 (L2)* or *external cache* made up of fast SRAM located on the motherboard. The speed and static characteristics of SRAM makes it an excellent device for memory cache systems.

Again, however, it takes a finite amount of time for the data to move from the CPU over the bus at an external frequency to the SRAM cache. The Pentium Pro lessened this problem by building a L2 cache in the same enclosure as the CPU. The L2 cache is closely coupled to the CPU and communicates with it over a very short 64-bit interface or special bus at the internal CPU frequency. The L2 cache will either be 256K or 512K. Caches made up of SRAM transistors are very fast, but they require a single transistor for each bit, so 256K cache requires 15.5 million transistors, and 512K requires 31 million.

### Disk cache

Cache memory should not be confused with disk caching. Often, while a program runs, it might need to access a hard disk. Again, certain chunks of data might be used over and over. If a small disk cache is set up in RAM, the CPU can import the data from a RAM cache much quicker than reading it from even the fastest hard disk. So a disk cache set up in RAM can help a program to run much faster.

If you have installed Windows 3.x or Windows 95, it will have set up a *swapfile* in an area on your hard disk. If you are running a large program and it happens to point to an address that is not in memory, it will go to the hard disk for it. It will then remove a *page* that is in memory, swap it to the hard disk, and bring in to RAM the address that is needed.

Of course, having to use a swapfile slows things down. This can be avoided if you have lots of RAM. Most programs can be run in a minimum of 4MB; however, if you can afford it, you should have at least 16MB. Even with 16MB, there will probably be times when the system will have to use the swapfile, but not nearly as often.

Some SCSI and IDE hard disk interface controllers might have a disk cache.

### Hit rate

A well-designed cache system might have a "hit rate" of over 90%. This means that, each time the CPU needs a block of data, it will find it in the nearby, fast cache. A good cache system can increase the speed and performance considerably.

## Motherboard memory

The old XT motherboard could only accept 640K of memory on the motherboard. The chips were large dual-inline pin (DIPs) that took up about one-fourth of the entire motherboard. Many of the new Pentium Pro motherboards can accept up to 512MB in about half the space required for the old 640K.

## SIMMS

Your computer motherboard will have sockets for single in-line memory modules (SIMMs). SIMMs take up very little space and can store enormous amounts of memory. Older motherboards had sockets with 30 contacts that would accept SIMM assemblies of 256K, 500K, 1MB, or 4MB.

Figure 4-1 shows a couple of the older 30-contact SIMMs at the top and a couple of 72-contact SIMMs at the bottom. Most of the newer motherboards have sockets with 72 contacts.

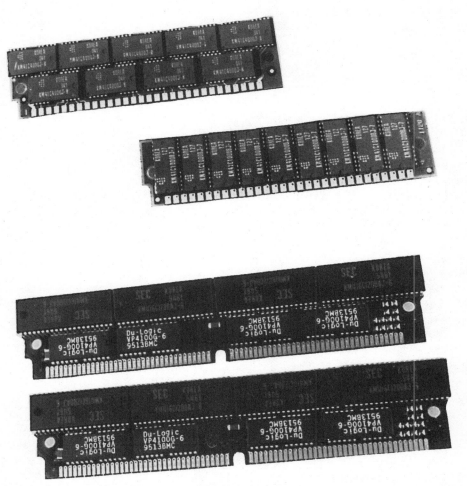

**Fig. 4-1** Two different types of SIMMs: older 30-contact at the top and newer 72-contact at the bottom.

The 72-contact SIMMs use the designation "$n$ x 36" to designate the amount of memory on the SIMM. To find the amount of memory, multiply the first number times 4. For example, $2 \times 36$ is 8MB, $4 \times 36$ is 16MB, and $8 \times 36$ is 32MB. What this means is that there are four times nine chips for each megabyte of memory. The ninth chip is for parity, which is discussed in the following section.

The SIMM assemblies are made up of chips on a small board that is plugged slantwise into a special connector.

### Parity

The old DIP chips have two rows of 8 pins, or 16 pins total. It requires nine chips of whatever type of memory designated. For example, for 64K, it takes 8 64K × 1-bit chips plus 1 64K × 1-bit chip for parity checking. If 256K chips are used, it takes 8 256K × 1-bit chips, plus 1 256 × 1-bit chip for parity checking. Even with the high-capacity SIMMs, it still takes nine chips to make up the designated memory. For a 4MB SIMM, it takes 8 4096 × 1-bit plus 1 4096 × 1-bit for parity checking. The nine chips would all be on the one small SIMM plug-in board. The same system is used even for the $n \times 36$ SIMM chips.

The Macintosh systems do not use the parity checking chip, so they have only the 8 × whatever the SIMM designation. Memory is one of the few areas where the components for Macintosh can be less expensive than those for ISA machines. A memory ad in a current computer magazine listed a price for an 8 chip Macintosh SIMM of $4 \times 8$, 70 ns at $120. For a 9 chip ISA SIMM of $4 \times 9$, 70 ns, the price was $137. Some have said that the 9th chip for parity checking is not necessary. Some of the Pentium Pro motherboards are now using nonparity $4 \times 8$ SIMMS.

Memory must be configured in banks. Most motherboards are designed for four banks: bank 0, 1, 2, and 3. Check the documentation that came with your motherboard. You must fill the lowest numbered bank before filling other banks.

Because memory is interleaved on most systems, you must install the SIMMs in multiples of two. You cannot intermix SIMMs of different values. For example, for 16MB, you would have to install two 8MB modules. If you install a single module instead of the required two, the computer might not boot up. The screen might be completely blank.

*Caution!* It is possible to have a module that is not seated properly. If this happens, the computer might not boot up. The screen might be completely blank with no error messages or any indication of the problem.

Before buying memory, check your documentation for the type and speed that you need. The 1 x 36 SIMM can give you 4MB in one 72-contact slot. The $2 \times 36$ will give you 8MB in each slot. There are also $4 \times 36$ for 16MB and $8 \times 36$ for 32MB. You can install 128MB in just four slots by using $8 \times 36$ SIMMs. Simple Technology (800-367-7330) makes a "stacked" Tower 64MB SIMM. They simply stacked four 16MB chips atop each, other times eight, to get 64MB of nonparity memory. With four of these SIMMs, you could have 256MB of memory.

Depending on what you are going to use your computer for, you could probably get by with two 1 × 36, which would give you 8MB. I would recommend against it unless you can't possibly afford more memory. Windows 95 and most other programs will run with only 8MB, but most programs will run much faster with more memory. If you start out with 1 x 36 SIMMs, if you want to add more memory, you will be limited to 1 x 36 SIMMs. However, if all you can afford is $1 \times 36$, and you wanted to add more later, you could use the memory socket expanders, which will be discussed in the following section.

I would suggest that you buy the largest modules that you can afford. Memory is somewhat like money in that you can never have too much.

The SIMMs will have speeds of 70 and 60 nanoseconds (ns). The smaller the number of ns, the faster. You should buy the speed recommended by your documentation. It is possible to mix SIMMs with different speeds, but the system will be limited to the speed of the slowest SIMM.

Because the memory comes in modules and is socketed, you can add as much as your motherboard allows. It is possible that a memory chip can fail. The BIOS does a power on self test (POST) every time the computer is booted. During this test, all of the memory chips are tested. If an assembly becomes defective, it is easy enough to replace it. One disadvantage of having large capacity SIMMs is that, if a chip fails, you have to replace the whole SIMM. The price in a current magazine for an $8 \times 36$, or 32MB, SIMM is $905. Another company advertises a $16 \times 36$, or 64MB, for $2025. (The prices listed are for comparison only. They will be different by the time you read this.)

Because memory must be installed in pairs, you would need two of these SIMMs. Fortunately, memory chips don't fail very often. Most dealers will give you a lifetime replacement guarantee if one of their modules fail. Be sure to ask for this guarantee if you are buying high capacity SIMMs.

You might have to set some switches or install some jumpers to configure your motherboard to the amount of memory that you have installed. Check the documentation that you got with your motherboard.

The Pentium Pro CPU can address 4 gigabytes ($2\wedge32$ = 4,294,967,296 bytes). A gigabyte is also the same as a billion bytes.

Incidentally, 4GB of DRAM, in 1MB SIMM packages, would require 4096 modules. You would need a fairly large board to install that much memory. It would also be rather expensive. At $35 per megabyte, 4096 modules would cost $143,360. If 64MB DRAM SIMM chips were used, you would only need 64 SIMMS to make 4GB. The cost of 4GB using 64MB SIMMS at $2025 each would be $129,600.

A few companies are developing 256MB SIMMs, which should be available by the time you read this. It would only take 16 of these chips to make 4GB.

While 4GB might seem like a lot of memory, at one time, we thought that 640K was a lot. However, the more memory a computer has, the more powerful it can be. The Pentium Pro can have one, two, or four CPUs in a single glueless system, all working together. 4GB of DRAM might not be unreasonable for a system such as this.

### Memory socket expanders

Most motherboards come with only four sockets for SIMMs. If you started out with a low capacity SIMM such as the 4MB modules, you might want to add more. A few companies—the Minden Group (800-746-3973), SIMMSTACK (800-209-7126), and SIMMSaver (800-636-7281)—have memory socket expansion boards that plug into the original sockets. Each plug-in expansion board has four additional sockets to allow you to add more SIMMs. Some of these boards will allow you to use the old 30 pin modules in the newer 72 pin sockets. If you are upgrading, the expansion sockets might let you use your old memory if it is fast enough.

If your old memory is not fast enough, you might be able to trade it in or sell it to some of the memory chip vendors. Several vendors are buying used memory. After all, it doesn't ever wear out. Just don't expect to get a whole lot of money for your old memory.

## DIMMs

Dual Inline Memory Modules (DIMMs) are very high density, fast memory chips. They look very much like the SIMMs, but they have two banks of chips soldered to a circuit board. Because they require less space for the same amount of memory, it is expected that DIMMs will become the chip of choice eventually. Most SIMMs now have 72 pins. DIMMs might have 72 pins or 168 pins. The motherboard has to be designed to accept the chips.

## Flash memory

A few years ago, Intel developed flash memory, which is similar to Erasable Programmable Read Only Memory (EPROM). AMD and several other companies now also manufacture it. Flash memory is fairly slow compared to DRAM and SRAM, so it can't replace them. However, it can be equivalent to hard disk memory. The hard disk is a mechanical device that will eventually wear out or fail. The flash memory is strictly electronic and should last several lifetimes. A disadvantage is that flash memory is still rather expensive and limited in the amount of memory that can be installed on a card. Most Pentium Pros now use flash memory for the BIOS chip.

## Video RAM

Video RAM (VRAM) chips are a bit different than DRAM chips. They are special memory chips that are used on the better (and more expensive) monitor adapter cards. The VRAM chips are unusual in that they have double ports so that they can be accessed and refreshed at the same time.

A new memory standard Unified Memory Architecture (UMA) is being used on many of the high-end graphics and video accelerator adapters.

## Printer memory

Your laser printer probably came with a minimum amount of memory or about 512K. A laser printer determines where each dot on a printed page should be, then prints the whole page. Most printers require memory that is installed on special proprietary boards. You might need to add more memory for better printing speed. Most lasers will perform much better if they have a minimum of 2MB.

# How much memory do you need?

This will depend primarily on what you intend to use your computer for. For word processing or small applications, you can get by with 640K. If you have more time than money, you can get by with a minimum of 4MB. However, you will be much better off with at least 16MB if you expect to use Windows, large databases, or spreadsheets. If your Pentium Pro is to be used as a large workstation, you might need to install up to 512MB of memory. Two of the most important things that makes a computer powerful is the speed of the CPU and the amount of memory available.

Having lots of memory is like having a car with a large engine. You might not need that extra power very often, but it sure feels great being able to call on it when you do need it.

# Prices

Prices of almost all computer components have dropped except for memory. Software and systems are being designed to use more and more memory, so there is a big demand for it. Eventually the prices should start coming down. At the present time, memory costs about $35 per megabyte. Hopefully, it will be less by the time you read this, but don't count on it. I have checked prices in some back issues of computer magazines, and they are higher at the present time than they were a couple of months ago.

# Installing the chips

One of the first things that you should do before touching your expensive memory chips, or any sensitive electronic device, is to discharge any static electric charge that you might have on you. To discharge yourself, touch some metal object, such as an unpainted metal case of a computer, a metal lamp, or some other object that is plugged into an outlet. The object that you touch does not have to be turned on.

The SIMM chips are very easy to install. If you refer back to the 72 contact SIMMs in Fig. 4-1, you will see a cutout on one end and a notch in the bottom center so that it can only be inserted one way. There is a small hole in each end of the SIMM board. There is a projection on the socket that fits in this hole when the SIMMs are inserted in the socket. Just lay the assembly slantwise in the socket, then push it to an upright position. Spring loaded clamps on each end of the socket lock the assembly in place. See Fig. 4-2. To remove the assembly, press the clamps on each end.

When you install the SIMMs make sure that they are completely seated. If not, your computer will not boot up.

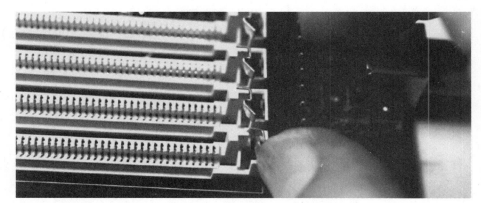

**Fig. 4-2** The spring clamps on each end of the SIMM sockets that hold the SIMMs in place.

# 5
# Floppy drives and disks

Some of the original PCs used a cassette recorder for data storage. When IBM developed the floppy system, it was a tremendous contribution to the computer revolution. However, the old floppy system is gradually being replaced by the recordable CD-ROM, magneto-optical disks, and high-density removable magnetic disks. At the present time, however, there is still a great need for floppy systems, especially in home offices and small businesses.

If you have used a computer for some time, you probably have a large stack of floppies. I have about 500 of them with programs that I might never use, but just in case, I am installing both 5.25" and 3.5" floppies in my 200MHz Pentium Pro.

## The floppy evolution

In the early days, it was possible to run a PC program with a single 140K floppy disk drive. Floppy disks were all that we had in those days. Most software programs were very small compared to those of today. Almost all of the early drives used single-sided floppy disks that held from 140K to 180K. It was a great leap forward when IBM introduced a PC with two floppy drives that could handle double-sided floppy disks. Even if you were fortunate enough to have a PC with two floppy drives, doing any kind of computing involved an endless amount of disk swapping and took forever to get anything done.

The 140K systems were soon replaced with 320K double-sided systems, then 360K, then 1.2MB, then 3.5" 720K, 1.44MB, and 2.88MB drives. The 2.88MB 3.5" drive and disks are still rather expensive. I just looked through the 1000 pages of ads in the latest *Computer Shopper*. They have hundreds of ads for the 1.44MB drive, some for as little as $26. I only saw one ad for a 2.88MB TDK drive. The cost was $79 for the drive and $2 each for the disks. I have seen ads for 1.44MB disks for as little as $.30 each. The 2.88MB system is supported by built-in controllers on most Pentium Pro motherboards. The 2.88MB system doesn't offer that much more advantage over the 1.44MB.

Most software programs today are very user friendly. The more user friendly they are, the larger they are. Today most programs are shipped on several 1.44MB disks in a compressed form. They must be uncompressed before they can be used. Many of the programs require from 25MB up to 60MB or more of hard disk space to be installed and to be able to run. It would be impossible to run programs such as these with a floppy disk system.

Many companies are beginning to use CD-ROMs instead of floppies to distribute software. One CD-ROM disc can store about 650MB. A CD-ROM disc can hold all of the software programs and include a very large instruction manual on disc. Eventually all software will be distributed on the high capacity CD-ROMs. It is much less expensive for the vendor to stamp out one CD-ROM rather than have to copy 25 floppy disks. Many of the companies now charge more if you want the software on floppy disks.

# How floppy drives operate

Computers rely to a very large extent on magnetism and voltage. Magnetism and voltage are closely interrelated. Magnetic lines of force can be produced when voltage is passed through a coil of wire that is wrapped around a piece of iron. The process can be reversed by passing a coil of wire through a magnetic field to produce voltage.

The amount of magnetism or voltage produced in these processes varies enormously depending on such factors as the voltage level, the number of turns of wire, the properties of the iron core, the frequency of the voltage, and many other factors.

The floppy drive spins a disk much like a record player. The disk is made from a type of plastic material called polyethylene terephthalate, which is coated with a magnetic material made primarily of iron oxide. It is similar to the tape that is used in cassette tape recorders.

The drive has a head that is basically a piece of iron with a coil of wire around it. The iron core for the head is shaped somewhat like a *C*. (Actually, the modern head is somewhat more complicated than a simple iron core and is made from a ferromagnetic material.) When voltage is passed through the coil of wire, a magnetic field is produced between the ends of the *C*. When a pulse of voltage passes through the head, the spot on the disk beneath the head is magnetized. During play back, when the magnetized spot on the disk passes beneath the head, it will cause a small voltage to be produced in the head.

Of course, the voltage produced by the magnetism on the disk is very small, so it must be amplified. Placing this small voltage on the base of a transistor can cause it to act like a switch to turn on a larger voltage. Most of the voltages used in computers is direct current, usually 3 to 5 volts dc. Transistors can be used to turn the direct current on and off. When the current is on, it can represent a 1; when it is off, it can represent a 0. A transistor can be switched on and off millions of times per second. Computer software programs control the various transistors causing them to turn on or off.

A pulse of electricity that represents a 1 causes the head to magnetize that portion of track beneath the head. If the next spot of the same track is not magnetized, it can represent a 0. When the tracks are read, the head detects whether each portion of the track is magnetized or not. If the spot is magnetized, it creates a small voltage signal to represent a 1, or represents a 0 if it is not magnetized. Writing over a previously recorded track automatically erases the previous data as the new data is written.

Computers operate with a very precise clock rate based on internal crystal oscillators. If a voltage remains high for a certain length of time, it can represent one or more 1s, or if it is off for a certain length of time, it can represent one or more 0s.

The floppy disks are divided into several concentric tracks. Each track is then divided into sectors. See Fig. 5-1. It is amazing that the head can find any one byte on a floppy disk that might have over a million bytes. It is even more amazing that the same system can find any one byte on a hard disk that might have over 2 billion bytes (2GB). I'll have more to say about disk organization later.

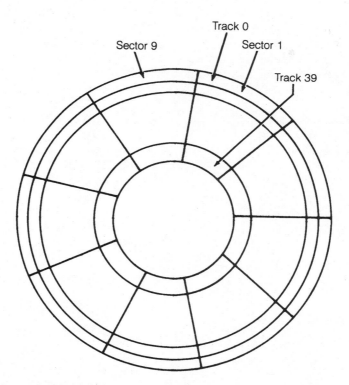

**Fig. 5-1** A diagram showing how the tracks and sectors are laid out on a floppy disk.

# The 5.25" and 3.5" floppy drives

The 5.25" 360K floppy drive is as obsolete as the horse-drawn buggy. (Of course the horse and buggy is still used by the Amish people in Pennsylvania, and there are some people who still use the 360K floppy drives.) The 360K drive was replaced by the 1.2MB floppy drive, which can read and write to either format. Even the 1.2MB floppy system is very nearly obsolete.

The 3.5" 720K drive is also obsolete. It was replaced by the 3.5" 1.44MB drive, which can read and write to both 720K and 1.44MB floppy disks.

The 3.5" drive is actually much smaller than the 5.25"; however, to fit in some of the older bays, it had to be installed in a 5.25" mounting chassis. Most of the newer cases now have bays that are designed for the 3.5" floppy drive and for 3.5" hard drives.

# The All-Media or combination floppy drive

The 5.25" floppy drives will eventually be phased out, but it will be some time before it happens. There is still a lot of software on 5.25" disks, especially shareware and public domain. Depending on what you intend to use your computer for, you can probably get by with just a 3.5" drive. However, just in case you do need a 5.25" drive, you can install a combination 5.25" and a 3.5" drive in a single bay. Many of the desktop computers provide only three or four bays to mount drives. You might not have space to mount two floppies, two hard drives, a tape backup drive, and a CD-ROM.

The CMS Enhancements Company (714-222-6316) noted this problem. They created an All-Media floppy drive by combining a 1.2MB and a 1.44MB floppy drive into a single unit. The 5.25" part of the drive can handle 5.25" 360K and 1.2MB floppies; the 3.5" part handles 720K and 1.44MB floppy disks. The two drives are never both used at the same time, so there is no problem. They can even share most of the drive electronics.

Teac, Canon, and several other companies are now manufacturing the combo drives. At the present time, the combo drives cost less than $100. Figure 5-2 shows a standard 5.25" drive on the left and a combination floppy drive on the right.

**Fig. 5-2** A standard 5.25" floppy drive on the left, and a combination drive on the right.

# Disk drive motors

Disk drives have two motors. One motor drives the spindle that rotates the disk. Then a stepping motor, or *actuator*, moves the heads back and forth to the various tracks.

## Spindle motor

Some of the old 5.25" floppy drives used an "O" ring belt to drive the spindle. Modern floppy drives use a direct drive where the spindle is just an extension of the motor shaft. When a disk is inserted, a plastic cone is lowered onto the disk that centers and locks it to the spindle.

The motors are regulated so that the speed is usually fairly constant. The speed of the old 5.25" 360K floppy drive is 300 RPMs. The 5.25" 1.2MB drive rotates at 360 RPMs, even when reading and writing to a 360K disk. The 3.5" floppy drives rotate at 300 RPMs. If, for some reason, the speed changes, you might not be able to read the disk. You could take the drive to a repair shop, which can test and adjust the speed. However, it would probably cost you more than $50 an hour for the service. You can buy a new drive for about $25.

## Head actuator motor

The head actuator motor is electronically linked to the File Allocation Table (FAT). If a request is received to read data from a particular track, say track 20, the actuator motor moves the heads to that track. Floppy drives have two heads: one on top and one on the bottom. They are connected together and move as a single unit.

Several large companies—such as Sony, Toshiba, Fuji, Teac, and others—manufacture the floppy drives. Each company's prices are within a few dollars of the others. Most of them are fairly close in quality, but there might be minor differences.

On some of the older drives, a fairly large actuator stepping motor is used to position the heads. It is very quiet and works smoothly as it moves the heads from track to track. It has a steel band around the motor shaft that moves the heads in and out.

The actuator stepping motors on most of the newer drives are small cylindrical motors with a worm screw. The heads are attached to the worm screw, much like a large nut, and as the screw turns, the heads move in or out. The motors groan and grunt as they move the heads from track to track. Other than being a bit noisy, they work perfectly.

In Fig. 5-2, the large square object in the lower-left corner of the old 5.25" drive is an actuator motor. The combo drive has two actuator motors; the round tubular object at the bottom center is for the 5.25" drive. The smaller round actuator motor for the 3.5" drive is seen in the top center. Figure 5-3 is a close-up of the 3.5" drive with the cover removed to show the head actuator worm gear. The black assembly in the center with the numbers is the head.

## Head misalignment

If the software tells the actuator motor to move the heads to track 20, it knows exactly how far to move the heads. If, for some reason, the steel band or the worm screw that is attached to the actuator motor shaft becomes worn, loose, or out of ad-

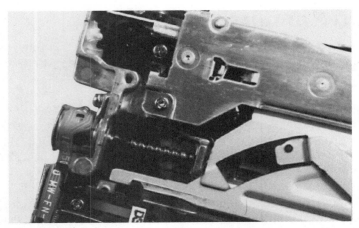

**Fig. 5-3** A 3.5" drive with the cover removed to show the worm gear that moves the heads from track to track. The heads are located in the black section with the numbers.

justment, the drive might not be able to find the proper tracks. If the hub of a 5.25" disk that you are trying to read has become worn or not centered exactly on the spindle by the cone, the heads might not be able to find a track that was previously written or one that was written on another drive.

If your heads are out of alignment, you can write and read on your own machine, because you are using the same misalignment to write and read. However, another drive might have trouble reading a disk recorded with misaligned heads. You might not be able to read disks recorded on another drive. Again, you could take such a drive to a repair shop, and they could align the heads, but it would probably cost more for the repair than for a new floppy drive.

# Floppy controllers

A floppy drive must have a controller to direct it to go to specific tracks and sectors. In the early days, the controller was a large board full of chips. Later manufacturers integrated the floppy disk controller (FDC) onto the same board as the hard disk controller (HDC). These were large full-length boards that were rather expensive (at about $250). Now the floppy drive controllers (FDCs) are usually built into a single very large scale integration (VLSI) chip and integrated onto a board along with a hard disk controller or integrated disk electronics (IDE) interface. An equivalent controller that cost as much as $250 a few years ago might now cost as little as $10 to $20. Many of these modern floppy controllers are integrated on multifunction input/output (I/O) boards that also have serial and parallel ports.

You probably won't need to worry about a floppy controller or I/O board. Most of the Pentium Pro motherboards have the FDC and the EIDE interfaces built-in. These motherboards usually have a set of upright pins for the flat ribbon cable connectors. This saves having to use one or more of your plug-in slots. Note that it is possible to plug a cable in backwards or improperly on the upright pins. Usually there is some indication of pin one on the boards and the cables will have a different colored stripe to indicate pin one.

Most of the Pentium Pro motherboards now use plug-and-play (PnP) BIOS. When a board or component that was made to the PnP specification is plugged in, the system can automatically recognize and configure the board or component. However there might be times when the PnP cannot work properly.

Floppy drive controllers are often integrated on SCSI and IDE interface boards. So it is possible to have a multifunction I/O board with a floppy controller, have a floppy controller built-in on the motherboard, and have a floppy controller on a SCSI or IDE interface all in one system. This could cause a major problem unless all of the controllers that were not to be used were disabled. The boards usually have configuration jumpers that can be used to disable or enable any function. It is very important that you keep any documentation that you get with your boards so that you will know how to enable, disable, or configure the board.

Many of these boards, especially the I/O boards and motherboards with built-in functions, also might have serial ports, printer ports, and other functions. These functions must also be enabled or disabled depending on which ones you choose to use.

# Drive select jumpers

It is possible to have four different floppy drives connected to one controller. The floppy drives have a set of pins with small jumpers so that each drive can be set for a unique number. The pins might be labeled DS0, DS1, DS2, and DS3. Some manufacturers might label them DS1, DS2, DS3, and DS4. The vast majority of systems use only two drives, so two of the sets of pins are hardly ever used.

These jumpers will also let you determine which drive is A: or B:. In most cases, you will use them as they come from the factory and never have to worry about these jumpers. Most drives are received with the second set of pins jumpered, which means they are set for drive A:.

If you install a second floppy drive, it will also have a set of pins jumpered just like the A: drive. Don't change it. The floppy cable has some twisted wires on the end cable for drive A:. The controller automatically recognizes whatever is plugged into this connector as drive A: and anything in the middle connector as drive B:. If you want your drive A: to be a 5.25" drive, just plug the connector end with the twisted wires into whatever drive you want to be A:, then plug the B: drive into the middle connector. The main difference in the A: drive and the B: drive is that you can boot from the A: drive but not from the B: drive. Fortunately, most drives work fine as received from the factory without ever having to change the jumpers.

The 5.25" drives are being phased out. Many of the new systems have only a 3.5" floppy drive. I recently bought a 3.5" drive and tried to install it as drive B:, but it did not work at all. I attached it to the end of the cable that has the twists, and it worked fine as drive A:. I looked for a set of pins to reconfigure the drive, but there were none. The factory configured the drive to be drive A:, and there was no way it could be changed.

The combination drives usually have configuration jumper pins near the miniature power cable connector. The combos have two columns of pins—one for each drive. There are six pins in each column, and four pins in each column are jumpered. Again, you should never have to reset or bother with these pins. The two drives share a single controller cable connector. If you want to use the 5.25" drive as drive A:, then plug the end of the cable with the twisted wires into the cable connector. If you want the 3.5" 1.44MB drive to be drive A:, then plug in the middle connector that has no twists. Again, fortunately, there is usually no need to move the jumpers.

# Extended density drives

The 3.5" Extended Density (ED) 2.88MB floppy drives have been available for some time. The 2.88MB disks have a barium ferrite media and use perpendicular recording to achieve the extended density. In standard recording, the particles are magnetized so that they lay horizontally in the media. In perpendicular recording, the particles are stood vertically on end for greater density.

The ED drives require a controller that operates at 1MHz. The other floppy controllers operate at 500KHz. Several companies are now integrating the ED controller with the other floppy controllers. Most of the Pentium Pro motherboards now have built-in floppy controllers for 2.88MB and other floppy drives.

The ED drives are downward compatible and can read and write to the 720K and 1.44MB disks. At the present time, the ED drives and disks are still rather expensive. Not many people are using them. They don't offer that much more advantage over the 1.44MB drives. With the introduction of the Iomega Zip 100MB and the Compaq 120MB drives, the 2.88MB system will probably just fade away.

# The virtual drive

DOS reserves the letters A and B for floppy drives. If you have only one drive, you can call it both. For example, you can say, "copy A: to B:." The drive will copy whatever is in the drive, then prompt you to insert a disk in drive B:, which is actually your A: drive because you only have one drive. Of course, you could have said "copy A: to A:" and got the same results.

# Very high density drives

Some of the floppy systems can almost rival the hard disk systems in storage capacity.

## Bernoulli drives

See chapter 6 for information on Bernoulli drives.

## The Iomega 100MB Zip floppy disk and drive

The Iomega Zip drive uses a 3.5" disk that can store 100MB. This system is much less expensive than the Bernoulli. With a few disks, you would never have to worry about running out of hard drive space.

See chapter 6 for more information on Zip drives.

## The 120MB floppy system

Although they were not generally available at the time of this writing, you can see chapter 6 for information on the 120MB floppy systems.

### SyQuest 135

As the name implies, the SyQuest 135 system can record 135MB on a removable cartridge. The drive can be mounted internally or externally as a SCSI device, or there is a model that can operate off the parallel port. This system can be used to backup several computers.

See chapter 6 for more information on SyQuest drives.

# Data compression

Data compression can double your disk capacity. One of the most popular compression programs is Stacker from Stac Electronics (800-522-7822). Windows 95, MS-DOS 6.2, and IBM PC DOS 7.0 come with the Stacker compression utility. It can be used on floppy disks as well as hard disks. Compression can be the least expensive way to increase disk capacity.

# Differences between floppy disks

The 5.25" 360K and the 3.5" 720K disks are called double-sided double-density (DS/DD). The 5.25" 1.2MB and the 3.5" 1.44MB are called high-density (HD). The 3.5" 720K double-density disks are usually marked DD; the high-density disks are usually marked HD.

However, the 5.25" 360K and the 1.2MB disks usually have no markings. They look exactly alike, except that the 360K usually has a re-enforcing ring or collar around the large center hole. The high-density 1.2MB disks do not have the ring. See Fig. 5-4. The 360K disk shown on the top right in the photo has a white collar or ring; most of the new disks have a black ring. One of the major differences between the 720K and the 1.44MB is that the high-density 1.44MB in the bottom left of Fig. 5-4

**Fig. 5-4** Some floppy disks. A 5.25" 1.2MB floppy at the top left, a 360K at the top right, a 3.5" 1.44MB at the bottom left, and a 720K at the bottom right.

has two small square holes at the rear of the plastic shell, while the 720K on the right bottom has only one. The 3.5" drive has a small media sensor microswitch that protrudes upwards. If it finds a hole on that side of the disk, it knows that it is a 1.44MB disk. If there is no hole, it is treated as a 720K.

When looking at the back side of a 3.5" disk, the square hole on the right rear of the shell has a small black slide that can be moved to cover the hole. A small microswitch on the drive protrudes upward and checks this hole when the disk is inserted. If the hole is covered, the switch is pressed downward, allowing the disk to be written on. If the hole is open, the switch protects the disk so that it cannot be written on or erased. The 3.5" write protect system is just the opposite of the system used by the 5.25" disks.

The 5.25" disks have a square notch that must be covered with opaque tape to prevent writing or unintentionally erasing the disk. (Incidentally, you must use opaque tape. The 5.25" system uses a light to shine through the square notch. If the detector in the system can see the light through the notch, then it can write on the disk. Some people have used clear plastic tape to cover the notch with disastrous results.)

There might be a time when you would want to make a diskcopy of a 720K and all you have are 1.44MB disks. Also, for some reason, you might want to use a 1.44MB as a 720K. You can cover the hole with any kind of tape, and it will format as a 720K.

Another difference between the 5.25" and the 3.5" disks is that the 5.25" floppy has a small hole near the center. A light shines through this hole to indicate where track one will begin. The 3.5" disks don't need this hole.

## Comparison of floppy disks

Table 5-1 shows some of the differences in the various types of floppy disks. Notice that the maximum number of root directories is the same for the 720K, 1.2MB, the 1.44MB. The 2.88MB has four times the capacity of the 720K yet allows only 16 more root entries. This means that you can enter 224 different files on a 1.2MB disk; however, if you try to enter one more, it will not accept it, even though you might have hundreds of unused bytes.

**Table 5-1.  Capacities of various disk types.**

| Disk type | Tracks per side | Sectors/ track | Unformatted capacity | System use | Available to user | Max. dirs |
|-----------|-----------------|----------------|----------------------|------------|-------------------|-----------|
| 360K  | 40 | 9  | 368,640   | 6144   | 362,496   | 112 |
| 1.2M  | 80 | 15 | 1,228,800 | 14,898 | 1,213,952 | 224 |
| 720K  | 80 | 9  | 737,280   | 12,800 | 724,480   | 224 |
| 1.44M | 80 | 18 | 1,474,560 | 16,896 | 1,457,664 | 224 |
| 2.88M | 80 | 36 | 2,949,120 | 33,792 | 2,915,328 | 240 |

The reason is that the DOS file allocation table was designed for this limited number of files. There is an easy way around this problem. Just create subdirectories like those created on a hard disk. Just type MD for "make directory." If necessary, you can even make subdirectories of the subdirectories.

## Read accuracy

The 5.25" disks have a 1⅛" center hole. The drives have a flexible plastic cone that presses down through the center hole of the disk when the drive latch is closed. This centers the disk so that the heads will be able to find each track. The plastic material that the disk is made from is subject to environmental changes and wear and tear. The flexible cone might not center each disk exactly, so head-to-track accuracy is difficult with more than 80 tracks. If you have trouble reading a disk, it might be off center. It might help if you remove the disk and re-insert it.

If your drive consistently has trouble reading your disks, or especially reading disks recorded on another machine, the heads might be out of alignment.

The 3.5" disks have a metal hub on the back, which is used to center the disks. The tracks of the 3.5" floppies are narrower and greater in density per inch. However, because of the metal hub, the head tracking accuracy is much better than that of the 5.25" systems.

## 360K & 1.2MB

Although the 360K and 1.2MB disks look exactly alike except for the hub ring on the 360K, there is a large difference in their magnetic media formulation. Several materials, such as cobalt or barium, can be added to the iron oxide to alter the magnetic properties. Cobalt is added to increase the oersted (Oe) of high-density floppy disks. Barium is used for the 2.88MB extra high density (ED) disks.

The Oe is a measure of the resistance of a material to being magnetized. The lower the Oe, the easier it is to be magnetized. The 360K has an Oe of 300, the 1.2MB is 600 Oe. The 360K disks are fairly easy to magnetize or write to, so they require a fairly low head current. The 1.2MB is more difficult to magnetize, so a much higher head current is required. The 1.2MB system can switch the current to match whatever type of disk that you tell the system you are using.

If you place a 360K floppy in a 1.2MB drive and just type FORMAT, it will try to format it as a 1.2MB. However, it will find several bad sectors, especially near the center where the sectors are shorter. These sectors will be marked and locked out. The system might report that you have over a megabyte of space on a 360K disk. This disk could be used in an emergency (for example, to move data from one machine to another), but I would not recommend that you use such a disk for any data that is important. The data is packed much closer together when it is recorded as 1.2MB. Because the 300 Oe of the 360K disks are so easy to magnetize, it is possible that nearby data might migrate and eventually deteriorate and become unusable.

## 720K & 1.44MB

The 3.5" disks have several benefits and characteristics that make them superior to the 5.25" disks. The 720K disk can store twice as much data as a 360K in a much smaller space. The 1.44MB can store four times as much as a 360K disk in the same small space.

The 3.5" floppy disks have a hard plastic protective shell, so they are not easily damaged. They also have a spring loaded shutter that automatically covers and protects the head opening when they are not in use.

The 3.5" systems are much more accurate than the 5.25" systems in reading and writing. If 5.25" disks are used for any length of time, it is possible for the hole to become stretched or enlarged. If the disk is not centered exactly on the hub the heads will not be able to find and read the data.

The 3.5" floppies have a metal hub on the back side. This gives them much greater accuracy in reading and writing, even though the tracks on the 3.5" systems are much closer together.

Figure 5-4 shows a 1.2MB floppy at the top left, a 360K at the top right, a 1.44MB at the bottom left, and a 720K at the bottom right.

## One-way insertion

It is possible to insert a 5.25" floppy upside down, backwards, or sideways. When I first started using computers, I inserted a floppy that had some original expensive software on it into a drive. I waited for a while and nothing happened. Then I got an error message, Not ready reading drive A. Abort, Retry, Fail? I almost panicked. I thought for sure that I had destroyed the software. I finally discovered that I had inserted the floppy upside down. I was still scared that I had damaged the disk, so I did what I should have done when I first got the program. I put a piece of tape over the square notch to write protect it, then I made a diskcopy backup of the disk. I found that the software was still okay.

You can't actually damage a disk by inserting it upside down. You can't read it because the small hole that tells DOS where track one begins is on the wrong side when inserted upside down. You can't write to it or format because of the small hole and also because the write protect notch is on the other side.

The 3.5" disks are designed so that they can only be inserted properly. They have arrows at the left top portion of the disks that indicate how they should be inserted into the drive. They have notches on the backside that prevents them from being completely inserted upside down.

# Disk format structure

Before a disk can be used, it must be formatted into tracks and sectors.

## Tracks

Formatting consists of laying out individual concentric tracks on each side of the disk. If it is a 360K disk, each side is marked or configured with 40 tracks, numbered from 0 to 39.

If it is a 1.2MB, 720K, or 1.44MB disk, each side is configured with 80 tracks, numbered from 0 to 79 on the top and bottom of the disk. The top is side 0 and the bottom is side 1. When the head is over track 1 on the top, it is also over track 1 on the bottom. The heads move as a single unit to the various tracks by a head actuator motor or positioner. When data is written to a track, as much as possible is written on the top track, then the head is electronically switched, and it continues to write to the same track on the bottom side. It is much faster and easier to electronically switch between the heads than to move them to another track.

## Cylinders

If you could strip away all of the other tracks on each side of track 1 on side 0 and track 1 on side 1, it would be very flat, but it might look like a cylinder. So if a disk has 40 tracks, such as the 360K, it has 40 cylinders; the 1.2MB and 1.44MB each have 80 cylinders.

## Sectors

Each of the tracks are divided up into sectors. Each track of the 360K is divided into 9 sectors, each of the 1.2MB tracks are divided into 15 sectors, each of the 720K tracks are divided into 9 sectors, each of the 1.44MB tracks into 18 sectors, and the 2.88MB tracks are divided into 36 sectors. Each sector can contain 512 bytes. Multiplying the number of sectors times the number of bytes per sector times the number of tracks times two sides gives the amount of data that can be stored on a disk. For example, the 1.2MB has 15 sectors times 512 bytes times 80 tracks times two sides ($15 \times 512 \times 80 \times 2 = 1,228,800$ bytes). The system uses 14,898 bytes to mark the tracks and sectors during formatting, so there are actually 1,213,952 bytes available on a 1.2MB floppy.

## Clusters or allocation units

DOS allocates one or more sectors on a disk and calls it a *cluster*, or *allocation unit*. On the 360K and 720K disks, a cluster or allocation unit is two sectors. On the 1.2MB and 1.44MB, each allocation unit is one sector. Only single files or parts of single files can be written into an allocation unit. If two different files were written into a single allocation unit, the data would become mixed and corrupted.

## File allocation table (FAT)

During formatting, a file allocation table (FAT) is created on the first track of the disk. This FAT acts like a table of contents for a book. Whenever a file is recorded on a disk, the file is broken up into allocation units. The head looks in the FAT to find empty units, then records the parts of the file in any empty units it can find. Part of the file might be recorded in sector 5 of track 10, part in sector 8 of track 15, and anyplace else that it can find empty sectors. It records the location of all the various parts of the file in the FAT. With this method, parts of a file can be erased, changed, or added to without changing the entire disk.

## TPI

The 40 tracks of a 360K are laid down at a rate of 48 tracks per inch (TPI), so each of the 40 tracks is $\frac{1}{48}$" wide. The 80 tracks of the high-density 1.2MB are laid down at a rate of 96 TPI, so each track is $\frac{1}{96}$". The 80 tracks of the 3.5" disks are laid down at a density of 135 per inch, or .0074" per track.

# Some differences between floppies and hard disks

Hard disks have very accurate and precise head tracking systems. Some hard disks have a density up to 3000 or more tracks per inch, so much more data can be stored on a hard disk.

Floppy disks have a very smooth lubricated surface. They rotate at a fairly slow 300 RPMs. Magnetic lines of force deteriorate very fast with distance. So the closer the heads, the better they can read and write. The floppy heads are in direct contact with the floppy disks. Hard disks rotate at speeds from 3600 up to 7200 RPMs. The heads and surface would be severely damaged if they came in contact at this speed. So heads "fly" just a few millionths of an inch above the surface of each disk.

## Formatting

To format a 360K disk with the 1.2MB drive, type FORMAT A /4. To format a 1.2MB disk, you only have to type FORMAT A:. If you try to format a 360K disk without the /4, it will try to format it to 1.2MB. It will probably find several bad sectors.

To format a 720K disk on a 1.44MB B: drive, type FORMAT B: /f:720. To format a 1.44MB disk, just type FORMAT B:.

The format command in newer versions can take a very long time before it starts. It searches the floppy disk, then will save any information that it finds on the disk. If you decide later that you want to unformat the disk, just type UNFORMAT. However, for most cases, I don't want to unformat a disk. Especially if it is one that has never been formatted before. You can speed up the formatting process by typing FORMAT A:/U. This performs an unconditional format. If the disk has been formatted and used previously, you can type FORMAT A:/Q. This gives you a quick format by just erasing the first letter of the files in the file allocation table of the disk.

The MS-DOS manual is not too much help for many commands, including help for formatting. The on-disk help is much better for most commands. If you have trouble with the format command, just type HELP FORMAT. For any command that you need help with, just type HELP then the command.

## Cost of disks

All floppy disks are now quite reasonable. The 1.2MB HD disks are selling at discount houses for as little as $.21 apiece, or $.25 each if preformatted. The 1.44MB are selling for as little as $.35 each, or $.39 each if preformatted. There are several discount mail-order floppy disk stores. The prices might be different when you read this. Check the computer magazines for ads. Most vendors now offer floppy disks that have been preformatted for just a few cents more for each disk. It is well worth the extra money to buy the preformatted.

These are real bargains. At one time, I paid as much as $2.50 each for 360K floppy disks. How times have changed.

# 6

# Choosing and installing a hard disk

Large books have been written about hard disks. A whole book probably wouldn't cover all of the questions that you might have about hard disks; however, this chapter covers most of the basics about hard drives and some of the different types of hard drives.

Just like floppy disks, hard drive disks must be formatted before they can be used. However, formatting a hard disk is a bit more complicated than for a floppy. The formatting and installation of hard drives will be discussed in detail in chapter 10.

The IBM term for hard disk drives is *Direct Access Storage Devices* (DASD, pronounced *dazdee*). The hard drives are also called *Winchester drives*. The IBM plant that developed the first hard drives is located near the Winchester House in San Jose, California. The house was built by the widow of the famous inventor of the Winchester .30-.30 repeating rifle. The first IBM hard disk had 30 tracks and 30 sectors per track. Because the IBM system was a 30/30, someone hung the name Winchester on it. You don't hear it too often nowadays; however, for several years, all hard drives were called Winchester drives.

A hard disk is a precise piece of machinery. The tracks might be only a few millionths of an inch apart. The head actuator must move the heads quickly and accurately to the specified track. In the early 1980s a 20MB hard disk cost over $2500. You can buy a 2GB hard disk today for less than $500. That is 100 times greater capacity for about one-fifth of the cost. I have seen ads for 1.05GB drives for less than $200. Prices might be even less by the time you read this.

## Floppy and hard drive similarities

A hard disk drive is similar to a floppy disk drive in some respects. Floppy drives have a single disk; the hard drives can have an assembly of one or more rigid disks. The hard disks platters are coated with a magnetic plating that is basically similar to magnetic coating of the floppy disks. Depending on the capacity, there might be several disks on a common spindle. A motor turns the floppy spindle at 300 RPMs; the hard disk spindle can turn from 3600 RPMs up to 7200 RPMs.

Just like the floppy, there is a read/write head on the top and on the bottom of each disk. On floppy disk systems, the head actually contacts the disk; on a hard disk system, the head "flies" just a few millionths of an inch from the disk on a cushion of purified air. The air has to be purified because the smallest speck of dust could cause a "head crash." If the head contacts the disk at the high speed that it turns, it would cause a lot of damage. A crash can destroy the disk, the head, and all the data that might be on the disk.

## Tracks and sectors

Like the floppy disk, the hard disk is formatted into several individual concentric tracks. A 360K floppy has 40 tracks on each side; a high-capacity hard disk might have 3000 or more tracks per side. Also like the floppy, each hard disk track is divided into sectors, usually of 512 bytes. The 360K floppy system divides each track into 9 sectors; a hard disk system might divide each track into as many as 84 or more sectors.

## Clusters and allocation units

A sector is only 512 bytes, but most files are much longer than that, so DOS lumps two or more sectors together and calls it a *cluster*, or *allocation unit*. If an empty cluster is on track 5, the system will record as much of the file as it can there, then move to the next empty cluster, which could be on track 20. DOS combines sectors into allocation units depending on the capacity of the hard disk. For a 100MB disk, DOS combines four sectors, or 2048 bytes, into each allocation unit; for a 200MB disk, each allocation unit is composed of 8 sectors, or 4096 bytes. The higher the capacity of the disk, the more sectors will be assigned to each allocation unit.

One slight disadvantage to this is that, if you have a lot of short files, it might waste a lot of disk space because no two files can be written in the same allocation unit. So, if a file is only 96 bytes long, depending on the cluster configuration, you might have space for 4000 or more unused bytes in an allocation unit.

## File allocation table

The location of each part of the file, and which cluster it is in, is recorded in the file allocation table (FAT). The hard disk FAT is basically about the same as the floppy FAT except that the hard disk FAT is more complex. Like the floppy FAT, it is somewhat similar to a table of contents in a book. If part of a file is recorded on track 5, sectors 3, 4, and 5, and part on track 9, sectors 7, 8, and 9, this information is recorded in the FAT. If a request for that file is entered, the computer reads the FAT, then sends the heads to that location. It has no trouble finding it.

Usually the larger the hard disk partition, the more sectors are assigned to each cluster or allocation unit. A 500MB hard disk would actually have 524,288,000 bytes. Dividing this number by 512 bytes to find the number of actual sectors gives 1,024,000 sectors. If DOS had to search through over a million entries in the FAT each time that it accessed the hard disk, it would slow things down considerably. The FAT is updated and rewritten each time the disk is accessed. A large FAT would take a lot of time and disk space.

The FAT is very important. If it is damaged or erased, you will not be able to access any of the data on the disk. The heads just wouldn't know where to look for the data. The FAT is usually written on track 0 of the hard disk. Because it is so important, a copy is also written near the center of the disk so that, if the original is damaged, it is possible to use the copy.

So a large FAT could slow the disk's access and seek time. To help solve this problem, DOS assigns several sectors to each allocation unit. If each allocation unit is made up of four sectors on a 500MB hard disk, there would only be 256,000 allocation units. If eight sectors are used, then DOS would only have to worry about the location of 128,000 allocation units.

## Cylinders

Just like the floppy, each same numbered track on the top and bottom of a disk platter is called a *cylinder*. Because a hard disk can have up to 10 or more platters, the concept of cylinders is a bit more realistic than that of a single floppy disk. Incidentally, the BIOS chips in some of the older computers would not allow you to install a hard disk that had more than 1024 cylinders and 63 sectors, which is about 504MB. One of the reasons for developing the Enhanced Integrated Disk Electronics (EIDE) specification was to overcome this limitation. The BIOS in the Pentium Pro will allow you to install hard disk drives with up to several gigabytes.

## Head actuators or positioners

Like the floppy, a head motor, or head actuator, moves the heads from track to track. The head actuator must move the heads quickly and accurately to a specified track, then detect the small variations in the magnetic fields in the specified sectors. Some of the older hard disks used a stepper motor to move the head from track to track. These motors moved, or stepped, the heads in discrete increments from track to track. A 20MB disk would have about 600 tracks per side of a 5.25" disk. The tracks were far enough apart that it wasn't too difficult to have the motor move the heads to any track. Most of the hard disks today are only 3.5" in diameter but can have up to 3000 or more tracks. Almost all hard disks now use a voice coil motor, which is much smoother, quieter, and faster than the stepper motors.

The voice coil of a loudspeaker is made up of a coil of wire that is wound on a hollow tube that is attached to the material of the speaker cone. Permanent magnets are then placed inside and around the outside of the coil. Whenever a voltage is passed through the coil of wire, it will cause magnetic lines of force to be built up around the coil. Depending on the polarity of the input voltage, these lines of magnetic flux will be either the same or opposite the lines of force of the permanent magnets. In magnetism, like poles repel each other, and opposites attract. The polarity of the voltage then causes the magnetic lines to move the voice coil in or out.

Figure 6-1 shows a 3.5" Seagate 4GB hard drive with the cover removed to show the heads and disks. The head is at the end of the triangular shaped arm. The voice coil actuator is the section in the bottom left corner of the assembly. By passing precise values of positive or negative dc voltage through the voice coil, it can quickly and accurately swing the arm and head to any track on the disk.

**Fig. 6-1** A 3.5" hard disk drive from Seagate with the cover removed. This small drive can store 4.294GB.

## Speed of rotation and density

Just like the floppy system, as the disk spins beneath the head, a pulse of voltage through the head coil will cause the area of the track that is beneath the head at that time to become magnetized. If this pulse of voltage is turned on for a certain amount of time, then turned off for some amount of time, it can represent the writing or recording of 1s and 0s. The hard disk spins much faster than a floppy, so the duration of the magnetizing pulses can be much shorter at a higher frequency.

The recording density depends to a great extent on the changes in magnetic flux. The faster the disk spins, the greater the number of changes. This allows much more data to be recorded in the same amount of space.

## Head spacing

The amount of magnetism that is placed on a disk when it is recorded is very small. It must be small so that it will not affect other recorded bits or tracks near it. Magnetic lines of force decrease as you move away from a magnet by the square of the distance. So it is desirable to have the heads as close to the disk as possible, within millionths of an inch.

# Disk platters

The surface of the hard disk platters must be very smooth. Because the heads are only a few millionths of an inch away from the surface, any unevenness or a microscopic speck of dust could cause a head crash. Hard disks are assembled in a clean room, then sealed so that they cannot be contaminated from outside air. You should never take one apart. The hard disk platters are usually made from aluminum, which is nonmagnetic, and lapped to a mirror finish. They are then coated or plated with a magnetic material. Some companies also use tempered glass as a substrate for the platters. A few companies are experimenting with plastic such as that used for CD-ROM discs as a substrate.

The platters must be very rigid so that the close distance between the head and the platter surface is maintained. The early 5.25" hard disks were fairly thick to achieve the necessary rigidity. Because they were thick and heavy, they required a fairly large spindle motor and a lot of wattage to move the large amount of mass.

If the platter is made smaller, it can be thinner and still have the necessary rigidity. If the disks are thinner, then more platters can be stacked in the same area. The smaller disks also need less power and smaller motors. With smaller diameter disks, the heads don't have to travel as far between the outer and inner tracks. This improves the access time tremendously. Most drives today are 3.5" or less in size.

You should avoid any sudden movement of the computer or any jarring while the disk is spinning because it could cause the head to crash onto the disk and damage it. Most of the newer hard disk systems automatically move the heads away from the read/write surface to a parking area when the power is turned off.

# How they can make smaller drives

There has been a fantastic evolution in hard disk drives. They keep making them smaller and smaller and increasing the capacity. Figure 6-2 shows four hard disks. The large MFM disk on the left has a capacity of 40MB, which was a whole lot just a few years ago. Next to it is an 85MB IDE drive, then a 540MB IDE, and on the right is a 1.05GB SCSI drive. One of the reasons that they can make the hard disks smaller now is because we have better plating materials, thinner disks, better motors, and better electronics.

## Zone bit recording

The old MFM drives divided each track into 17 sectors. A track on the outer edge of a 5.25" platter would be over 15" long if it were stretched out. You can determine this by using the simple math formula for pi times the diameter. So pi, or 3.14159, times 5.25 is 16.493" in length. A track on the inner portion of the disk might have a diameter of only 1.5 inches, times pi, or 4.712" in length if stretched out.

It is obvious that you should be able to store more data in the outer longer tracks than in the short inner tracks. That is exactly what the newer drives do by using zone bit recording (ZBR). The platters on the Maxtor 540MB drive is divided up into eight different zones. Zone 1 has the inner tracks that are shorter. This zone has 48 sectors per track; the outer zone 8 has 87 sectors per track.

**Fig. 6-2** Some hard drives. The large drive on the left is an early 40MB, the next one is a later 85MB, then a 540MB and a 1.05GB on the right.

## Rotational speed and recording density

The recording density, or bits per inch (bpi), for each zone also changes from the inner tracks to the outer tracks. The reason for this is that the speed at which the inner tracks pass beneath the heads are faster than that of the outer tracks.

The overall drive speed is still another way of increasing the amount of storage. The old MFM drives spun at 3600 RPMs. The newer drives can have a rotational speed of up to 7200 RPMs or more. The higher the speed of the disk, the higher the recording frequency and the higher the data density.

Of course, the rotational speed of the disk is also one of the factors that determines the seek, access, and transferal time. If you want to access data on a certain track, the faster the disk rotates, the sooner that sector will be available for reading.

The hard disk technology has improved tremendously over the last ten years.

## Partial response, maximum likelihood system

Another reason they can make the drives smaller is because of their partial response, maximum likelihood (PRML) system. This system was first developed by IBM several years ago. This system involves electronics that allows them to store up to 25% more data on a disk. The PRML system is being used by Seagate, Quantum, Western Digital, and several other companies. Figure 6-3 shows a 2.5" Seagate 810MB drive that uses the PRML technology.

**Fig. 6-3** A Seagate 2.5" 810MB drive that uses the PRML technology.

# Factors to consider in choosing a hard drive

You have the option of a very large number of different types and capacities of disks to choose from. Of course, what you choose will depend on what you need to do with your computer and how much you want to spend.

## Capacity

When you consider capacity, buy the biggest you can afford.

You might have heard of Mr. C. Northcote Parkinson. After observing business organizations for some time, he formulated several laws. One law says, "Work expands to fill up available employee time." A parallel law that paraphrases Mr. Parkinson's immutable law might say, "Data expands to fill up available hard disk space."

Don't even think of buying anything less than a 500MB hard drive. Better yet would be a minimum of two 500MB drives. New software programs have become more and more friendly and offer more and more options. Most of the basic application programs that you will need—such as spreadsheets, databases, CAD programs, word processors, and many others—will each require 10MB to 30MB of disk storage space. Windows 95 itself requires about 60MB of disk space.

Most of the major hard disk drives are fairly close in quality and price. My recommendation is to buy the highest capacity drive that you can possibly afford. Hard disk drives are now selling for less than $.50 per megabyte.

### Speed or access time

Speed or access time is the time that it takes a hard disk to locate and retrieve a sector of data. This includes the time that it takes to move the head to the track, settle down, and read the data. For a high end, very fast disk, this might be as little as 9 milliseconds (Ms). Some of the older drives and systems required as much as 100 Ms.

### IDE or AT drives

The most popular drives today are those with Integrated Drive Electronics (IDE). They are sometimes called ATA (for Advanced Technology Attachment) IDE drives because they were first developed for use on the 286 AT. The drives are similar to the SCSI drives in that all of their controller electronics is integrated on the drive. You do not need a controller card, such as those required by the older MFM, RLL, and ESDI drives, but you do need an interface. The interface might be a plug-in card, or it might be a set of upright pins on the motherboard.

### Enhanced IDE

The BIOS in some older systems could not recognize a hard disk with more than 1024 cylinders, so until recently, many IDE drives had a maximum capacity of 540MB. The Enhanced IDE (EIDE) specification can handle drives with up to several gigabytes of storage capacity.

The EIDE specification is somewhat similar to SCSI. It will support up to four IDE devices, including CD-ROM and tape drives. The IDE hard disks and other devices are usually considerably less expensive than similar SCSI devices.

The old IDE specification has a transfer rate of 4.3MB per second. The newer EIDE specification allows data transfers up to 13.3MB per second. Of course, to achieve this transfer rate, you must have a hard disk that can meet the specification.

Most of the Pentium Pro motherboards have a built-in EIDE interface with two sets of upright pins that will support up to four different IDE devices. However, to take full advantage of the speed of some of the newer drives, you might want to install a fast PCI IDE interface.

# Installation configuration

Most of the Pentium Pro motherboards have a Plug-and-Play (PnP) BIOS that can recognize the hard disk and automatically configure your PC. You might still have to set some of the jumpers to determine master and slave drives. If your motherboard does not have the PnP BIOS, then use the following configuration instructions.

You should receive some instructions with your drive documentation. If you are only installing a single IDE drive, the installation might be very simple. The drive will probably have jumpers set at the factory that makes it drive #1, or the master drive. Check your documentation and the jumpers, then just plug the 40-pin cable into the drive connector and the other end into a board interface or into a set of pins on the motherboard. If you use the upright pins on the motherboard, the first two hard disks are connected to the set of pins marked "Primary." If you are connecting an IDE CD-ROM or other IDE device, it should be connected to the set of pins marked "Secondary." You must make sure that the colored side of the ribbon cable goes to pin one on the drive and on the interface.

If you are installing a second IDE drive, you will need to set some jumpers so that the system will know which drive to access. When two IDE drives are installed, the IDE system uses the term *Master* to designate the C: or boot drive and the term *Slave* to designate the second drive. You will have to place small jumpers on the drives to configure them. If the drives are not configured properly, you will get an error message that might tell you that you have a hard disk or controller failure. You will not be able to access the drives. Your documentation should tell you which pins to jumper for your configuration.

Some drives have pins that can be jumpered so that they will be read only. This is a type of write protection that is similar to write protecting a floppy. This could be used on a hard disk that had data that should never be changed or written over.

You should have received some documentation with your drive. If you don't have the configuration information, call the company or dealer. The following paragraphs provide technical support numbers for some of the more popular companies.

Conner Peripherals has technical support at 408-456-3388. They have a BBS at 408-456-4415 and FaxBack information at 800-426-6637.

The Maxtor Corp. has technical support at 800-262-9867. They have a BBS at 303-678-2222 for 2400 baud or 303-678-2020 for 9600 baud. The modem should be set for 8 data bits, one stop bit, and no parity.

Quantum Corp. offers free technical support at 800-826-8022. Quantum also has a Fax on Demand System. If you call 800-434-7532 from your fax machine, they can send you documentation and configuration specifications for all of their products. When you call, you should ask for their Product Catalog, which lists all available documents by number. You can review the catalog and order whatever document you might need. Quantum also has a BBS at 408-894-3214.

You can call the Seagate Technology Corp. at 800-468-3472 for 3.5" drive technical support; for 5.25" drives, call 800-852-3475. Seagate also has a bulletin board that has a Technical Desk Reference file that lists most of their hard disk configurations. Their BBS is at 408-438-8771. Set communications software for 8 bits, no parity, and one stop bit (8-N-1). The Seagate BBS also has some free software that can be downloaded. Their FINDTYPE and FINDINIT can help make installation of ATA IDE drives easier.

You can call Western Digital at 800-832-4778. They have a BBS for 2400 baud at 714-753-1234. For 9600 baud and up, they have a BBS at 714-753-1068.

# The IDE or EIDE interface board

Because the IDE and EIDE interface is so simple and inexpensive, many vendors have built it onto the motherboard by providing a set of upright pins on the motherboard. A single cable can be plugged into these pins to control two IDE drives. For EIDE systems, there will be two sets of pins. This saves the cost of a controller and also saves one of your slots. These motherboards usually also have a built-in controller for floppy drives, pins for the LPT1 printer port, and pins for serial ports.

The two sets of pins on the EIDE boards might have markings "Primary Channel" and "Secondary Channel." The primary channel pins are for the cable connections of your first two IDE hard disks. The secondary channel is for one or two IDE CD-ROM drives or an IDE tape drive.

When plugging the connectors into the pins, be very careful that you locate pin 1 on the board and plug the cable in so that the colored wire goes to the pin 1 side. If you plug the cable in backwards, you could possibly damage some of the fragile transistors and electronics.

The built-in EIDE interfaces on the motherboard might not be fast enough for some high-speed hard disks. There are EIDE Peripheral Component Interconnect (PCI) bus interface boards that are available. Some of these interfaces might have up to 2MB or more of RAM cache that can vastly accelerate the hard disk operations. Of course, the extra memory adds to the cost of the interface.

If you use a PCI interface board, then the EIDE upright pins on the motherboard must be disabled. Check your motherboard documentation. There should be a set of jumpers to enable or disable the pins.

# EIDE drivers

When connecting an IDE CD-ROM drive or other IDE device to an EIDE interface, you must have special software drivers. Usually the software is included with the EIDE interface. Software drivers might also be included with the IDE CD-ROM drive.

# SCSI

Most companies who manufacture IDE and EIDE drives also make identical small computer system interface (SCSI, pronounced *scuzzy*) drive models. The built-in electronics on IDE and SCSI drives are very similar.

A SCSI board can interface up to seven different intelligent devices to a computer. SCSI devices are called *logical units*. Each device is assigned a logical unit number (LUN). The devices have switches or jumpers that must be set to the proper LUN. In Fig. 6-4, the pen points to pins that are jumpered to set the LUN on this SCSI hard drive.

A SCSI interface board can handle up to seven devices. It is possible to install up to four different SCSI interface boards in a PC; however, each host SCSI interface board is counted as one of the seven devices, so you could have a maximum of 24 SCSI devices in a PC. This works out just right because DOS only allows one device per each of the 26 letters of the alphabet. DOS reserves A and B for floppy drives and C for the boot drive, so we are limited to a maximum of two floppies and 24 other drive devices.

**Fig. 6-4** The pen points to the jumper pins that set the LUN of this SCSI hard drive.

The different devices can be two or more IDE or SCSI hard disk drives, one or more CD-ROM drives, a scanner, a tape backup unit, and other SCSI products. For a small business or a home office, you probably won't need that many drives.

Besides handling up to seven SCSI products, many of the interface boards also have a built-in controller for two floppy drives. If you have a built-in floppy controller on the motherboard or any other board, all other controllers must be disabled except for the one you use. Usually there are nearby jumpers for disabling or enabling functions. Check your documentation.

You should be aware that not all SCSI interfaces are equivalent. There are some that are made for special purpose devices, so they might not have all of the functionality of other SCSI interfaces. The different SCSI interfaces can cost from $50 to $200. There are some high-end SCSI interfaces that can cost up to $500 or more. The original SCSI interface was for the 8-bit bus. Most are now for 16-bit and PCI buses. Figure 6-5 shows a Future Domain SCSI interface with a 50-wire ribbon cable connected. This board also has upright pins for controlling floppy disks.

## Fast SCSI-2 and Wide SCSI-2

SCSI-1, as defined in 1986, is an 8-bit bus with a transfer rate of 5MHz. In 1992, ANSI added the SCSI-2, which can allow data transfer rates up to 10MHz. It is backward compatible so that it can also support SCSI-1 devices.

Wide SCSI-2 is a 16-bit bus that allows twice as much data to be transferred. The transfer rate can be as high as 20MHz. This specification will also allow as many as 16 devices, counting the host adapter. The wide SCSI-2 will have a 68-pin connector.

**Fig. 6-5** A Future Domain SCSI interface board with a 50-wire ribbon cable connected.

UltraSCSI adapters can provide a transfer rate of up to 40MB per second. Most of these newer adapters, such as the Adaptec PCI Ultra Wide SCSI kit, have PnP capability for easy installation.

## SCSI drivers

Most hard drives require that you enter the drive type into the CMOS setup. The setup lists several drive types that describe the hard disk characteristics. The setup allows only two drives, and they must be the same particular type, such as two IDE, two ESDI, two RLL, or two MFM drives. The SCSI interface has its own drivers, so it does not have to be entered into the CMOS setup. Most SCSI interface come with the necessary drivers.

## Advanced SCSI Programming Interface

Advanced SCSI Programming Interface (ASPI) is a set of standards that was first developed by the Adaptec Company. Adaptec has been one of the foremost companies in the design of SCSI products. The ASPI standard has been widely accepted by most other manufacturers. You still need a separate driver from each manufacturer for individual devices. These drivers are set up in your CONFIG.SYS file, then the ASPI driver is installed in the CONFIG.SYS. If the device drivers are software compatible to the ASPI specification, the ASPI driver then controls the other drivers. It is much easier to install SCSI devices that comply with the ASPI standard.

The Corel Company has one of the best drawing and graphics software programs available. Corel (800-836-7274) has also developed one of the better programs for installing SCSI devices. CorelSCSI is ASPI software that supports hundreds of SCSI devices. It makes it very easy to daisy chain up to seven devices and install the device software drivers. CorelSCSI supports hard drives, removable hard drives, CD-ROM drives, CD-ROM Juke Boxes, DAT tape drives, QIC tape drives, WORM and Magneto-Optical hard drives, and other SCSI devices.

An industry committee designed another SCSI specification that they called Common Access Method (CAM).

Both Adaptec (408-945-8600) and Future Domain (714-253-0400) manufacture almost any type of adapter interface you could want.

## Cables and connectors

The standard SCSI cable is a 50-wire flat ribbon cable. The standard connectors are Centronics types, but some devices might have a small miniature connector. Most devices have two connectors in parallel for attaching and daisy chaining other devices.

Not all of the 50 wires in a flat ribbon cable are needed for data. Many of the wires are ground wires placed between the data wires to help keep the data from being corrupted. The better and more expensive cables are round cables with twisted and shielded wires. This type of cable might be necessary for distances greater than 6'.

You should be aware that the advertised price of a SCSI device usually does not include an interface or cables. It might not even include any software drivers. Be sure to ask about these items whenever you order a SCSI device.

# Removable disk drives

There are several companies that manufacture removable disk drives. There are several different models and types. There are some advantages and disadvantages in removable drives.

## Bernoulli drives

The Iomega Corporation (800-697-8833) has a high-capacity Bernoulli floppy disk system. They first began with a 20MB floppy cartridge, then 40MB, 90MB, and 150MB. Now their system allows the recording of up to 230MB on special 5.25" sfloppy disks. Using the Stacker compression software, the 230MB floppy will hold 460MB. With a Bernoulli drive, you need never run out of hard disk space. The Bernoulli can be used instead of a hard disk or in conjunction with a hard disk.

The Bernoulli disks spin much faster than a standard floppy, which forces the flexible disk to bend around the heads without actually touching them. This is in accordance with the aerodynamics principle discovered by the Swiss scientist, Daniel Bernoulli (1700-1782).

The Bernoulli floppy disks spin at 2368 RPMs. The ordinary floppy spins at 300 RPMs. To keep the Bernoulli from flexing too much at the high speed, the floppy is placed within two steel plates. The Bernoulli system stores data on one side of the floppy only. For the lower-capacity systems, a single floppy is used; for the higher-capacity disks, two floppy disks are sandwiched together and each is recorded on the outer side.

The average seek time for the Bernoulli systems are 32 Ms. The better hard drives work at about 10 Ms. They have both external and internal drives. For an interface, the drives can use a parallel port, IDE, or SCSI.

Because the floppies can be removed and locked up, they are an excellent tool for security. They are also an excellent tool for making backups of your hard disks. You can backup 460MB in just seconds with Bernoulli. It would take hours using floppy disks and a lot of intensive swapping of disks.

One disadvantage is that the Bernoulli drives and disks are a bit expensive. At the present time, a Bernoulli drive can cost from $300 to $450, and the removable disks can cost from $70 up to $100 each.

Look in the computer magazines, such as the *Computer Shopper* or *PC World*, for ads and current prices, or call Bernoulli for brochures and your nearest dealer.

## The Iomega 100MB Zip floppy disk and drive

The Iomega Zip drive uses a 3.5" disk that is similar to a floppy. However, this 3.5" disk can store 100MB. This system is much less expensive than the Bernoulli. At this time, the Zip drives cost less than $200, and the disks cost less than $20. With a few disks, you would never have to worry about running out of hard drive space.

## The Compaq 120MB floppy drive

The Compaq, 3M, and Matsushita-Kotubuki Companies are developing a 120MB floppy system. The very high density drives will be downward compatible so that they can also read and write to the 720K and 1.44MB format. These drives could be used as a second hard drive. With enough floppy disks, you could have an unlimited capacity. You could even install two or more 120MB floppy drives.

At the time of this writing, the 120MB floppies are still not generally available. When they hit the market, it will make the standard 1.44MB drive just about obsolete.

## SyQuest drives

SyQuest (800-437-9367) has several models of removable hard disk cartridges. Each cartridge is actually a single hard disk platter. SyQuest uses zone bit recording (ZBR) on some of their disks. At the present time, the maximum SyQuest cartridge capacity is 270MB. Data compression can be used to double the capacity.

For the increased capacity, they use ZBR to divide the disks into zones. The 105MB disk is divided into two zones. The outer, longer tracks are divided into 52 sectors per track, with 512 bytes per sector. The inner zone tracks are divided into 72 sectors per track, but each sector is only 256 bytes. This is unusual because almost all systems use 512 bytes per sector.

SyQuest has a 135MB EZ135 drive that costs less than $200. Each removable cartridge costs about $20. The EZ135 comes as an EIDE, SCSI II, or external parallel drive that connects to the printer port. A parallel drive could be moved to several different computers to back them up or to transfer large amounts of data. Figure 6-6 shows a SyQuest EZ135 parallel system.

The SCSI hard drives must have an adapter. Read the ads carefully; some vendors advertise these drives at a very low price, then in very small letters at the end of the ad it might say "Controller card optional."

**Fig. 6-6** A SyQuest EZ 135 parallel port system with 135MB removable cartridges.

## PCMCIA hard drives

Several companies have developed 60MB to 340MB 1.8" drives that fit in the type III PCMCIA slots. These drives are ideal for laptop and notebook computers that have the PCMCIA slots. Many desktop computers are now installing PCMCIA slots. The small plug-in PCMCIA hard disks are much smaller than floppies, can store an enormous amount of data, and are very fast. Of course, they are ideal for security, for backup, or for transfer of data from one computer to another.

The PCMCIA specification allows *hot swapping*, which means that a card or hard disk can be inserted or removed without having to shut off the power to the main system.

## Magneto-optical drives

The Magneto-Optical (MO) drives are a combination of the magnetic and optical technologies. Magnetic disks, especially floppies, can be easily erased. Over a period of time, the data on a magnetic disk, hard or floppy, will gradually deteriorate. Some critical data must be renewed about every two years. Some tests indicate that MO drives can retain their data for as long as 390 years.

If a magnetic material has a high coercivity, or a high resistance to being magnetized, it will also resist being demagnetized. (Coercivity is measured in oersteds, or Oe.) However, the higher the Oe, the more current that is needed to magnetize the area. A high current could magnetize a large area. To pack more density, the magnetized area must be very small. To solve this problem, heat is used with a small current.

The Oe of a material decreases as it is heated. Most materials have a Curie temperature whereby the Oe can become zero. By heating the magnetic medium with a laser beam, a very small current can be used to write data to a disk. The heated spots cool very quickly and regain their high coercivity. The disks can be easily written over or changed by heating up the area again with the laser beam.

Figure 6-7 shows a 4.6GB removable MO drive system from Pinnacle Micro (800-553-7070). It is almost as fast as standard hard disks. The cartridges can be erased and rewritten up to 10 million times. At this time, the drive and a single cartridge costs about $1500, or about $.37 per megabyte. An equivalent 4.3GB hard disk costs about $.47 per megabyte.

**Fig. 6-7**
A 4.6GB Magneto-Optical
removable disk drive system.

This single disk can hold more data than six CD-ROM discs. It would be ideal for archiving or backing up large amounts of data. The contents of several file cabinets could be stored on this one disk.

The standard magnetic disk begins to deteriorate almost immediately after it has been recorded. It should be refreshed every two or three years. MO disks have a minimum lifetime of more than 30 years without degradation of data.

## Parallel port hard drives

SyQuest, Iomega, and other companies have parallel port models that can be used with laptops, PS/2s, or any computer with a parallel port. These drives are great for such things as backup, presentations, removal and security, data transport, and many other uses.

Because these drives plug into the computer's only parallel port, the hard drives usually provide a parallel port connector for the printer.

## Recordable CD-ROMs

There are several companies that now offer drives that can record CD-ROM discs. When first introduced, the recordable drives cost up to $10,000. There are some that are available today for less than $1000. They might be even less by the time you read this.

The CD-ROM blank disc can hold up to 650MB of data. This is a great way to back up or archive data and records that should never change. One disadvantage of the recordable CD-ROM system is that it cannot be changed or written over like a hard disk. I have seen some blank CD-ROM discs for as little as $6 each. So, if you wanted to change some of the data, just throw away the old disc and record the data onto another disc.

Unlike magnetic media that deteriorates or can be erased, data on a CD-ROM should last for many years.

## WORM drives

Write Once, Read Many (WORM) drives use the optical technology similar to the CD-ROM. However, a CD-ROM disc is standard and can be read by any CD-ROM drive. In the WORM systems, there are no standards. There are several different manufacturers, and there are different size disks from 5.25" up to 12" in diameter. A disk recorded on one machine might not be able to be read by another. Another difference is that the WORM systems usually have larger discs and can store up to several gigabytes.

Unlike the CD-ROM system, which uses a single winding track from the center outward, the WORM drives use the same system used by hard drives; that is, separate concentric tracks and sectors.

The WORM drive systems and blank disks are much more expensive than the recordable CD-ROM systems and discs.

Many large companies are now using WORM systems for archiving the mountains of data that accumulate. A new acronym, COLD, has been coined for Computer Output to Laser Disc. A COLD system can recover acres of file cabinet space.

## Advantages of removable disks

The following sections cover some of the advantages of removable disks or cartridges.

### Security

There might be data on a hard disk that is accessible to other people. If the data is sensitive data, such as company design secrets or personal employee data, the removable disks can be removed and locked up for security.

### Unlimited capacity

With enough cartridges, you will never have to worry about running out of disk space. If you fill one cartridge, just pop in another and continue.

### Fast backup

One reason that people don't like to backup their data is that it is usually a lot of trouble and takes a lot of time. It can take several hours to back up a large hard drive onto tape; it can take only seconds or minutes to backup the same data onto a removable drive. A big advantage of the removable cartridge backup is that the data can be randomly accessed; a tape backup can only be accessed sequentially. If you want a file that is in the middle of the tape, you must run through the tape to find it.

### Moving data to another computer

If you have two or more computer systems with the same type of removable drives, you can easily transfer large amounts of data from one machine to another. It is possible to send the data on a cartridge through the mails to other locations that have the same type system.

### Multiple users of one software copy

Most people don't bother to read the license agreements that come with software, and who can blame them. The agreements can be one or more pages long in small type and filled with lawyer-type jargon. Essentially, most of them simply say:

> You are granted the right to use one copy of the enclosed software on a single computer.

However, supposing that you have several computers in an office. Some of the people might be doing nothing but word processing most of the time. Others might be running databases or spreadsheets. Occasionally, these users might have need to use one of the other programs for a short time. If these users all have standard hard disks, then legally, you need a separate copy of all the software used on the computers. Some software programs can cost from $500 up to $1000 or more. If you have several computers in an office, providing individual packages for each machine can be quite expensive. (Check chapter 16 for ways to save on software.)

If these computers had removable disks, then a copy of a software program could be installed on the cartridge and the cartridge could be used on the different machines when needed.

### Archiving

I have hundreds of software programs on my hard disks that I will probably never use. However, it seems that every time I throw something away or delete a program, I need it the next day. The removable disks are a great way to archive old data and programs that are not used very often, but you don't want to delete them.

### Limit access

You might have things on a large hard disk that are of a sensitive nature, such as the boss's salary. You might want to limit access to this type of information. An employee can be limited to whatever is on the removable disk.

### Organization of data

If a company has several large clients, each account could be placed on a separate removable disk. This system could also be used for special projects or plans.

### Presentations

Many of these drives can be plugged into the parallel port or printer connection so that they can be used with almost any computer, including laptops. Instead of having to lug a large desktop computer to make a presentation, just take a parallel port drive, such as the Iomega Zip.

## Some disadvantages of removable disks

### Limited cartridge capacity

Some of the removable cartridges might not have enough capacity to store all of the data that you need to operate some of today's large programs. You could have the program on two separate cartridges; however, in accordance with Murphy's law, there will always be times when you need to access a file that is on the other cartridge.

### Cost of cartridges

Another disadvantage is that the removable drives can cost a bit more than a standard hard drive. Except for the Zip and SyQuest drive disks, which cost less than $20, the cost for other cartridges can be from $70 to over $100 each. The second least expensive of all the disks are the MO cartridges, but the initial cost of the drive itself is usually much higher than other drives.

The expense of cartridges might be well worth the cost if you consider that, with enough cartridges, your disk capacity is unlimited.

### Access speed

Still another disadvantage is that some of the removable drives are a bit slower than most standard hard drives. The MO drives are slower because it takes time to heat the area with the laser. However, if you don't mind waiting a few microseconds, it shouldn't be too much of a problem.

### Data compression

The capacity of all the hard drives mentioned in this chapter can be doubled by using data compression with them. MS-DOS and IBM PC DOS come with the disk compression utility. Using data compression is certainly less expensive and easier than installing a second, or larger, hard disk.

### Mean Time Between Failures (MTBF)

Disk drives are mechanical devices. If used long enough, every disk drive will fail sooner or later. Manufacturers test their drives and assign them an average lifetime that ranges from 40,000 up to 150,000 hours. Of course, the larger the figure, the longer they should last (and the more they cost).

These are average figures, much like the figures quoted for a human lifespan. The average man should live to be about 73 years old. However, some babies die very young, and some men live to be over 100. Likewise, some hard disks die very young, some older ones become obsolete before they wear out. At one time, I thought that MTBF meant *Mean Time Before Failure*. However, because it means *Mean Time Between Failures*, there is no guarantee that a new disk won't be defective the first time it is turned on.

# Partition and formatting procedure

Before you can use an IDE or EIDE hard drive, you must enter its type into the CMOS setup. Then it must be partitioned and formatted. SCSI hard drives are not entered into the CMOS setup, but they must be partitioned and formatted. See chapter 10 for these instructions.

# Sources

Local computer stores and computer swap meets are a good place to find a hard disk. You can at least look them over and get some idea of the prices and what you want. Mail order is a very good way to buy a hard disk. There are hundreds of ads in the many computer magazines listed in chapter 17.

# 7

# Backup:
# Disaster prevention

Making backups is a chore that most people dislike; however, if your data is worth anything at all, you should be making backups of it. You might be one of the lucky ones and never need it. However, there are thousands of ways to lose data. Data can be lost due to a power failure or a component failure in the computer system. In a fraction of a second, data that might be worth thousands of dollars could be lost forever. It might have taken hundreds of hours to accumulate the data and might be impossible to duplicate it. Yet many people do not back up their precious data. Most of these people are those who have been fortunate enough not to have had a major catastrophe. Just as sure as we have earthquakes in California, if you use a computer long enough, you can look forward to at least one unfortunate disaster. However, if your data is backed up, it doesn't have to be a catastrophe.

By far, most losses are the result of just plain dumb mistakes. I have made lots of mistakes in the past. No matter how careful I am, I will make mistakes in the future. When the poet said, "To err is human," he could have been talking about me and, possibly, thee.

## Write protect your software

When you buy a software program, you should make a diskcopy of the program and store the original away. If you should ruin the copy, you can always make a new copy from the original. However, the very first thing that you should do before you make a diskcopy is write protect the original floppies. It is very easy to become distracted and write on a program diskette in error. This would ruin the program. The vendor might give you a new copy, but it would probably entail weeks of waiting and much paperwork.

If you are using 5.25" floppies, you should cover the square write-protect notch with a piece of opaque tape. Don't use Scotch or clear tape. The drive focuses a light through the square notch. If the light detector can sense the light, it will allow the diskette to be written on, read, or erased. If the notch is covered with opaque tape, the diskette can be read but cannot be written on or erased. Some vendors distribute their programs on diskettes without the square notch.

If you are using 3.5" diskettes, you should move the small slide on the left rear side so that the square hole is open. The 3.5" write-protect system is just the opposite of the 5.25" system. The 3.5" system uses a small microswitch. If the square hole is open, the switch will allow the diskette to be read, but not written on or erased. If the slide is moved to cover the square hole, the diskette can be written on, read, or erased. Some vendors distribute software on diskettes that have had the slide removed so that it cannot be written on or erased.

It takes only a few seconds to write protect a diskette. It might save months of valuable time. If a program diskette is ruined because it was not protected, it might take weeks to get a replacement for the original. You might even have to buy a complete new program.

# Protect your original floppies and CD-ROM discs

Your valuable original program floppy disks should be protected from dirt and dust, especially the 5.25" floppies. There is a simple, easy way to protect them. Just seal them in plastic sandwich bags such as the Ziploc baggies from the Dow Company.

A lot of software is now distributed on CD-ROM discs. The software is usually loaded onto the hard disk and the CD-ROM disc is stored away. The Ziploc baggies are also great for protecting these discs from dirt, dust, and moisture.

Of course, you know that the original floppies should not be placed near any magnet or magnetic source. They also should not be exposed to heat or left in a closed car on a hot summer day. I ruined a half dozen disks one day by leaving them in a closed car where the sun could hit them.

If the files are critical, the disks should be protected from dirt and dust and stored in a temperature-controlled environment. The magnetic data on a disk can deteriorate over time. If the data is critical, it might be a good idea to copy it onto a new disk every so often.

# .BAK files

There are functions in many of the word processors and some other programs that create a .BAK file each time you alter or change a file. The .BAK file is usually just a copy of the original file before you changed it. You can call a .BAK file up, but you might not be able to edit it or use it unless you rename it. Usually, just changing the .BAK extension is all that is necessary.

WordStar and several other word processors can be set up to automatically save any file that you are working on. The programs can be set to create a backup at whatever times you determine when there is no activity from the keyboard. If there is a power outage or you shut the machine off without saving a file, chances are that there is a backup of your saved disk.

# Unerase software

One of the best protections against errors is to have a backup. The second best protection is to have a good utility program, such as Norton's Utilities from Symantec. DOS and Windows 95 also have undelete utilities. These programs can unerase a file or even unformat a disk.

When a file is erased, DOS goes to the FAT and deletes the first letter of each file name. All of the data remains on the disk *unless a new file is written over it*. If you have erased a file or formatted a disk in error, *do not do anything to it until you have tried* using a recover utility. To restore the files, most of the utilities ask you to supply the missing first letter of the file name.

# MS-DOS delete protection

Erasing or deleting files by mistake is so common that Microsoft licensed the undelete technology from one of the major utility companies and includes an UNDELETE command in late versions of MS-DOS. There are three levels of protection with Delete Sentry, Delete Tracker, and the standard Undelete. PC DOS 7.0 from IBM also has similar undelete utilities.

The UNDELETE command is available immediately from any DOS prompt and any directory. To find out more about the UNDELETE command, type HELP UNDELETE at any DOS prompt and any directory.

The early versions of MS-DOS made it very easy to format your hard disk in error. If you happened to be on your hard disk and typed FORMAT, it would immediately begin to format your hard disk and wipe out everything. Later versions will not format unless you specify a drive letter.

The early versions of DOS would also let you copy over another file. If two files were different, but you told DOS to copy one to a directory that had the file with the same name, the original file would be gone forever. MS-DOS 6.2, IBM PC DOS 7.0, and Windows 95 now ask if you want to overwrite the file.

# Jumbled FAT

The all-important file allocation table (FAT) was discussed in the previous chapter about disks. The FAT keeps a record of the location of all the files on the disk. Parts of a file might be located in several sectors, but the FAT knows exactly where they are. If, for some reason track 0, where the FAT is located, is damaged, erased, or becomes defective, then you will not be able to read or write to any of the files on the disk.

Because the FAT is so important, a program such as Norton Utilities can make a copy of the FAT and store it in another location on the disk. Every time you add a file or edit one, the FAT changes. So these programs make a new copy every time the FAT is altered. If the original FAT is damaged, you can still get your data by using the alternate FAT.

Norton Utilities from Symantec (408-253-9600) is an excellent utility software package. If you accept the defaults when installing Norton Utilities, it causes Norton to scan your disk and analyze the boot record, file allocation tables (FAT), analyze directory structure, analyze file structure, and check for lost clusters or crosslinked files. It then reads the FAT and stores a copy in a different place on the hard disk.

# Reason for smaller logical hard disks

Early versions of DOS would not recognize a hard disk larger than 32MB. DOS can now handle hard drive capacities up to several gigabytes. Most programs seem to be designed to be installed on drive C:. You could have a very large drive C:; however, if this large hard disk crashed, you might not be able to recover any of its data. DOS allows you to use the FDISK command when formatting your disk to divide it up into as many as 24 logical drives. If the same disk was divided into several smaller logical drives and one of the logical sections failed, it might be possible to recover data in the unaffected logical drives.

A very fast way to back up is to copy the data from one logical drive to another. This type of backup is very fast and very easy. However, it doesn't offer the amount of protection that a separate hard drive would offer. Still it is much better than no backup at all.

# Head crash

The heads of a hard disk "fly" over the disk just a few microinches from the surface. They have to be close to detect the small magnetic changes in the tracks. The disk spins at 3600 RPMs on some older drives and up to 7200 RPMs on some of the newer drives. If the heads contact the surface of the fast spinning disk, it can scratch it and ruin the disk.

A sudden jar or bump to the computer while the hard disk is spinning can cause the heads to crash. Of course, a mechanical failure or some other factor could also cause a crash. You should never move or bump your computer while the hard disk is running.

Most of the newer disks have a built-in safe park utility. When the power is removed, the head is automatically moved to the center of the disk where there are no tracks.

The technology of the hard disk systems has improved tremendously over the last few years. However, hard disks are still mechanical devices. As such, you can be sure that eventually they will wear out, fail, or crash.

I worked in electronics for over 30 years and am still amazed that a hard disk will work at all. It is a most remarkable mechanical device. It is made up of several precision components. The mechanical tolerances must be held to millionths of an inch in some devices, such as the flying head and the distances between the tracks. The magnetic flux changes are minute, yet the heads detect them easily and output reliable data.

Despite all of the things that could go wrong with a hard disk, most hard disks are quite reliable. Manufacturers quote figures of several thousand hours *mean time between failure* (MTBF). However, these figures are only an average, so there is no guarantee that a disk won't fail in the next few minutes. I made a mistake in one of my earlier books and described the acronym MTBF as meaning *mean time before failure*. Several people wrote and pointed out my mistake, that it should be *between*, not *before*. If a disk should fail and you get it repaired, it should last as long as their guarantee says before it fails again. A hard disk is made up of several mechanical parts. If the disk is used long enough, eventually it will wear out or fail.

# Crash recovery

Despite the MTBF claims, hard drives do fail. There are lots of businesses who do nothing but repair hard disks that have crashed or failed. A failure can be frustrating, time-consuming, and make you feel utterly helpless. In the unhappy event of a crash, depending on its severity, it is possible that some of your data can be recovered, one way or another.

There are some companies that specialize in recovering data and rebuilding hard disks. Many of them have sophisticated tools and software that can recover some data if the disk is not completely ruined. If it is possible to recover any of the data, the Ontrack Computer Systems (800-752-1333) can probably do it. There are several others. Look in the computer magazine ads.

The cost for recovery services can be rather expensive. However, if you have data that is critical and irreplaceable, it is well worth it. It is a whole lot cheaper to have a backup.

# Preventing hard disk failures

During manufacturing, the hard disk platters are coated or plated with a precise layer of magnetic material. It is almost impossible to manufacture a perfect platter. Most all hard disks end up with a few defective areas after being manufactured. When the vendor does the low-level format, these areas are detected and marked as bad. They are locked out so that they cannot be used. However, there might be areas that are borderline bad that won't be detected. Over time, some of the areas might change and lose some of its magnetic characteristics. They might lose some of the data that is written to them.

There are several companies that manufacture hard disk utilities that can perform rigorous tests on the hard disk. These software programs can exercise the disk and detect any borderline areas. If there happens to be data in an area that is questionable, the programs can usually move the data to another safe area.

The ScanDisk command in MS-DOS 6.2 basically does what some of the stand-alone utilities do. It does a surface test of the hard disk and will report on any areas that are questionable. It can move any data from those areas to safer areas. It will then mark the questionable areas as bad. The bad areas are listed in the FAT just as if they were protected files that cannot be written to or erased.

Disk Technician from Prime Solutions (619-274-5000) is a much more sophisticated and comprehensive software program than ScanDisk. It can be set up to automatically check your hard disk every time you boot up. It can detect errors, recover data, and relocate data that is in danger.

SpinRite from Gibson Research (714-348-7100) was developed by Steve Gibson who writes a very interesting column for *InfoWorld*. Version 4.0 is a complete data-recovery and disk-repair system. It can read and recover most data from both hard and floppy disks that DOS might tell you is unreadable. It analyzes and tests the disks for surface defects and moves endangered data to safe areas. SpinRite can work with most types of hard disks and disk compression systems.

The SpinRite user manual is about the briefest of any that I have ever seen. It only has six pages with very brief instructions; however, don't let the brief manual fool you. You don't really need a lot of instructions. It is a robust program and has extensive help on disk.

# A few reasons why they don't backup and why they should

Here are a few of the lame excuses used by some people who don't backup their software.

## Don't have the time

This is not a good excuse. If your data is worth anything at all, it is worth backing up. It takes only a few minutes to back up a large hard disk with some of the newer software. It can take just seconds to copy all of the files to a directory on another logical drive of the disk or to another hard drive.

## Too much trouble

It can be a bit of trouble unless you have an expensive tape automated backup system or a second hard disk. If you backup to floppies, it can require a bit of disk swapping, labeling, and storing. However, with a little organizing, it can be done easily. If you keep all of the disks together, you don't have to label each one. Just stack them in order, put a rubber band around them and use one label for the first one of the lot.

It is a bit of trouble to make backups. However, if you don't have a backup, consider the trouble it would take to redo the files from a disk that has crashed. The trouble that it takes to make a backup is infinitesimal.

## Don't have the necessary disks, software, or tools

If you use floppy disks, depending on the amount of data to be backed up and the software used, it might require 50 to 100 disks. However, it might take only a few minutes and just a few disks to make a backup of only the data that has been changed or altered. In most cases, the same disks can be reused the next day to update the files.

## Failures and disasters only happen to other people

People who believe this way are those who have never experienced a disaster. There is nothing you can say to convince them. They just have to learn the hard way.

Outside of ordinary care, there is little one can do to prevent a general failure. It could be a component on the hard disk electronics, in the controller system, or any one of a thousand other things. Even things such as a power failure during a read/write operation can cause data corruption.

### Theft and burglary

Computers are easy to sell, so they are favorite targets for burglars. It would be bad enough to lose a computer, but many computers have hard disks that are filled with data that is even more valuable than the computer.

Speaking of theft, it might be a good idea to put your name and address on several of the files on your hard disk. It would also be a good idea to scratch identifying marks on the back and bottom of the case. You should also write down the serial numbers of your monitor and drives.

I heard of a story where a man took a computer to a pawn shop. The dealer wanted to see if it worked, so he turned it on. A name came up on the screen that was different from the name the man had given to the dealer. He called the police, and the man was arrested for burglary. The owner of the computer was very happy to get it back. He was also quite fortunate. Most burglaries don't have a happy ending.

Another good idea is to store your backup files in an area away from your computer. This way there would be less chance of losing both computer and backups in case of a burglary or fire. You can always buy another computer; however, if you had a large database of customer orders, files, and history, how could you replace that?

An article in a recent *Information Week* magazine says that PC theft has increased over 400% in the last few years. (*Information Week* magazine is free to qualifying subscribers. See chapter 17 for the address.)

### Archival

Another reason to backup is for archival purposes. No matter how large the hard disk is, it will eventually fill up with data. Quite often, there will be files that are no longer used or only used once in a great while. I keep copies of all the letters that I write on disk. I have hundreds of them. Rather than erase the old files or old letters, I put them on a disk and store them away.

### Data transfer

There are often times when it is necessary to transfer a large amount of data from one hard disk on a computer to another. It is quite easy to use a good backup program to accomplish this. Data on a disk can be used to distribute data, company policies and procedures, sales figures, and other information to several people in a large office or company. The data can also be easily shipped or mailed to branch offices, customers, or others almost anywhere. If more companies used disks in this manner, we could save thousands of trees that are cut down for paper.

# Types of backup

There are two main types of backup: the image and file oriented. An *image backup* is an exact bit-for-bit copy of the hard disk copied as a continuous stream of data. This type of backup is rather inflexible and does not allow for a separate file backup or restoration. The *file oriented* type of backup identifies and indexes each file separately. A separate file or directory can be backed up and restored easily. It can be very time-consuming to have to backup an entire 40MB or more each day. However, with a file-oriented backup system, once a full backup has been made, it is necessary only to make incremental backups of those files that have been changed or altered.

DOS stores an *archive attribute* in each file directory entry. When a file is created, DOS turns the archive attribute flag on. If the file is backed up by using DOS BACKUP or any of the commercial backup programs, the archive attribute flag is turned off. If this file is later altered or changed, DOS will turn the attribute back on. At the next backup, you can have the program search the files and look for the attribute flag. You can then backup only those that have been altered or changed since the last backup. You can view or modify a file's archive attribute by using the DOS ATTRIB command.

There are several very good software programs on the market that let you use a 5.25"or 3.5" disk drive to back up your data. Again, you should have backups of all your master software, so you don't have to worry about backing up that software every day. Because DOS stamps each file with the date and time it was created, it is easy to backup only those files that were created after a certain date and time.

Once the first backup is made, all subsequent backups need only to be made of any data that has been changed or updated. Most backup programs can recognize whether a file has been changed since the last backup. Most of them can also look at the date that is stamped on each file and back up only those within a specified date range. So it might take only a few minutes to make a copy of only those files that are new or have been changed. Of course, it is usually not necessary to backup your program software. You do have the original software disks safely tucked away, don't you?

## Windows 95 backup accessory

Windows 95 has a very good built-in backup program. To use it, push the Start button, then choose Programs, then Accessories, then System Tools, then Backup. The Microsoft Backup Wizard will be displayed. Then just follow the simple directions.

## Windows 3.1 and DOS BACKUP.COM

Early versions of MS-DOS included a BACKUP.COM program that was very slow and rather difficult to use. MS-DOS 6.0 and later versions have MSBackup for DOS and Windows Backup that are fast and easy to use. The MS-DOS backup can now compete with some of the commercial backup programs.

The MSBackup and Windows Backup can let you make full, incremental, or differential backups. DR DOS and IBM PC DOS also have backup commands that are as good as or better than the MS-DOS commands.

The XCOPY command can also be used for backup. There are several switches that can be used with XCOPY. For example, XCOPY C:\*.* A:/A will copy only those files that have their archive attribute set to on. It does not reset the attribute flag. XCOPY C:\*.* A:/M will copy the files, then reset the flag. Whenever a disk on A: is full, you merely have to insert a new floppy and hit F3 to repeat the last command. This will continue to copy all files that have not been backed up. XCOPY C:\*.* A:/D:01-15-96 will copy only those files created after January 15, 1996. There are several other very useful switches that can be used.

Check your MS-DOS, DR DOS, or IBM PC DOS manuals for more details on backup. All of these systems have built-in online help for all commands.

The MSBackup, Windows Backup, and XCOPY commands cannot be used with most tape backup systems. Tape backup systems usually have their own proprietary backup software.

There are several commercial backup programs available.

## XTree

XTree is an excellent shell program for disk and file management. It has several functions that make computing much easier. You can use it to copy files from one directory or disk to another very easily. I often use it to make backups when I only have a few files to back up. XTree is now a division of Central Point and PC Tools, which is now a division of Symantec (408-253-9600).

## Tape

There are several tape backup systems on the market. Tape backup is easy, but it can be relatively expensive: $250 to over $500 for a drive unit and $10 to $20 for the tape cartridges. Some of them require the use of a controller that is similar to the disk controller, so they will use one of your precious slots. However, there are some SCSI systems that can be daisy chained to a SCSI controller. There are also enhanced IDE tape systems that can be controlled by an EIDE interface.

Unless the tape drives are external models, they will also require the use of one of the disk mounting areas. Because it is only used for backup, it will be idle most of the time.

There are some tape systems that run off the printer parallel port. These systems don't require a controller board that takes up one of your slots. Another big plus is that these systems can be used to back up several different computers by simply moving it from one to the other.

Like floppy disks, tapes have to be formatted before they can be used. However, unlike a floppy disk, it can take over two hours to format a tape. You can buy tapes that have been preformatted, but they cost quite a bit more than the unformatted tapes.

Tape systems are very slow, so the backups should be done at night or during off hours. Most systems can be set up so that the backup is done automatically. If you set it on auto, you won't have to worry about forgetting to backup, or wasting the time doing it.

Another disadvantage of tape is that data is recorded sequentially. If you want to find a file that is in the middle of the tape, it has to search until it finds it. Because disk systems have random access, they are much faster than tape both in recording and reading.

## DAT

Several companies are offering the digital audio tape (DAT) systems for backing up large computer hard disk systems. DAT systems offer storage capacities as high as 1.3GB on a very small cartridge. The DAT systems use a type of helical scan recording that is similar to that used for video recording. The DAT tapes are 4 millimeters wide, or about .156".

# Removable disks

One of the better ways for data backup and for data security is to backup to a disk that can be removed and locked up. There are several different systems and companies that manufacture such systems.

## Bernoulli drives

The Iomega Company has several different models. Disk compression can be used with the floppies, so their 150MB floppy can actually store about 300MB. These drives can be used instead of a hard drive for most purposes.

One disadvantage is that the Bernoulli drives are rather expensive, and the cartridges are also a bit costly.

See chapter 6 for more information about Bernoulli drives.

## The Iomega Zip drive

The Iomega Zip drive is much less expensive than the Bernoulli. At this time, the Zip drives cost less than $200, and the disks cost less than $20. The Zip system is ideal for backup or for any type of data storage.

See chapter 6 for more information on the Iomega Zip drive.

## The 120MB floppy system

In chapter 6, I mentioned that Compaq, 3M, and Matsushita-Kotubuki Companies are developing a 120MB floppy system. The very high density drives will be downward compatible so that they can also read and write to the 720K and 1.44MB format. These drives will be ideal for backup.

At the time of this writing, they are still not generally available, but you can find more information about them in chapter 6.

## SyQuest Corp.

SyQuest drives were discussed in chapter 6. These drives use removable disks that can store up to 270MB. Of course, data compression can be used to almost double this amount of storage.

SyQuest also has a 135MB EZ135 drive and 60MB and 80MB 1.8" removable drives that can be used in the PCMCIA type III slots (see the following section). Any of these drives could be used to make an excellent backup system.

See chapter 6 for more information on the EZ135 drives.

## PCMCIA

The Personal Computer Memory Card International Association (PCMCIA) cards were originally developed to add memory to portable computers. However, many desktops are now using the cards. Several different products have been developed using the card format, such as modems, faxes, network cards, and hard disk drives. These very small hard disk drives can have a capacity up to 400MB or more. They are ideal for making backups.

See chapter 6 for more information on the PCMCIA hard drives.

## Magneto-optical drives

The magneto-optical drives (MO) are rather expensive, but the removable cartridges are fairly low cost. They are a good choice for use as a normal hard drive and for backup.

See chapter 6 for more information on MO drives.

## Recordable CD-ROM

If you have a lot of data that needs to be permanently backed up, a CD-ROM can store over 650MB. An advantage of CD-ROM over magnetic systems is that data on a CD-ROM will last for many years.

For more information on recordable CD-ROMs, see chapter 6.

## WORM drives

WORM systems usually have larger discs than recordable CD-ROMs and can store up to several gigabytes. They are great for backing up and archiving data.

See chapter 6 for more information on WORM drives.

## Second hard disk

The easiest and the fastest of all methods of backup is to have a second hard disk. It is very easy to install a second hard disk. An IDE interface can control two high-capacity hard disks; the EIDE interfaces can control up to four hard drives. You can add as many as seven hard drives to a SCSI interface.

A good system is to have an IDE drive for the C: boot drive and have one or more SCSI drives. You can back up several megabytes of data from one hard drive to another very easily and quickly. The chances are very good that both systems would not become defective at the same time. So, if the same data is stored on both systems, it should offer very good RAID-like protection.

At one time, tape backup systems were less expensive than a hard disk, but the cost of hard disks have come way down. One of the advantages of using a hard disk for backup is that, unlike tape, any file is available almost immediately.

## LapLink

LapLink allows you to connect two computers together and access either one. It is very simple to use the parallel port cables that come with the package and transfer files from one computer to the other. LapLink allows you to update only those portions of a file that have changed. If you are updating or backing up files that are already on the disk, it takes very little time.

LapLink can also be used over a modem. If you are on the road and need to back up a laptop, you can easily send the data back to the desktop.

## RAID systems

RAID is an acronym for Redundant Arrays of Inexpensive Disks. There is some data that is absolutely critical and essential. To make sure that it is saved, data is written to two or more hard disks at the same time. Originally, five different levels were suggested, but only three levels (1, 3, and 5) are in general use today.

Some RAID systems will allow you to *hot swap*, or pull and replace a defective disk drive without having to power down. You don't lose any information because the same data is being written to other hard disk drives.

To prevent data losses due to a controller failure, some RAID systems use a separate disk controller for each drive. A mirror copy is made of the data on each system. This is called *duplexing*. Some systems use a separate power supply for each system. All systems use uninterruptible power supplies.

RAID systems are essential for networks or any other area where the data is critical and must absolutely be preserved. However, no matter how careful you are and how many backup systems you have, you might still occasionally lose data through accidents or some other act of God. You can add more and more to the backup systems to make them fail-safe, but eventually you will reach a point of diminishing returns.

Depending on how much is spent and how well it is engineered, the system should be system fault tolerant (SFT); that is, it will remain fully operational regardless of one or more component failures.

# Uninterruptible power supplies

Uninterruptible Power Supplies (UPS) were discussed briefly in chapter 2. They are mentioned here again because they are so important to backup. If you have a power failure or brownout while working on a file, you could lose a lot of valuable data. In areas where there are frequent electrical storms, it is essential that you use a UPS.

The basic UPS is a battery that is constantly charged by the 110v input voltage. If the power is interrupted, the battery system takes over and continues to provide power long enough for the computers to save the data that might happen to be in RAM, then shut down.

There are several companies who manufacture quite sophisticated UPS systems for almost all types of computer systems and networks. Of course, for a single user, you only need a small system. On a network or for several computers, it will require a system that can output a lot of current.

There are several UPS companies. Here are just a few:

American Power Conversion    800-788-2208
Best Power Technology        800-356-5794
Sola Electric                800-289-7652
Tripp-Lite Mfg.              312-329-1777

Again, if your data is worth anything at all, it is worth backing up. It is much better to be backed up than to be sorry.

# 8
# Monitors

There are many different types of monitors with many different qualities and, of course, many different prices. A few of the monitor basics will be discussed to help you make a better decision in buying your monitor.

## The CRT

A monitor is similar to a TV. The main component is the cathode ray tube (CRT), or picture tube. In some respects, the CRT is like a dinosaur that is left over from the vacuum tube era. Before the silicon age of semiconductors, vacuum tubes operated almost all electronic devices. Like all vacuum tubes, the CRTs use enormous amounts of power and generate lots of heat.

Vacuum tubes have three main elements: the cathode, the grid, and the plate. These elements correspond to the emitter, the base, and the collector of a transistor. In a vacuum tube, the cathode is made from a metallic material that causes electrons to be boiled off when heated. The cathode is heated by the filament that is made from resistive wire similar to that used in light bulbs. Also, very much like light bulbs, the filaments burn out, which causes the tube to fail. Burned out filaments are the single greatest cause of failure in vacuum tubes. The filaments of computer CRTs are designed a bit better now so that they don't burn out as often as they did in the early days.

If a positive direct current (dc) voltage is placed on the plate of a vacuum tube, the negative electrons boiled off from the heated cathode will be attracted to the plate. A control grid is placed between the cathode and plate. The grid acts like a valve that can be opened and closed. (The British call vacuum tubes *valves*.) If a small negative voltage is placed on the grid, it will repel the negative electrons and keep them from reaching the plate. Zero voltage or a small positive voltage on the grid will let the electrons go through to the plate.

The plate in a vacuum tube might have as much as 400 volts on it; the face plate or screen of a monitor or TV might have as much as 2500 volts. As the analog voltage swings up and down on the grid, it acts as a switch that allows the large voltage from the plate to pass through the vacuum tube. A voltage as small as a millionth of a volt on the grid of a vacuum tube can create a much larger exact voltage replica on the output of the plate. Figure 1-5 in chapter 1 is a diagram of a vacuum tube circuit.

With the proper voltages on the emitter, base, and collector, a transistor operates much like a vacuum tube, acting as a switch or as an amplifier. A transistor is much smaller, uses less voltage, and creates very little heat and lasts a lifetime; a vacuum tube can be quite large, requires a lot of space and energy, produces a lot of heat, and eventually burns out.

Like the vacuum tube, the CRT has a filament that heats up a cathode to produce electrons. It also has a grid that can shut off the passage of the electrons or let them pass through. The corresponding plate of the CRT is the back of the picture screen, which has about 2500 volts on it to attract the electrons from the cathode. The back of the screen is coated with a phosphor. Because of the high attracting voltage, the electrons slam into the phosphor and cause it to light up and glow.

A very small thin beam of electrons are formed. This electronic beam acts very much like a piece of iron in a magnetic field. If four electromagnets are placed around the neck of the CRT—one on top, one on the bottom, and one on each side—the beam of electrons can be directed to any area of the screen by varying the polarity of the voltage fed to the electromagnets. If we wanted the beam to move to the right, we would increase the plus voltage on the right magnet. If we wanted the beam to move up, we would increase the plus voltage on the top magnet. With these electromagnets, we can move the beam to any spot on the screen.

The small input signal voltage on the grid of the CRT turns the electron beam on and off to cause portions of the screen to light up. The beam can be caused to move and write on the screen just as if you were writing with a pencil. Alphabetic characters, numbers, or any kind of graphics, can be created in an exact replica of the input signal.

Many laptops and notebook computers have excellent color screens using transistors. The active matrix type uses thousands of transistors to light up each individual pixel. However, these active matrix systems are very expensive because just one defective transistor out of many thousands can ruin the whole panel. Some companies have already developed screens as large as 21", but they are still too expensive to be practical.  Eventually the cost will come down, and we will have large low- energy flat screens that can produce a good high-resolution picture. Soon, even the large television CRTs will be replaced with flat screens that can be hung on a wall.

# Monochrome versus color

In a monochrome TV or a monitor, there is a single "gun" that shoots the electrons toward the back of the screen. Color TVs and color monitors are much more complicated than monochrome systems. During the manufacture of the color monitors, three different phosphors—red, green, and blue (RGB)—are deposited on the back of the screen. Usually a very small dot of each color is placed in a triangular shape. If you use a magnifying glass and look at a color monitor or color TV, you can see the individual dots.

The different phosphors used to make color monitors are made from rare earths. They are designed to glow for a certain period of time after they have been hit by an electron beam.

In a color TV or monitor, there are three guns, each shooting a beam of electrons. The electrons from each gun have no color. However, each gun is aimed at a particular color: one to hit only the red dots, one the blue dots only, and one the green dots. They are very accurately aimed so that they will converge or impinge only on their assigned color dots. To make sure that the beams hit only their target, the beam must go through the holes of a metal shadow mask. Being hit by stray electrons causes the shadow mask to heat up. The heat can cause fatigue and loss of focus. Many of the newer monitors use shadow masks made from Invar, an alloy that has good heat resistance.

By turning the guns on or off to light up and mix the different red, green, and blue dots of phosphor, any color can be generated.

The Sony Trinitron monitors and TVs use a system that is a bit different. Its three guns are in a single housing and fire through a single lens. Instead of a shadow mask, the Trinitron uses a vertical grill that allows the beams to pass through. The Trinitron system was actually invented in this country, but no one in the TV industry was interested until Sony adopted it.

# Dot pitch

If you look closely at a black-and-white photo in a newspaper, you can see that the photo is made up of small dots. There will be a lot of dots in the darker areas and fewer in the light areas. The text or image on a monitor or a television screen is also made up of dots very similar to the newspaper photo. You can see the dots and spaces with a magnifying glass. This is much like the dots of a dot matrix printer.

The more dots and the closer together they are, the better the resolution. A good high-resolution monitor will have solid, sharply defined characters and images. However, the more dots and the closer together they are, the more difficult it is to manufacture a CRT. The red, blue, and green dots must be placed very accurately and uniformly for their specific electron beam to hit them. Dot pitch is the distance between two dots of the same color. Most standard monitors will have a dot pitch of .28 millimeters (mm). The better monitors will have dots that are as close as .24 mm. Some of the low-cost color monitors might have them from .39 mm up to .52 mm. Such monitors might be all right for playing games. However, they wouldn't be very good for anything else.

# Pixels

Resolution is also determined by the number of picture elements (pixels) that can be displayed. A *pixel* is the smallest unit that can be drawn or displayed on the screen. A pixel can be turned on or off with a single bit. However, to control the intensity and color depth, it might take several bits per pixel.

The following figures relate primarily to text, but the graphics resolution will be similar to the text. Most monitors are designed to display 80 characters in one row or line across the screen. By leaving a bit of space between each row, 25 lines of text can be displayed from top to bottom.

The old color graphics monitor (CGA) could display $640 \times 200$ pixels. If we divide 640 by 80, we find that one character will be 8 pixels wide. There can be 25 lines of characters, so $200 \div 25 = 8$ pixels high. The entire screen will have $640 \times 200 = 128,000$ pixels. EGA monitors have $640 \times 350$ pixels, so each cell is 8 pixels wide and 14 pixels high. The Video Electronics Standards Association (VESA) chose $640 \times 480$ to be the VGA standard and $800 \times 600$ to be the Super VGA (SVGA) standard. For SVGA, it is $800 \div 80 = 10$ pixels wide and $600 \div 25 = 24$ pixels high. Many of the newer systems are now capable of $1024 \times 768$, $1280 \times 1024$, $1664 \times 1200$, and more. With a resolution of $1664 \times 1200$, we would have 1,996,800, or almost 2 million, pixels that could be lit up. We have come a long way from the 128,000 pixels possible with CGA.

# Painting the screen

To put an image on the screen, the electron beam starts at the top-left corner. Under the influence of the electromagnets, it is drawn across to the right of the screen lighting up a very thin line as it moves. Depending on what the beam is depicting, it will be turned on and off by the grid as it sweeps across the screen. When the beam reaches the right side of the screen, it is turned off and sent back to the left side. It drops down a bit and begins sweeping across the screen to paint another line.

On a TV set, it paints 262.5 lines in $\frac{1}{60}$ of a second. These are all of the even numbered lines. It then goes back to the top and interlaces the other 262.5 odd numbered lines in between the first 262.5. It does this fairly fast, at a frequency of 15,750 Hz (15750 divided by 60 = 262.5). So it takes $\frac{1}{60}$ of a second to paint 525 lines. This is called a *frame*, so 30 frames are written to the screen in one second. When one of the dots is struck by the electron beam, it lights up and remains lit up for a certain length of time depending on the type of phosphor it was made from.

When we watch a movie, we are seeing a series of still photos, flashed one after the other. Due to our persistence of vision, it appears to be continuous motion. It is this same persistence of vision phenomenon that allows us to see motion and images on our television and video screens.

## The vertical scan rate

The time that it takes to fill a screen with lines from top to bottom is the *vertical scan rate*. This might also be called the *refresh rate*. The phosphor might start losing some of its glow after a period of time unless the vertical scan refreshes it in a timely manner. Some of the multiscan, or multifrequency, monitors can have several fixed or variable vertical scan rates. The Video Electronics Standards Association, (VESA) specifies a minimum of 70Hz for SVGA and 72Hz for VGA systems.

## Interlaced versus non-interlaced

The higher scan frequencies requires that the adapter have more precise and higher quality electronics. The monitor must also be capable of responding to the higher frequencies. Which, of course, requires higher costs to manufacture. To avoid this higher cost, IBM designed some of their systems with an interlaced horizontal system. Instead of increasing the horizontal frequency, they merely painted every other line across the screen from top to bottom, then returned to the top and painted the lines that were skipped. This is the same system used on TV sets.

Theoretically, this sounds like a great idea. Practically, however, it doesn't work too well because it causes a very annoying flicker. It can be very irritating to some people who have to work with this type of monitor for very long.

This flicker is not readily apparent, but some people have complained of eye-strain, headaches, and fatigue after prolonged use of an interlaced monitor. If the monitor is only used for short periods of time, by different persons, then the interlaced type would probably not be a problem.

Some companies make models that use interlacing in some modes and non-interlacing in other modes. The system can provide a bit more resolution in the interlaced mode. Most companies do not advertise the fact that their systems use interlacing; some might use the abbreviation N/I for their non-interlaced adapters. The interlaced models are usually a bit lower in price than the non-interlaced. You might have to ask the vendor what system is used.

## Multiscan

The multiscan monitors can accept a wide range of vertical and horizontal frequencies. This makes them quite versatile and flexible. Many of the early multiscans could accept both digital and analog signals. Almost all monitors sold today are the analog type.

The VGA system introduced by IBM on their PS/2 systems in 1987 used a fixed frequency instead of a multiscan adapter and monitor. A multiscan design costs more to build, so many of the low-cost VGAs are designed to operate at a single fixed frequency. They are not as versatile or flexible as the multiscan, but the resolution can be as good as the multiscan.

Many companies are manufacturing monitors with *multifixed frequencies* with two or more fixed frequencies. Again, they are not quite as flexible as the true multiscan, but they can cost less. I am using a 19" Sampo TriSync, which has three different frequencies. For my purposes, it does everything that I need to do.

The multiscan monitors can sell for as little as $250 and up to as much as $3500 or more for some of the large 19" to 30" sizes.

# Adapter basics

You can't just plug a monitor into your computer and expect it to function. Just as a hard disk needs a controller, a monitor needs an adapter to interface with the computer. Our computer monitors are a bit different than a TV. A TV set usually has all of its controlling electronics mounted in the TV console or case and is assembled and sold as a single unit. A computer monitor might have some electronics within its case, but its main controller, the adapter, is usually on a plug-in board on the PC motherboard. This gives us more versatility and utility because we can use different or specialized adapters if needed.

There are several manufacturers that make monitor adapters, so there is quite a lot of competition. This has helped to keep the prices fairly reasonable. Most monitors can operate with several different types of adapters. Adapters can cost as little as $40 and up to $1000 or more.

It would be foolish to buy a very expensive monitor and an inexpensive adapter, or vice versa. You should try to match the capabilities of the monitor and the adapter.

Most monitor adapters have text character generators built onto the board, which are similar to a built-in library. When we send an A to the screen, the adapter goes to its library and sends the signal for the preformed A to the screen. Each character occupies a cell made up of a number of pixels. The number of pixels depends on the resolution of the screen and the adapter. In the case of the VGA, if all the dots within a cell were lit up, there would be a solid block of dots 10 pixels wide and 24 pixels high. When an A is placed in a cell, only the dots necessary to form the outline of the A will be lit up. It is very similar to the dots formed by the dot matrix printers when it prints a character.

With the proper software, a graphics adapter can allow you to place lines, images, photos, various text fonts, and almost anything you can imagine on the screen. Almost all adapters sold today have both text and graphics capability.

# Analog versus digital

Most all monitors and adapters sold today are analog systems. Up until the introduction of the PS/2 with VGA, most displays used the digital system. However, the digital systems have severe limitations.

The digital signals are of two states: either fully on or completely off. The signals for color and intensity require separate lines in the cables. It takes six lines for the EGA to be able to display 16 colors out of a palette of 64. The digital systems are obsolete.

The analog signals that drive the color guns are voltages that are continuously variable. It takes only a few lines for the three primary colors. The intensity voltage for each color can then be varied almost infinitely to create as many as 256 colors out of a possible 262,144. To display more than 256 colors requires the true color adapters.

# Video accelerator boards

The fixed-function cards have accelerator chips with several built-in graphics functions. Because they have built-in functions, they can handle many of the Windows graphics tasks without having to bother the CPU. Because they don't often have to go back and forth to the CPU over the I/O bus at the slow speed of 8MHz, they are usually much faster than the dumb frame buffer type. Examples of the graphics chips used in these cards are S3 86CXXX, IIT AGX014, and the ATI 68800. Some that have a limited fixed-function can cost as little as $50 and up to $400. There is a wide price range for these cards.

Another type of adapter has its own coprocessor chip on board, such as the Texas Instruments 34010 or the Hitachi HD63483. By using an onboard coprocessor, it frees up the CPU for other tasks. The coprocessor boards are usually more expensive than any of the other types of boards.

Newer and better boards are being developed every day to meet the strenuous demands of multimedia for digital video, 3D technology, and full motion. Most of these boards are available for the VLB or PCI bus. One of the boards that has received some of the highest ratings by magazine laboratories is the Diamond Multimedia Stealth 64. It can play digital video from several different formats such as Indeo, Motion JPEG, and MPEG. (JPEG is a set of standards set up by the Joint Photographers Expert Group; MPEG is a similar set of standards set up by the Motion Picture Expert Group. Both standards concern compression of video and motion pictures.)

An optional daughter board can be added to the Diamond Stealth 64 Video Multimedia Accelerator to provide hardware MPEG decoding of both audio and video. The module provides capabilities to accept both NTSC (the American TV standard) and PAL (the standard used in many European countries) signals. It will accept a camcorder, VCR, and several other input devices. The board comes bundled with Corel Draw, Turbo DLD, and PanaStation CAD accelerators. These software accessories alone are worth the cost of the board.

This Diamond adapter has a S3 Vision969 controller, 2MB of VRAM (upgradeable to 4MB VRAM), horizontal sync 31.5KHz to 96.6KHz, vertical refresh of 43.5Hz to 120Hz. It comes with several software utilities.

Diamond also manufactures the DTV 1100 that is a hardware option for their Stealth 64 Video 2001 series. The hardware provides a 125-channel TV tuner and the MPEG Video Player. This board can accept broadcast video or a TV signal from a camcorder, VCR, laser disc, or camera. It also provides video capture capability.

## 3D adapters

Much of the newer software for games and animation is now 3D. There are several companies who are manufacturing special adapters for 3D. At the present time, there are no standards for 3D software or hardware, but Microsoft, Creative Labs, and several other companies are working to create a standard. Here are a couple of the 3D software companies:

Lightwave 3D, NewTek      800-847-6111
Microsoft 3D Movie Maker      800-426-9400

A couple of 3D adapter companies are:

3D Blaster, Creative Labs      800-998-1000
Edge 3D, Diamond Multimedia      800-468-5446

Here are a couple of Virtual Reality products:

SimulEyes VR, Stereo Graphics      800-746-3937
Virtual I-Glasses, Virtual I-O      800-646-3579

There are many other companies who are working on 3D hardware and software. There are usually articles in several magazines, such as the *New Media Magazine*, *CD-ROM Today*, and *Virtual Reality*. See the addresses listed in chapter 17.

## PCI bus adapters

You could use an old 8- or 16-bit ISA adapter on your Pentium Pro, but it would be about like hitching up a horse to pull a Cadillac. Many of the 486 and Pentium motherboards have either a VL bus or a PCI bus. The PCI offers some advantages over the VLB, so most Pentium Pro motherboards will have three or four PCI connectors. They might also have three or four ISA plug-in slot connectors.

The PCI bus adapters are much faster than the older graphics and accelerator boards because they have a 32- or 64-bit path that is used to directly communicate with the CPU. This direct path also allows them to communicate at the CPU speed or frequency. The ISA I/O systems are limited to the 8- or 16-bit bus and operate at a speed of 8MHz to 10MHz no matter how fast the CPU is.

Some Windows, most graphics, and many other applications, require a lot of interaction with the CPU, so many of the true color adapters are made for motherboards with a VLB or PCI bus. Most of the newer adapters are now designed for 64 bits and a few even operate at 128K, such as the Number Nine Imagine 128 Pro.

In Fig. 8-1, the top photo shows the highly rated Diamond Multimedia Stealth 64 VLB and some of the software that comes with it. The bottom photo shows the PCI version of the Diamond Stealth 64 adapter. Both units come with an extensive software bundle. The PCI version is shown with an optional MPEG decoder daughterboard. The VLB adapters have 2MB of VRAM memory, and the PCI has 4MB of VRAM.

# Video memory

Having memory on the adapter board saves having to go through the bus to the conventional RAM. Some adapter boards even have a separate plug-in daughterboard for adding more memory. With the older dumb frame buffer cards, even with a lot of memory, the adapter had to go back and forth over the 16-bit bus to communicate with the CPU. Many of the applications, especially under Windows, were painfully slow. An accelerator card with lots of onboard memory and a VESA local bus (VLB) or Peripheral Component Interconnect (PCI) bus system can speed up the processing considerably.

You should have at least 1MB of memory to display 256 colors in 1024 × 768 resolution. Of course, the more colors displayed and the higher the resolution, the more memory is required. To display 64,000 colors at 1024 × 768 requires 2MB, and for 24-bit true color it takes about 4MB.

# Adapter memory chips

Many of the high-resolution adapters have up to 4MB or more of Video RAM (VRAM) memory on board. The VRAM chips look very much like the older DRAM DIP memory chips, but they are not interchangeable with DRAM. The DRAM chips have a single port; they can only be accessed or written to through this port. The VRAM chips have two ports and can be accessed by one port while being written to in the other. This makes them much faster and a bit more expensive than DRAM. Some of the less expensive adapters use DRAM memory.

Many of the less expensive adapter boards are sold with only 512K of DRAM or less. They often have empty sockets for adding more memory. Some cards have space to install as much as 40MB of DRAM. It is not likely that you would need that much for ordinary use.

It is very easy to install the memory chips in the sockets. Just be sure that you orient them properly. They should be installed the same way as other memory on the board. Make sure that all legs are fully inserted in the sockets.

**Fig. 8-1** Two monitor adapters: a Diamond Stealth 64 VLB at the top and a Diamond Stealth PCI at the bottom.

If you expect to do any high-resolution graphics, you should have a minimum of 1MB of VRAM on the adapter, and 2MB would be even better.

# Installation

Installing a monitor and adapter is usually fairly easy. Just plug the adapter board into an empty slot and plug in the monitor cable. Then run whatever software drivers that might have come with the board.

A new Plug-and-Play (PnP) standard should be available by the time you read this. The monitors and adapters that conform to the PnP standard will have a special connector that will include a display data channel (DDC) that can be used by the system to automatically choose the optimum settings for highest refresh rates and resolution.

The Video Electronics Standards Association (VESA) is also working on a new Enhanced Video Connector (EVC) that will support higher bandwidths and let the monitor accept multimedia input devices such as cameras and microphones.

Windows 95 lets you easily customize your display. Just click the right mouse button anywhere on the desktop, then choose Properties. Display Properties has four different tabs: Background, which lets you set or change the desktop's pattern or wallpaper; Appearance, which lets you modify the color scheme; Screen Saver, and Settings, which lets you change the color depth, resolution, and drivers for the monitor and adapter.

# SVGA colors

The number of colors that a SVGA card can display is dependent on the resolution displayed. Here are the numbers for a low cost SVGA: 16.7 million colors at 640 × 480, only 64,000 colors at 800 × 600, and only 16 colors at 1280 × 1024.

Of course, there are adapters that can display a much greater number of colors than that listed here, but they are also more expensive.

### True colors

Most of the standard low-cost VGA cards are capable of only 16 colors. True colors, or pure colors, requires a video board with lots of fast memory, a coprocessor, and complex electronics. True color means that a video board can drive a monitor to display a large number of shades in separate, distinct hues or pure colors. Remember that a pixel can be turned on or off with a single bit; however, for color intensity or shades and depth, it might take several bits per pixel. (See Table 8-1.) A good adapter for true color can cost more than the monitor.

**Table 8-1.  Pure color.**

| Bits | Shades | Depth |
|------|--------|-------|
| 4 ($2^4$) | 16 | |
| 8 ($2^8$) | 256 | |
| 15 ($2^{15}$) | 32,768 | 5:5:5 |
| 16 ($2^{16}$) | 65,536 | 5:6:5 or 6:6:4 |
| 24 ($2^{32}$) | 16.7 million | 8:8:8 |

## Depth

True color usually refers to displays with 15-, 16-, or 24-bit depths. *Depth* means that each of the individual red, green, or blue (RGB) color pixels will have a large amount of information about each color. The 15-bit system will have 5 bits of information for each of the three colors. The 16-bit system can have 6 bits for red, 6 bits for green, and 4 bits for blue or a combination of 5:6:5. The 24-bit system will have 8 bits for each color.

Table 8-2 can give you an idea of how much memory is needed for the various resolutions and colors.

**Table 8-2. Memory and resolution.**

| Bits/Pixel | Color | 640×480 | 800×600 | 102×768 |
|---|---|---|---|---|
| 4 | 16 | 150K | 234K | 386K |
| 8 | 256 | 300K | 469K | 768K |
| 16 | 35,536 | 600K | 938K | 1.536MB |
| 24 | 16,777,216 | 900K | 1.406MB | 2.304MB |

## Dithering

If a board doesn't have enough power to display the true distinct colors, it might use dithering to mix the colors to give an approximation.

Dithering takes advantage of the eye's tendency to blur colors and view them as an average. A printed black-and-white photo uses all black dots, but several shades of gray can be printed depending on the number of black dots per inch. A mixture of red dots with white ones can create a pink image. Gradual color transitions can be accomplished by using dithering to intersperse pixels of various colors.

# Anti-aliasing

Some low-resolution systems have a "stair-step" effect when a diagonal line is drawn on the screen. Some adapters have the ability to use anti-aliasing to average out the pixels so that a smooth line appears.

# Sources

There are hundreds of adapter manufacturers. I hesitate to mention models because each manufacturer has dozens of different models with different features and resolutions. They are constantly designing, developing, and introducing new models. I have used several different models of the Diamond adapters, and I think they are one of the best. Several computer magazines have tested and rated the following to be among the best. Call the companies for brochures and more information:

Diamond Multimedia Systems     800-468-5846
ASUSTek                        408-956-9077
Boca Research                  407-997-6227
Orchid Technology              510-683-0300
Matrox Graphics                800-361-1408
STB Powergraph 64              214-234-8750
ATI Technologies               905-882-2600
Number Nine Imagine 128        800-438-6463

# Adapter software

Most adapter cards will work with any software that you have. However, many adapter vendors provide special software drivers that are necessary for high resolution and speed with certain applications. Make sure that the adapter has drivers for all popular graphics software.

# MPEG boards

The Motion Pictures Expert Group (MPEG) devised a specification for compressing and decompressing graphics and video. Ordinarily, a single frame in a moving picture requires about 25MB to digitize and store. The MPEG system allows a compression up to 100 to 1 so that it is possible to store as much as 72 minutes on a 650MB CD-ROM.

Several companies have developed plug-in boards that will allow you to capture and play back video from several different sources such as a VCR, camcorder, CD-ROM, TV, laser disk, and others. Some cards have built-in sound systems, and some can even be supplied with a TV tuner so that you can watch TV on your monitor.

There are a few feature movies that have been compressed to the MPEG specifications. With a MPEG board, you can watch the movies on your high-resolution monitor. It is possible that, as the MPEG system becomes more widespread, the PC might become the home entertainment center.

Here are a few companies who manufacture MPEG boards. Call them for brochures and information:

| | |
|---|---|
| Diamond Multimedia Systems | 800-468-5846 |
| Genoa GVision DX | 800-934-3662 |
| Orchid Kelvin MPEG | 510-683-0300 |
| Sigma Real Magic Rave | 510-770-0100 |
| Prolink | 213-780-7978 |
| High Technology | 800-697-8001 |

# Choosing a monitor

The primary determining factor for choosing a monitor should be what it is going to be used for and the amount of money you have to spend. Try to get a good 15" as a minimum. If you can afford it, buy a large 21" monitor with super high resolution and a good SVGA board to drive it. Look for monitors with a refresh rate of at least 72Hz. Look for a dot pitch of no more than .28 mm; .26 mm or .24 is even better but more expensive. The resolution should be at least 800 × 600; 1024 × 768 is better.

Make sure the controls are near the front and easily accessible.

The stated screen size of a monitor is very misleading and almost fraudulent. The stated size is a diagonal measurement. There is a border on all four sides of the screen. The usable viewing area on a 14" monitor is about 9.75" wide and about 7.75" high. One reason is because the screen is markedly curved near the edges on all sides. This curve can cause distortion, so the areas are masked off and not used.

If you expect to do any kind of graphics or CAD/CAM design work, you will definitely need a good large-screen color monitor with very high resolution. A large screen is almost essential for some types of design drawings so that as much of the drawing as possible can be viewed on the screen.

You will also need a high-resolution monitor for close tolerance designs. For example, if you draw two lines to meet on a low-resolution monitor, they might look as if they are perfectly lined up; however, when the drawing is magnified or printed out, the lines might not be anywhere close to one another.

Most desktop publishing (DTP) is done in black-and-white print. The high-resolution paper-white monochrome monitors might be all you need for these applications. These monitors can usually display several shades of gray.

Many of these monitors are the portrait type; that is, they are higher than they are wide. Many of them have a display area of 8½" by 11". Instead of 25 lines, they will have 66 lines, which is the standard for an 11" sheet of paper. Many have a phosphor that will let you have black text on a white background so that the screen looks very much like the finished text. Some of the newer color monitors have a mode that will let you switch to pure white with black type.

Most of our monitors are wider than they are tall. These are called landscape styles.

## What to look for

If possible, go to several stores and compare various models. Turn the brightness up and check the center of the screen and the outer edges. Is the intensity the same in the center and the outer edges? Check the focus, brightness, and contrast with text and graphics. There can be vast differences even in the same models from the same manufacturer.

Ask the vendor for a copy of the specs. Check the dot pitch. For good high resolution, it should be no greater than .28 mm., even better would be .26 mm. or .24 mm.

Check the horizontal and vertical scan frequency specifications. For a multiscan, the wider the range, the better. A good system could have a horizontal range from 30KHz to 40KHz or better. The vertical range should be from 45Hz to 70Hz or higher.

## Controls

You might also check for available controls to adjust the brightness, contrast, and vertical/horizontal lines. Some manufacturers place them on the back or some other difficult area to get at. It is much better if they are accessible from the front so that you can see what the effect is as you adjust them.

## Glare

If a monitor reflects too much light, it can be like a mirror and be very distracting. Some manufacturers have coated the screen with a silicon formulation to cut down on the reflectance. Some have etched the screen for the same purpose. Other screens are tinted to help cut down on glare. If possible, you should try the monitor under various lighting conditions.

If you have a glare problem, several supply companies and mail-order houses offer glare shields that cost from $20 up to $100.

# Cleaning the screens

Because there are about 25,000 volts of electricity hitting the back side of the monitor face, it creates a static attraction for dust. This can distort and make the screen difficult to read.

Most manufacturers should have an instruction booklet that suggests how the screen should be cleaned. If you have a screen that has been coated with silicon to reduce glare, you should not use any harsh cleansers on it. Usually, plain water and a soft paper towel will do fine.

# Monitor radiation

Almost all electrical devices emit very low frequency (VLF) magnetic and electrical fields. There have been no definitive studies that prove that this radiation is harmful to a person. In some cases, the emissions are so weak that they can hardly be measured. However, the government of Sweden developed a set of guidelines to regulate the strength of emissions from video display terminals (VDTs).

Several people in this country are also concerned that the VDT radiation might be a problem, so many monitor manufacturers now add shielding to control the emission. If you are worried about VDT emissions, look for monitors that are certified to meet MPR II specifications.

Incidentally, if you use a hair dryer, you will get much more radiation from that than from a monitor.

# Green monitors

The monitor can use 100 to 150 watts of energy. The EPA Energy Star program demands that the energy be reduced to no more than 30 watts when they are not being used.

I sometimes sit in front of my monitor for 10 or 15 minutes doing research, or more likely with writers block. All this time, the monitor is burning up lots of watts of energy. Many of the new monitors meet the Energy Star specifications; therefore, when there is no activity, they go into a sleep mode where they use very little energy. A small amount of voltage is still applied to the monitor, and it will come back online almost immediately.

None of my monitors comply with the Energy Star specification. However, I am saving energy by using the PC ener-g saver from the NEI Company (800-832-4007). The PC ener-g saver acts as an on/off switch for the monitor and printer. The keyboard cable connector is removed from the motherboard connection and plugged into the box. A cable from the box replaces the keyboard connection to the motherboard. Using software that comes with the unit, you can set the PC ener-g saver to shut down your monitor and printer if there is no activity from the keyboard. You can set the time interval for no activity from just a few seconds up to several minutes. As soon as any key on the keyboard is pressed or the mouse is moved, the monitor comes back on. It comes back to the same place where you were working when it shut down.

To re-activate the printer, just send it a print command.

# Software for monitor testing

If you are planning to buy an expensive high-resolution monitor, you might want to buy a software program called DisplayMate for Windows from Sonera Technologies (908-747-6886). It is a collection of utilities that can perform several checks on a monitor. It lets you measure the resolution for fine lines, the clarity of the image, distortion, gray and color scales, and a full range of intensities and colors. The software can actually help tweak and fine-tune your monitor and adapter. The setup also helps a person set the controls for the optimum values. If you plan to spend $1500 or so for a monitor, it could be well worth it to test the monitor first.

# Other resources

A monitor is a very important part of your computer system. I couldn't possibly tell you all that you need to know in this short chapter. One of the better ways to keep up on this ever-changing technology is to subscribe to one or more computer magazines. They frequently have articles about monitors. Of course, they also have many ads for monitors and adapters. I have listed several computer magazines in chapter 17.

# 9
# Input devices

Before you can do anything with a computer, you must input data to it. There are several ways to input data, such as from a keyboard, disk, modem, mouse, scanner, barcode readers, voice-recognition input, fax, and online from a bulletin board, mainframe, or a network. This chapter will discuss a few of the ways to input data to a computer.

## Keyboards

By far, the most common way to get data into the computer is by way of the keyboard. For most common applications, it is impossible to operate the computer without a keyboard.

The keyboard is the most personal connection with your computer. If you do a lot of typing, it is very important that you get a keyboard that suits you. Not all keyboards are the same. Some have a light mushy touch; some heavy. Some have noisy keys; others are silent with very little feedback.

### A need for standards

Typewriter keyboards are fairly standard. There are only 26 letters in the alphabet and a few symbols, so most QWERTY typewriters have about 50 keys. However, I have had several computers over the last few years, and every one of them has had a different keyboard. The main typewriter characters aren't changed or moved very often, but some of the very important control keys—like the Esc, Ctrl, PrtSc, \, function keys, and several others—are moved all over the keyboard.

For the last few years, most keyboards had 101 keys. Windows 95 and multimedia functions have caused several more keys to be added. Keyboards can now have up to 109 or more keys. The extra keys provide application shortcuts for Windows 95 and other task functions.

There are well over 400 different keyboards in the U.S. Many people make their living by typing on a keyboard. Many of the large companies have systems that count the number of keystrokes that an employee makes during a shift. If the employee fails to make a certain number of keystrokes, then that person can be fired. Can you imagine the problems if the person has to frequently learn a new keyboard? I am not a very good typist in the first place. I have great difficulty using different keyboards. There definitely should be some sort of standards.

Innovation—creating something new that is useful and needed and makes life better or easier—is great. That type of innovation should be encouraged everywhere; however, many times, changes are made just for the sake of differentiation without adding any real value or functionality to the product. This applies not only to keyboards, but to all technology.

## How a keyboard works

The keyboard is actually a computer in itself. It has a small microprocessor with its own ROM. The computerized electronics of the keyboard eliminate the bounce of the keys, can determine when you hold a key down for repeat, can store up to 20 or more keystrokes, and can determine which key was pressed first if you press two at a time.

In addition to the standard BIOS chips on your motherboard, there is a special keyboard BIOS chip. Each time a key is pressed, a unique signal is sent to the BIOS. This signal is made up of a direct current voltage that is turned on and off a certain number of times within a definite time frame to represent zeros and ones.

Each time a 5 volt line is turned on for a certain amount of time, it represents a 1; when it is off for a certain amount of time, it represents a 0. In the ASCII code, if the letter A is pressed, the code for 65 will be generated: 1000001.

## Reprogramming key functions

Most word processors, spreadsheets, databases, and other software programs usually designate certain keys to run various macros. A macro is a word, or several words, that can be input by just pressing one or more keys. By pressing a certain key or a combination of keys, you could input your name and address or any other group of words that you use frequently.

These programs also use the function keys to perform various tasks, such as moving the cursor, underlining, bolding, and many other functions. The problem is that there is no standardization. Changing from one word processor or software program to another is about like having to learn a new foreign language. It sure would be nice if you could go from one program to another as easily as you can drive different automobiles.

## Keyboard sources

Keyboard preference is strictly a matter of individual taste. The Key Tronic Company of Spokane (509-928-8000) also makes some excellent keyboards. They are the IBM of the keyboard world. Their keyboards have set the standards. The Key Tronic keyboards have been copied by the clone makers, even to the extent of using the same model numbers.

Quality keyboards use a copper-etched printed circuit board and keys that switch on and off. The keys of quality keyboards have a small spring beneath each key to give them a uniform tension. Key Tronic offers several models. On some models, they can even let you change the little springs under the keys to a different tension. The standard is 2 ounces, but you can configure the key tension to whatever you like. You can install 1-, 1.5-, 2-, 2.5-, or 3-ounce springs for an extra fee. They can also let you exchange the positions of the CapsLock and Ctrl keys. The Key Tronic keyboards have several other functions that are clearly described in their large manual. Call them for a copy.

Many of the less expensive keyboards use plastic with conductive paint for the connecting lines instead of an etched copper printed circuit board. Instead of springs beneath each key, they use a rubber cup. The bottom of each key is coated with a carbon conductive material. When the key is depressed, the carbon allows an electrical connection between the painted lines. The keys are part of, and are attached to, the main plastic board by strips of flexible molded plastic. These low-cost keyboards can have as few as 17 parts. The keyboards work fairly well.

I recently saw new clone keyboards being sold at a swap meet for $10 each. The keyboards looked very much like the Key Tronic 101 key types. The assembly snapped together instead of using metal screws. They also had several other cost-saving features. However, there is quite a lot of electronics in a keyboard. I don't know how they can possibly make a keyboard to sell for $10. At that price, you could buy two or three of them. If you ever had any trouble with one, just throw it away and plug in a new one.

There are several keyboard manufacturers and hundreds of different models with many different special functions. Prices range from $10 up to $400 or more. Look through any computer magazine.

## Specialized keyboards

Several companies have developed specialized keyboards. I have listed only a few of them in this section.

Quite often, I have the need to do some minor calculations. The computer is great for calculations. Most of the word processor, database, and spreadsheet programs have built-in calculator functions. However, to use the calculator, most of these programs require that the computer to be on and be using a file. There are some keyboards that have a built-in calculator, such as the one shown in Fig. 9-1. It has a calculator built into the number pad. It has a battery so that it can be used whether the computer is on or not.

All newer keyboards now have the extra Windows 95 keys, even the $10 clones that I saw at a swap meet. You don't really need the extra keys to run Windows 95. I have several older keyboards that work just fine with Windows 95.

The Maxi Switch Company (520-746-9378), NMB Technologies (800-662-8321), and SC&T International (800-408-4084) have multimedia keyboards that come with a microphone, speakers, input jacks, and volume control.

Another Key Tronic model has a bar code reader attached to it. This can be extremely handy if you have a small business that uses bar codes. This keyboard would be ideal for a computer in a point of sale (POS) system.

If you have been in the computer business for a while, you might remember the PCjr from IBM. It had a wireless keyboard that used an infrared system similar to a TV remote control. The Casco Products Company (800-793-6960) thinks it is still a good idea. They have developed the LightLink, a wireless keyboard that communi-

**Fig. 9-1** A keyboard with a calculator in the number pad.

cates by infrared with a small receiver that plugs into the motherboard keyboard socket. One use for this keyboard is for presentations. The person can operate the computer from across the room.

## Carpal tunnel syndrome

Businesses spend billions of dollars each year for employee health insurance. Of course, the more employee injuries, the more the insurance costs. Carpal tunnel syndrome (CTS) has become one of the more common complaints. CTS causes pain and/or numbness in the palm of the hand, thumb, and index and ring fingers. The pain can radiate up into the arm. Any movement of the hand or fingers can be very painful. CTS is caused by pressure on the median nerve where it passes into the hand through the carpal tunnel and under a ligament at the front of the wrist. Either one or both hands can be affected. Treatment often requires expensive surgery that might or might not relieve the pain.

CTS most commonly affects those people who must use a computer for long periods of time. Keying in data is a very important function in this computer age. That is the job of many employees, eight hours a day, every day. CTS is usually caused by the way the wrist is held while typing on the keyboard. There are several pads and devices to help make the typing more comfortable. I have a foam rubber pad that is the length of the keyboard and is about 4" wide and .75" thick. See Fig. 9-2. I can rest and support my wrists on this pad and still reach most of the keys. Many of the vendors give them away at shows like COMDEX.

Repetitive strain injury (RSI) is about the same as CTS. Many employees are asking for workers compensation insurance and taking companies to court because of RSI. At the time of this writing, there are several cases in court against IBM, Apple, and several other large computer manufacturers. CTS and RSI injuries have cost millions of dollars in loss of work days. They have become a serious problem.

Before the computer revolution, thousands and thousands of people, mostly women, sat at a typewriter eight or more hours a day typing on keyboards that are similar to computer keyboards. Yet there were few, if any, cases of CTS or RSI ever

**Fig. 9-2** A foam rubber pad that can help prevent RSI and CTS injuries.

reported. It is a disorder that has become prevalent only in the last few years. It could be that typewriter keyboards have more slant and were usually placed at a different height. Another factor might have been that the typewriter limited the typist's speed and repetition. Some data-entry workers can do as many as 13,000 keystrokes per hour.

Joan Stigliani has written a book titled "The Computer User's Survival Guide" (O'Reilly & Associates). She claims that, in the last 15 years, RSI has gone up from 14% of all occupational illnesses to 60%.

Some of the things that are suggested to help prevent RSI and CTS is to pause frequently and stretch your hands and upper body. The desk and chair should be adjusted so that both feet rest easily on the floor.

## Ergonomic keyboards

The Key Tronic Company has an ergonomic keyboard that breaks in the middle and each half can be elevated from the center. The center can be separated and angled to fit the angle of your hands. The B and N keys might be separated by as much as an inch or more, while the Y and T keys might be touching. The elevation and the angle should help prevent CTS and RSI.

This Key Tronic keyboard is rather expensive at about $300. The Key Tronic company developed the ergonomic keyboard for Microsoft shown in Fig. 9-3. Like most products with a brand name, it is a bit expensive at $99.

Several other companies have also developed similar ergonomic keyboards for less than half that price.

ALPS Electric (800-825-2577), Cirque Corp. (800-454-3375), and Northgate (800-548-1993) all have Glidepoint keyboards with pads that can take the place of the mouse. They have a square pad below the arrow keys. You use your finger on the

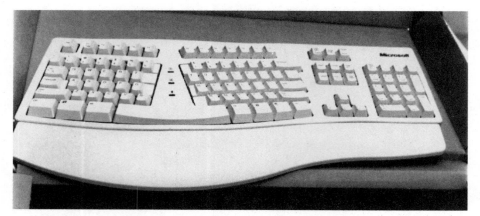

**Fig. 9-3** The Microsoft ergonomic keyboard that was developed by the Keytronics Company.

pad to move the cursor. To click, just tap the pad with your finger or press one of the three nearby buttons. The Northgate OmniKey is ergonomically shaped with the keys separated and angled similar to the Microsoft Natural keyboard. Mitsumi (800-648-7864) also has a low-cost ergonomic-shaped keyboard.

Figure 9-4 shows a clone ergonomic keyboard with a touch pad. It is quite similar to the keyboards mentioned previously. The main difference is that those keyboards are listed at this time for $139 to $149 each. I paid $49 for this clone. It has a PS/2-type keyboard connector, which is much smaller than a standard AT keyboard connector. However, it comes with an adapter so that it can be used on either system. The touch pad must be connected to one of the serial ports, just like a normal mouse. This port connector and cable is part of the keyboard cable.

**Fig. 9-4** An ergonomic keyboard with a glide point touch pad that takes the place of a mouse.

Some of the advantages of the touch pad are that it does not have the mouse cable on the desktop and does not require desktop space for a mouse pad. The keyboard has a switch that will allow you to switch off the touch pad and use a standard mouse if you want to.

This clone keyboard has the new Windows 95 extra keys. It also has an extra Tab and Backspace key. Most of the other keys are the same as the standard 101-key keyboard, but they are angled, separated, and raised in the center. It has taken me a bit of time to become accustomed to it.

Even though some of the ergonomic keyboards are a bit expensive, they are a lot less expensive than having to go to a doctor for a painful operation that might or might not be successful. Other than surgery, the other alternative is to rest the hands and miss several months of work. If you work for a large company, the company might save money by installing these ergonomic keyboards. Many people are now suing the companies for CTS and RSI injuries. Of course, the insurance companies are increasing their rates to help pay for any damages that might be awarded.

# Mouse systems

One of the biggest reasons for the success of the Macintosh is that it is easy to use. With a mouse and icons, all you have to do is point and click. You don't have to learn a lot of commands and rules. A person who knows nothing about computers can become productive in a very short time.

The people in the DOS world finally took note of this and began developing programs and applications such as Windows for the IBM and compatibles.

There are now dozens of companies that manufacture mice. There are some mice that can cost up to $100 or more; others can cost less than $10. What is the difference in a mouse that costs $100 and one that costs $10? The answer is $90. The low-cost mouse does just about everything that most people would need from a mouse. After all, how much mouse do you need just to point and click? Of course, if you are doing high-end drafting and designing and very close tolerance work, then you definitely need one that has high resolution.

## The ball mice

Most mice have a small round rubber ball on the underside that contacts the desktop or mouse pad. As the mouse is moved, the ball turns. Inside the mouse, two flywheels contact the ball—one for horizontal and one for vertical movements. The flywheels are mounted between two light sensitive diodes. The flywheels have small holes in the outer edge. As the flywheels turn, light shines through the holes or is blocked where there are no holes. This breaks the light up into patterns of 1s and 0s which then control the cursor movement.

The ball and flywheels pick up dirt, which can affect their operation. On most mice, the ball can be easily removed and cleaned.

## Mouse interfaces

You can't just plug in a mouse and start using it. The software—whether Windows, WordPerfect, or a CAD program—must recognize and interface with the mouse. So, mouse companies develop software drivers to allow the mouse to operate with various programs. The drivers are usually supplied on a disk. The Microsoft Mouse is the closest to a standard, so most other companies emulate the Microsoft driver. Most mice drivers are now included in Windows. Most mice today come with a small switch that allows you to switch between the Microsoft emulation or the IBM PC. If the switch is not in the proper position, the mouse might not work.

The mouse plugs into a serial port: COM1 or COM2. This might cause a problem if you already have two serial devices using COM1 and COM2. DOS also allows for COM3 and COM4, but these two ports must be shared with COM1 and COM2, so they must have special software to be shared.

The serial ports on some systems use a DB25 socket connector with 25 contacts. Others might use a DB9 socket with 9 contacts. Many of the mice now come with the DB9 connector and a DB25 connector adapter. The DB25 connector looks exactly like the DB25 connector used for the LPT1 parallel printer port except that the serial port connector is a male connector with pins, the LPT1 printer port is a female with sockets. Figure 9-5 shows a mouse and several adapters.

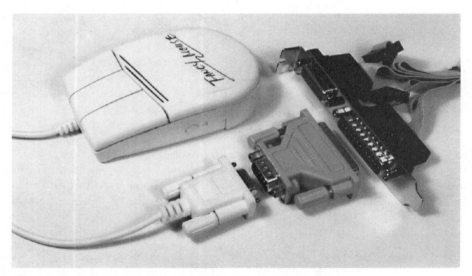

**Fig. 9-5** Some DB 25 connectors and adapters for a mouse cable.

There might be times when you have a cable that is a male when what you need is a female or vice versa. (A male connector is one that has pins; a female connector has sockets.) You can buy DB25 "Gender Bender" adapters that can solve this type of problem. If you simply need an extension so that you can plug two similar cables together, straight-through adapters are also available. There are many different kinds of combinations. The Cables To Go Company (800-225-8646) has just about every cable and accessory that you would ever need. The Dalco Electronics Company (800-445-5342) also has many types of cables, adapters, and electronic components.

Before you buy a mouse, you might check the type of serial port connector you have and order the proper type. You can buy an adapter for about $3.

### Wireless mice

One of the disadvantages of operating a keyboard, such as the wireless LightLink mentioned earlier, is that you also need a wireless mouse.

Several companies have developed wireless mice. They operate with infrared rays similar to the remote control of a TV. Some operate using a radio frequency, such as the wireless mouse made by Mitsumi Electronics (800-648-7864). Logitech (800-231-7717) also has wireless models. Even though they are wireless, they still need a receiver and an interface to connect to a serial port.

# Trackballs

A trackball is a mouse that has been turned upside down. Like the mouse, the trackballs also require a serial port.

One advantage of the trackball is that you don't need the square foot of desk space that a mouse requires. The trackballs are usually larger than the ball in a mouse, so it is possible to have better resolution. They are often used with CAD and critical design systems.

Constant use of a mouse can also lead to CTS and RSI. The Itac Systems (800-533-4822) claim that their ergonomically designed trackball Mouse-Trak can help prevent those injuries.

There are several companies who manufacture trackballs. Look through the computer magazines for ads.

# Touch screens and light pens

Some fast-food places now have a touch screen with a menu of several items. You merely touch the item that you want and the order is transmitted to the executive chef who is usually a young high school kid. The same type of system is sometimes found in kiosks in shopping malls and large department stores. Some systems use an image of a keyboard so that you can touch the various keys almost as if you were typing. The touch system is accurate, saves time and money, and is convenient.

The touch screen operation is similar to using a mouse and pointing. Most of them have a frame installed on the bezel of the monitor. Beams of infrared light crisscross the front of the monitor screen. For ordinary text, most monitors are set up so that they have 80 columns left to right and 25 rows from top to bottom. Columns of beams originate from the top part of the frame and pass to the bottom frame. Rows of beams originate from the left portion of the frame and pass to the right frame. If one of the beams is interrupted by an object, such as a finger or pencil, the computer can determine exactly what character happens to be in that portion of the screen.

# Joysticks

Joysticks are used primarily for games. They are serial devices and need an interface. Many of the multifunction boards that have COM ports also provide a game connector for joysticks.

Joysticks are fairly reasonable and can cost from $10 up to $30. There are usually several ads for them in magazines such as the *Computer Shopper*.

# Digitizers and graphics tablets

Graphics tablets and digitizers are similar to a flat drawing pad or drafting table. Most of them use some sort of pointing device that can translate movement into digitized output to the computer. Some are rather small; some can be as large as a standard drafting table. Some can cost as little as $150 or up to over $1500. Most of them have a very high resolution, are very accurate, and are intended for precision drawing.

Some of the tablets have programmable overlays and function keys. Some will work with a mouse-like device, a pen light, or a pencil-like stylus. The tablets can be used for designing circuits, CAD programs, graphics designs, freehand drawing, and even text and data input. The most common use is with CAD software. The Wacom Technology Corp. also has a digitizer pad that uses a cordless, batteryless, pressure sensitive pen.

Most of the tablets are serial devices, but some of them require their own interface board. Many of them are compatible with the Microsoft Mouse systems.

The CalComp Company (800-932-1212) has developed several models. These tablets use a puck that is similar to a mouse except that it has a magnifying glass and cross-hairs for very high resolution. They have both corded and cordless pucks. Call CalComp for a brochure and more information.

## Signature capture

It is very easy to generate a fax with a computer, but most letters and memos need a signature. The Inforite Company (800-366-4635) has a small pad and a stylus that will let you input a signature into a file. The signature can then be attached to a fax or to other documents. With the Inforite, you can add notes, comments, or drawings to other documents in the computer.

## Pressure-sensitive graphics tablets

Several companies have developed pressure-sensitive tablets. Wacom has developed several different models. The Wacom tablets use an electromagnetic resonance system. This allows the use of a special stylus that requires no wires or batteries. The tablet has a grid of embedded wires that can detect the location of the stylus and the pressure that is applied. The tablets sense the amount of pressure and can draw a thin line or a heavy line in response.

The tablets can be used with different graphics software programs to create sketches, drawings, designs, and art.

Here are some of the companies who manufacture pressure-sensitive tablets:

| | |
|---|---|
| Wacom Technology | 800-922-6613 |
| Communication Intelligence | 800-888-9242 |
| Kurta Corp. | 602-276-5533 |
| Summagraphics | 800-337-8662 |

Call the companies for brochures or more information.

# Scanners

Scanners with Optical Character Reader (OCR) software can scan a line of printed type, recognize each character, and input that character into a computer just as if it were typed in from a keyboard. A beam of light sweeps across the page and the characters can be determined by the absorption and reflection of the light.

One problem with the early scanners was that they could only recognize a few different fonts. They could not recognize graphics at all. The machines today have much more memory, and the technology has improved to where the better scanners can recognize almost any font or type.

Scanners have been around for several years. When they first came out, they cost from $6000 to more than $15,000. Many full-page flatbed scanners are now fairly inexpensive, starting at about $500. Scanners now have the ability to recognize a large number of fonts, and they can copy and digitize color graphics and images. Many of the early scanners had a 100 dot per inch resolution (DPI). Later ones had 300 to 400 DPI. Many of the newer high-end ones now have a DPI as high as 800.

Some of the early low-cost color scanners had to make three passes—one for each primary color. Most of the newer and more expensive ones can now scan all three colors in one pass.

Many of the flatbed scanners have 24-bit color. Some of the newer ones now have 30- to 36-bit color. The 36-bit resolution means that 12 different bits of information is possible for each of the three primary colors. Some high-end, very high resolution scanners that are needed for color graphic image processing and publishing can cost from $12,000 up to $95,000.

The flatbed scanners have a glass panel that is similar to those found in copy machines. The sheet to be scanned is laid on the glass panel, and the machine sweeps the scanning heads across the sheet from top to bottom. Scanners have a lot in common with copy machines, printers, and fax machines. Many companies are now manufacturing multifunction machines that include the capability to scan, copy, print, and fax. These machines will be discussed in more detail in chapter 12.

## Personal scanners

Several companies are manufacturing small-page pass-through compact scanners, such as the Logitech ScanMan shown in Fig. 9-6. This scanner is quite versatile. It attaches to the parallel port of the computer, so it doesn't need a separate board. It can scan in text, drawings, or even photos into the computer. If you need a copy of a page, scan it into the computer, then print it out. It can input printed text, signatures, drawings, or graphic images to a fax/modem board or to a hard disk.

Here are a few of the compact scanner vendors:

| | |
|---|---|
| Delrina WinFax Scanner | 800-268-6082 |
| Envisions Personal PageVacuum | 800-365-7226 |
| Epson Personal Document Station | 800-626-4686 |
| Logitech ScanMan PowerPage | 800-231-1717 |
| Microtek Lab PageWiz | 800-654-4160 |
| Plustek USA PageReader 800 | 800-685-8088 |
| Umax Technologies PageOffice | 800-562-0311 |
| Visioneer PaperPort | 800-787-7007 |

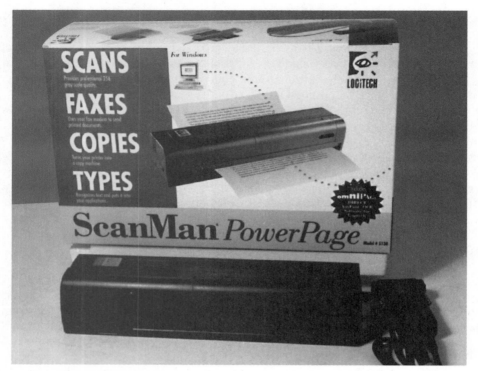

**Fig. 9-6**  The Logitech ScanMan personal scanner.

The IRISPen Company (800-447-4744) has a small pen that can scan a single line at a time. There are times when you don't want or need to scan in a whole page, so the IRISPen is very handy for those occasions.

The Envisions, Epson, Microtek, and Umax companies listed here also manufacture several other models and the higher quality flatbed scanners. The Umax Mirage D-16 is a 12" by 17" format with 30-bit color and 800 DPI. There are many other scanner companies. Look for ads and articles in the computer magazines listed in chapter 17.

## What to look for when buying a scanner

What to look for will depend on what you want to do with your scanner and, of course, how much you want to pay. There are several manufacturers of scanners and hundreds of different models, types, resolutions, bus types, and prices. A monochrome scanner is fine for text. Many of the monochrome scanners are relatively inexpensive. They can recognize text and graphic images in up to 256 different shades.

If you are buying a color scanner, there will be a lot more options to consider. Some of the lower priced ones might have to make three passes—once each for red, green, and blue. For each pass, the light is sent through filters that can recognize 256 levels of red, green, or blue.

The less expensive scanners might have a resolution of only 300 DPI or 400 DPI; however, they may use interpolation software that fills in the spaces between the dots to give two or three times the true resolution. As you might expect, some ads might list the interpolated resolution in large letters and the true resolution in small letters (if it is mentioned at all).

The more expensive color scanners can capture all three colors in one pass. They can also scan at a true 24-bit color depth to yield 16.7 million colors. That means that there can be 8 bits of color information about each of the red, green, or blue colors.

You should try to find a system that conforms to the TWAIN specification. The word TWAIN is an acronym for *Technology Without An Interesting Name.* (Mark Twain would have appreciated this acronym.) It is an Application Programming Interface (API) specification that was jointly developed by Aldus, Caere, Eastman Kodak, Hewlett-Packard, and Logitech.

A different device driver is needed for each of the hundreds of different printers. Before TWAIN, you needed a different device driver from every manufacturer for each model and type of scanner. TWAIN helps to standardize some of the device drivers. We really need something like TWAIN for printers.

Some of the less expensive scanners use a proprietary interface board. It is much better to buy one that uses the SCSI interface.

There are many manufacturers of scanners and, of course, many different prices. Look at the ads in any of the computer magazines listed in chapter 17.

## OCR software

The OCR capabilities of a scanner allows it to recognize each character of a printed document and input that character into a computer just as if it were typed in from a keyboard. Once the data is in the computer, a word processor can be used to revise or change the data, then print it out again.

Faxes are received as graphical documents. It requires a lot of disk space to store a fax; however, a scanner can convert faxes to text, which takes up much less disk space. Some of the OCR software programs, such as OmniPage Pro, supports over 100 different scanners. In most cases, it can match text to the original fonts. It can read degraded text by reading it in context. It has a large internal dictionary that helps in this respect. It yields excellent OCR accuracy. OmniPage Pro can automatically convert scanned text into any of the most popular word processor formats. It has the Image Assistant, which is an integrated 24-bit color editor for graphic editing. OmniPage Pro 6.0 is one of the better OCR packages available. It has a list price of $695; street price should be about $499. If you have any earlier version of OmniPage or WordScan, you can upgrade for $149.

Surplus Software (800-753-7877) advertises OmniPage 5.0 for $99. You could trade the 5.0 version in for the 6.0 for a total cost of $248. You would save at least $250 off the street price. (See the write-up in chapter 16 about Surplus Software and other low-cost early versions of software that can be traded in for current versions.)

Once data is entered into a computer, it can be searched very quickly for any item. Many times, I have spent hours going through printed manuals looking for certain items. If the data had been in a computer, I could have found the information in just minutes.

Several companies have developed advanced software to work with their scanners and, in some cases, those manufactured by other companies.

Here is a brief list of the companies who have OCR software:

| | | |
|---|---|---|
| Caere Corp. | 800-535-7226 | OmniPage Professional |
| Logitech Corp. | 510-795-8500 | Catchword Pro |
| Ocron, Inc. | 408-980-8900 | Perceive |
| Recognita Corp. | 408-241-5772 | Recognita Plus |
| Delrina Company | 408-363-2345 | WinFax PRO |

## COLD

About 10 years ago, just about everyone was getting computers installed in their offices. There was a lot of excitement about the forthcoming age of the paperless office. However, instead of reducing the large stacks of paper, the amount of paper increased. The reason was that most people insisted on having paper printouts along with the files on disk. A discouraged vice president of a large company made the observation that we would probably see paperless offices at about the same time we had paperless bathrooms. He was right, but we are making a bit of progress.

Most large companies have thousands of file cabinets overflowing with memos, manuals, documents, and files that must be saved. Most of the documents will never be needed again. However, from time to time, a few items stored in these files must be retrieved. Even with a good indexing system, it can take a lot of time to find a particular item. A good filing system and document management system using scanners, OCR, and a computer to laser disc (COLD) can be very helpful. Acres of file cabinets can be replaced by just a few small optical discs. As an added bonus, a good COLD system can help you find and retrieve any document within seconds.

Worm and optical laser discs systems used for COLD were discussed in chapter 6.

## Business card scanners

If you depend on business cards to keep in contact with prospective buyers or for other business purposes, you might have several rolodexes full of cards. You can take each card and enter the information into your computer database. However, there is an easier way. Some companies have developed card scanners that can read the information off a business card and input it to a computer.

At this time, they are still a bit expensive; however, if you depend on business cards, they are well worth it. Like most computer products, the prices will come down very soon.

Here are three of the companies that offer business card scanners:

| | | |
|---|---|---|
| CypherTech, Inc. | 408-734-8765 | CyperScan 1000 |
| Microtek Labs | 800-654-4160 | Scan-in-Dex |
| Cognitive Technology | 415-925-2367 | Cognitive BCR |
| Pacific Crest Tech. | 714-261-6444 | CardGrabber |

## Large-format scanners

Several companies manufacture large-format scanners that are similar to the large plotters. They can be up to 4' wide and stand about 3' high. The scanners can be used to copy and digitize blueprints, CAD, architectural drawings, and even large signs and color images. These scanners are rather expensive and are often used with high-end workstations.

Here are a few companies who manufacture them:

| | |
|---|---|
| ANAtech | 303-973-6722 |
| Ideal Scanners | 301-468-0123 |
| Intergraph | 205-730-8008 |
| Scangraphics | 610-328-1040 |
| The WideCom Group | 905-712-0505 |
| Vidar Systems | 703-471-7070 |

## Installing a scanner

Most of the scanners, especially the high-end color scanners, use a SCSI interface. However, some scanners might come with a plug-in board and software drivers, and some of them are serial devices, so they will require the use of one of your COM ports and one of your motherboard slots.

You might have to set switches or jumpers to configure the board so that it does not conflict with other devices in your system. You should get some sort of installation documentation and driver software with your scanner.

# Digital cameras

Digital cameras might someday replace the standard cameras and film. After all, you don't have to buy film for them or pay to have your pictures developed. You can take the photos, download them into your computer hard disk for viewing, or print them out if you have a good quality color printer. They make it very easy to add a photo to a presentation or just for an album. Because they are digitized, you can also send the photos over the telephone line by modem.

Unfortunately, at this time, the cameras and the printers still don't have the resolution that is possible with film. Another disadvantage is that the initial cost of the cameras are rather high, especially for the better ones. It is expected that the costs will come down as more vendors enter the market.

Here are a few of the manufacturers of digital cameras:

| | |
|---|---|
| Apple QuickTake | 800-538-9696 |
| Casio QV-10 | 201-361-5400 |
| Chinon ES-3000 | 800-441-0222 |
| Dycam Digital 10-C | 800-883-9226 |
| Kodak Digital DC40 | 800-235-6325 |
| Logitech FotoMan | 800-231-7717 |

Connectix's QuickCam (800-950-5880) is a small, low-cost camera that plugs into your computer. It is black and white only and can give you still pictures or movies. It can be set up as a surveillance camera with images stored on a hard disk.

The Sony DCR-VX1000 Digital Handycam is rather expensive but has very high resolution.

The Snappy from Play Incorporated (800-306-7529) is a small device that lets you grab a still photo from a camcorder, VCR, or TV. Snappy plugs into the printer port of a computer, and you can capture and send to disk any scene that you want.

# Voice-recognition input

Another way to input data into a computer is to talk to it with a microphone. Of course, you need electronics that can take the signal created by the microphone, detect the spoken words, and turn them into a form of digital information that the computer can use.

The early voice data input systems were very expensive and limited. One reason was that the voice technology required a lot of memory. However, the cost of memory has dropped considerably in the last few years, and the technology has improved in many other ways. Eventually, the voice input technology will replace the keyboard for many applications.

Voice technology usually involves "training" a computer to recognize a word spoken by a person. When you speak into a microphone, the sound waves cause a diaphragm, or some other device, to move back and forth in a magnetic field and create a voltage that is analogous to the sound wave. If this voltage is recorded and played through a good audio system, the loudspeaker will respond to the amplified voltages and reproduce a sound that is identical to the one input to the microphone.

A person can speak a word into a microphone that creates a unique voltage pattern for that word and that particular person's voice. The voltage is fed into an electronic circuit, and the pattern is digitized and stored in the computer. If several words are spoken, the circuit will digitize each one of them and store them. Each one of them will have a distinct and unique pattern. Later when the computer hears a word, it will search through the patterns that it has stored to see if the input word matches any one of its stored words.

Of course, once the computer is able to recognize a word, you can have it perform some useful work. You could command it to load and run a program or perform any of several other tasks.

Because every person's voice is different, ordinarily the computer would not recognize the voice of anyone who had not trained it. Training the computer might involve saying the same word several times so that the computer can store several patterns of the person's voice. Some of the new systems will now recognize the voices of others who have not trained the computer.

In most of the older systems, the computer had to be trained to recognize a specific word. Memory limitations and computer power was such that the vocabulary was quite limited. Today we have computers with a lot of memory and power. Because the English language has only 42 phonemes, several companies—such as IBM, Verbex Voice Systems, and Dragon Systems—are working on systems that will use a small sample of a person's voice that contains these phonemes. Using the phonemes from this sample, the computer could then recognize any word that the person speaks.

## Uses for voice recognition

Here are just a few uses: letters, reports, and complicated business and technical text. Voice recognition can be used by doctors, nurses, lawyers, reporters, loan officers, auditors, researchers, secretaries, and business executives; in manufacturing; in language interpreters; and by writers.

Computer voice recognition is very useful whenever you must use both hands for doing a job but still need a computer to perform certain tasks.

Voice recognition is also useful on production lines where the person does not have time to manually enter data into a computer. It can also be used in a laboratory where a scientist is looking through a microscope and cannot take his eyes off the subject to write down the findings or data. There might be times when the lighting must be kept too dim to input data to a computer manually. In other instances, the person might have to be several feet from the computer and still be able to input data through the microphone line or even with a wireless mike. The person might even be miles away and be able to input data over a telephone line.

Voice recognition and a computer can help many of those who have physical limitations to become productive and independent. Carnegie-Mellon University is working on a system that would allow a person using English to call someone in Germany and the spoken conversation could be understood. The spoken English would be translated into German, and the spoken German would be translated into English. The system would recognize the spoken word, then use computerized speech to translate it for the parties, so the parties would actually be talking to a computerized mechanical interpreter. Similar systems are being developed for Japanese and other foreign languages.

The same type of system can be built into small handheld foreign language interpreters. Speak an English word into the machine, and it gives you the equivalent spoken foreign word.

Many luxury automobiles now come with cellular phones with voice-activated dialing. This lets the driver keep his or her eyes on the road while the number is being dialed.

The designers of computers are constantly looking for new ways to differentiate and improve their product. In the very near future, you can be sure that many of them will have voice recognition built in.

Chips that use very large scale integration (VLSI) are combining more and more computer functions onto single chips. They are making computers smaller and smaller. We now have some very powerful computers that can fit in a shirt pocket. One of the big problems is that there is not room for a decent keyboard. To fit them all on a keyboard, the keys have to be very small. You can only use a single finger to type on the keyboards. Even then, if your fingers are very large, you might end up pressing two keys at once. A solution would be to build in voice recognition so that the keyboard would not be needed.

## Limitations

For most systems, the computer must be trained to recognize a specific discrete individual word. So the computer vocabulary is limited to what it is trained to recognize, the amount of memory available, and the limitations imposed by the software and hardware.

There are many basic systems available today that are very good at recognizing discrete words. Ordinarily, however, when we speak, many words meld together. There are not many systems around that can recognize continuous speech.

Another problem is homonyms—words that are pronounced the same, and sometimes spelled the same, but that have different meanings. For example, *him*, *hymn*, *hem* are all pronounced the same but have very different meanings. Another example includes the words *to*, *too*, and *two*. Many people misspell and confuse the words *there* and *their*, *your* and *you're*, and *it's* and *its*.

A lot of our words have many different meanings, such as: *set*, *run*, *round*, *date*, and many others.

One of the solutions to this problem would be to have software and hardware with enough intelligence that it could not only recognize the words but recognize the meaning due to the context in which they are used. That requires more intelligence than some human beings have.

## Security systems

The voice of every person is as distinct and different as fingerprints. Voice prints have been used to convict criminals. Because no two voices are alike, a voice-recognition system could be used to practically eliminate the need for keys. Most automobiles already have several built-in computerized systems. You can be sure that, sometime soon, you will see autos that have a voice-recognition system instead of ignition keys. Such a system could help reduce the number of car thefts and carjackings.

A voice-recognition system could also be used for any place that required strict security. If they installed voice recognition at Fort Knox, they could probably eliminate many of their other security measures.

## Basic systems

Verbex Voice Systems (800-275-8729) has developed a fairly sophisticated system that almost makes the keyboard obsolete. Their Listen for Windows application uses special software and a 16-bit plug-in board with a Digital Signal Processor (DSP) on it. After a bit of training, this system can recognize continuous speech. Of course, it is still not perfect, so there are times when you will have to slow down to discrete words and make corrections for words it does not understand. Call Verbex for more information and current pricing.

The Covox Company (503-342-1271) has several less expensive voice recognition systems. Call the Covox Company for a brochure and current prices.

# Computers and devices for the handicapped

Several computer devices have been developed that can help the disabled person live a better life. Just because they have a physical impairment, doesn't mean that they have a brain impairment. Nature often compensates. For example, the hearing and tactile senses of many blind people is much more acute than those who can see.

There are devices that allow the blind, deaf, quadriplegic, and other severely disabled victims to communicate. There are special braille keyboards and keyboards with enlarged keys for the visually impaired. The EyeTyper from the Sentient Systems Technology of Pittsburgh, PA, has an embedded camera on the keyboard that can determine which key the user is looking at. It then enters that key into the computer. Words Plus of Sunnyvale, CA, has a sensitive visor that can understand input from a raised brow, head movement, or eye blinks.

The Speaking Devices Corp. (408-727-5571) has a telephone that can be trained to recognize an individual's voice. It can then dial up to 100 different numbers when the person tells it to. The same company has a tiny earphone that also acts as a microphone. These devices would be ideal for a person who can speak but cannot use his or her hands.

Devices for the disabled can allow many people to lead more active, useful, and productive lives. Some have become artists, programmers, writers, and scientists.

IBM has a number of products that they call the *Independence Series* that are designed to aid those people with physical disabilities. They have a DOS-based utility, AccessDOS, that can be used to add functions to the keyboard, mouse, and sound boards. Call IBM at 800-426-4832 for more information.

Windows 95 has a bit of help for disabled persons. Click on the Start button, highlight Settings, click on Control Panel, then double-click on the Accessibility Options. You will see several window tabs:

- StickyKeys lets you press one key at a time instead of having to press two or three, such as Ctrl, Alt, and Del.
- FilterKeys tells Windows 95 to disregard keystrokes that are not held for a certain length of time.
- The SoundSentry lets you substitute a visual cue for an audible alert. ShowSounds can be used with programs that use digitized speech to display captions on screen.
- Display is an option that allows one to select colors, fonts, and high contrast.
- MouseKeys lets one control the cursor with the numeric keypad instead of a mouse.
- The SerialKey option makes it easy to attach special equipment to the serial port.

Here are some other companies who supply devices for the handicapped:

- Wrist and arm support
  Bucky Products (800-692-8259)
  DeRoyal/LMB (800-541-3992)
- Miniature keyboards
  InTouch Systems (800-332-6244)
  TASH (800-463-5685)

- Programmable keyboards
  Don Johnston (800-999-4660)
  IntelliTools (800-899-6687)
- Onscreen keyboards
  Don Johnston (800-999-4660)
  Words+ (800-869-8521)
- Wands and pointers
  Extensions for Independence (619-423-1478)
  North Coast Medical (800-821-9319)
- Electronic pointers
  Ability Research (612-939-0121)
  Madenta (800-661-8406)
- Switches
  AbleNet (800-322-0956)
  Toys for Special Children (800-832-8697)
- Touch Screens
  Edmark (800-426-0856)
  MicroTouch Systems (800-642-7686)
- Voice Recognition
  Dragon Systems (800-825-5897)
  Speech Systems (303-938-1110)

*Speech Technology Magazine* is a free magazine to qualified subscribers. If you are in any kind of business that involves speech, you can probably qualify. Call 203-834-1430 or send e-mail to Speechmag@AOL.COM for information and a qualifying form.

Several organizations can help in locating special equipment and to lend support. If you know someone who might benefit from the latest technology and devices for the handicapped, contact these organizations:

| | |
|---|---|
| AbleData | 800-344-5405 |
| Accent on Information | 309-378-2961 |
| American Foundation for the Blind | 212-620-2000 |
| Apple Computer | 408-996-1010 |
| Closing The Gap, Inc. | 612-248-3294 |
| Direct Link for the Disabled | 805-688-1603 |
| Easter Seals Systems Office | 312-667-8626 |
| IBM National Support Center | 800-426-2133 |
| National ALS Association | 818-340-7500 |
| Trace Research and Development Center | 608-262-6966 |

Some of these organizations will be glad to accept your old computers. Of course, you can write it off your income tax as a donation. You will be helping them and yourself, and you will feel better helping someone else.

# 10
# System assembly

If you have now bought all of your major internal components, this chapter will show you how to assemble them.

## Ease of assembly

You might think that, because the Pentium Pro is so much more powerful than a 386, 486, or Pentium, it would be more difficult to assemble. However, there is very little difference in the assembly of a Pentium Pro and the assembly of any other computer, even the early XT. In fact, the Pentium Pro can be even easier to assemble than the old XT because it uses fewer screws and even fewer components. Your motherboard might have several integrated and built-in goodies, such as the serial ports, the EIDE and floppy drive interfaces, and sockets for memory modules that were not available 10 years ago.

Some motherboards might be slightly different than others because of the built-in utilities and functions. They also might have the components placed differently on the motherboard. For example, note the differences in the two Pentium Pro motherboards in Fig. 10-1. The motherboard on the left is a 200Mhz from ASUS and the one on the right is a 150MHz from Micronics. The different placement of the chips and sockets is not because of the frequency of the CPU. Either motherboard can operate at several different frequencies, depending on the CPU installed and how they are configured with the jumpers.

It doesn't matter how the board is laid out and designed. Every company tries to differentiate their product and add things to make it better than the competition. These differences have nothing to do with the assembly of the computer. They are all assembled into the system in the same basic way. Note also that they are still assembled the same way no matter whether the CPU on the motherboard is made by Intel, Cyrix, or AMD/NexGen.

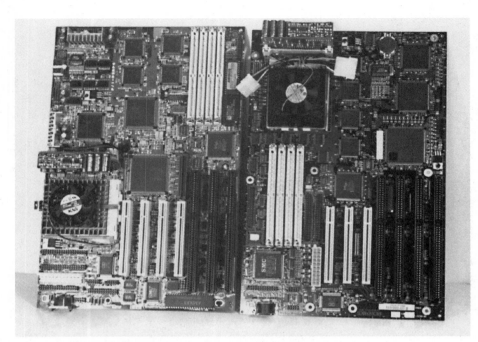

**Fig. 10-1** Two different Pentium Pro motherboards. The assembly is the same for both boards.

# Bench-top assembly

When I assemble a computer, I usually gather all of the components and assemble them on a bench top or kitchen table. I then turn on the power and try it before I install it in the case. If there is any problem or trouble, it is fairly easy to find it while it is still in the open. (Note that the backside of the motherboard and other plug-in boards, have sharp projections from the cut and soldered component leads. I usually lay a couple of newspapers on the table or bench top to prevent scratching or marring the table or bench.)

If you bought a case, you probably received a small plastic bag with the necessary hardware, screws, and plastic standoffs. A white plastic standoff is shown in Fig. 10-2. There is also a small brass standoff shown that is needed to ground the motherboard to the case. There might be several extra holes in the motherboard for the plastic standoffs. Determine which ones will be needed to match the slots in the case, then push the standoffs into place so that they lock in.

Here is a list of the major components that will be needed for a minimum system:
- Case and power supply
- Motherboard
- Floppy drives
- Hard drives
- Controllers for drives (if they are not built-in on the motherboard)
- Keyboard

- Mouse
- Monitor and adapter board

Later you might also want to add several other components, such as a modem/fax board, network card, and several other goodies. However, it is best to start out with a minimum system.

Before you start, gather all of your components and tools. You will need a Phillips and a flat-blade screwdriver and a pair of long-nose pliers. Figure I-1 in the Introduction shows all of the tools that you might need.

*Caution!* I mentioned electrostatic voltage earlier. Remember that you can build up thousands of volts on your body, so touch something to discharge yourself before touching any of the sensitive electronic components.

Detailed assembly instructions are listed in the following section; however, in a few words, here is a basic benchtop assembly: Plug the power supply cables into the motherboard, making sure that the four black ground wires are in the center, then connect the keyboard, the floppy drives, hard disk drives, and the monitor. Then apply power, boot the computer up, and see if it works.

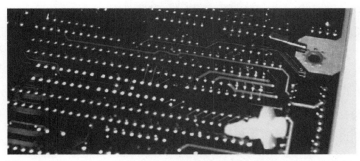

**Fig. 10-2** A white plastic standoff along with a brass standoff for mounting the motherboard.

# Assembly instructions

Here are detailed instructions for the assembly. Note that there are also photos that show the assembly process.

## Step 1: Set all switches and jumpers

Motherboards from different manufacturers can have several alternate options and different ways that they can be configured. The many different possible configurations are part of what makes the computer so versatile and valuable. Some of the Pentium Pro motherboards can accept several different versions of the Pentium Pro CPU. You might have to set some configuration jumpers on the motherboard, plug-in boards, disk drives, and other components.

If you are new to computers and electronics, a jumper is usually a small block or cap that is placed over a set of pins. The jumper creates a short, or solid path, between the two pins. The jumpers are very small. It is almost impossible for a person with large fingers to handle one. That is one of the reasons you need the long-nose pliers. The long-nose pliers in Fig. 10-3 point to jumpers on an IDE hard drive that must be set to configure the drive as a master or slave. If you don't have long-nose pliers, you should be able to use a pair of tweezers. The jumpers are usually numbered from JP1 on up.

**Fig. 10-3**
The long-nose pliers point to small white jumpers on this IDE hard drive that are used to configure the drive as either a Master or Slave.

You should have received some sort of documentation with your motherboard and each of your components. Check the documentation and determine if there are any switches and jumpers that should be set to configure the component.

Jumpers and switches are often used on plug-in boards to set them for a specific interrupt request (IRQ) line or the system memory address. Jumpers can be used to set the COM ports for the mouse, modem, sound card, and other peripherals.

Your motherboard will probably have built-in utilities, such as on-board COM serial ports. If you plug in an I/O board with COM ports, you must set jumpers to disable the COM ports either on the motherboard or on the plug-in board. You can't have both of them enabled.

The improper setting of jumpers and switches is the source of a large number of problems when assembling a system or upgrading one. Most newer motherboards and plug-in boards are manufactured to the Plug-and-Play (PnP) specifications. This will eliminate many of the problems that we suffered previously. PnP will cause most of the configurations to be done automatically by software and built-in firmware on the components.

## Step 2: Install the memory

The 486 and Pentium motherboards had L2 SRAM cache memory onboard. The Cyrix 6x86 and the AMD/NexGen motherboards will also have an L2 SRAM cache. If you are building a Cyrix or AMD/NexGen system, you might have to add or install the SRAM. However, the Pentium Pro CPU has an L2 SRAM cache built into the CPU enclosure.

If the SIMM memory chips have not been installed, you should install them now. Again, they are very susceptible to damage from electrostatic electricity, so make sure that you discharge yourself before handling them. Check your documentation. There should be a diagram of the motherboard showing how the memory is to be installed. You will probably have to install them in pairs. For example, for 16MB of memory, you will need to install an 8MB Single Inline Memory Module (SIMM) in bank 0 and an 8MB SIMM in bank 1.

Make sure that your SIMMs are fast enough. Your documentation should tell you which speed to use. Depending on your system, you might be using Dual Inline Memory Modules (DIMMs) instead of SIMMs.

There are several different types of memory and new types are being introduced almost daily. Some motherboards are designed for Extended Data Out (EDO) memory or burst EDO (BEDO), and others for fast page mode (FPM) or synchronous DRAM (SDRAM). Check your documentation to make sure that you buy the proper memory chips.

The memory modules are very easy to install. See Fig. 10-4. Just place them in the proper slot on a slant, then lift them to an upright position, and they will lock in.

**Fig. 10-4** Installing memory modules. Just lay the SIMM in a slot on a slant, then pull upright, and it will lock in.

There is a cutout on one end of the module assembly so that they can only be installed the proper way. However, it is possible to have one end of the SIMM not inserted fully. If a SIMM is not completely seated or if they are not in the proper bank, the computer might not boot up.

## Step 3: Connect the power supply to the motherboard

The power supply will have two 6-wire cables that are plugged in side by side to the 12-pin motherboard connector. These cables are sometimes marked P8 and P9.

*Caution!* It is possible to install these cables improperly. Each of the cables have two black wires for ground. When installed properly, the four black wires are in the center of the connector. If installed improperly, you could severely damage the motherboard components. You can see the four black wires in the center of the white connector in Fig. 10-5.

**Fig. 10-5** The power supply connection to the motherboard from standard power supply. The two connectors, P8 and P9, can be transposed. When connected properly the four black wires are in the center.

Some of the motherboards such as the one from Micronics, are now using an ATX power supply. This power supply has a special connector that plugs into the motherboard power socket. You cannot use the older standard power supplies with this motherboard. The power connector on this ATX supply can only be plugged in properly. Refer back to Fig. 3-6 in chapter 3.

The Micronics motherboard also had one other feature that wasn't listed in their preliminary M6Pi System Board Manual. When I turned on the power, nothing happened. I knew that a power supply will not come on if there is a short anywhere. So I unplugged everything except for the floppy drive. Still no power. I called Micronics, and they said that a small power cable plugs into jumper pins on the motherboard. The other end of this cable then attaches to the power switch on the front panel of the case. They apologized for not sending me the cable and for not updating the manual.

Actually I didn't need the cable as long as the unit was on the bench. I had only to use a screwdriver or other metal object to momentarily short out the jumper pins to start the power.

## Step 4: Install the floppy drives

The older floppy drives have edge connectors for the 34-wire ribbon cable. Newer floppy drives have pins, but many of them come with an edge connector adapter such as that shown in Fig. 10-6. Figure 10-6 shows a universal floppy cable that has both edge connectors and pin connectors. Your cable might have pin connectors only.

One end of the cable will have several wires that were split and twisted. The connector on this end goes to the drive that you want to be your drive A:. See Fig. 10-7. Be careful because these connectors can be plugged in backwards. The floppy ribbon cable will have a different color wire on one edge. This wire might be red, blue, or black or might have intermittent red marks on it. This indicates that this wire goes to pin 1 on the connectors. Make sure that this side goes to pin 1 on the floppy drive connectors.

**Fig. 10-6** An adapter that allows an edge connector cable to be used.

**Fig. 10-7** A 34-wire ribbon cable with both edge and pin connectors so that it can be used on either. Make sure that the colored wire side of the cable goes to pin one.

      The connector in the middle of the cable goes to floppy drive B:. See Fig. 10-8. This connector can also be incorrectly plugged in. Make sure the colored wire side goes to pin 1 on the drive connector.

**Fig. 10-8** Connecting the middle connector to the B: drive. The colored wire side goes to pin 1.

I recommend that you install a combination floppy drive that has both 1.2MB and 1.44MB drives, such as the one shown in Fig. 10-9. One of the advantages of the combo drive is that it requires only one bay, one power cable and one controller connection. The combination drive has a single connector that serves both the 3.5" and 5.25" drives. Again, make sure the colored wire side of the cable goes to pin 1 on the drive connector.

**Fig. 10-9**  A combination floppy with both 3.5" and 5.25" drives.

Figure 10-10 shows the rear of the drive and its single connector for both drives. If you want to make the 5.25" drive your A: drive, attach the connector with the twisted wires. The 3.5" drive will be the B: drive. To reverse this and make the 3.5" drive the A: drive, connect the middle connector.

The other end of the ribbon cable plugs into the upright pins on the motherboard or to a floppy disk controller board. See Fig. 10-11. Make sure that the colored wire of the ribbon cable goes to pin 1 on the board. There should be some marking or indication on the board as to which is pin 1. If the floppy drive cable is plugged in backwards, when you try to boot up from floppy drive A:, the disk will spin, and it will erase the boot system from the floppy. (Never use your original software floppies except to make diskcopies of them. Even then you should make sure that the originals are write protected).

**Fig. 10-10**  Connecting the ribbon cable to the combination drive. Connect the end connector with the twist to make the 5.25" drive the A: drive or the middle connector to make the 3.5" drive the A:. Make sure the colored wire goes to pin 1. The small white connector in the center is for power. It can only be plugged in one way.

It is also possible to plug these connectors in so that only one row of pins are plugged in or have it shifted so that two pins on one end are not plugged in. Some boards will have a square outline around the pins, which can be seen in Fig. 10-11. It is easy to see if the connector is within the outline.

If you are using a floppy controller board, it will probably be an integrated multifunction input/output (I/O) board. If it is an I/O board, it will probably also have an EIDE connector for a hard disk interface, a connector LPT1 for the printer, and one or two port connectors for COM1 and COM2. The COM port connectors are for the mouse, modem, or other serial devices. The controller board can be plugged into any of the ISA slots on the motherboard. I usually try to install the controller boards near the drives so that the cables don't have to be draped over other boards.

If you use an I/O board for the floppies or other device and your motherboard also has built-in interfaces for these devices, then you must set the jumpers to disable the interfaces on the motherboard. You might even have a floppy controller on a SCSI board. Any of the interfaces or controllers that are being used must be enabled by setting jumper pins; those not being used must be disabled by jumpers. Check your documentation.

Figure 10-12 shows the power connector being attached to a 5.25" hard drive. The white plastic shell of the power connectors are shaped so that they can only be plugged in properly. The same type of power connectors are used on the hard drives and CD-ROM drives.

**Fig. 10-11** Connecting the floppy drive cable to the upright pins on the motherboard. Make sure the colored wire side goes to pin 1. Note that the motherboard has the figures 33 and 34. Note also that there is an outline around the pins. When plugged in properly, the connector should be within the outline.

**Fig. 10-12** Connecting the power to a hard drive. The power connectors can only be plugged in properly.

The small fan that sits on the CPU also needs power. Some motherboards, such as the one from ASUS, don't have a power connector because the power wires are soldered into the motherboard power. If you refer back to Fig. 3-2, you can see that the small fan on the Micronics motherboard has a power connector.

Some of the older power supplies only provided four power cables. However, if you need more, you can use a Y cable to hook two units to one cable. The newer power supplies, such as the ATX in Fig. 2-3, have six standard size and two miniature connectors. The small fan in Fig. 3-2 has a pass-through cable where the power is supplied to the fan and passes through. Another device can be plugged into the other end of this cable. The 3.5" drives and the combination drives use a miniature power connector. It can be seen in Fig. 10-13. It can only be plugged in properly.

**Fig. 10-13** The keyed connector and shell on an IDE drive. This guarantees that the connector can only be plugged in properly.

## Step 5: Install the hard disk drives

If you install an IDE hard drive, you will have a 40-wire ribbon cable that is very similar to the 50-wire SCSI cable shown in Fig. 10-14. The IDE ribbon cable is also similar to the 34-wire floppy disk cable. Unlike the floppy disk cable with twisted wires at one end, the three connectors on the IDE cable will all be the same. Like the floppy and SCSI cables, it will have a colored wire on one edge that indicates pin 1. Most connectors on the drives have a plastic shell around them with a square notch on one side of the shell. The connectors on the cable have a square elevation that fits the notch on the drive connector plastic shell. This keys the connector so that it can only be plugged in properly. See Fig. 10-14. The 50-wire cable and connectors for the SCSI devices have the same type of keying. If the connectors are not keyed, then

**Fig. 10-14** A 50-wire SCSI ribbon cable. Note the elevation in the center of the connector. This elevation fits in the slot on the drive connector shell and keys it so that it can only be connected properly.

look for some indication of pin 1 on the drive and connect the cable so that the colored wire goes to that side. Then plug in the power cable to the hard drive.

If you are installing a second IDE hard drive, it will be plugged into the center connector. The other end plugs into an IDE interface or into motherboard upright pins.

### IDE drive configuration

The configuration instructions will be similar whether you are installing IDE or EIDE drives. You should have received some instructions with your drive documentation. If you are only installing a single IDE drive, the installation might be very simple. The drive will probably have jumpers set at the factory that makes it drive #1, or the master drive. Check your documentation and the jumpers, then just plug the 40 wire cable connector into the drive connector and the other end into a board interface or into a set of pins on the motherboard. You must make sure that the colored side of the ribbon cable goes to pin 1 on the drive and on the interface.

There will probably be two sets of EIDE pins on the motherboard or interface. One will say "Primary" and the other "Secondary." The cable from the master and slave IDE goes to the primary pins. If you are installing an IDE CD-ROM, tape drive, or other device, that cable will go to the pins marked secondary.

Even though you have an EIDE interface on the motherboard, you might want to install a fast EIDE interface that plugs into one of the PCI connectors. One reason to install a PCI interface is because you can have a disk cache on the board that will make the system much faster. Again, if you use a plug-in board, you must use the jumpers to disable the built-in interface.

If you are installing a second IDE drive, you will need to set some jumpers so that the system will know which drive to access. When two IDE drives are installed, the IDE system uses the term *Master* to designate the C: or boot drive and the term *Slave* to designate the second drive. You will have to place small jumpers on the drives to configure them. If the drives are not configured properly, you will get an error message that might tell you that you have a hard disk or controller failure. You will not be able to access the drives. In Fig. 10-3, the long-nose pliers point to the small configuration jumpers on a Maxtor 540MB IDE drive.

Ordinarily, you will have to do a setup when you first turn on your computer. You will have to tell the system what kind of drive you have and the number of cylinders, sectors, and heads it has. However, your Pentium Pro will probably have a Plug-and-Play (PnP) BIOS that will recognize the IDE drive and automatically configure it.

You should have received some documentation with your drive. If you don't have the configuration information, call the company or dealer. The following paragraphs provide technical support numbers and related information for some of the more popular companies.

Conner Peripherals has technical support at 408-456-3388. They have a BBS at 408-456-4415 and FaxBack information at 800-426-6637.

The Maxtor Corp. has technical support at 800-262-9867. They have a BBS at 303-678-2222 for 2400 baud or 303-678-2020 for 9600 baud. The modem should be set for 8 data bits, no parity, and one stop bit.

Quantum Corp. offers free technical support at 800-826-8022. Quantum also has a Fax on Demand System. If you call 800-434-7532 from your fax machine, they can send you documentation and configuration specifications for all of their products. When you call, you should ask for their Product Catalog, which lists all available documents by number. You can review the catalog and order whatever document you might need. Quantum also has a BBS at 408-894-3214.

You can call the Seagate Technology Corp. at 800-468-3472 for technical support. Seagate also has a bulletin board that has a Technical Desk Reference file that lists most of their hard disk configurations. Their BBS is at 408-438-8771. Set communications software for 8 bits, no parity, and one stop bit (8-N-1). The Seagate BBS also has some free software that can be downloaded. Their FINDTYPE and FIND-INIT utilities can help make installation of ATA IDE drives easier.

You can call Western Digital at 800-832-4778. They have a BBS for 2400 baud at 714-753-1234; for 9600 baud and up, they have a BBS at 714-753-1068.

### Hard drive activity indicator

The older hard drives used a stepping motor head actuator, and they could be easily heard as they stepped from track to track. The newer drives use the voice coil technology. They are usually very smooth and silent. If you did not have some sort of indicator, you might not know that they are working.

Your front panel will have a small light emitting diode (LED) that will flash on and off to indicate hard disk activity. There will probably be a small 2-wire cable that plugs into a set of pins on the motherboard for this LED. Note that the LEDs are sensitive to plus and negative voltage. The motherboard might be marked with a + sign near one of the pins, or one set of pins might have a 1 nearby. The two wires will be different colors, usually red and black, yellow and white, or blue and white. Usually the colored wire will go to pin 1, and the black or white wire will go to the negative pin. There will be several other sets of pins near the front of the motherboard for front panel LEDs for power, reset, and speaker connections. Check your documentation.

### Installing SCSI drives

If you are installing one or more SCSI drives, you will need to check your documentation to set any switches or jumpers. Because the SCSI interface can handle up to seven devices, the drive will probably need to be set to a logical unit number (LUN) between 0 and 6. In Fig. 10-15, the pen points to the jumper pins for setting the LUN on a Seagate 1.05GB drive.

The SCSI hard disk and CD-ROM drives will have a 50-wire ribbon cable that is similar to the 40-wire IDE cable. See Fig. 10-14. Like other cables, it will have a different colored wire on one edge that indicates pin 1. The cable will have three connectors that will probably be keyed with elevations so that they can only be plugged in properly. If they are not keyed, then look for pin 1 and make sure that the colored wire goes to that side. The connector on the other end of the 50-wire cable is connected to the SCSI card. See Fig. 10-15. Again, this connector is usually keyed so that it can only be plugged in properly. The pen in the photo points to jumpers that might have to be set. Check your documentation.

**Fig. 10-15** A SCSI interface board with the 50-wire cable connected. The pen points to jumpers that might have to be set. Check your documentation.

Figure 10-16 shows a 50-wire cable being connected to a quad-speed Toshiba SCSI CD-ROM. Note the notch in the drive connector shell and the elevation on the cable connector, which prevents it from being plugged in backwards. At the left of this connector are the LUN pins and jumpers. These jumpers have a .5" plastic extension so that they are easy to change. The small white connector is for the audio cable.

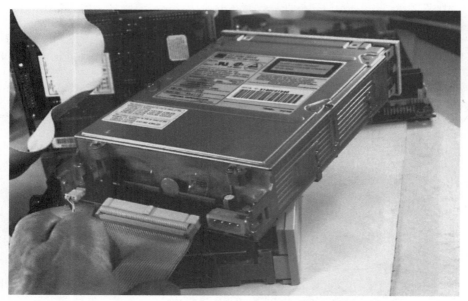

**Fig. 10-16** Connecting a 50-wire SCSI cable to a CD-ROM drive.

If you are installing more than one SCSI device, such as a second hard drive or a CD-ROM drive, check your documentation and set any necessary jumpers for the correct LUN. You might also have to remove or install termination resistors if you have more than one SCSI device.

Install the power cable to the SCSI devices. They can only be plugged in properly. Most power supplies have only four cables. If you install more than four devices, you will need a small Y cable that allows two devices to be attached to one cable. The ATX power supply that came with the Micronics motherboard had six standard and two miniature power connectors.

## Step 6: Connect the mouse and printer cables

You should receive a bracket with two short cables for the printer and mouse. See Fig. 10-17. The mouse cable plugs into the pins for one of the COM ports and the printer cable into pins for the printer. Again, look for the colored wire, and make sure that side of the cable goes to pin 1. The bracket will be mounted on the rear of the case.

## Step 7: Install the monitor

The next step is to plug your monitor adapter into a slot and connect the monitor cable to the adapter. You will probably have PCI slots and a PCI adapter, such as

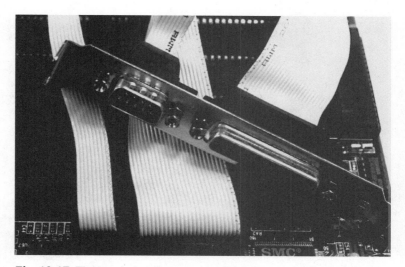

**Fig. 10-17** The bracket and connectors for the mouse and printer cables. The short cables from this bracket connects to the motherboard upright pins.

that shown in Fig. 10-18. However, you can use one of the older ISA adapters and plug it into any ISA slot. You can also have a VLB motherboard and adapter.

## Step 8: Plug in the keyboard

The keyboard cable is plugged into a connector on the back of the motherboard. It has a rounded connector that is keyed so that it can only be connected properly. It can be seen in Fig. 10-19.

## Step 9: Turn on the power and boot up

Figure 10-20 shows the benchtop assembly completed and running. If everything was connected properly, the system should boot up. You will need a floppy disk that can boot up your system. If you have DOS 6.0 or later, the disk that says *Disk 1-Setup* will have the files necessary for booting up. Later you will want to boot from your hard drive C:. Once the computer starts to boot up, the CMOS system screen will come up. You can then enter the date, hour, type of floppy and hard drives, and other information into your CMOS setup. You will have to partition and format your hard drives before you can use them. The formatting procedures are listed in the following section.

I usually install a combination drive with both 1.2MB and 1.44MB floppy drives. If your boot disk is on a 3.5" floppy, then you must make the 3.5" drive the A: drive. You can only boot up from the A: drive with a floppy. Your floppy drives will be either A: or B: depending on how you plug them in to the controller cable. The A: drive will be the drive that is connected to the end of the cable that has several wires that are split and twisted.

**Fig. 10-18** A PCI monitor adapter board installed.

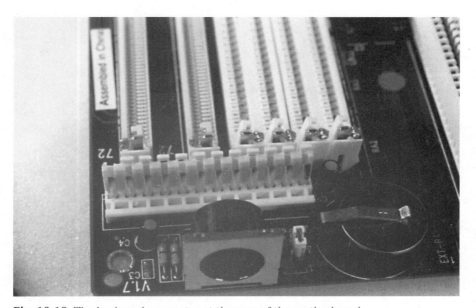

**Fig. 10-19** The keyboard connector at the rear of the motherboard.

**Fig. 10-20** The completed benchtop assembly.

### Software installation and formatting of hard drives

Once the drives and plug-in boards are installed and connected, you can plug in the power cable. Put your boot disk in drive A:, and turn on the power. Check your motherboard documentation and press the required keys on the keyboard to enter the setup mode. The keys to enter the setup mode will depend on the BIOS that is installed on the motherboard. Often a message will tell you which keys to press as the computer is booting up.

Besides the system files needed for booting up, the boot floppy should have the FDISK and FORMAT commands on it.

**Setup routine** When you install a hard disk, your BIOS must be told what type it is. The BIOS must also know the number and type of floppies you have, the time, the date, type of monitor, and other information. The setup routine asks several questions, then configures the BIOS for that configuration. This part of the BIOS configuration is stored in low-power CMOS semiconductors and is on all the time. Even when the computer is turned off, a small lithium battery on the motherboard supplies power for the CMOS semiconductors.

In the early 1980s, IBM determined that there were only 15 different types of hard drives available. This information was made into a standard table that listed all of the characteristics of each drive. This table was included in the ROM BIOS of the IBM and all compatible clones. When you installed a hard disk, you just looked at the table to find which one of the 15 fit your hard disk and typed in the number. However, pretty soon more and more different type drives were developed. The first 15 drive types remained standard; however, as new types were introduced, each BIOS manufacturer produced different tables. It soon reached the number 46 when it became apparent that there was no end in sight. There are now hundreds of different drives, each one a bit different than others. Most setup routines will now allow you to enter type 46 or 47 and then type in data for any drive that does not fit any of the listed types.

The setup usually allows you to enter only two drives, C and D. However, you might have two very large drives that are divided into several smaller partitions. So your D drive might be a partition of the hard disk that is your C drive. So ignore the designation for drive D. You should enter the information for your first drive, the C drive, then enter the information under the D drive for your second drive. The CMOS setup would be less confusing if it asked for information about hard drive number 1, then number 2 instead of C and D.

I don't know why anyone would want to do it, but you can still use any of the original MFM drive types. The Micronics motherboard manual has a listing of the old types. For example, type 1 has 306 cylinders, 4 heads, and 17 sectors and is a whopping 10MB. You would not be able to do any worthwhile computing at all with a 10MB hard disk. Type 39 has 925 cylinders, 9 heads, and 17 sectors for 72MB. You wouldn't even be able to load Windows 95 on this disk. You should have at least 540MB or more.

You will probably have to use type 46 or 47, which will let you input whatever number of cylinders, heads, and sectors you have on your drive. Check your documentation. Both ASUS and Micronics have a PnP BIOS that can automatically recognize the type of drive so that you do not need to input the information.

*Caution!* If your motherboard does not have the PnP, you should write your drive type down somewhere. (In fact, you should have a copy of your entire CMOS setup.) If you have data on your hard drive and, for some reason, you remove the drive or your onboard CMOS battery goes completely dead, you will not be able to access your hard drive unless you tell the CMOS setup exactly what type it is or whatever data you used to format the drive.

This information is for IDE type drives. The SCSI type drives are controlled by device drivers and are not entered into your CMOS tables.

**Booting from a floppy** *Another caution!* Never boot up with a floppy disk version that is different from the DOS version used to format the hard disk. There is a short boot record on the hard disk. If a different version is used to boot up, you might lose all of your data on the disk.

**Disk partitions and formatting** The early versions of DOS would not allow a hard disk with a greater capacity than 32MB. DOS can now recognize and handle hard disks that have a capacity of several gigabytes. To handle large capacity hard disks, DOS allows you to partition them into smaller logical units by using the FDISK command. Each partition then appears to DOS to be a separate hard drive.

**FDISK options** When you type FDISK, if you are using MS-DOS 6.2 or later, this message will be displayed:

```
MS-DOS Version 6.2
Fixed Disk Setup Program
Copyright Microsoft Corp. 1983, 1993
FDISK Options
Current Fixed Disk Drive: 1
Choose one of the following:
1. Create DOS partition or Logical DOS Drive
2. Set active partition
3. Delete Partition or Logical DOS Drive
```

```
4. Display partition information
5. Change current fixed disk drive (Option 5 is only displayed
   if you have more than one drive.)
Enter choice: [1]
Press ESC to exit FDISK
```

If you choose 1 and the disk has not been prepared, a screen like this comes up:

```
Create DOS Partition or Logical DOS Drive
Current Fixed Drive: 1
Choose one of the following:
1. Create Primary DOS partition
2. Create Extended DOS partition
3. Create logical DOS drive(s) in the Extended DOS partition
Enter choice: [1]
Press ESC to return to FDISK Options
```

If you want to boot from your hard drive (I can't think of any reason why you would not want to), then you must choose 1 to create a primary DOS partition and make it active.

**Partition size**  I would recommend not making a partition of more than 200MB. If there are several partitions on a disk and one of them fails, you might be able to recover the data in the other partitions. If your disk is one large partition and it fails, you might not be able to recover any of the data, especially if the FAT is destroyed. Norton Utilities for Windows 95 can be set up to make a mirror image of the FAT. If the primary FAT is destroyed, you can still use the mirror image to reconstruct the FAT.

Using FDISK can be a bit confusing. The manual that comes with MS-DOS 6.2 is no help at all. MS-DOS has on-disk help for all of its commands. Just type HELP and the command name. However, the FDISK help is not much help. There are several books on DOS that can help. The Microsoft Press is a division that prints hundreds of books about how to use Microsoft software. If their manuals were well written, you probably would not need to buy extra books to learn how to use the software.

To make several partitions you must first choose option 2 to Create Extended DOS partition. It will tell you how much space is available, which will be the entire drive. You cannot partition the drive at this point. Accept the figure given for the entire drive. If you try to partition the drive at this point, whatever you choose will be all that you can use. For example, with option 2, if you have a 500MB drive and you try to divide it into two 250MB partitions, it will figure that the entire drive is to be only 250MB. You will not be able to use the other 250MB. You must tell it to use the 500MB that is available. Then press Esc to return to the options, then choose option 3, Create Logical DOS Drives in the Extended DOS partition. You can now divide this partition into as many drives as you want.

**High-level format**  After the FDISK partitioning, the disk must be formatted. Formatting organizes the disk so that data can be stored and accessed easily and quickly. If the data was not organized, it would be very difficult to find an item on a large hard disk. I have about 3000 files on my two hard disks. Those files are on tracks and sectors that are numbered. A file allocation table (FAT) is set up to record the location of each track and sector on the disk.

A brief analogy of a disk organization would be similar to that of a developer of a piece of land. He would lay out the streets and create blocks. He would then partition each block into lots and build a house on each lot. Each house would have a unique address. A map of these streets and house addresses would be filed with the city. A track would be analogous to a street, and a sector number would be similar to a house number.

The FAT is similar to an index in a street atlas or a book. When a request is sent to the heads to read or write to a file, it goes to the file allocation table, looks for the location of that file, and goes directly to it. The heads can find any file, or parts of any file, quickly and easily.

Formatting is not something that is done every day and can be rather difficult in some cases. One reason the disks do not come from the manufacturer preformatted is that there are so many options. If you have a 540MB hard disk, you will probably want to divide or partition it into two or three different logical disks.

After the FDISK options have been completed, return to drive A: and high-level format drive C:. Because you want to boot off this drive, you must also transfer the system and hidden files to the disk as it is being formatted, so you must use a /S to transfer the files. Type FORMAT C: /S. DOS will display a message that says:

```
WARNING! ALL DATA ON NON-REMOVABLE DISK DRIVE C: WILL BE LOST!
Proceed with Format (Y/N)
```

If you press Y, the disk light should come on, and you might hear the drive stepping through each track. After a few minutes, it will display:

```
Format complete
System transferred
Volume label (11 characters, ENTER for none)?
```

You can give each partition a unique name, or volume label, if you want to. You can test your drive by doing a warm boot by pressing Ctrl, Alt, and Del at the same time. The computer should reboot.

Now that drive C: is completed, if you have other partitions or a second disk, format each of them.

### System test

Now that the disks are installed and formatted, try copying files to them. The first thing to do is to copy the DOS files onto drive C:. Try copying from one disk to another and then erase them. Exercise the system and look for any faults.

## Step 10: Install the system in the case

If the system seems to work properly on the bench, then install it in the case. You should have received a small bag of hardware with your case. You should have some white plastic standoffs that have a round head and a narrow groove, such as that in Fig. 10-2. In addition to the white standoffs, you should have one or two small brass standoffs, such as the one shown in Fig. 10-2. The brass standoff screws into the metal case to provide a ground path between the motherboard and case. One brass standoff is screwed into the front center of the case and one in the rear center.

Install the white plastic standoffs in the holes on the motherboard. When pressed into the holes, the standoffs have two ears that spread and lock them into place. If you need to remove them, just press the ears together with a pair of pliers. There might be extra holes in the motherboard that will not need standoffs. There should be three standoffs in the front (including the brass standoff), three across the center, and three across the rear (including the other brass standoff).

You then align the motherboard so that the round heads of the standoffs fit in the slots, then slide it into place. Figure 10-21 shows the back side of the motherboard mounted in a medium tower case. If you install your system in a desktop case, the bottom of the case will have slots that are similar to those seen in Fig. 10-21. Install a screw in the front and one in the back into the brass standoffs. This grounds the motherboard and also makes it secure.

**Fig. 10-21** The back side of the motherboard mounted in the case.

There will be several wires from the front panel with small connectors that plug into pins on the front of the motherboard. The long-nose pliers are handy for inserting these connectors on the pins. There will be wires for the small speaker and for the light emitting diodes (LEDs) on the front panel to indicate power on and hard disk activity, for the speaker, and several other functions. The motherboard might or might not have labels or markings as to where each wire connects. Because the cases and motherboards are made by different companies, there might be some wires that are not needed for your particular motherboard.

Install the floppy and hard drives in the bays. Reconnect the cables and install the boards in the slots on the motherboard. Try the system once more and if everything still works, then install the cover. Figure 10-22 shows all components mounted in the case, ready for the cover to be installed.

Your system should now be up and running perfectly at this time.

**Fig. 10-22** All components mounted in the case ready for the cover.

# 11
# Communications

Even if you read several large books on communications, it still wouldn't begin to cover this far reaching industry. The marriage of computers to the telephone technologies has brought about a tremendous increase in functions, utilities, services, and applications.

## Infoglut

At one time, long-distance communications was limited to as loud as one could yell, to beating on hollow logs, and to smoke signals. Today, we have more means of communicating than at any time in history.

The reason for communications is to share information. We need information for pleasure, health, business, and every aspect of our daily lives. Some people think that today we have too much information, that it is overwhelming. Someone has coined the term *infoglut*. Whether you like it or not, the infoglut is going to continue to grow. What we all need is enough information to be able to determine what we need without being overwhelmed.

## Telephones

Telephones are one of the most important communications devices ever invented. They are be a critical part of our personal life as well as for almost all business. By adding a modem to your computer, you can make the telephone even more useful and important. You can use your computer and the telephone line to access online services and bulletin boards, for telecommuting, for the Internet, and to communicate with anyone else in the world who also has a computer and modem.

Many of the modem boards are now integrated with fax capability. A modem board with a fax might not cost much more than the modem alone. Communicating by fax is fast and efficient.

# Reaching out

There are over 100 million personal computers installed in homes, offices, and businesses worldwide. About half of them have a modem or some sort of communications capability. This capability of the computer is one of its most important aspects.

If your computer has a modem, you can access over 10,000 bulletin boards in the U.S. You can take advantage of electronic mail, faxes, up-to-the-minute stock market quotations, and a large number of other online services, such as home shopping, home banking, travel agencies, business transactions, many databases, data services, and even dating services.

For some types of work, a person can use a modem and work from home. Someone has called this *telecommuting*. It is a whole lot better than commuting by auto and sitting in traffic jams on the crowded freeways.

Communications covers a wide range of activities and technologies. Many books have been written that cover all phases of communications. Just a few of the many technologies will be discussed in this chapter.

# The Internet and World Wide Web

One of the hottest topics at the moment is the Internet and World Wide Web (WWW). The Internet started off as a government project in 1973 with the Advanced Research Projects Agency (ARPA), an agency of the Department of Defense (DOD). It was a network designed to facilitate scientific collaboration in military research among educational institutions. ARPAnet had some similarities to peer-to-peer networking. It allowed almost any system to connect to another through an electronic gateway.

The ARPAnet is no longer primarily concerned with military research. It is now known as the *Internet*. It is possible to access the Internet or WWW from several of the larger online services. Here are some voice numbers:

| | |
|---|---|
| CompuServe | 800-848-8990 |
| Prodigy | 800-776-3449 |
| America Online | 800-827-6364 |
| Delphi | 800-695-4005 |
| Microsoft Network | 800-386-5550 |

Besides these large online service providers, there are hundreds of smaller Internet service providers (ISPs). The larger online companies might have a higher hourly or monthly rate than the small ISPs, but the larger companies can offer more utilities. You can access anyone on the Internet or WWW from any of the online providers or ISPs.

Many books have been written about the Internet. Three very good ones, published by Osborne/McGraw-Hill (800-227-0900), are *Internet Essentials and Fun List*, *The Internet Complete Reference*, and *The Internet Yellow Pages*. If you are just getting started, *The Internet Complete Reference* would help you immensely. It has over 800 pages of information about getting on the Net. It has addresses and numbers of hundreds of local, state, national, and international access gateways. There are valuable helpful hints on almost every page. There are many other books about the Internet, published by companies other than McGraw-Hill.

There are now millions of people who access the Internet. There is something on the Internet for everyone. There are encyclopedias, up-to-the-minute news, people chatting with another, online romance, and X-rated photos and talk. You can post notes or send e-mail. You can send a message to anyone in the world for just the cost of the dial-up connection and your hourly rate from the ISP. I recently sent several e-mail messages to friend in England for less than it would have cost me to send a letter.

There are several companies who are now making software and hardware that will let you use voice over the Internet. The telephone companies are a bit worried. If a person can make a long-distance call to anywhere in the world by just dialing a local access number, then the telephone companies might stand to lose some money. One of the software packages for Internet voice is WebTalk from Quarterdeck (310-309-3700).

Because there is such a large amount of information on the Internet, search and browsing software is essential. The most popular navigational software at this time is Netscape Navigator. Microsoft also has a browser, and Prodigy and CompuServe provide browsers as part of their service.

# Modems

A *modem* is an electronic device that allows a computer to use an ordinary telephone line to communicate with other computers that are equipped with a modem. Modem is a contraction of the words *modulate* and *demodulate*. The telephone system transmits voice and data in analog voltage form. Analog voltages are sine waves that vary continuously up and down. Refer back to Fig. 1-6 to see what a sine wave looks like. Computer data is usually in a digital voltage form, which is a series of on and off voltages.

The modem takes the digitized bits of voltage from the computer and modulates, or transforms, it into analog voltages to transmit it over the telephone lines. At the receiving end, a similar modem will demodulate the analog voltage and transform it back into a digital form.

## Transmission difficulties

Telephone systems were originally designed for voice and have a very narrow bandwidth. A person with perfect hearing can hear 20 cycles per second, or Hertz (Hz), all the way up to 20,000 Hz. For normal speech, we only use about 300 Hz up to 2000 Hz.

The telephone analog voltages are subject to noise, static, and other electrical disturbances. Noise and static takes the form of analog voltages. So do most of the other electrical disturbances, such as electrical storms and pulses generated by operating electrical equipment. The analog noise and static voltages can be mixed in with any analog data voltages that are being transmitted. The mixture of the static and noise voltages with the data voltages can corrupt and severely damage the data. The demodulator might be completely at a loss to determine which voltages represent data and which are noise.

## Baud rate

These problems, and the state of technology at the time, limited the original modems to about 5 characters per second (CPS), or a rate of 50 baud.

We get the term *baud* from Emile Baudot (1845-1903), a French inventor. Originally, the baud rate was a measure of the dots and dashes in telegraphy. It is now defined as the actual rate of symbols transmitted per second. For the lower baud rates, it is essentially the same as bits per second. Remember that it takes 8 bits to make a character. Just as we have periods and spaces to separate words, we must use one *start bit* and one *stop bit* to separate the on/off bits into characters. A transmission of 300 baud would mean that 300 on/off bits are sent in one second. For every 8 bits of data that represents a character, we need one bit to indicate the start of a character and one bit to indicate the end. We then need another bit to indicate the start of the next character. So counting the start/stop bits, it takes 11 bits for each character. If we divide 300 by 11 it gives us about 27 CPS.

Some of the newer technologies can actually transmit symbols that represent more than one bit. For baud rates of 1200 and higher, the CPS and baud rate can be considerably different.

There have been some fantastic advances in the modem technologies. A few years ago, 2400 baud systems were the standard. Today, they are obsolete. The industry leaped over the 4800 and 9600 baud systems to the 14.4K systems. These units incorporate the V.42bis compression standard. This allows them to use 4:1 data compression and thus transmit at 57,600 bps. The 14.4K systems are now obsolete, but a lot of vendors are still selling them at very low prices. I would recommend that you spend a little more and get a 28.8K V.34 systems.

When communicating with another modem, both the sending and receiving units must operate at the same baud rate and use the same protocols. Most of the faster modems are downward compatible and can operate at the slower speeds. If you use a modem frequently, a high-speed modem can quickly pay for itself. We have sure come a long way since those early 50 baud standards.

## How to estimate connect time

You can figure the approximate length of time that it will take to transmit a file. For rough approximations of CPS, you can divide the baud rate by 10. For example, a 14.4K modem would transmit at about 1400 CPS. Look at the directory and determine the number of bytes in the file. Divide the number of bytes in the file by the CPS to give a rough approximation. For example, to transmit a file with 144,000 bytes at 1400 bytes per second, it would take 103 seconds.

## Data compression

One way to reduce modem phone charges is to use file compression. Bulletin boards have been using a form of data compression for years. There are several public-domain programs that compress and uncompress the data. The newer modems take advantage of compression using the standard V.42bis for 4:1 compression. Using 4:1 compression, a 14.4K modem can send at 57,600 bits per second (bps).

With a 14.4K baud modem, and 4:1 compression, a 40K file that takes 3.6 minutes when transmitted at 2400 baud can be sent in less than one second.

At this time, the 28.8K is the fastest modem available unless you have a digital ISDN system. Cable modems might be able to operate at up to 10MB per second.

## Protocols

Protocols are procedures that have been established for exchanging data, along with the instructions that coordinate the process. Most protocols can sense when the data is corrupted or lost due to noise, static, or a bad connection. It will automatically resend the affected data until it is received correctly.

There are several protocols, but the most popular ones are Kermit (named for Kermit the frog), Xmodem, and Ymodem. Each of these protocols transmits a block of data along with an error-checking code, then waits for the receiver to send back an acknowledgement. It then sends another block and waits to see if it got through okay. If a block does not get through, it is resent immediately. Protocols such as Zmodem and HyperProtocol send a whole file in a continuous stream of data with error checking codes inserted at certain intervals. It then waits for confirmation of a successful transmission. If the transmission is unsuccessful, then the whole file must be resent.

Both the sending and receiving modems must use the same protocol and baud rate. You cannot send a file at 28.8K to someone who only has a 2400 baud modem. However, the faster modems are able to shift down and send or receive at the lower speeds.

## ITU recommended standards

The communications industry is very complex. So there have not been many real standards. There are many different manufacturers and software developers. Of course all of them want to differentiate their hardware or software by adding new features.

A United Nations standards committee was established to help create worldwide standards. If every country had different protocols and standards, it would be very difficult to communicate. The original committee was called the *Comite Consulatif International de Telephone et Telegraphique* (CCITT). The name has now been changed to *International Telecommunications Union* (ITU). This committee has representatives from over 80 countries and several large private manufacturers. The committee makes recommendations only. A company is free to use or ignore them. However, more and more companies are now adopting the recommendations.

All ITU recommendations for small computers have a *V* or *X* prefix. The V series is for use with switched telephone networks, which are almost all of them. The X series is for systems that do not use switched phone lines. Revisions or alternate recommendations have *bis* (second) or *ter* (third) added.

The *V* prefixes can be a bit confusing. For example, a V.32 modem can communicate at 4800 or 9600 bits per second (bps). It can communicate with any other V.32 modem. A V.32bis can communicate at 14,400 bps. The V.32bis standard is a modulation method and is not a compression technique. The V.34 standard is for 28.8K modems.

The V.42bis standard is a method of data compression plus a system of error-checking. A V.42bis can communicate with another V.42bis at up to 57,600 bps by using compression and error-checking.

## Basic types of modems

There are two basic types of modems, the external desktop and the internal. Each type has some advantages and disadvantages.

A disadvantage is that the external type requires some of your precious desk space and a voltage source. It also requires an external cable from a COM port to drive it. The good news is that most external models have LEDs that light up and let you know what is happening during your call.

Both the external and the internal models have speakers that let you hear whether the phone is ringing or if you got a busy signal. However, the internal modem might have a very small speaker, and you might not even be able to hear the dial tone and the ringing. Some of the external models have a volume control for the built-in speaker.

The internal modem is built entirely on a board, usually a half, or short, board. The good news is that it doesn't use up any of your desk real estate, but the bad news is that it uses one of your precious slots. It also does not have the LEDs to let you know the progress of your call. Of course, not being able to see the LEDs flashing might not be that important to you. The only thing most people care about is whether it is working or not. The fewer items to worry about, the better.

Even if you use an external modem, if your motherboard does not have built-in COM ports, you will need an I/O board that will require the use of one of your slots for a COM port.

The external modems can cost up to $100 more than an equivalent internal modem. By far, the most popular modems are the internal types.

## Hayes compatibility

One of the most popular early modems was made by Hayes Microcomputer Products. They became the IBM of the modem world and established a de facto standard. There are hundreds of modem manufacturers. Except for some of the very inexpensive ones, almost all of them are Hayes compatible.

## Installing a modem

If you are adding a modem on a board to a system that is already assembled, the first thing to do is to check your documentation and set any jumpers or switches needed to configure the board. There are usually jumpers or small switches that must be set to enable COM1, COM2, COM3, or COM4. Once the switches and jumpers have been set to configure the modem, remove the computer cover. Find an empty slot, and plug the board in.

Normally, most systems only allow for two ports: COM1, which uses IRQ 4, and COM2, which uses IRQ 3. However, COM1 and COM3 can share IRQ 4 and COM2 and COM4 can share IRQ 3 if the software or hardware will allow it. One of the biggest problems of installing serial hardware—such as network cards, mice, modems, fax boards, sound cards, serial printers, plotters, and other serial devices—is that there just aren't enough IRQs. The ISA machines only have 16 IRQs, and most of them are reserved for other uses.

The interrupt requests cause the BIOS and CPU to stop whatever it is doing and give its attention to the current request. The IRQs have a hierarchical arrangement so that the lower-numbered IRQs have priority. If you would like to see how your IRQs are arranged, if you have DOS 5.0 or later, just type MSD (for Microsoft Diagnostics), and it will show you several things about your computer, including your IRQ uses. Table 11-1 shows how my IRQs are arranged.

**Table 11-1.**
**IRQ arrangement.**

| IRQ | User |
|-----|------|
| 0 | Timer click |
| 1 | Keyboard |
| 2 | Second 8259A |
| 3 | COM2: COM4 |
| 4 | COM1:COM3 |
| 5 | LPT2 |
| 6 | Floppy disk |
| 7 | LPT1 |
| 8 | Real-time clock |
| 9 | Redirected IRQ2 |
| 10 | (Reserved) |
| 11 | (Reserved) |
| 12 | (Reserved) |
| 13 | Math coprocessor |
| 14 | Fixed disk |
| 15 | (Reserved) |

It is permissible to use any of the IRQs marked Reserved for things like sound boards and network cards, but serial devices, such as mice and modems, must be connected to one of the COM ports.

If you have an I/O board in your system with external COM ports and you have built-in COM ports on your motherboard, you can only use two of them. You must set the switches or jumpers to configure your system for whichever port that will be used by the modem and the port used by a mouse or other device. Any port on the motherboard or on a plug-in board that is not being used should be disabled. Ordinarily jumpers are used to enable or disable the ports.

If you are installing an external modem, you must go through the same procedure to make sure the COM port is accessible and does not conflict. If you have a mouse, a serial printer, or some other serial device, you will have to determine which port they are set to. You cannot have two serial devices set to the same COM port unless you have special software that will allow them to share the port.

## A simple modem test

It is often difficult to determine which COM port is being used by a device. You can use the AT command to determine if your modem is working with this simple test.

Switch to your communications software directory. At the DOS prompt C:>, type the following using uppercase:

```
ECHO AT DT12345>COM1:
```

The AT is for modem *attention*, the DT is for *dial t*one. If you have a pulse phone system, the command would be AT DP12345. If the modem is set properly, you will hear a dial tone, then the modem will dial 12345. The modem will then emit a continuous busy signal. You can stop the busy signal by invoking the command ECHO ATHO. The HO tells it to hang up.

If two devices are both set for the same COM port, there will be a conflict. The computer will try for a while, then give an error message and the familiar Abort, Retry, Ignore, Fail?. If the modem is connected to COM1 and you invoke the command ECHO AT DT12345>COM2, you will get the message, Write fault error writing device COM2. Abort, Retry, Ignore, Fail?

You might not get any message and not hear the dial tone if the COM ports on both the I/O board and motherboard are enabled. You must disable those ports that are not used.

A diagnostic program, such as Check-It Pro from TouchStone (714-969-7746), can determine which ports are being used. It also does several other very helpful diagnostic tests. Another good program for finding port conflicts is the Port Finder from the mcTronic Systems (713-462-7687).

It is very important that you keep any documentation that you get with your various plug-in boards. Many of the I/O boards have dozens of pins and jumpers. If you don't have the documentation, you might never be able to determine how the board should be configured. It is also necessary that you write down and keep a log of which ports and addresses are enabled. It can save a lot of time.

Your Pentium Pro motherboard will have a Plug-and-Play (PnP) BIOS. If you buy a modem that was manufactured to the PnP specifications, it will be very easy to set up your system. When you plug in a modem board, the BIOS will check to determine which IRQs are free and automatically set itself so that there is no conflict.

Plug in the modem board, and hook it up to the telephone line. Unless you expect to do a lot of communicating, you might not need a separate dedicated line. However, you will need some sort of switching device, such as those from Command Communications (800-288-6794). They have several different devices that can recognize an incoming voice, modem, or fax signal and route the call.

There should be two connectors at the back end of the board. One might be labeled for the line in and the other for the telephone. Unless you have a dedicated telephone line, you should unplug your telephone, plug in the extension to the modem and line, then plug the telephone into the modem.

After you have connected all of the lines, turn on your computer and try the modem before you put the cover back on. Use the simple test that was mentioned previously.

Make sure you have communications software, then call a local bulletin board. Even if you can't get through or have a wrong number, you should hear the dial tone, then hear it dial the number.

# Communications software

To use a modem, it must be driven and controlled by software. There are dozens of communication programs that can be used.

Crosstalk (404-998-3998) was one of the earlier modem programs.

ProComm Plus from DataStorm (314-474-8461) is an excellent communications program. Qmodem from Mustang Software Company (805-873-2500) is another very good program. At one time, both ProComm and Qmodem were low-cost shareware programs. They were among the most popular communication programs available. Both of them are now commercial programs but are still reasonably priced.

Mustang Software also provides software for setting up bulletin boards. If you would like to start your own BBS, contact them for the details.

One of the most comprehensive communications programs is the Delrina Win-Comm PRO from Delrina (800-268-6082). It operates under Windows and handles both modem and fax communications. It can be used to access all of the online services, other modems, and can even be set up as a mini-BBS to let other users log on to your computer. You can set up passwords and access privileges. Because it works under Windows, a mouse can be used to point and click on the many icons and buttons. WinComm PRO is much like the Plug-and-Play software in that it can automatically detect and avoid port conflicts. Call Delrina and ask for a brochure. It is one of the better communication software packages available.

## Low-cost communication software

If you buy a modem or modem/fax board, many companies include a basic communications program. If you subscribe to one of the large online services such as CompuServe or Prodigy, they provide special software for their connections.

You can get copies of communication shareware programs from bulletin boards or from any of the several companies who provide shareware and public-domain software.

Remember, shareware is not free. You can try it out and use it, but the developers ask that you register the program and send in a nominal sum. For this low cost, they will usually provide a manual and some support. Some of the shareware companies are listed in chapter 17. You should be very careful and check for viruses when downloading or using any public domain or shareware.

## Fax/modem software

Most fax/modems come with several communication software packages. The fax/modem that I had been using for the last couple of years died on me. I bought a new one and installed it along with some communication software that came with it. It screwed up my system completely. I could no longer access Prodigy or CompuServe. I sweated for half a day before I discovered that the software that was included is Terminate and Stay Resident (TSR). It loads itself into memory each time I boot up. With that software in memory, I could not access CompuServe or Prodigy.

(*Note:* You can find out if there any TSRs loaded into memory on your computer when in Windows by pressing the Control key plus Escape: Ctrl–Esc. This will show you any TSRs programs in memory. You can then close them.)

After closing the TSR programs, I was able to access Prodigy, but I could not access CompuServe. After several hours of frustration, I called CompuServe Support. They determined that the modem initialization string had somehow become damaged. I reinstalled the CompuServe software, and everything now works.

There are thousands of little things that can go wrong. PnP will go a long way to help solve some of the problems, but it can't possibly solve all of the thousands of little things that can go wrong.

# Bulletin boards

If you have a modem, you have access to several thousand computer bulletin boards. At one time, most bulletin boards were free of any charge. You only had to pay the phone bill if they are out of your calling area. However, a lot of low-down scum have uploaded software with viruses, pirated commercial software has been loaded onto some bulletin boards, stolen credit card numbers have been posted, and many other loathsome and illegal activities have occurred. Because of this, the Sysops (systems operators) have had to spend a lot of time monitoring their BBSs. Many of the bulletin boards now charge a nominal fee to join; some just ask for a tax-deductible donation.

Some of the bulletin boards are set up by private individuals, and some by companies and vendors as a service to their customers. Some are set up by users groups and other special interest organizations. There are over 100 boards nationwide that have been set up for doctors and lawyers. There are gay bulletin boards, X-rated boards, and several for dating.

Many of the bulletin boards are set up to help individuals. They usually have lots of public-domain software and a space where you can leave messages for help, advertising something for sale, or just plain old chit-chat.

If you are just getting started, you probably need some software. There are all kinds of public-domain and shareware software packages that are equivalent to almost all of the major commercial programs. The best part is that the public domain software is free and the shareware is practically free. Another good source of software is from the Surplus Software Company (800-753-7877). Call them for a free catalog. You can save hundreds of dollars on essential software.

## Viruses

A few years ago, you could access a bulletin board and download all kinds of good public-domain or shareware software. You never had to worry about the software destroying your data. Because a few sick psychopaths have created computer viruses, you now have to use safeguards. You now must be quite selective and very careful about where you get your software and who you get it from.

A computer virus is not a live thing; it cannot harm you, only the data in a computer or on a disk. However, you might have invested a lot of time creating that data. A computer virus is usually a bit of program code that is hidden in a piece of legitimate software. The virus is usually designed to redirect, corrupt, or destroy data. The computer virus can resemble an organic virus in that it can cause a wide variety of virus-type symptoms in the computer host.

The virus code might be written so that it can replicate or make copies of itself. When it becomes embedded on a disk, it can attach itself to other programs that it comes in contact with. Whenever a floppy disk is inserted into the drive, it can come away with a hidden copy of the virus.

Infected software might appear to work as it should for some time. Eventually, however, it might contaminate and destroy many of your files. If a virus gets on a workstation or network, it can infect all of the computers in the network. The McAfee Associates (408-988-3832) has one of the best shareware antivirus programs available. McAfee has a bulletin board at 408-988-4004 from which you can download the latest version. They constantly revise the program to try to keep up with the latest viruses.

## Where to find the bulletin boards

Several computer magazines devote a lot of space to bulletin boards and user groups. In California, the MicroTimes and Computer Currents magazines have several pages of bulletin boards and user groups each month. The Computer Shopper magazine has the most comprehensive national listing of bulletin boards and user groups of any magazine. The Computer Shopper alternates each month with a listing of user groups one month and bulletin boards the next.

If you have a bulletin board or belong to a user group and want them listed in the *Shopper*, use your modem and submit your entry to 913-478-3088, 8NI at 2400 bps.

## Online services

The bulletin boards are not nearly as popular today as the Internet and online services. The online services provide forums for help and discussions, mail boxes, and a large variety of information and reference services. A caller can search the databases and download information as easily as pulling the data off his own hard disk.

They have phone service to most areas in the larger cities so that there is not even a toll charge. They have an impressive list of services, including home shopping, home banking, airline schedules and reservations, stock market quotations, a medical bulletin board, and many others.

## Banking by modem

Many banks offer systems that will let you do all your banking with your computer and a modem from the comforts of your home. You would never again have to drive downtown, hunt for a parking space, then stand in line for a half hour to do your banking.

Intuit (415-322-0573) developed Quicken, an excellent financial software program. Intuit offers CheckFree, a service that allows you to pay all of your bills electronically. It also will allow you to print your checks from your computer on a laser printer. This requires special checks that are imprinted with your account number in magnetic ink.

CheckFree costs about $10 a month. However, if you spend about 4 hours a month paying bills, the $10 is not very much compared to the time spent. Another advantage to CheckFree is that the bills are paid automatically, but not until they are due. This lets your account accrue interest until the last moment. If you ordinarily write a lot of checks, CheckFree and Quicken can quickly pay for themselves.

Intuit is now merged with ChipSoft (602-295-3070). ChipSoft is the developer of TurboTax, one of the better software packages for doing your taxes. The marriage of these two companies means that they can offer the most complete financial software available for your computer system. With a good financial program, you can get rid of the shoe boxes full of canceled checks. The data that is in your computer can automatically flow onto the TurboTax forms. It can make the onerous task that occurs on April 15 each year a bit easier to accomplish.

# Facsimile machines

Facsimile (fax) machines have been around for quite a while. Newspapers and businesses have used them for years. The early machines were similar to the early acoustic modems. Both used foam rubber cups that fit over the telephone receiver-mouthpiece for coupling. They were very slow and subject to noise and interference. Fax machines and modems have come a long way since those early days.

A page of text or a photo is fed into the facsimile machine and scanned. As the scanning beam moves across the page, white and dark areas are digitized as 1s and 0s, then transmitted out over the telephone lines. On the receiving end of the line, a scanning beam sweeps across the paper. The dark areas cause it to print as it sweeps across the paper. The finished product is a black-and-white image of the original.

When a text file is sent by modem, the digitized bits that make up each character is converted from digital voltage to analog voltage. A modem sends and receives bits that make up each character.

A fax machine or board sends and receives scanned whole pages of letters, graphics, images, signatures, etc. Because a modem recognizes individual characters, a computer program can be sent over a modem but not over a fax. A fax sends and receives the information as digitized graphic data. A modem converts the digital information that represents individual characters into analog voltages, sends it over the line, then converts it back to individual digital characters.

There are times when a modem or fax is needed. Both units could not be in use at the same time on the same phone line. Otherwise a single phone line can be used for both fax and modems.

There are millions of facsimile machines in use today. There are very few businesses that cannot benefit from the use of a fax. It can be used to send documents that include handwriting, signatures, seals, letterheads, graphs, blueprints, photos, and other types of data around the world, across the country, or across the room to another fax machine.

Express mail can cost from $8 to $10 or more. A fax machine can deliver the same letter for about 40¢ and do it in less than three minutes. Many of the software programs will let you delay sending a fax until late at night to get the best long-distance rates. Depending on the type of business and the amount of critical mail that must be sent out, a fax system can pay for itself in a very short time.

Most of the fax machines use thermal paper for printing, especially the lower-cost machines. The thermal paper does not provide very good resolution and fades when exposed to light. The better, and more expensive, fax machines use ink jet or laser technology and print on plain paper.

They are usually a bit slow, but almost all of the fax machines can be used as a copier. Fax machines have a lot in common with copy machines, scanners, and printers. Several companies have added these features to their machines so that one machine can do the work of several. More about these combo machines in chapter 12.

# Fax/modem computer boards

Several companies have developed fax systems on circuit boards that can be plugged into computers. Most of the fax boards are now integrated with a modem on the same board. The modem and fax combination costs very little more than either board separately. This combination also saves having to use an extra plug-in slot.

For some time, the standard baud rate for fax was 9600. However, many of the newer fax-modem boards are now capable of a 14,400 speed for both modem and fax. However, just like the modem connections, both the sender and receiver must be operating at the same speed. Also like the modem, the fax can shift down to match the receiver if it is slower.

Special software allows the computer to control the fax boards. Using the computer's word processor, letters and memos can be written and sent out over the phone lines. Several letters or other information can be stored or retrieved from the computer hard disk and transmitted. The computer can be programmed to send the letters out at night when rates are lower.

The computer fax boards have one disadvantage. They cannot scan information—such as signatures, graphics, or drawings—that are not in the computer. However, with a scanner, this information can be stored as a file on a hard disk then added to a document that is to be faxed. There are several scanners that can be used to input data.

With the proper software, a computer can receive and store any fax. The digitized data and images can be stored on a hard disk, then printed out.

## Fax-On-Demand

Several companies have set up fax machines that can supply information to you 24 hours a day. You simply call them with your voice phone, tell them what documents you want, and give them your fax number. The documents will be sent immediately.

Most of the companies have a catalog that lists all of their documents and the document number. You should first ask to have the catalog faxed to you. You can then determine which documents to order.

The FaxFacts Company (708-682-8898) publishes a small booklet that lists several companies who have the Fax-On-Demand or Faxback capability. They list topics such as medical, computers, travel, trade shows, and many more.

Most Faxback information is free, but some companies, such as Consumer Reports (800-766-9988), ask for a credit card number and charge a fee for articles you request.

Here are just a few of the other companies who offer Faxback or Fax-on-Demand:

| | |
|---|---|
| Borland TechFax | 800-822-4269 |
| Cyrix Direct Connect | 800-215-6823 |
| IBM | 800-426-4329 |
| Novell Support Line | 800-638-9273 |
| Symantec Corp. | 800-554-4403 |
| WordStar Fax Support | 404-514-6333 |

(When you call, ask for their new users instructions and navigation map.) If you prefer, most will send the information to you by mail rather than by fax.

## Fax/modem/phone switch

Having the modem and telephone on the same line should cause no problems unless someone tries to use the telephone while the modem is using it. Life will be a lot simpler though if you have a switch that can detect whether the incoming signal is for a fax, modem, or voice. Fax and modem signals transmit a high-pitched tone, called the CNG (Calling) signal. A fax/modem switch can switch and route the incoming call to the proper device.

You should be aware that there are a few old fax systems that do not use the CNG signals. My Command Communication system will let me manually transfer the call in that case. If I know the incoming call is a fax, I can press 1 1, and it will be switched to the fax machine. If it is a modem call, I can press 2 2, and it will be switched to the modem.

Of course, I have to be there to answer such a call. One solution to this problem, for those people who have machines without the CNG signal, is to have them punch in the 1 1 or 2 2 on their end after they dial the number. I can also put this instruction on my answering machine if I am not available. Fortunately, not many of the old systems without the CNG signals are still in existence.

There is another solution for the problem of those people who have machines without the CNG signal. The telephone company can set up two or more numbers with different and distinctive rings on a single line. The Command Communications switchers can be programmed to recognize the distinctive ring and route the call to the proper device. The South Tech Instruments Company (800-394-5556) has a FoneFilter device that can recognize the distinctive rings and route the call to a fax, modem, or answering machine.

Of course, there is a charge by the telephone company for the extra numbers added to your line. At this time, in the Los Angeles area, it costs $7.50 to set up a separate distinctive ring on your line, then $6.00 a month thereafter. This is still less expensive than adding a second line.

If you still have one of the older fax machines, I would suggest that you scrap it and buy a later model. Most of them are now very inexpensive, but they are faster and handle the paper much better. If you do a lot of faxing, they will pay for themselves quickly.

Command Communications (800-288-6794) has several different model switchers that are suitable for homes, small offices, and even large businesses. They have connections for a telephone answering device (TAD), telephone extensions, a fax machine or fax board, and a connection for an auxiliary or modem. The alternative to a switcher would be to install a dedicated telephone line for the fax machine, another line for the modem, and another line for voice. If you don't do a lot of transmissions by fax and modem, you can get by with a single telephone and a good switcher. It can pay for itself many times over.

Many of the standalone fax machines have a built-in detector that can determine if the incoming call is for voice or fax.

# Telephone outlets for extensions

You need a telephone line or extension to hook up a computer modem or a fax. You might also want telephone outlets in several rooms or at one or more desks or at another computer. You can go to almost any hardware store, and even some grocery and drug stores, and buy the telephone wire and accessories needed. However, you might have trouble running telephone wires to the computer, desks, and other rooms. It can be a lot of work cutting holes in the walls and running the wires up in the attic or under the floor.

There is a much simpler way. Just use the 110-volt wiring of the building. The Phonex Company (801-566-0100) developed special adapters that plug into any wall plug outlet. It requires at least two adapters: one for the telephone input line and another adapter for where you want the extension. More adapters can be plugged into any other 110-volt outlet to provide as many telephone extensions as needed. If you need an extension in another location, just unplug an adapter and plug it into another nearby wall outlet. You could even use a standard electrical extension cord and a Phonex adapter to provide a telephone extension. Electronic circuitry in the adapters blocks the ac voltage from getting into the telephone lines but allows voice and data to go through. The device is being marketed and sold by Comtrad Industries (800-704-1211).

# Combination devices and voice mail

The fax machines, copiers, printers, and scanners all have a lot in common. Several companies are now taking advantage of this commonality and offering combination devices.

Some companies are starting to use color for fax. If you have one of the combination devices with a color scanner, the Laser Today International (415-961-3015) has software that will let you send and receive color faxes.

The Compex International Company (800-626-8112) has an all-in-one fax, scanner, printer, and copier.

The Speaking Devices Corporation (408-727-2132) has a unit with a fax, fax/phone switch, scanner, voice mail, and caller ID.

Boca Research (407-997-6227) has a multimedia voice modem that has up to 1000 password-protected voice and fax mailboxes, private and public fax-on-demand, remote message and fax retrieval, professionally recorded greetings and voice prompts, and personalized greetings for individual mailboxes.

Tiger Software (800-888-4437) publishes a catalog that has hundreds of software and hardware items. They advertise the Vomax 2000, which is a fax, voice, and modem system. It has 1MB of digital storage, which can store up to 20 minutes of voice mail messages or up to 50 sheets of faxes. It has message forwarding so that it can call another number and play your messages. It can also call your pager and relay messages. Call Tiger Software for a catalog and more information.

I recently upgraded my 14.4K fax/modem to a U.S. Robotics Sportster Vi 28.8K V.34 system. This system has Personal Voice Mail that can be used as an answering machine. It also came with a book on the World Wide Web and several software packages for exploring the WWW. See Fig. 11-1.

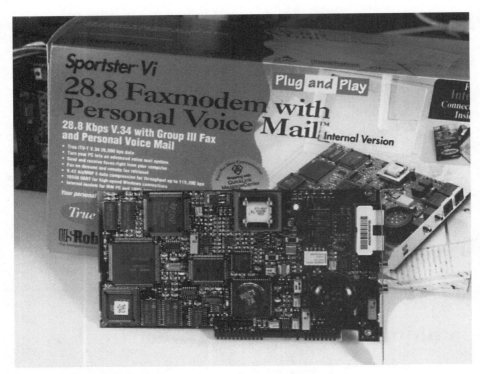

**Fig. 11-1** A 28.8K Robotics Fax/Modem with voice mail.

The AnyWhere Associates (617-522-8102) has software that allows you to send e-mail to faxes. Delrina's WinFax 7.0 integrates fax, e-mail, and voice mail. Cylink (408-735-5800) and Syntel Sciences (800-499-1469) have software that lets you encrypt faxes so that your nosy neighbor will not be able to read them.

# Telecommuting

Millions of people risk their lives and fight frustrating traffic every day. Many of these people have jobs that could allow them to stay home, work on a computer, then send the data to the office over a modem or a fax. Even if the person had to buy their own computer, modem, and fax, it might still be worth it. You could save the cost of gasoline, auto maintenance, and insurance. Thousands are killed on the highways; telecommuting can be a life saver.

Being able to work at home would be ideal for those who have young children, for the handicapped, or for anyone who hates being stuck in traffic jams. It is expected that about half of all PCs sold in 1996 will be for home use. A large percentage of those computers will be used for telecommuting.

There is one other very big plus for working at home in that you can be an "open-collar worker" unlike a "blue-collar worker" or a "white-collar worker." Many people spend thousands of dollars buying new outfits so that they can wear a different one to work each day of the week. They can save that money if they work at home. If you are working at home you can wear any old clothes as often as you like. If you are living alone, you don't have to wear anything at all. (However, you probably should remember to put on a robe or something when answering the door for the UPS or Fed Ex man.)

There are several technological tools such as the new fast modems/fax/voice/ whatever machines, remote access software, conference calling software, cellular telephones, and many other goodies that can make working from home almost like being at the office. A telecommuter can have a first-class virtual office in a bedroom or den. A plus for the company is that they will be saving office space, parking space, and wear and tear on the coffee machine.

There are a few disadvantages. You might miss the face-to-face interaction of your co-workers. In some cases, you might be overlooked when it comes time to hand out raises and perks. Out of sight, out of mind. On the other hand, you might be required to wear a beeper and stay close to a telephone or computer. You might feel like you are on a short leash. However, the advantages far outweigh the few disadvantages. Telecommuting or virtual offices will be adopted by more and more companies.

## Remote-control software

If you are on the road or working from home and have a computer at the office, it is often necessary to access the data on that computer. There are several software packages that will allow you to connect from remote locations. You can be sitting in a distant hotel room or at a PC at home and dial up a computer at the office. You can take control across a phone line or across a network and work just as if you were sitting in front of the office computer. You can review documents, update files, edit reports, do print outs, or download files.

## LapLink

For many years, LapLink (800-343-8088) has had one of the best ways to connect a laptop to a desktop or to connect any two computers together. Their software usually comes with a cable for linking computers together. LapLink for Windows 95 still does all the good things it did in the past; in addition, it is now one of the better ways to remotely access and connect two or more computers. It has SmartXchange and will let you transfer only those files that have been changed. You can also update a file by sending only that portion of it that has changed, which can save a lot of connect time. You can connect via cable, modem, Internet, a network, or even with infrared. LapLink comes with a cable for the parallel port or for a serial port. See Fig. 11-2.

Here are a few other software packages for remote control:

Reachout from Ocean Isle
Norton pcAnywhere from Symantec
Carbon Copy from Microcom
Close-Up from Norton Lambert
CO/Session from Triton

You should be able to find this software at most software stores or listed in software catalogs, such as the MicroWarehouse (800-367-7080) or DellWare (800-847-4051).

All of these packages will only work if the computer is turned on and booted up. Server Technology has Remote Power On/Off + AUX. This device plugs into the power line between the computer and the wall plug. The telephone line plugs into

**Fig. 11-2** LapLink software and cables for connecting two computers. Software can also be used for remote access.

this device. When the device detects an incoming call, it will automatically turn on and boot up the PC. When the call is ended, it can turn off the PC. It can even let you reboot if the computer hangs up for some reason. Some companies bundle the Remote Power On/Off with pcAnywhere and other remote software. It is available from Dellware, Microwarehouse, and other discount catalog stores.

## Telephony

There have been some important advances in computers and telephones in the last few years. Even greater changes can be expected soon. All of the items listed in this section can be used in a large business or a small office or home office (SOHO). The SOHO has become a very important element of business today.

*Computer Telephony* is a magazine that is devoted entirely to telephone computer technology and Computer Telephone Integration (CTI). The magazine is free to qualified subscribers. If you work for a company or yourself and use a telephone or computer, then you can probably qualify for a free subscription. Call 800-677-3435 and ask them to send you a qualifying form.

The telephony business has become so important and widespread that Computer Telephony Conferences and Expositions are being held twice a year. The conferences are sponsored by *Computer Telephony* magazine. At these shows, they have hundreds of vendors displaying and demonstrating the latest computer and telephone technology plus dozens of informative seminars. For the next show date and location, call 800-677-3435.

Another free magazine that deals with telephony is *InfoText* (218-723-9437). Hello Direct is a free catalog that is devoted to telephone products. A current issue has 72 pages full of descriptions of telephone-related products, such as all kinds of telephones, headsets, computer and telephone integration products, and many other items. A couple of items actually do away with a standard telephone. The telephone line is plugged into your computer, then with a headset and microphone, you can use a mouse to point to an address list or to dial the number by pressing the keys of the keyboard. There are several different models with different features.

The products handled by Hello Direct are rather expensive, but they have many items that are difficult to find elsewhere. Hello Direct is at 800-444-3556. Call them for a catalog.

Universal Serial Bus (USB) is a new standard that will allow telephones and other telephone technologies to be connected to computers and operate at up to 12 megabits per second.

Several companies provide hardware and software for Interactive Voice Response (IVR) that can be used in many different business functions.

The computer industry is rife with hundreds of acronyms. The CTI portion of the industry has greatly increased the number.

## Telephone conference

It is very simple to have a telephone conference with as few as two persons or as many as several hundred. In the conference calls, everyone on the line can talk to anyone else on the line. You can do teleconferences from anywhere: home, a small office, a large office, or even a pay telephone booth.

U.S. Robotics (800-949-6757) has developed a PC-adaptable conference speakerphone: the ConferenceLink CS 1500. It can be connected to a computer as a speakerphone for teleconferences or for video conferencing or for use on Internet telephony applications.

## Fax conferences

If you have a fax machine, you can send out a graphics design, plans, or any number of business papers and have other persons review the plan or whatever, make changes or sign it, and return it. You can have an interactive meeting with others in the same building, or almost anywhere in the world, over a simple telephone line. One disadvantage is that it is not in real time. You have to send the fax then wait for a reply.

## Modem teleconferences

With a computer modem, you can have a desktop conference. You send data, graphics, and other materials over the telephone line to other computers over a local area network (LAN), in the same building or almost anywhere in the world. Other persons sitting at the computer can view the text data, spreadsheets, graphics, and other materials. The persons can change the material or interact with the other persons on the line in real time.

One of the better products that can help with a desktop conference is called TALKShow, from Future Labs (415-254-9000; fax 408-736-8030). This small simple program works under Windows. Each person in the conference must have a copy of TALKShow installed on their computer. TALKShow connects everyone together and automatically handles all of the computer communications.

The same data appears on all the computer screens that are on the line. Many live conferences use a large white board in front of the conference room. The leader writes on the board while the attendees watch, and perhaps make comments for changes. With TALKShow, each computer screen becomes a white board. Each individual can suggest changes or additions to the material on the screen. (Of course, if it is the president of the company who is leading the desktop conference, you may have to be careful of what you suggest.)

With TALKShow, anything that appears on the screen can be saved on the hard disk or printed out.

# Educational

Several universities, colleges, and specialized training facilities are using telecommunications to offer many different courses. Some courses might lead to degrees; others might be for specialized training for a large company. You could sit at home in front of your computer and take a course from a college or training facility on the other side of the country.

# National telephone directories

I live in the Los Angeles area. In Los Angeles and Orange Counties, there are over 100 suburban cities with over 12 million people. Can you imagine a single telephone directory that would list all of these people? How about a telephone directory that would list all of the millions of people in New York, Boston, or San Francisco? Believe it or not, there are such directories, and these directories are smaller than one that you might find in a small town. These national directories are small because they are on CD-ROM discs.

The ProPhone, from New Media Publishing (617-631-9200), has 7 CD-ROM discs: 6 discs for the "white pages" and one disc for businesses in the U.S. There is over 600MB of data on each disc, which lists telephone numbers, the address, and zip codes. The separate disc for business makes it very easy to look up a company anywhere in the country.

The PhoneDisc, from Digital Directory Assistance (800-284-8353), only has 5 CD-ROM discs. See Fig. 11-3. It has over 90 million listings of residential and businesses. It does not have a separate business disc but lists businesses along with the general population in the white pages.

Not every person in the country is listed on the discs. Of course, many people move and change phone numbers. Most phone companies only update their directo-

**Fig. 11-3** A telephone directory of the whole country on CD-ROM discs.

ries once a year. However, these CD-ROM disc directory companies do quarterly updates. Once you are a registered owner, the updates are very reasonable.

If you are in a business where you have to contact a lot of people, then you need these two directories. You might also need them if you live in the Los Angeles area.

## ISDN

ISDN is an acronym for Integrated Services Digital Network. Most of the ISDN networks are made up of fiber optic cable. Eventually the whole world will have telephone systems that use this concept. It will be a system that will be able to transmit voice, data, video, and graphics in digital form rather than the present analog. When this happens, we can scrap our modems.

ISDN is already installed in several cities. However, don't throw your modem away just yet. The new service might not be available at all locations for some time, and it will be rather expensive.

## Cable modems

At the present time, ISDN allows modems to operate at up to 128K bits per second, which is more than four times faster than a 28.8K modem. However, it is not nearly as fast as communicating over coax cable, which can operate at up to 10 megabits per second. Many of the Internet Web sites have lots of graphics. It might take several megabytes to create a good graphic image. Over the plain old telephone service (POTS), it might take several minutes to download a graphic. With a cable modem, it would only take seconds.

At the time of this writing, Congress has just passed a law giving cable TV companies the right to enter the phone business and vice versa. You can expect to see a lot of competition from the cable and telephone companies for your business. Motorola and several other companies are busy making new cable modems.

# Sources

I have not listed the names and manufacturers of modems and faxes because there are so many. Look in any computer magazine, and you will see dozens of ads. A recent copy of the Computer Shopper had ads for about 200 modem/fax boards from several different companies.

One modem company that I do want to mention is U.S. Robotics. They manufacture a large variety of modems, especially the high-end, high-speed type. They will send you a free 110-page booklet that explains about all you need to know about modems. For a free booklet, call 800-342-5877.

I suggest that you subscribe to several of the computer magazines listed in chapter 17. A good magazine that is free to qualified subscribers is *Telecommunications*. Almost anyone can qualify. For a qualification form, call them at 617-769-9750 or write to:

Telecommunications
P.O. Box 850949
Braintree, MA 02185

# 12
# Printers

For the vast majority of applications, a computer system is not complete without a printer. There are several manufacturers of computer printers and hundreds of different models. You will have a vast number of options and choices when choosing a printer. This chapter discusses some of the features and functions of those different types.

## Printer life expectancy

Printers usually have a long life. I have an HP LaserJet III that is about eight years old and still going strong. Although printers usually last a long time, like most other industries, the printer manufacturers constantly work to obsolete the printer that you might already have so that you will buy a new and improved model. There are dozens and dozens of printer companies. Each company produces dozens of different models. Because the models change so frequently, when I mention a product, I don't usually mention the model name.

## Dot matrix printers

Except for a few specialized applications, the dot matrix is practically obsolete. Dot matrix printers are fairly low priced, but they are limited in fonts and graphics capability. The laser printer speed is measured by the average number of pages per minute it can print; dot matrix printer speed is measured by the characters per second (CPS) it can print. Dot matrix printers can print much faster in the draft mode than in the Near Letter Quality (NLQ) mode. There are some high-end dot matrix line printers that can print a whole line at a time. Some of them can print up to 1000 lines per minute. To get the high speed, some dot matrix printers might have four or more heads, with each head printing out a different line.

# Advantages of dot matrix

One of the distinct advantages that dot matrix printers have over the lasers is the low cost. Some dot matrix printers cost less than $150. Of course, there are some high-end dot matrix printers, such as the very fast line printers, that can cost close to $10,000.

There are many applications where a dot matrix printer is needed to accomplish a task. Wide continuous sheets are necessary for some spreadsheet printouts. My LaserJet can't handle anything wider than 8.5". With the wide carriage on my Star dot matrix, the wide sheets are no problem.

Another advantage is the number of sheets that can be printed. Most lasers have from 100 to 250 sheet bins. The dot matrix can print up a whole box of 5000 sheets of fanfold continuous sheets. (It has been my experience though, if I start a job that requires a lot of printed sheets, as long as I stand there and watch the printer, it will work perfectly. If I walk away and start doing something else, the printer will immediately have a paper jam or some other problem. This is probably one of Murphy's many laws.)

Many offices and businesses still use multiple sheet forms. A laser printer can't handle these forms, but a dot matrix can easily print them.

The dot matrix can also print on odd sizes, shapes, and thicknesses of paper. There are many times when I use mine to address large manila envelopes.

The U.S. Post Office has adopted a Postnet bar code that helps sort and speed up mail. If you look at some of the envelopes that you receive in the mail, you might see the Postnet bar codes below the address. Many of the companies that send out bulk mail use this code. Several of the dot matrix printers have the Postnet bar code built-in; some others offer it as an option. The Post Office gives a discount when the envelopes have the Postnet code on them. If you do a lot of mailing, a printer with the Postnet option could save you some money.

## Maintenance costs

Maintenance costs of dot matrix printers are usually much less than that for lasers and inkjets. The main costs for a dot matrix is to replace the ribbon about every 3000 sheets. A dot matrix ribbon can cost from $3 to $10. A laser toner cartridge also lasts for about 3000 sheets and can cost from $30 to $75 to replace.

## Number of pins

There are still a few 9-pin dot matrix printers being sold today, but most people are buying those with a 24-pin print head. The 24-pin head has much better resolution and might cost only a few dollars more. The 24-pin printer forms characters from two vertical rows of 12 pins in each row.

There are small electric solenoids around each of the wire pins in the head. An electric signal causes the solenoid to push the pins forward. Dot matrix printers are also called *impact printers* because the pins impact against the ribbon and paper. The solenoids press one or more of the various pins as the head moves in finite increments across the paper so that any character can be formed.

Figure 12-1 shows a representation of the pins if it were a 7-pin print head and how it would form the letter A.

The numbers on the left represent the individual pins in the head before it starts moving across the paper. The first pin to be struck would be number 7, then number 6, then 5, 4, both 3 and 5, 2, 1, both 2 and 5, 3, 4, 5, 6, then 7.

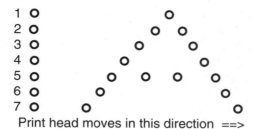

Fig. 12-1
Forming the letter A on a 7-pin
dot matrix printer.

A 24-pin head would be similar to the 7-pin representation in Fig. 12-1, except that it would have two vertical rows of 12 pins, side by side, in each row. The pins in one row would be slightly offset and lower than the pins in the other row. Because the pins are offset, they would overlap slightly and fill in the open gaps normally found in a 9-pin system.

There is a lot of competition between the dot matrix and laser companies for your dollar. Some vendors are now selling laser printers for about the same price as some of the dot matrix printers. This low cost of the lasers has forced the dot matrix people to lower their prices. In addition to lower prices, many dot matrix companies are also adding more features, such as more memory and more fonts, to attract buyers.

## Some disadvantages of dot matrix

One of the disadvantages is that the dot matrix can't come close to the quality printing of a laser. In the draft mode, if the printer has a 24-pin print head, only half of the pins will be hit. There will be noticeable spacing between the dots. For NLQ, all of the pins will be hit. In draft mode, with a 9-pin head, all of the pins will be hit, but there will be spaces between the dots. For NLQ on a 9-pin system, the printer makes a second run with the head slightly displaced so that the pins will hit different spots and fill in the open spaces. So, in draft mode, the printing can be fairly fast but has poor quality. In the NLQ mode, they slow down considerably but have much better quality.

Most 24-pin dot matrix printers have a resolution of 360 × 360 dots per inch (DPI). Until recently, the standard laser was rated at 300 × 300 DPI. However, if you compare the dot matrix output to the laser, you will see that the laser has a much higher resolution. The reason is that the laser produces a much smaller dot than the dot matrix dot. So, if an *A* is printed out on a dot matrix, the jagged edges from the large dots are very apparent.

Most lasers can use scalable type fonts; only a very few of the high-end dot matrix printers can use scalable fonts.

Most dot matrix printers have only 8K or less of memory. A few of the high-end dot matrix printers might have as much as 64K or even up to 128K. The memory on a dot matrix can be used as a print buffer. The computer can download a file to the printer, then go about its business doing other things. Laser printers use memory a bit differently. They take the file and format the whole page in memory before they start printing. Most lasers come with a minimum of 512K, and you have the option to add more. For higher speed and graphics, the laser should have a minimum of 2MB.

If you can get by with a dot matrix, you should be able to find one at a very good price. Look for ads in *Computer Shopper* or any of the other computer magazines.

# Inkjets

Hewlett-Packard developed the first inkjet printer. Now there are many companies—such as Brother, Canon, Epson, Texas Instrument, Lexmark, and several others—that are manufacturing inkjet printers. Some of the companies call them by a different name such as Canon's Bubble Jet, but they are all basically inkjets. The inkjet printers have a print output that approaches that of the laser but at a lower cost. Most of the inkjet manufacturers have one or more color models. Those models that can print in color usually have a C in the model number, such as the HP DeskJet 660C or the Canon Bubble Jet BJC-70.

The inkjet printers use a system that is similar to the dot matrix printers. However, instead of pins that press a ribbon onto the paper, they use a matrix of small inkjets that spray dots of ink on the paper. They also have a much larger number of inkjets; the dot matrix can have from 9 to 24 pins; the inkjet can have from 48 to 128 small jets. The head moves across the paper much like the dot matrix system, and dots of ink are sprayed onto the paper to form text or graphics. To print color, they have three or more color inkjets. Of course, those with a larger number of jets produce more and smaller dots that yields higher resolution.

Most of the inkjet printers come with one or more fonts, but they might be able to use several more that are available on plug-in font cartridges. Some of the inkjets can use scalable fonts.

Like the dot matrix, the speed of the inkjets is measured in characters per second. Depending on the type of print the average speed is about 2 pages per minute.

## Inkjet color

Most inkjet printers sold today are color. Because black is used most often, most of them have a large black cartridge along with the three primary color cartridges. It is now possible to buy color inkjet printers for less than $300. Figure 12-2 shows a low-cost Canon color inkjet. Some of the color machines can be very slow. About the best they can do is 2 pages per minute just printing black text. Lasers can print 4 to 8 pages per minute. A color graphics printout might take several minutes on an inkjet machine.

The inkjet color printers use a system of three different colored ink cartridges—cyan, magenta, and yellow—to print color. Some systems also have a black cartridge for standard text; some use the mixture of the three colors to make black. Some low-cost systems use a single cartridge with three colors. I recommend that you look for a printer that uses a separate cartridge for black and each of the primary colors.

As the head moves across the paper, the software can have any of the various colors sprayed onto the paper. The three colors blend to produce any color of the rainbow.

The black inkjet cartridges are good for about 700 pages of text. The color cartridges might yield about half this many pages. They must then be replaced or refilled. The Signal Computing Company (800-454-2288) has refill kits for most inkjet printers.

If you do any presentations using an overhead projector, the inkjets can handle transparencies very well. The color inkjet printers are ideal for creating low-cost colored transparencies for presentations, graphs, and schematic plotting and drawings.

**Fig. 12-2** A low-cost Canon ink jet color printer.

Compared to the less than $300 inkjets, there are some inkjet printers that are rather expensive, such as the HP DeskJet 885C, the Epson Stylus Pro, and the Canon BJC-610. These printers are about equivalent in speed, graphics capabilities, and cost. The HP DeskJet 1200C is a more sophisticated machine, has more memory, and can print faster. HP also has a 1200C-PS, which has PostScript. The IBM Jetprinter PS 4079 is also a PostScript printer and about equivalent to the HP 1200C-PS.

Of course, there are several options and features not listed here. Many of the companies have several different models of their products. Models and prices listed are for comparison only and might be different when you read this. Check through the ads in the computer magazines.

Here are some of the color inkjet companies and their numbers:

| | |
|---|---|
| Canon Corp. | 800-848-4123 |
| Hewlett-Packard | 800-752-0900 |
| Lexmark International | 800-232-2000 |
| Okidata Okijet | 609-235-2600 |

Call the companies for brochures and specifications.

There are several inkjet and color inkjet printers that I did not mention. There are many different models, from different companies with different features, functions and prices. Look for ads in the major computer magazines.

## Wide-format printers

There are several companies who make wide format color printers that can print such things as large posters, signs, banners, point of sale (POS) displays, trade show materials, advertisements, business and presentation graphics, and billboards. Most of the printers can print on 36" wide cut sheets or roll sheets as long as 50 feet. Usually the paper has to be specially coated. Most of the printers use a high resolution inkjet technology. The cost of these printers range from $6000 and up to $20,000.

Using standard silk-screen techniques or large four-color printers to make a large poster or banner can cost from $1000 up to $6000 or more. The same poster can be printed on a wide-format inkjet printer for $200 to $300 or less. Figure 12-3 shows a CalComp TechJet wide-format printer.

**Fig. 12-3**  A CalComp wide-format inkjet color printer.

Another type of wide-format printers use an Electrostatic process with special cyan, magenta, yellow, and black (CYMK) toners. The special paper is electrostatically charged and the toners adhere to the charged areas. The high-speed printers have a very high resolution that is suitable for life-size posters, banners, or several types of signs. The signs and posters can be used in exterior areas where they can withstand temperature changes and sun and rain. The electrostatic printers are rather expensive at $30,000 and up to $100,000.

Most of the wide format printers use a raster image processor (RIP), a software controller. The RIPs act as color and ink control managers, handle enlargement, rotation, tiling and paneling, previewing, screening, and other tasks. The RIP software is made by several different companies, so it is not all the same.

Here are just a few companies:

| | |
|---|---|
| CalComp | 714-821-2100 |
| Hewlett-Packard | 800-367-4772 |
| Houston Instrument | 512-835-0900 |
| Encad | 619-452-0891 |

## Inkjet supplies

The original cost of a printer is not the end. If you do much printing, the cost of supplies can be more than the cost of the printer. Ink cartridges can cost from $30 to $35. Some cartridges only last for about 300 pages. It is possible to refill some of the cartridges.

# Laser printers

The Hewlett-Packard LaserJet was one of the first lasers. It was a fantastic success and became the *de facto* standard. There are now hundreds of laser printers on the market. Most of them emulate the LaserJet standard. Even IBM's laser printer emulates the HP standard.

Laser printers are a combination of the copy machine, computer, and laser technologies. They have excellent print quality, but they have lots of moving mechanical parts and are rather expensive.

Laser printers use synchronized, multifaceted mirrors and sophisticated optics to write the characters or images on a photosensitive rotating drum. The drum is similar to the ones used in copy machines. The laser beam is swept across the spinning drum and is turned on and off to represent white and dark areas. As the drum is spinning, it writes one line across the drum, then rapidly returns and writes another. It is quite similar to the electron beam that sweeps across the face of a TV screen or computer monitor one line at a time.

The spinning drum is sensitized by each point of light that hits it. The sensitized areas act like electromagnets. The drum rotates through the carbon toner. The sensitized areas become covered with the toner. The paper is then pressed against the drum. The toner that was picked up by the sensitized areas of the drum is left on the paper. The paper then is sent through a heating element where the toner is heated and fused to the paper. Except for the writing to the drum, this is the same thing that happens in a copy machine. Instead of using a laser to sensitize the drum, a copy machine takes a photo of the image to be copied. A photographic lens focuses the image onto the rotating drum, which becomes sensitized to the light and dark areas projected onto it.

## Engine

The drum and its associated mechanical attachments is called an *engine*. Canon is one of the foremost makers of engines. They manufacture them for their own laser printers and copy machines and for dozens of other companies, such as Hewlett-Packard and Apple. There are several other companies who manufacture laser engines.

## Low-cost laser printers

Because of the large number of companies manufacturing laser printers, there is a lot of competition, which is a great benefit to us consumers. The competition has driven prices of both lasers and dot matrix printers down. It has also forced many new improvements.

Until recently, most laser printers had a resolution of only 300 x 300. Most lasers now have a resolution of 600 x 600. Some vendors are selling them for less than $1000.

## Memory

If you plan to do any graphics or desktop publishing (DTP), you will need to have at least 1MB of memory in the machine. Before it prints the first sheet, the printer loads the data into its memory and determines where each dot will be placed on the sheet. Of course, the more memory, the better.

Not all lasers use the same memory configuration. For some machines, you must buy a special plug-in board for the memory. Check the type of memory that you need before you buy.

Several companies offer laser memories. Here are a couple:

ASP     800-445-6190
Elite    800-942-0018

Look in computer magazines for ads from other companies.

## Page description languages

If you plan to do any complex desktop publishing, you might need a page-description language (PDL) of some kind. Text characters and graphics images are two different species of animals. Laser printer controllers are somewhat similar to monitor controllers. The monitor adapters usually have all of the alphabetical and numerical characters stored in ROM. When you press the letter A from the keyboard, the monitor dives into the ROM chip, drags out the A and displays it in a precise block of pixels wherever the cursor happens to be. These are called bitmapped characters. If you wanted to display an A that was twice as large, you would have to have a complete font set of that type in the computer.

Printers are very much like monitors and have the same limitations. They have a library of stored discrete characters for each font that they can print. My dot matrix Star printer has an internal font and two cartridge slots. Several different font cartridges can be plugged into these slots, but they are still limited to those fonts that happen to be plugged in.

With a PDL, the laser printer can take one of the stored fonts and change it, or scale it, to any size you want. These are *scalable fonts*. With a bitmapped font, you have one type face and one size. With scalable fonts, you can have one typeface with an infinite number of sizes. Most of the lasers printers will accept ROM cartridges that can have as many as 35 or more fonts. You can print almost anything that you want with these fonts if your system can scale them.

## Speed

Laser printers can print from 4 to over 10 pages per minute depending on the model and what they are printing. Some very expensive high-end printers can print over 30 pages per minute.

A dot matrix printer is concerned with a single character at a time. The laser printers compose, then print, a whole page at a time. With a PDL, many different fonts, sizes of type, and graphics can be printed. However, because the laser must determine where every dot that makes up a character, or image, is to be placed on the paper before it is printed, the more complex the page, the more memory it will require and the more time needed to compose the page. It might take several minutes to compose a complex graphics. Once composed, it will print out very quickly.

A PDL controls and tells the laser where to place the dots on the sheet. Adobe's PostScript is the best known PDL.

## Resolution

Most lasers now print 600 x 600 dots per inch (DPI) resolution, which is very good. However, it is not nearly as good as 1200 x 1200 DPI used for typeset in standard publications. The LaserMaster has models that can print at 1200 x 1200 and some that go as high as 1800 DPI. They also have upgrade kits for the HP LaserJet III and LaserJet 4 that can increase the resolution to 1200 DPI. Call LaserMaster at 800-327-8946 for details and brochures.

Most lasers print in the 8.5" by 11" A size format. CalComp (714-821-2000), a division of Lockheed, has developed a 600 x 600 high-resolution laser that can print in the 8.5" × 17" B size format. QMS, Xerox, and several other companies have also developed large-format printers.

## Maintenance

Most of the lasers use a toner cartridge that is good for 3000 to 5000 pages. The cost of an original cartridge is about $75. Several small companies are now refilling the spent cartridges for about $30 each. It might be a good idea to keep an extra cartridge as a spare. The toner cartridge is sealed, so it will last for some time on the shelf. I had a cartridge go out on a weekend when I was working on a tight deadline. Most stores that sell cartridges were closed. Since then I've kept a spare on hand.

Most laser printers keep track of the number of sheets that have been printed. If you have a HP LaserJet, you can use the front panel buttons to run a self test. This tells you the configuration, how much RAM is installed, font cartridges installed, type of paper tray, how many pages have been printed, and other information.

When the toner gets low, most lasers will display a warning message in the digital readout window. Also, if the print is very light, the toner might be low. If you remove the toner cartridge and turn it upside down and shake it vigorously, you sometimes can get a few more copies out of it. This might help until you can get a replacement.

Of course, there are other maintenance costs. Because these machines are very similar to the copy machines, they have a lot of moving parts that can wear out and jam up. Most of the larger companies give a mean time between failures (MTBF) of 30,000 up to 100,000 pages. However, remember that these are only average figures and not guarantees. Most of the lasers are expected to have an overall lifetime of about 300,000 pages.

## Paper

There are many different types and weights of paper. Almost any paper will work in your laser. However, if you use cheap paper in your laser, it could leave lint inside the machine and cause problems in print quality. Generally speaking, any bond paper or a good paper made for copiers will work fine. Colored paper made for copiers will also work fine.

Some companies are marking copier paper with the word "Laser" and charging more for it. The lasers will accept paper from 18 pound up to 24 pound easily. I have even used 67 pound stock for making up my own business cards. It is a bit heavy for wrapping around the drums, and it jams once in a while. Some lasers use a straight through path, so the heavier paper should not cause any problems in these machines.

Many of the laser printers are equipped with trays to print envelopes. Hewlett-Packard recommends envelopes with diagonal seams and gummed flaps. Make certain that the leading edge of the envelope has a sharp crease.

## Labels

The Avery Company (818-858-8245) and a few other companies make address labels that can withstand the heat of the fusing mechanism of the laser. There are also other specialty supplies that can be used with your laser. The Integraphix Company (800-421-2515) carries several different items that you might find useful. Call them for a catalog.

Here are some other companies that make small special printers for labels:

Brother International P-Touch PC     800-284-4357
CoStar LabelWriter                   800-426-7827
Seiko Instruments Smart Label        800-688-0817

# Color "laser" printers

There are several color printers that are available. They can cost from less than $1000 up to $15,000. These printers are often referred to as *laser color printers*; however, at this time, only a few actually use the laser technology.

The other companies use a variety of thermal transfer technologies using wax or rolls of plastic polymer. The wax or plastic is brought into contact with the paper, then heat is applied. The melted wax or plastic material then adheres to the paper. Very precise points, up to 300 dots per inch, can be heated. By overlaying three or four colors, all of the colors of the rainbow can be created.

The Fargo Electronics Company offers a color printer for less than $1000. Of course, it does not have all of the goodies that you would find on the Tektronix Phaser or the CalComp ColorMaster.

Another type of color printer uses dye-sublimation, also called *thermal dye transfer* or *dye diffusion*. These systems use a ribbon with continuous series of four different color ink stripes across the ribbon. The paper that is to be printed is forced against the ink ribbon. Dots of heat are applied to the various colors, which causes the color to diffuse onto the paper. The higher the temperature, the more color that can be diffused. The dots of heat can be accurately controlled for up to 256 different shades for each color.

The dye-sublimation printers provide the best resolution and can provide prints that are near photographic quality. However, as you might suppose, these printers are also the most expensive. Again, the least expensive dye-sublimation printer is the Fargo.

There are several companies who now make digital cameras. The photos taken with these cameras can be downloaded directly onto a hard disk and viewed on the monitor. However, what if you wanted a copy of a photo for an album or to sit on your desk? Fargo Electronics has developed the FotoFUN, which is a small personal color printer that uses the thermal dye-sublimation technology. See the section "Color photo printers" for more information.

The QMS ColorScript Laser 1000 was one of the first true laser color printers. It blends four different color toners—black, cyan, magenta, and yellow—to print out color. The drum is sensitized for each color, and that color toner is transferred to it. Once all of the colors are applied to the drum, it then prints out on ordinary paper or on transparencies. The QMS ColorScript is still rather expensive.

The Hewlett-Packard LaserJet 5M was introduced a couple of years after the QMS. Basically, the technology is about the same as the QMS, but it is a bit less expensive.

The Xerox Corp. also has a true laser color printer. Call them for a brochure and pricing information.

Most of the color printers have PostScript, or they emulate PostScript. The Tektronix Phaser CP can also use the Hewlett-Packard Graphics Language (HPGL) to emulate a plotter. These color printers can print out a page much faster than a plotter.

One disadvantage of the color printers is the cost. Thermal wax can cost up to 45¢ per page, dye-sublimation can cost up to $2.75 per page. Most of this cost is for the ribbons and wax rolls that are used by the color machines.

The color printers are rather slow, but the technology is improving. There will be several other color printers on the market soon. There is a lot of competition, so the prices are coming down.

Here are just a few of the companies who have color printers:

| | |
|---|---|
| CalComp, Lockheed | 800-932-1212 |
| Fargo Electronics | 800-258-2974 |
| General Parametrics | 800-223-0999 |
| Hewlett-Packard | 800-257-3783 |
| QMS | 800-523-2696 |
| Tektronix | 800-835-6100 |
| GCC Technologies | 800-422-7777 |
| Kodak | 800-344-0006 |
| Xerox | 800-248-6550 |

General Parametrics has a desktop film recorder attachment for their printer. This allows one to make 35mm color slides for presentations. Some of the other companies also provide features such as this. Call them for a brochure.

# Multifunction machines

There are many times in a small office or home office (SOHO) when you might need to make one or more copies or to scan something. A large office can afford to have high-end copiers, scanners, plain paper fax machines, and printers; however, each of these items is rather expensive, and if not used very often, the cost cannot be justified. Besides, in a SOHO, especially one like mine, there just isn't room for all of these separate machines.

Several companies have noted the fact that most of these machines have a lot in common. There are now many multifunction machines that can copy, scan, fax, and print. Most of them are fairly reasonable in cost when you consider what they can do. Another big plus is that this four-in-one machine takes up very little space.

Many of the machines come with several software packages such as document management that can help you organize scanned data. Some of them come with business card readers and organizers, with OCR software and faxing software.

Many of the multifunction machines print and copy in black and white only. Here are few:

| | |
|---|---|
| Canon MultiPASS 1000 | 800-828-4040 |
| Epson Personal Document Station | 800-289-3766 |
| Hewlett-Packard OfficeJet LX | 800-752-0900 |
| Lexmark Medley 4x | 800-358-5835 |
| Xerox Document WorkCenter 250 | 800-832-6979 |

All of these machines use inkjet technology. Brother International (800-284-4357) has a multifunction laser machine: model MFC-4500ML. The Panasonic Company (201-348-9090) also has a laser multifunction unit: model KX-SP100. Of course, the laser provides a bit better resolution than the inkjet. It is comparably priced to the inkjet machines.

There are a few that can print and copy in color, such as the Scanpaq Color Scan FX (800-335-5533). It has high resolution 24-bit true color and comes bundled with several software packages.

The Hewlett-Packard CopyJet is a high-end color copier/printer combination. It has a flatbed glass panel surface that is similar to standard copy machines and can copy originals up to 8.5" by 14". It also has the ability to reduce the size of the originals. It provides 300 x 300 DPI full feature color copies. The printer part of the combination is Hewlett-Packard's 1200c, which provides good color resolution. It would have been great if they had added a scanner and fax to this machine.

# Color photo printers

Digital cameras are now becoming quite reasonable in cost, and many people are buying them. The photos taken with these cameras can be downloaded directly onto a hard disk and viewed on the monitor. However, what if you wanted a copy of a photo for an album or to sit on your desk?

Fargo Electronics (800-327-4622) has developed the FotoFUN, which is a small personal color printer that uses the thermal dye-sublimation technology. It can print 4 x 6 photos, post cards, or even use a transfer system to put a photo on a coffee mug.

The photos are very near to the photo quality of film. At the present time, the FotoFUN printer costs $399. However, you will need separate kits for print film, postcards, or FotoMug. The print film kits cost $35.95 for 36 prints. A kit for 36 postcards costs $39.95, and a kit for four FotoMugs costs $29.95. The prices might be different by the time you read this. They are listed to give you an idea of what it costs for color printing.

Nikon Electronic has developed a dye sublimation color photo printer that they call the Coolprint. It also is limited to about 4 × 6 prints. It is much more expensive than the Fargo at about $2000.

# Plotters

Plotters can draw almost any two-dimensional shape or design under the control of a computer. The plotters are a bit like a robot. An arm selects a pen. The pen can be moved from side to side, while at the same time the sheet of paper can be moved from top to bottom. The computer can direct the pen to any point across the paper and can move the paper up or down for any point on an X-Y axis.

The motors are controlled by predefined X-Y coordinates. They can move the pen and paper in very small increments so that almost any design can be traced out.

Values can be assigned of perhaps 1 to 1000 for the Y elements and the same values for the X or horizontal elements. The computer can then direct the plotter to move the pen to any point or coordinate on the sheet. Some of the newer plotters use inkjet technology instead of pens. This makes them faster. The different colored ink cartridges can be activated much quicker than moving an arm to a rack, selecting a pen, then replacing it and selecting another.

Some less expensive plotters use a thermal paper such as that used by fax machines. An advantage is that they can be much faster than the pen plotters. Two disadvantages are that this system does not provide any color and the resolution might not be very good. The thermal paper also fades when exposed to light.

Plotters are ideal for such things as printing out circuit board designs, architectural drawings, graphs, charts, and many CAD/CAM drawings and for making transparencies for overhead presentations. All of this can be done in many different colors. The different colors can be very helpful if you have a complex drawing such as a multilayered motherboard. A different color could be used for each layer.

A plotter can have from one up to eight or more different colored pens. There are several different types of pens for various applications, such as writing on different types of paper or on film or transparencies. Some pens are quite similar to ballpoint pens; others have a fiber type point. The points are usually made to a very close tolerance and can be very small so that the thickness of the lines can be controlled. The line thicknesses can be very critical in some precise design drawings. The plotter arm can be directed to choose any one of the various pens.

There are several different sized plotters. Some desktop units are limited to only A- and B-sized plots. There are other large floor models that can accept paper as large as 4' wide and several feet long. Many of the floor models are similar to the wide-format CalComp inkjet printer/plotter shown in Fig. 12-4.

There are many very good graphics and Computer Aided Design (CAD) programs available that can use plotters.

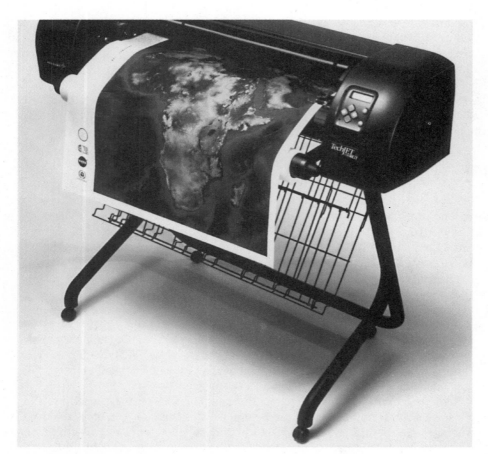

**Fig. 12-4** A CalComp wide-format inkjet color plotter and printer.

One of the disadvantages of the early plotters was that they were rather slow. There are now some software programs that allow laser printers to act as plotters. Of course, they are much faster than a plotter; however, except for the colored printers, they are limited to black and white. Most of the laser printers are also limited to the A size, or 8.5" × 11".

Here are a few of the plotter manufacturers. Call them for a product list and latest prices:

| | |
|---|---|
| Alpha Merics | 818-999-5580 |
| Bruning Computer | 415-372-7568 |
| CalComp | 800-225-2667 |
| Hewlett-Packard | 800-367-4772 |
| Houston Instrument | 512-835-0900 |
| Ioline Corp. | 206-775-7861 |
| Roland DG | 213-685-5141 |

# Printer and plotter supplies

It is important that a good supply of toner cartridges, plotter pens, special paper, film, and other supplies be kept on hand. Plotter supplies are not as widely available as printer supplies. A very high-priced plotter might have to sit idle for some time if the supplies are not on hand.  Most of the plotter vendors provide supplies for their equipment. One company that specializes in plotter pens, plotter media, accessories and supplies is the Plotpro Company (800-223-7568). Another company that has all kinds of printer, plotter, and office supplies is the Numeridex Company (800-323-7737). Call these companies for a current catalog.

# Installing a printer or plotter

Most IBM-compatible computers allow for four ports: two serial and two parallel. No matter whether it is a plotter, dot matrix, or laser printer, it will require one of these ports. Most printers use the parallel port LPT1; most plotters use a serial port. Some printers have both serial and parallel connections.

If the serial port is used, the printer can be up to 50' from the computer. If the parallel is used, normally the cable can only be about 10'. There are special devices that will allow longer cables to be used. The serial printers use a RS232C connector. The parallel printers use a Centronics type connector. When you buy your printer, buy a cable from the vendor that is configured for your printer and your computer.

# Printer sharing

Ordinarily a printer will sit idle most of the time. There are some days when I don't even turn my printer on. There are usually several computers in most large offices and businesses. Almost all of them are connected to a printer in some fashion. It would be a terrible waste of money if each computer had a separate printer that was only used occasionally. It is fairly simple to make arrangements so that a printer or plotter can be used by several computers.

### Sneaker net

One of the least expensive methods of sharing a printer is for the person to generate the text to be printed out on one computer, record it on a floppy diskette, then walk over to a computer that is connected to a printer. If it is in a large office, a single low-cost XT or 286 clone could be dedicated to running a high-priced laser printer.

It doesn't matter whether the person carrying the floppy disk is wearing sneakers, brogans, or wing tips, the sneaker net is still one of the least expensive methods of sharing printers.

### Switch box

If there are only two or three computers and they are fairly close together, you can use a simple switch box to switch between the computers. If you use a simple switch box and the computers use the standard parallel ports, the cables from the computers to the printer should be no more than 10' long. Parallel signals will begin to degrade if the cable is longer than 10', which could cause some loss of data. A serial cable can be as long as 50'.

If an office or business is fairly complex, then there are several electronic switching devices available. Some of them are very sophisticated and can allow a large number of different types of computers to be attached to a single printer or plotter. Many of them have built-in buffers and amplifiers that can allow cable lengths up to 250' or more.

### Printer sharing device sources

Here are a few of the companies that provide switch systems. Call them for their product specs and current price list:

| | |
|---|---|
| Altek Corp. | 301-572-2555 |
| Arnet Corp. | 615-834-8000 |
| Belkin Components | 310-515-7585 |
| Black Box Corp. | 412-746-5530 |
| Buffalo Products | 800-345-2356 |
| Crosspoint Systems | 800-232-7729 |
| Digital Products | 800-243-2333 |
| Fifth Generation | 800-225-2775 |
| Server Technology | 800-835-1515 |
| Quadram | 404-564-5566 |
| Rose Electronics | 713-933-7673 |
| Western Telematic | 800-854-7226 |

# Wireless connections

Many of the Pentium Pro motherboards now have an infrared (IrDA) built-in port. The IrDA systems are similar to TV remote controls. The IrDA ports can be used to connect keyboards, notebook computers, and printers. The JetEye from Extended Systems Company (800-235-7576) is two small devices: one plugs into the parallel printer port on the computer and the other plugs into the printer connector.

The Merrit Computer Products Company (800-627-7752) has a wireless printer sharing kit. Instead of IrDA, it uses a radio frequency. The system can support up to 16 computers and 4 printers.

# Network printers

Almost any printer can be attached to a network and called a network printer; however, several companies make fast, high-end, heavy-duty laser printers specifically for networks. The prices can range from $3000 up to $30,000. Many of the printers come bundled with special network printer management software and internal network interfaces. The print speed can range from 12 pages per minute (ppm) up to 32 ppm. Some of them are capable of duplex printing, or printing on both sides of the paper. The resolution can be from 300 dots per inch (DPI) up to

1200 DPI. They might come with several different page description languages (PDLs), such as PostScript, Hewlett-Packard HPGL, Intellifont, or True Image. They can have a paper tray that can hold as many as 3000 sheets.

Here are some of the companies:

| | |
|---|---|
| Dataproducts Corp. | 800-980-0374 |
| Digital Equipment Corp. | 800-777-4343 |
| Hewlett-Packard | 800-752-0900 |
| Kyocera Electronics | 800-232-6797 |
| Lexmark International | 800-891-0331 |
| QMS Inc. | 800-523-2696 |
| Xerox Corp. | 800-349-3769 |

Call the companies for more information.

## Green printers

The entire industry is under pressure to produce energy-conservation products. The federal government will no longer buy computer products that do not meet Energy Star standards. Printers, especially laser printers, are notorious for being energy hogs. Hewlett-Packard and most of the other manufacturers are designing newer models that go into a "sleep mode" after a period of inactivity. Ordinarily, it takes from 20 to 30 seconds for a printer to warm up. Some of these models maintain a low-voltage input so that they can warm up almost instantly.

For those people with older printers, they can purchase a *PC ener-g saver* from the NEI Company (800-832-4007). See Fig. 12-5. The printer, monitor, and keyboard can be plugged into this unit. After a period of inactivity from the keyboard, the printer and monitor shut down. You can choose and set whatever length of inactive period that you desire by software. The printer and the monitor can be set for different times. To reactivate the monitor, just press any key. To reactivate the printer, just send a print request.

The PC ener-g saver can pay for itself many times over in saved electricity bills. Besides, you will be doing your part for energy conservation. Call the companies for brochures and details.

## Progress

If Gutenberg were around today, you can bet that he would be quite pleased with the progress that has been made in the printing business. We have come a long way since 1436.

**Fig. 12-5** The PC ener-g saver that can turn off the printer and monitor during periods of inactivity.

# 13
# CD-ROM

Today, a CD-ROM drive is an essential part of your computer. Almost every computer sold within the next year will have a CD-ROM as standard equipment. It has become almost as necessary as a hard disk drive.

A CD-ROM offers some very important benefits to the individual end user for entertainment, education, business, and industry. There are thousands of CD-ROM disc titles that cover just about every subject imaginable that are available.

## CD-ROM titles

A short time ago, CD-ROM disc titles were very expensive. However, every day, there is more competition. There are just too many titles to even try to review them in a book like this. There are several CD-ROM and PC magazines that can help you be aware of what is available. Here are just a few:

| | |
|---|---|
| *CD-ROM Today* | 415-696-1688 |
| *CD-ROM Power* | 800-328-6719 |
| *CD-ROM Multimedia* | 800-565-4623 |
| *New Media* | 415-573-5170 |
| *Mr. CD-ROM* (Catalog) | 800-444-6723 |

Because of the thousands of companies that are producing CD-ROM titles, the enormous amount of competition is forcing the prices down. Some CD-ROM titles that cost as much as $100 a few months ago can now be bought for as little as $5 to $10. The prices are still going down. It is great for us the consumers.

### Home entertainment

A large number of CD-ROM titles are designed for entertainment for both young and old. There are titles for arcade-type games and chess and other board games. There are titles for music, opera, art, and a large variety of other subjects to entertain you. Many of the titles are both educational as well as entertaining.

## Digital videodisc

It takes a tremendous amount of memory to store digital images. Just one digitized frame of a movie can require over 25MB to store. At this rate, you could only store a few seconds of a movie on a standard CD-ROM disc. However, it is possible to store up to 3 hours of movies on the digital videodisc (DVD) systems. The discs for this system will be the same size as the present CD-ROM discs; however, instead of 650MB, the new disc will be able to store 4.7GB. Eventually, the discs will be able to store up to 17GB.

Besides being able to store complete movies, the new system will be great for business use. There is always the need for more information. However, chances are that, even with 4.7GB of data, what you are looking for will be stored on some other disc. Several companies have developed systems that can have four or more discs loaded in the drive. If what you want is on another disc, it can easily and quickly switch to that disc. These companies should be able to do the same with the DVD system.

The DVD system will be able to read all of our present CD-ROM discs, but our present CD-ROM drives will not be able to read the new DVD discs.

## Home library

At the present time, only one side of the CD-ROM discs are used for recording, but this single side can hold over 650MB of data. You can have a multitude of different programs on a single CD-ROM disc and a world of information at your fingertips. More books and information can be stored on just a few CD-ROM discs than you might find in an entire library. A 21-volume encyclopedia can be stored in just a fraction of the space on one side of a single CD-ROM disc. When data compression is used to store text, several hundred books can be stored on a single disc.

It might take only seconds to search through an entire encyclopedia or through several hundred books to find a subject, sentence, or a single word.

## Easier way to learn

Text, graphics, sound, animation, and movies can be stored on CD-ROM discs. We have several avenues to the brain. The more avenues used to input information to our brain, the easier it is to learn and to remember. We can learn by reading; however, we can learn much better if sound is added to the text. We have all heard the old saying that a picture is worth a thousand words. It is so very true. We learn much better and retain more if graphics and motion are added. Rather than trying to remember just dry text, the many advantages of CD-ROM can make learning fun and pleasurable. Schools can use CD-ROM for teaching; businesses can use CD-ROM to train their personnel.

## Lawyers

Lawyers might have to spend hours and hours going through law books to find precedents, some of the finer points of the law, or loopholes. A few CD-ROM discs could replace several law clerks.

## Health and medicine

The human body is a fantastic machine. There is more written about medicine and computers than any other subject. There are several CD-ROMs published for the home user, such as the Family Doctor, published by Creative Multimedia Corp. (503-241-4351); the Mayo Clinic Family Health Book, published by Interactive Ventures (507-282-2076); and several others.

A doctor must keep abreast of all of the scientific advances and new drugs and treatments. A busy doctor can't possibly read all of the published papers. A CD-ROM can help. *The American Family Physician* is the official journal of the American Academy of Family Physicians. It is available from the Bureau of Electronic Publishing at 800-828-4766.

The A.D.A.M. (for Animated Dissection of Anatomy for Medicine) Software Company (800-755-2326) has developed several discs that show the various parts of the anatomy, both male and female. This CD-ROM is very good for students and families to learn about the human body. If you are a bit prudish, you are given an option to cover certain parts of the anatomy with fig leaves.

# How CD-ROMs work

CD-ROM is an acronym for *Compact Disc-Read Only Memory*. The system was first developed by Sony and Philips using lasers for recording and playing back music. (LASER is an acronym for *Light Amplification by Stimulated Emission of Radiation*.) Almost all CD-ROM drives can also play the music compact discs. Most of the drives have a plug for earphones and an audio connector on the back so that it can be plugged into a sound card. You can set up a very good hi-fi system using a CD-ROM and a computer. Basically, the music compact disc systems are quite similar to the CD-ROM systems, but the CD-ROM drives are usually more expensive.

When a CD-ROM disc is created, a powerful laser is turned on and off in response to data (0s and 1s). The laser burns holes in the disc material. When the beam is switched on to create a hole, it is called a *pit*; when left off, the area of the track is called a *land*. When played back, a laser beam is focused on the track. The pits do not reflect as much light as the lands so it is easy to distinguish the digital data.

## High Sierra/ISO 9660

The Philips and Sony companies developed the audio CD in 1982. It wasn't long before the importance of the technology was recognized and adopted for CD-ROMs.

It was a fast growing technology, but there were no standards. Every company wants to make their products a bit different, so there were several different formats. In 1985, a group of industry leaders, including Microsoft, met at a hotel in Lake Tahoe to hammer a set of standards. The standard that they devised defined the table of contents and directory structure. It also defined the logical, file, and record structures. Microsoft provided their Microsoft Compact Disc Extensions (MSCDEX) software, a driver that allows DOS to access the CD-ROM through conventional DOS commands. All CD-ROMs used in PCs use the Microsoft MSCDEX driver.

There were several other specifications adopted at this meeting. Because they were meeting at Tahoe, which is in the Sierra Mountain range, they called the new standard the *High Sierra Specification*. The specification was later adopted, with minor modifications, by the International Organization for Standards as *ISO 9660*. Unless otherwise stated, most all CD-ROM drives and discs conform to the ISO 9660.

Besides the standards set forth in ISO 9660, several other standard specifications have been developed. There are thousands of pages of specifications in each of four books. Some of the books are more than a foot thick. The specifications were originally issued in books with different colors. The standards have been named for the color of the original book:

- The *Red Book* sets forth the standards for audio or compact disc digital audio (CD-DA).
- The *Yellow Book* sets forth the ISO 9660 standards for storing files that can be translated to DOS, Apple, or Amiga files. The Microsoft MSCDEX drivers are used to accomplish the translation. Of course, every time someone uses the MSCDEX drivers, they are making Bill Gates a little bit richer.
- The *Green Book* covers CD-Interactive (CD-I) and CD-ROM extended architecture (CD-ROM/XA).
- The *Orange Book* covers write-once read-many (WORM) drives and magneto-optic (MO) drives. It also covers the multi-session Photo CD drives.

Sometimes a disc will have specifications from two or more books. For example, if the disc contains text, audio, and graphics, it might conform to specifications from the Red Book, the Yellow Book, and the Green Book.

## How the discs are made

Data that is to be stored on a CD-ROM disc is usually assembled and organized, then copied onto a large-capacity hard disk. The data can be copied onto the large hard disk from floppies, hard disks, tape, or almost any medium. A table of contents, an index, and error-detection and -correction and retrieval software are usually added to the data.

A *One-off* disc can be made from the organized data. A CD-ROM recorder similar to the Philips CCD 521 can be used to make this first test disc. The disc can be tested and tried. If it meets the client's specifications, then the data will be laser etched onto a glass master disc. All of the duplications will come from this disc.

All CD-ROM discs are pressed much like the vinyl phonograph records. However, a disc that is pressed from the original master would be a mirror image of it. The pits and the lands on the copy would be just the reverse of those on the master. To make it identical to the master a copy of a copy is made. The pits and lands are then in the proper order.

The first copy of the master is called a *mother*. A working copy of the mother is made, which is called the *father*. *Virgin* blank discs are pressed against the father to make all of the commercial discs.

The blank discs are 120 millimeters, about 4.75", in diameter and are made from a polycarbonate plastic. Each blank disc costs less than $1.

After being pressed, the discs are coated with reflective aluminum. This coating is 1 micron thick. The discs are then coated with a thin layer of lacquer to prevent oxidation and contamination. The same process is used for both audio compact discs and CD-ROM discs.

## Laser color

As you know, white light encompasses all of the colors of the rainbow. Each color has its own frequency of vibration. The slower frequencies are at the dark red end; the frequencies increase as the colors move toward the violet end.

The particles that make up ordinary light are incoherent; that is, they are scattered in all directions. Lasers are possible because a single color of light can be sharply focused and amplified. All of the particles of one color are lined up in an orderly coherent fashion.

The laser effect can be obtained from several different gases and materials. Most of the present CD-ROM lasers use light at the lower-frequency dark end of the spectrum, such as the red or yellow. The Samsung Company has developed a green laser that has a shorter wave length and higher frequency. They claim that, by using this laser and their proprietary compression techniques, they can store up to 110 minutes of the MPEG 2 video on a disc, which is five times as much as usual. (MPEG is an acronym for *Moving Pictures Experts Group*, who developed a set of methods for video compression.)

An experimental blue laser has also been developed. It will have an even higher frequency than a green laser. At the time of this writing, neither the green or the blue have been incorporated into available units.

A hard disk might have several thousand separate concentric tracks with each track divided into several sectors. Usually each sector can store 512 bytes. A CD-ROM disc has a single spiral track that begins in the center and winds out to the outer edge. The track is similar to the groove on a phonograph record except that the groove on a phonograph record begins on the outer edge and winds to the center. The long spiral track of a CD-ROM disc is divided into about 270,000 sectors, each sector with 2048 bytes. The sectors are numbered and given addresses according to the time in minutes, seconds, and hundredths of a second. For example, the first sector is 00:00:00, and the second sector is 00:00:01.

Remember that the hard disk has a head actuator motor that moves the head to the various concentric tracks. The CD-ROM has a similar small motor that moves the laser beam to whatever sector on the spiral track that is to be read. Figure 13-1 shows a CD-ROM drive with the cover removed. The round object in the center is the spindle from the main motor that spins the disc. At the right is the white laser head assembly. This assembly has a small motor that moves it back and forth in the slot to read the various sectors of the track.

## Rotational speed

If you remember your high school physics, the speed of a spinning disk or object will be greater near the center than on the outer edge. If we took a track at the 2" diameter of the disk and stretched it out it would measure a little over 6" long. (Pi × D = circumference, so $3.1459 \times 2" = 6.28"$.) On the same disk, if a track at the 4" diameter is stretched out, it would measure over 12 inches long. At a constant speed, it is easy to see that an inner track passes beneath the head in about half the time that it takes for an outer track to pass beneath the head.

**Fig. 13-1** A CD-ROM drive with the cover removed. The object in the center is the spindle. The round white object in the slot is the laser head assembly. An actuator motor moves the laser head in the slot to read whatever sector on the track that is requested.

The CD-ROM uses a system that constantly changes the speed of the drive. The drive electronics speeds the disc up or slows it down depending on what area of the disk it is reading. When reading the inner portion, the original 1X drive spins at about 200 RPM. When reading the outer portion, it spins at about 530 RPM. This is called constant linear velocity (CLV).

The double-speed (2X) CD-ROMs rotate at 400 RPM near the center and at 1060 RPM on the outer edge. The quad-speed drives double these figures again from 800 to over 2000 RPM, 6X drives range from 1200 to over 3000 RPM, and 8X drives range from 1600 to over 4000 RPM. At 4000 RPM, there can be quite a bit of vibration from the spindle motor. The plastic disc is somewhat flexible. At the higher speeds, a slight imbalance can cause the spinning disc to wobble and vibrate. Even placing the label improperly on the disc can cause an imbalance at the high speed. This can cause errors in reading the small pits and lands. Unless these problems can be overcome, 8X is probably the fastest CD-ROM drive that will ever be made.

The 1X speed drives are as obsolete as the 350K floppy drives. Even the 2X is very nearly dead. I have seen double-speed drives for sale for as little as $35. Just a short time ago, the double-speed drives were selling for over $400. For some purposes, a 2X speed might be all you need. Quad-speed drives are very reasonable now; however, for just a bit more money, you can get a 6X speed drive.

Here are a few companies who make CD-ROM drives. In many cases, they make both 4X and 6X drives (Diamond makes an 8X drive):

| Diamond | 800-468-5846 |
| NEC | 800-632-4636 |
| Panasonic | 800-742-8086 |
| Pioneer | 800-444-6784 |
| Plextor | 800-886-3935 |
| Samsung | 800-726-7864 |
| Sony | 800-352-7669 |
| TEAC | 800-888-4293 |
| Toshiba | 800-678-4373 |
| UMAX | 800-562-0311 |

Call these companies for brochures and spec sheets.

## Transfer speed

The transfer speed, or the amount of time that it takes to read a track, on the original 1X CD-ROMs and all of the audio CDs was 75 sectors per second. A sector is 2048 bytes (2K), so the transfer speed was equal to 150K per second (75 × 2K).

Doubling the speed of the 1X drive doubled the transfer rate to 300K bytes per second. A quad-speed drive will transfer data at 600K/S; the 6X drives can transfer data at 900K/S. The faster transfer times allows video and motion to be displayed in a smooth fashion. The faster drives can read all of the CD-ROM discs that the slower drives can read, but read them faster.

The audio files must still be played back at the 150K rate. When playing audio, the speed must drop down to the original speed of 200 to 530 RPMs.

## Data buffers

The faster drives usually have a fairly large buffer system that also helps to smooth out video and motion and speed up the transfer rate. The buffer memory is located on chips on the drive. The firmware (software embedded on chips) portion of the buffer system decides what information will be used most often and stores it in the buffer. For example, the contents of the disk directory might be stored in the buffer.

Many of the newer drive systems have from 128K up to 2MB of DRAM for cache memory buffers.

## Access or seek time

The access or seek time is the time necessary to move the laser head to find a certain block or sector on the spiral track and begin reading it. The original MPC specification was that the drive should be able to find any block in 1000 milliseconds (ms), or 1 second. Most of the older drives had access times of 300 to 400 ms. Most of the newer machines now have an access time of 100 to 250 ms.

Generally speaking, the transfer rate or speed is more important than the access speed.

# CD-ROM differences

There are several different types of CD-ROM drives. Some mount internally, some are external, some use SCSI for an interface, and some use an enhanced IDE interface. Of course, there also are the various speeds. There are also a lot of different prices. The external drives can cost up to $100 more than an internal because they need a power supply and cables.

What you should buy will depend on what your needs are.

## Interface systems

Some of the earlier systems had their own proprietary interface. Often the interface was built-in on sound cards. Almost all drives today are either SCSI or EIDE. The EIDE interface is built-in on many of the Pentium Pro motherboards. If your EIDE interface is not built-in or you are buying an SCSI drive, the interface card and cable might not be included in the price of the system. Read the ads carefully if you are buying by mail order.

The interface card will be plugged into one of the bus slots. Before plugging the card in, make sure that any jumpers or switches on the board are set properly. The board must be configured so that it does not conflict with the address or interrupt (IRQ) of any of your other devices. Check your documentation.

(*Note:* Always turn your computer off before unplugging or changing the settings of any card. Never plug in or unplug a card, cable, or device while the power is on.)

If your system does not conform to the Plug-and-Play (PnP) specification, a CD-ROM drive interface can be difficult to set up and configure. It must be set to a specific IRQ and memory address location. If the board conflicts with any other device in your system, it will not work.

### Enhanced IDE interfaces

The Enhanced IDE (EIDE) interface can handle up to four devices. This can be any combination of EIDE hard drives, EIDE CD-ROMs, or EIDE backup tape drives. The IDE CD-ROM systems are considerably less expensive than the SCSI.

Your motherboard will probably have a built-in EIDE interface. If not, you will have to buy one. They are fairly inexpensive and can cost from $20 to $60.

The interface can be plugged into any one of the 16-bit ISA slots. Remember that the ISA system operates at 8MHz to 10MHz. For high-end work, you might want to buy an PCI IDE interface, which would be considerably faster and, of course, more expensive. IDE CD-ROM drives can cost from $50 to $100 less than an equivalent SCSI CD-ROM drive.

### SCSI interfaces

More companies are now manufacturing drives for the SCSI interface. If you have other SCSI products, such as a SCSI hard drive or tape backup, you already have an interface card. The SCSI interface cards can drive up to seven different devices. It is amazing how quickly the slots get used up. The SCSI can save having to install a separate interface for up to seven different devices. Most SCSI devices have two connectors: one for the input cable and an identical connector for the next item.

There are also several sound boards that have SCSI interfaces built-in, such as the Diamond Sonic Sound and the Adaptec Audio Machine. Not all SCSI interfaces are the same. Some of them are made for special-purpose SCSI devices and might not be able to completely control a hard disk. The Adaptec Audio Machine has complete control functions for hard disks and most other SCSI devices.

If you don't already have a SCSI interface, you might have to pay $100 to $200 extra for the interface. Again, these interfaces would plug into the 16-bit ISA slots and operate at 8MHz to 10MHz. If you are doing high-end work, you might want to buy a faster and more expensive PCI SCSI interface.

## Multidisc systems

Even though you have over 600MB on a disc, there will be many times when it doesn't have the programs or information that you need at the moment. For example, I have a telephone directory of the whole country on five discs from PhoneDisc (800-284-8353). Each disc covers a certain section of the country. Ordinarily, to change discs, you have to eject the disc, unload the caddy, and put the new disc in.

To solve this type of problem, several companies have developed multidisc systems. The MultiSpin 4x4 from NEC (800-632-4636) can hold four discs. The 4X drive is rather inexpensive and fits in the same half-height space as a standard drive. The DRM 624X from Pioneer (800-444-6784) can hold six discs and is fairly reasonable in cost. Alps Electric (800-825-2577) has a multidisc changer that can hold four discs. The CDJ 7004 changer from the Smart & Friendly Company (800-959-7001) can hold seven discs.

There will probably be more companies that offer multidisc systems by the time you read this.

## Multidrive systems

There are several companies that manufacture multidrive systems for network servers and other high-end users. Of course, anything that is high-end is usually highly expensive. They can have 4 to 14 drives or more and can cost from $2000 up to $18,000 or more.

Here are some of the companies who offer multidrive systems:

| | |
|---|---|
| JVC | 800-828-1582 |
| Logicraft | 800-308-8750 |
| Meridian | 800-755-8324 |
| Microtest | 800-526-9675 |
| SciNet | 800-653-1010 |
| TAC HotSwap | 205-721-1976 |
| Plasmon Data | 408-956-9400 |

JVC has several changers and network devices. Their CL-100 CD-Library gives you access to 100 different discs. The NSM Mercury Jukebox (800-238-4676) gives you access of up to 150 discs.

## Build your own multidrive/multidisc system

You can build your own system and save a bundle. The cost of CD-ROM drives is coming down every day. Some of the multidisc drives are selling for just a little more than $300. (Prices quoted are for comparison only and will probably be less by the time you read this.) With an enhanced IDE interface, you can install up to four multidisc drives, or up to 7 or more with a SCSI interface. You would need a tower case with several bays. You can put together a system with three or four of the multidisc drives for a whole lot less than $18,000 or even less than $2000.

## Caddies

Some of the CD-ROM drives just have a tray to hold the disc. You push a button, the tray comes out, and you drop the disc in with the label facing up and push the tray back in.

You should be very careful in handling the discs to prevent fingerprints, scratches, or other damage to the bright side of the disc.

Some of the CD-ROM drives use a caddy to hold the disc. The caddy has a clear plastic hinged cover. The caddy encloses the disc and protects it from dirt and dust and unnecessary handling. When the caddy is inserted into the drive, a metal sliding door moves to one side for the head access. It is similar to the 3.5" floppies. If your CD-ROM drive uses a caddy, you can buy several caddies, load them up, and not have to handle the discs thereafter. The caddies cost about $3 each and are available from several places. Look in the computer magazines. Figure 13-2 shows a caddy.

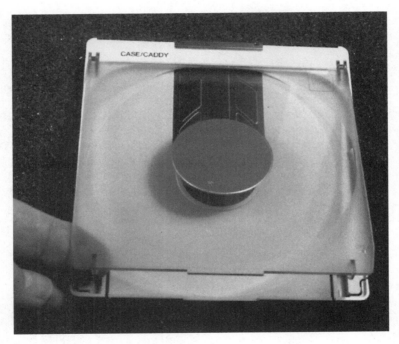

**Fig. 13-2**  A CD-ROM disc caddy.

## CD-ROM recorders (CD-R)

There are several companies that are now manufacturing CD-ROM recorders. When they were first introduced, they were very expensive at around $10,000 for a system. Some companies are now offering the CD-recorders for less than $1000. The blank discs cost from $5 to $20 at this time.

In 1989, Taiyo Yuden of Japan developed an organic dye that could be combined with a reflective gold plating on a blank disc. A laser could then be used to burn pits in the disc, and it would have the same qualities of a standard CD-ROM disc. In addition, this disc offered the capability of multisession; that is, data can be added from time to time. When a disc is stamped out at a factory, nothing further can be added. The data on the recordable disc has the same reflective characteristics as that of a standard CD-ROM.

There are several advantages of recordable CD-ROMs. If only one or two discs are needed, they can be made for the cost of the media. The disc is available immediately. You might have to wait for a week or more to have a disc made up at a factory. Of course, if a large number is needed, then it would be better to have a factory master made to replicate them. Even then, however, it would be advisable to record a single disc, check it for accuracy and content, then have a master made.

Another reason to record the disc inhouse is to guarantee the security of the data. Recording a small number of discs inhouse from time to time is much less expensive than having them mastered and replicated.

Some large businesses have huge databases of customers, invoices, prices, and other information. Businesses might also have large parts catalogs that must be updated frequently. They can use a single disc to replace parts catalogs. A CD-ROM disc can store millions of part numbers, descriptions, drawings, costs, locations, and any other pertinent information.

In addition to paperwork records that are stored, some businesses keep important records on backup tape and floppy disks. Tape and floppy disks are good for less than 10 years before they start to deteriorate. A CD-ROM disc should last for 75 to 100 years or more. It is much easier to search and find an item on a CD-ROM disc than on a backup tape or in a stack of paperwork.

Large organizations might have acres of file cabinets, overflowing with paper. Some studies have shown that 90% of the files are never looked at again after they are stored. What a terrible waste of space and paper. If businesses replaced the millions of file folders and cabinets with CD-ROM discs, they could regain millions of square feet of office space. We could save thousands of trees if businesses saved documents electronically or on CD-ROM discs instead of putting everything on paper.

CD-ROM recordings are ideal for data that should never be changed. CD-ROM discs are an excellent way to make backups and to store and archive data. A CD-ROM makes it very easy to share large files with other computers, across the room, across the nation, or anywhere in the world. It can be shipped for a very nominal price, and you won't have to worry too much about it being erased or damaged.

There are systems that can be used to scan all of this information into a computer, which can then compress it. It can then be indexed so that any item can be quickly found and accessed. The data can then be stored on a CD-ROM disc, a write-once, read-many (WORM) disc or other storage device.

COLD is a recent acronym for *Computer Output to Laser Disk*. With a good COLD system and the proper hardware and software, millions of documents can be placed on a few small discs. To learn more about this technology, subscribe to the following imaging magazines; they are free to qualified subscribers:

*Imaging Business Magazine*
301-343-1520

*Advanced Imaging*
445 Broad Hollow Rd.
Melville, NY 11747-4722

*Managing Office Technology*
1100 Superior Ave.
Cleveland, OH 44197-8092

If you are in any kind of business at all, you should be able to qualify. There are several other magazines listed in chapter 17.

Here are just a few of the many companies that offer recordable CD-ROM systems:

| | |
|---|---|
| Pinnacle Micro | 800-553-7070 |
| DataDisc | 800-328-2347 |
| JVC | 714-261-1292 |
| Alos | 800-431-7105 |
| Bering Technology | 800-237-4641 |
| Boffin | 612-894-0595 |
| CMS Enhancements | 800-327-5773 |
| DynaTek Automation | 800-461-8855 |
| Eastman Kodak | 800-235-6325 |
| Hewlett-Packard | 800-810-0134 |
| Philips Electronics | 408-453-7373 |
| Pioneer New Media | 800-444-6784 |
| Procom Technology | 800-852-1000 |
| Sony Electronics | 800-352-7669 |
| Yamaha System Tech. | 800-543-7457 |

Several companies manufacture blank discs for the CD-R systems. The ProSource Company (800-903-1234) offers blank discs from several companies. The discs can cost from $6 up to $9 each. They also have several other items that are needed, such as labels and label applicators.

A group of hardware manufacturers, led by Philips and IBM, are working on a CD-Erasable (CD-E) format.

Ordinarily, a CD-ROM disc can store about 650MB, but the Young Minds (909-335-1350) and EWB Companies (619-930-0440) have developed a compression system that lets you store up to 4GB of data on a disc.

## Kodak Photo CD

Eastman Kodak (716-742-4000) has developed a system that will display photos on a television set or on a computer monitor. A person can take a roll of film to a photo developer and have the photos copied onto a CD-ROM disc. The Kodak CD recorder is much too expensive for most small photo finishing labs, so they have to send them out to be done. It usually takes about a week to get the disc back.

It costs about $20 for a disk, and the cost for putting 24 photos onto a CD disc is about $20. If you later decide to add more photos to the disc, just take it back to the lab, and they will load them on.

Some of the advantages of the Photo CD system is that the photos can be recorded at a resolution of $128 \times 192$ and up as high as $4000 \times 6000$ pixels. There are no televisions or even computers that would allow you to view the photos at $4000 \times$

6000. At this resolution, less than 100 photos in the 4" × 5" format can be recorded on a disc. The lower the resolution and the smaller the photo, the more photos that can be stored on a disc. Most photos will be stored at 480 × 640. At a resolution of 128 × 192 as many as 6000 small thumbnail size photos can be stored on a disc. The 128 × 192 format is often used to make a small copy of each photo on the disc. These small copies are then used as an index or catalog for all photos on the disc. If you are using a computer, you can use a mouse to point and click on any of the small images to bring up the large photo.

The Kodak Photo CD player can be connected directly to a television or to a computer. The photos can be displayed and enlarged on a television screen, and they can be rotated, mirrored, flipped, cropped, copied to a computer file, and printed out or exported.

The Kodak Photo CD player is a great tool for business presentations. It would be much more versatile than using a slide projector.

The Kodak Photo CD player is also a high fidelity player for audio CD.

# Multimedia upgrade kits

Many companies are offering multimedia upgrade kits or bundles. Many of them sport the MPC logo, which means that they conform to the MPC specifications for any of the products in the kit.

Some of the kits can be a very good bargain. However, you should check them out carefully. Be aware that some of the kits might have older CD-ROM drives and components. At the minimum, the kit should have a late model double- or quad-speed CD-ROM drive; a 16-bit audio sound board; 22KHz mono and 11KHz stereo playback and recording (44KHz stereo playback and recording is better); multivoice MIDI synthesizer (boards with the Wave Table are better); internal audio mixer for CD audio, MIDI, and digitized sound; and MIDI and joystick ports.

In addition to the hardware components, some vendors include several multi-media titles. In some cases, the list price of the titles alone exceeds the cost of the entire bundle. Some kits might even include speakers and a microphone.

# Installing CD-ROM drives

There are two main types of CD-ROM drives at this time: IDE and SCSI. The following steps will walk you through the installation of a CD-ROM drive.

## Step 1: Remove the computer cover

The first step in installing any of these drives is to remove the cover from your computer. Then make sure that you have a standard 5.25" bay that is accessible from the front panel. Use two small screws on each side to mount the drive.

## Step 2: Set any jumpers or switches

You should have received some sort of documentation and installation instructions with your drive.

### IDE CD-ROM drives

Your Pentium Pro motherboard probably has a secondary EIDE interface built in. If not, you will have to buy an EIDE interface. The EIDE interface can support up to four devices. Set any jumpers or switches necessary, then perform the following instructions for plugging in cables and boards. The IDE CD-ROM drives come with driver software, so they are fairly easy to install.

### SCSI CD-ROM drive

You can have up to seven SCSI devices installed, but each device must be assigned a logical unit number (LUN), between 0 and 6. The LUN is usually determined by a set of jumpered pins. Check your documentation. If you already have other SCSI devices installed, you must determine which LUNs are assigned to them and configure the CD-ROM drive for a number not being used.

## Step 3: Install the interface board

After the jumpers are set, find an empty slot on the motherboard and insert the board.

## Step 4: Install cables

For proprietary and IDE CD-ROM drives, you should have a flat 40-wire ribbon cable. For IDE drives, you might have to use the middle connector on the cable that is connected to your IDE hard drive.

For SCSI drives, you will have a 50-wire ribbon cable that connects to the back of the CD-ROM and then to an SCSI interface board. Most SCSI interface boards have provisions for two cable connections. If you have more than two SCSI devices, you might need to buy a cable with two or more connectors in the center.

The flat ribbon cable will have a different colored wire on one side. This wire will go to pin 1 of the connectors. Some connectors might have a shell with a square slot on one side. The cable connector will have a square elevation that fits in the slot so that it can only be plugged in correctly. Otherwise, look for an indication of pin 1 on the CD-ROM drive and on the interface board.

Plug in one of the four power cables to the drive. Most computer power supplies only have four cables. If all four cables are already being used, you might have to buy a small Y power cable.

If you plan to use your CD-ROM drive with a sound card (I strongly recommend that you do), you will have to install a small audio cable. There is no standardization for the audio cables and sound cards. Because the CD-ROM drives and sound cards are made by different manufacturers, you must tell the vendor which sound card you are using to get the proper audio cable. Because there are so many variations, many vendors don't include the audio cable unless you specifically ask for it. The cable might cost an additional $5.

Figure 13-3 shows the power cable being attached to a Toshiba SCSI quad-speed drive. The 50-wire ribbon cable is already attached. To the left of this connector are pins for setting the Logical Unit Number (LUN) of the drive. On the far left is the small white audio connector and cable.

**Fig. 13-3** Attaching the power cable to a Toshiba SCSI CD-ROM drive for bench testing.

### Step 5: Install software drivers

All of the drives should come with some sort of installation and driver software, usually on a floppy disk. The vendor might not provide it unless you ask for it.

If you have other SCSI devices already installed, then you probably have SCSI driver software, such as the Corel SCSI. If not, then you should contact your vendor for SCSI driver software. Once the SCSI software is installed, it will automatically recognize the new drive when you boot up.

### Step 6: Test the system

Test the system with a CD-ROM disc. If everything works, then reinstall the computer cover.

## Sources

There are several companies and vendors for CD-ROM drives and CD-ROM disc titles. Just look in any computer magazine, and you will see dozens of ads. There are now several magazines that are devoted entirely to the CD-ROM technology, such as:

*New Media*
P.O. Box 1771
Riverton, NJ 08077-7331

*CD-ROM Today*
P.O. Box 51478
Boulder, CO 80302-1478

# 14
# Computer sound
# and music

Sound can be an important part of your computer system. You can run your Pentium Pro without a sound board and speakers, but you will be missing out on a lot of good stuff. Sound can add a lot more fun, function, and utility to your computer. There are some Windows applications that make great use of sound. The Windows Sound Recorder is an included utility that lets you record, edit, insert, mix, and play sound files that are in the .WAV format. You can add sound annotations to documents such as spreadsheets or to programs that support object linking and embedding (OLE).

## Teleconferencing

One important reason to have a sound board and speakers in your computer is for voice and data conferencing. Two computers can be linked together on a network or by modem on the other side of the country. Several modems and faxes are now capable of sending and receiving voice and data. A couple are WinFax Pro 7.0 from Delrina (800-268-6082) and Fax Center PC Server from SoftLinx (800-899-7724).

Figure 11-1 in Chapter 11 shows my 28.8K Sportster Vi fax/modem from U.S. Robotics with voice mail that will let me play and record voice messages. Here are a few others that do about the same thing:

| | | |
|---|---|---|
| Aztech Labs | Aztech Audio Telephony 2000 | 800-886-8859 |
| Best Data | ACE 5000 | 800-632-2378 |
| Boca Research | Sound Expression | 407-997-6227 |
| Creative Labs | Phone Blaster | 800-998-5227 |
| Diamond Multimedia | TeleCommander 2500XL | 800-468-5846 |
| IBM PC Options | Multimedia Modem | 800-426-2968 |
| Prometheus Products | CyberStereo | 800-477-3473 |
| Reveal Computer | Decathlon XL | 800-738-3251 |
| U.S. Robotics | Sportster | 800-342-5877 |

The OfficeF/X from Spectrum Signal Processing (800-667-0018) is a modem/fax, Sound Blaster-compatible sound card, voice mail, and speaker phone. It can distinguish between incoming voice, modem, or fax calls and route the call appropriately.

Microsoft has developed MS Phone, a telephony application for Windows 95 that functions as a telephone, speakerphone, answering machine, PBX, interactive voice response (IVR), and personal assistant. With this application, you will be able to use several voice commands to operate your computer.

The AT&T Computer Telephone 8130 connects to a serial port on the computer and provides several functions, such as contact management, logging of incoming and outgoing calls, and caller ID.

# Music

Computers have made enormous contributions to the creation and playing of music. It has been said that music is the universal language. Everybody likes music of one kind or another. There are many different kinds of music, and music can be used in many different ways. Music can be used to express just about every emotion known to man. There is music that makes us happy, elated, excited, and exhilarated. There is passionate music that can arouse you and make you feel amorous. There is music that can make you feel joyful, merry, and cheerful. There is music that is touching and sad and sorrowful. There is music that makes you feel sentimental and reminiscent. There is heartbreaking music of unrequited love that can make one feel so sad and forlorn. There is serious music that is solemn, sedate, and dignified. Then there is rock and roll and heavy metal music. All of this music can be played on your computer.

Not only can you play music through your computer, but even if you know nothing at all about music, you can use your Pentium Pro to compose and create music. A computer is very good at converting text and graphics into digital data. Music can also be represented as digital data just as easily. Once music is digitized, you can edit it, rearrange it, add new sounds to it, remove certain sounds, or change it in hundreds of different ways. The Pentium Pro, along with the proper software, is an excellent tool for this purpose.

Music software is available from most of the software discount companies. Egghead (800-344-4323) has several music software packages. Rhapsody lets you compose, edit, and print your music score. The low-cost Concertware will let you enter music, play it back, edit it, or change it. They have instruction software for the piano and for guitar.

There are lots of articles and ads for music software in the music magazines and catalogs listed near the end of this chapter.

# Sound boards

A good audio board should be able to digitally record narration, sound, or music and store it as *.WAV files. You should have the option of recording in mono or stereo and be able to control the sampling rate. The board should have chips to convert the stored digital signals for analog conversion (DACs). It should also have chips to convert analog sound to digital signals (ADCs).

A good board will have a Musical Instrument Digital Interface (MIDI). With MIDI capabilities, you can use the board with MIDI instruments, such as piano keyboards, synthesizers, sound modules, and other MIDI products.

The board should have an FM synthesis chipset that duplicates the 128 different MIDI voices and 46 percussion instruments. Instead of the synthesized sound, some of the more expensive cards might have samples of actual instruments and use a wave table for synthesis.

The board should have an audio mixer function that allows you to control the source and level of the audio signals. The better boards will have tone controls for the bass and treble ranges. The board should also have a joystick port connector, a microphone input, and a speaker output jack.

## Sound, microphones, and speakers

Sound is made by the pressure on air created by a vibrating object. The pressure of the vibrations causes the air to move back and forth creating sound. If a microphone is placed in the vicinity of the sound, it can capture an image of the sound and turn it into electrical impulses.

There are several different types of microphones. One basic type has a diaphragm that vibrates due to the pressure of the sound waves. The diaphragm is attached to a coil of wire that moves in and out of the field of a permanent magnet. The movement of the coil of wire in the magnetic field produces an analog voltage that varies according to the vibration of the sound. We can record the electrical pulses, then using electronics to amplify the small signals, we can cause a loudspeaker to reproduce the original sound.

Basically, a loudspeaker is quite similar to the microphone. The speaker has a coil of wire that is attached to the speaker cone. The coil of wire is surrounded by a strong permanent magnet. Moving a coil of wire through a magnetic field produces a voltage; passing voltage through a coil of wire produces a magnetic field. The polarity of the magnetic field thus created will vary plus or minus depending on the polarity of the voltage. As the positive and negative pulses of voltage are passed through the coil of wire it alternately attracts and pulls the coil into the magnet or repels it pushing the coil and cone outward. The movement of the speaker cone produces pressure waves that are a replica of the original sound.

## Digital sampling

Some large mainframe network computers operate by giving each person on a network a small slice of time, or time-sharing. If the time was divided into millionths of a second, a person might receive a couple of slices, then the next person would get a few slices, then a few millionths of a second later the first person would get a few more slices of data. It would be done so fast that the person would not realize that the data was being received only part of the time. Hundreds or even thousands of people could be on a single line, all receiving different data at the same time.

Digitizing an analog voltage is somewhat similar to time-sharing. Digital samples, or slices, are taken of the analog waves. If the number of digital samples per second is rather low, then there can be a lot of unrecorded space between each slice. When played back, the unrecorded space can usually be electronically reconstructed to some degree. However, if the sample rate is fairly low, with wide spaces between each sample, the output sound will be somewhat less than high fidelity. The higher the frequency of the sample rate, the more closely the output sound will match the original. Then why not take higher frequency samples? Because the higher the frequency of the digital sample rate, the more space it requires to be stored or recorded. High fidelity digital sound requires a tremendous amount of disk space to store.

## Sampling rates and bits

Sound can be digitized using 8- or 16-bit samples. An 8-bit system can chop a wave form into a maximum of 256 steps ($2^8$). A 16-bit system can save up to 65,000 ($2^{16}$) pieces of information about the same wave form. As you can imagine, the 16-bit system will offer much greater fidelity, but at a greater need for storage space.

Using an 8-bit mode with a sample rate of 11KHz, you will be recording 11,000 bytes of data each second, or 661K per minute. If you were recording in 8-bit stereo at the same rate, the storage requirement would double to 1.6MB for one minute. To record in 16 bits at 11KHz, it would be twice the bits per second, or 1.6MB for one minute.

Most speech has a frequency range from about 300Hz up to about 6KHz. Sampling at 11KHz and 8 bits is good enough for speech, but it would not be very good for high fidelity music. Most systems are capable of sampling at 22KHz and 44.1KHz in both monaural and stereo modes. A sample rate for 44.1KHz in monaural would be 82.2K bytes per second, or 5.292MB per minute. In stereo, it would be doubled to 10.5MB per minute. One hour of recording at this sample rate would require over 630MB. Most audio CDs have about 630MB of storage space and can play for about one hour.

Standard digital sampling rates in the audio industry are 5.0125, 11.025, 22.05, and 44.1KHz.

## Why 44.1KHz sample rate

If we had perfect hearing, we could hear sounds from 20 Hertz (Hz), or cycles per second, up to 20KHz. Most of us, especially older people, have a much narrower hearing range. So why should we worry about a 44.1KHz sample rate? This is more than twice the frequency that we could hear even if we had perfect hearing.

Many instruments and other sounds have unique resonances and harmonics that go beyond the basic sounds they produce. These resonances and harmonics are what makes a middle C note on a piano sound differently than the same note on a violin or trumpet. Many of the harmonics and overtones of sound is in the higher frequencies. In digital recording, the upper frequency must be at least twice of what you can expect when it is converted to analog. So 44.1KHz digital signal will produce a 22KHz analog signal.

## Resolution

We often speak of the resolution of our monitors. The more pixels displayed, the sharper the image and the higher the resolution. We also use resolution to describe digitized sound. The higher the sampling rate and the more bits of information about each sound wave, the higher the resolution and the better the fidelity. There is a limit to the resolution of an 8-bit system no matter how fast the sample rate. The maximum samples of a waveform that can be captured by an 8-bit system is $2^8$, or 256. Some people might think that a 16-bit system would only provide twice the resolution of an 8-bit system. Actually a 16-bit system can provide 256 times more resolution: $2^{16}$, or 65,536. It is apparent that a 16-bit system can give much better resolution and fidelity than an 8-bit system.

## Signal-to-noise ratio (SNR)

Analog audio is made up of voltage sine waves that vary up and down continuously. Noise and static are also made up of similar sine waves. Noise and static is everywhere. It is in the air, especially so during electrical storms. It is in our electrical lines and in almost all electronic equipment. It is very difficult to avoid it.

The signal-to-noise ratio is the ratio between the amplitude of the audio or video signal as compared to the noise component. The SNR is measured in dB, usually a negative dB. The larger the negative number the better.

Most sound boards, CD-ROM drives, and other sound systems list the SNR on their specifications. Most of the better systems will have at least a -90 dB SNR. Because noise is analog voltage, a good digital system will usually have less noise than the analog systems.

## Digital signal processors (DSP)

One of the things that helps make it possible to get so much music from the sound board is a digital signal processor (DSP). It can be a very large task just to assemble and determine which notes to output from a single instrument. However, it can be mind boggling to try to do it for several instruments.

The central processor unit (CPU) is the brains of your computer. Ordinarily, almost everything that transpires in your computer has to go through the CPU. However, there are certain things, such as intensive number crunching, that can be speeded up with a coprocessor.

The Digital Signal Processor (DSP) chips are quite similar in function to math coprocessors. A DSP can take over and relieve the CPU of much of its burdens. DSP chips can be configured and programmed for several specific tasks, such as high-quality audio or complex graphics and video. The DSP can be used for musical synthesis and many special digital effects.

At one time, the DSP chips were rather expensive, but now the chips are quite reasonable. Because they add very little to the cost, more manufacturers are adding DSP chips to their sound boards. Before you buy a sound board, check the specifications.

Turtle Beach Systems was one of the first to design and implement the DSP technology on their MultiSound boards. Creative Labs followed soon after with their Sound Blaster 16 ASP. Several other companies are now manufacturing boards with the superior DSP technology. These chips add so much more function and utility to the sound board that eventually every manufacturer will be using them. Figure 14-1 shows a Creative Labs Sound Blaster board.

## What sound board should you buy?

It all depends on what you want to do and how much you want to spend. If you can afford it, I would suggest that you look for a 16-bit card with a DSP chip. For sources,

**Fig. 14-1** A Creative Labs Sound Blaster card.

look in any computer magazine such as *Computer Shopper*, the *New Media*, *PC World*, *PC Computing*, *PC Magazine*, and any of the several other computer magazines.

## Installing a sound board

The CPU of your computer is always busy and can only be interrupted by certain devices that need its attention. The obvious reason for this is to keep order. If all of the devices tried to act at the same time, there would be total confusion. So computers have 16 interrupt or IRQ lines and each device is assigned a unique number. They are given a priority according to their ranking number. For example, if the CPU received an interrupt request from the keyboard, which is IRQ 1, and a request from a mouse on IRQ 4, the keyboard request would be answered first.

If two devices are set for the same IRQ, it will cause a conflict. You might have to set one or more jumpers or switches on your board before you install it. If it has been designed and manufactured to the Plug-and-Play (PnP) specifications, you might not have to worry about setting switches and jumpers.

Just as your house has a unique address, areas of RAM memory have distinct addresses. Certain devices use a certain portion of RAM to perform some of their processing. So you might have to set jumpers or switches for the Input/Output (I/O) address of the sound card. The default address, the one set by the factory, will probably be set to 220. This is the Sound Blaster standard, and it is used by many others.

There might also be a set of jumpers to set the Direct Memory Access (DMA) channel. On most PCs there are three or more DMAs, and they don't usually cause a conflict if two or more devices are set to the same channel.

Most of the newer audio boards now meet the PnP specification. If so, your Pentium Pro BIOS will recognize these boards and automatically configure them. Many of the older boards have built-in diagnostics that can detect a conflict with the IRQ or I/O settings. However, you might have trouble determining which other device is causing the conflict. If you have DOS 6.0 or later, you can use the Microsoft Diagnostics (MSD) command. It can show all of the IRQs and which components are using them.

One of the benefits of CD-ROMs are that they can play sound and music along with the text, graphics, and motion. You can play compact audio discs on most CD-ROM drives. Most CD-ROM drives have a small audio connector on the back panel. A special cable is used to connect to the sound board. Unfortunately, there are no standards for the audio connector for the CD-ROM. It might be different on sound boards from different companies. Because there are so many variations, the audio cable is often not included with the sound board or with the CD-ROM drive. You might have to order it special. They cost about $5. The audio cable plugs into a miniature connector on the back of the CD-ROM drive. The other end plugs into a small connector on the sound board.

## Speakers

Most of the sound cards have an output of about 4 watts. That isn't very much, but you're not going to be trying to fill a concert hall. You really don't need much for your computer. You can attach any small speaker, but several companies manufacture small speakers with a built-in amplifier. The speakers are powered by batteries or by a power supply. They can cost from $20 up to $100 for the larger ones. There are also high-end, high fidelity systems available. Of course, high fidelity usually means high cost. Figure 14-2 shows a couple of 75-watt speakers.

**Fig. 14-2** A couple of 75-watt computer speakers.

Just a few of the many companies who offer small computer speakers are Labtec, Media Vision, Koss, and Roland.  Look through computer magazines for others.

If you use good sound boards and speakers, your computer can be a major component in an excellent high fidelity system.

## Microphones

Many of the sound boards come with a microphone. The type needed for just voice annotations can be very inexpensive, such as those available from Radio Shack for about $5.

If you expect to do any kind of high fidelity recording, then you definitely need a good microphone. A sound system is only as good as its weakest link. A good microphone can cost from $35 up to $500 or more.

There are two basic types of microphones. The dynamic type uses a diaphragm and a coil of wire that moves back and forth in a magnetic field. The other type is the condenser, or capacitor, microphone. A capacitor is made up of two flat plates. When voltage is applied to the plates, a charged field, or a capacitance, will exist between the plates. The capacitance will depend on the voltage, the size of the plates, and the distance between the plates. If the plates are moved toward or away from each other, the capacity will change. In a capacitor microphone, one plate is fixed and the other is a flat diaphragm. Sound pressure on the flexible diaphragm will move the one charged plate in and out, which causes a change in the capacity. Capacitor mikes can be made very small, such as the lapel mikes.

Many professional type microphones sold today are the wireless kind. They have a small transmitter built into the microphone that feeds the sound to a small receiver that is connected to an amplifier or recorder.

Microphones can also be classified as to their pickup directionality. The omnidirectional picks up sound from all directions. The bidirectional picks up sound from opposite sides of the mike. The cardiod picks up sound in a heart shaped unidirectional pattern (*cardi* is a prefix for *heart*). The unidirectional supercardiod picks up sound on a very narrow straight in path.

# Musical Instrument Digital Interface (MIDI)

Electronic circuits can be designed to oscillate at almost any frequency. The output of the oscillating circuit is a voltage that can be amplified and routed through a loud speaker to reproduce various sounds.

In the early 1970s, Robert Moog used voltage controlled oscillators (VCOs) to develop the Moog Synthesizer. With a synthesizer, you can create synthetic musical sounds that imitate different instruments. The sounds from the early systems didn't sound much like real musical instruments.

Also in the early 1970s, John Chowning of Stanford University, developed Digital FM synthesis. The Yamaha Corporation licensed the technology from Stanford and introduced the first FM digital synthesizer in 1982. Since that time, there have been some tremendous technological advances. Today a person might not be able to discern as to whether a sound was synthesized or came from a real instrument.

In some instances, the music from a sound board does come from real instruments. Sample notes are recorded from instruments. Under computer control, any of the stored samples can be joined and played back. The notes can be held for a half note, shortened to a quarter note, or edited for whatever the music requires. Samples from several instruments can all be playing at the same time. The music can sound as if it is being produced by a live 100-piece orchestra. It all comes from a chip that is about 1" square. It is absolutely amazing.

The early voltage-controlled oscillators (VCOs) were rather crude. The electronic industry was still in its infancy. There were no integrated circuits. As the electronic industry and technology evolved, newer and better VCOs were developed and incorporated into musical instruments.

## The MIDI standard

There were no standards for the VCOs and new musical instruments. As usual, each vendor's product was a bit different than all others. In 1983, a group of companies got together and adopted a set of standards that they called the *Musical Instrument Digital Interface*. This was truly an historic agreement for the music industry. MIDI and the advances in electronic technology has made it possible to generate more new music in the last 10 years than was generated in the last 100 years. Synthesized music is not only used for rock and roll, but for television commercials, movies, and all types of music.

## How MIDI operates

MIDI itself does not produce music. It is only an interface, or controller, that tells other devices, such as a synthesizer or a sampler, which particular sound to produce. In some respects, MIDI is similar to the old-style player pianos that used a punched roll of paper to play.

Briefly, the MIDI specification says that a MIDI device must have at least two MIDI connectors: an input and an output. (These are DIN connectors that are the same type as that used for the computer keyboard connector on the motherboard.) A MIDI device can include adapter cards, synthesizers, piano type keyboards, various types of instrument pickups, digital signal processors, and MIDI-controlled audio mixers.

One of the great advantages of MIDI is that it allows many different electronic instruments to communicate with each other. When two MIDI instruments are connected, the devices exchange information about the elements of the performance, such as the notes played and how loud they are played. A master keyboard can be connected to two or more MIDI electronic keyboards or other MIDI devices. Any note played on the master can be also played on the connected MIDI "slaves." The electronic keyboards can emulate several different instruments. One person playing the master can use the slaves to make it sound as though a very large orchestra is playing. There are many options available, such as allowing you to record the notes played, then play them back or edit and change them.

## General MIDI standard signals

There are 128 common instrument sound signals for MIDI control; each signal is numbered 1 to 128. (You might also see them numbered 0 to 127.) The standard was originated by the Roland Corporation and is now coordinated by the MIDI Manufacturers Association (MMA).

If the MIDI receives a signal and it is connected to a synthesizer, keyboard, or any MIDI instrument, it will trigger the device to play a note corresponding to the signal number. For example, a signal on number 3 would cause a honky tonk piano sound, and number 40 would be a violin. Note that there are 16 different instrument classifications. Every 8 numbers represents sounds from a basic class of instrument. For example, the first 8 sounds are made by piano-type instruments, the next 8 are made by chromatic percussion instruments, then organs, etc.

There are an additional 46 MIDI Note numbers for nonmelodic percussion instruments. These numbers include such things as drums, a cowbell, wooden blocks, triangles, and cymbals.

## Synthesizers

The MIDI specification was primarily designed as a standard for controlling synthesizers. It did not specify how a synthesizer should create a sound or what sounds should be created.

The word *synthesize* means to combine or put together. Synthesizers can combine two or more wave forms to form new sounds. There are several types of sound waves or oscillations. Each musical note has a basic oscillation frequency. For example, A2 has a frequency of 220 oscillations per second, or 220Hz. Note that E3 vibrates at 330Hz, A4 at 440Hz, and E6 at 660Hz. We could generate pure single frequency sine waves of each of these notes, but they would be rather dull and uninteresting. The actual notes are a combination of oscillation frequencies.

Even though it has the same basic frequency, if a note is played on different instruments, there will be a distinct difference in the sounds. The note A4 played on a trombone sounds quite different than A4 played on a guitar. They all sound differently because they are not pure single sine wave frequencies. The vibrations of a basic note causes other vibrations in the metal of a trombone or the wood of a guitar. These extra vibrations are the timbre that adds tone color to a sound and distinguishes it from a note played on another instrument.

## Harmonics

An important cause for difference in sounds is the harmonics created. A guitar string that is plucked to play A4 will vibrate at 440Hz. If you photographed the vibrating string with a high-speed movie camera, then slowed it down, you could see a primary node of vibrations. However, there would also be several smaller nodes on the string. These smaller nodes would be vibrating at twice the frequency of the primary node, and some would even be vibrating at four times the primary frequency. The sounds made at the higher frequencies blend with the primary sound to give it tone and color. These higher frequencies are called harmonics.

Harmonics are even multiples of the fundamental oscillation of a note or its basic pitch.

## Envelope generator

Bob Moog determined that there were four main criteria in each sound. He identified them as *attack*, *decay*, *sustain*, and *release* (ADSR). The attack determines how fast the initial sound rises. It might hold at the initial height for a while, then start to decay. Sustain determines how long the sound is audible while a key is held down. Release is the rate at which the sound intensity decreases to zero after the key is released.

The ADSR electronic envelope is used in synthesizers to describe almost any sound.

## Wave tables

The FM synthesized sounds are usually not as good as the sound generated from an actual instrument. The more expensive sound cards and many of the better MIDI instruments use digital samples of real sounds. This requires some memory to store the samples, but actually not as much as you might think. For example, a piano has 88 notes or keys. However, it is only necessary to sample a few notes. Because they are all piano notes, the main difference is the pitch. Middle A, or A4, has a frequency of 440Hz; A2 has a frequency of 220Hz. A sample of a single A can be electronically altered to make it sound like any A on the piano keyboard. So they only need a sample of an A, B, C, D, E, F, and G. With a small sample of each of these notes, any note of the 88 on the piano can be created. It also would not matter whether the note was a quarter note, half note, or whole note. Once the note is simulated, it can be held for as long or as short a time as necessary.

The same type of system would be used to sample notes from other instruments. It would be a little simpler to store notes from other instruments because most of them don't have as many notes as a piano. A piano is one of the few instruments that allows more than one note to be played at the same time.

The samples are stored in ROM. When a note is called for, the sample is read from ROM, placed in RAM, electronically adjusted for whatever note is needed, then sent to an amplifier and loudspeaker.

The more instruments sampled and the more samples that are stored, the more memory that is required, both ROM and RAM. Some high-end keyboards might have 10MB or more of ROM and about 4MB of RAM.

## Sequencers

Sequencers are a type of recorder that uses computer memory to store information about a performance. Like the MIDI, it does not record the sound itself, but just the information about the sound.

Even if you know nothing at all about music, you can write and compose music with a sequencer that is connected to a synthesizer or other electronic instrument. If you know a little bit about music, you can become an expert composer with a sequencer. Most sequencers are software programs that allow you to create, edit, record, and playback on a hard disk musical compositions in the MIDI message format.

A sequencer memorizes anything you play and can play it back at any time. They are similar to multitrack recorders, except that they are much faster because the tracks are on a computer. The computer also lets you do hundreds of things better, quicker, and easier than a tape recorder. A sequencer lets you edit music in thousands of ways that are not possible with a tape machine. With a single MIDI instrument, an entire album could be recorded.

A sequence can be part of a song or a single track of a song or the whole song. The sequences are laid down in tracks. Several tracks of different instruments can be laid down separately, then all played back together. A single track can be played back and edited or changed. Tracks can be recorded at different times, then blended together. A song or an album can be created by a group even though one member might be in New York, one in Los Angeles, or others scattered all over the country. Each member of the group could record their part on a disk, then ship it to a studio where all of the tracks could be edited and blended together.

Some sequencers allow you to record channels while playing back existing channels. Tracks can be laid down over another track without erasing what is already there. Portions of a track can be erased and new material inserted. The editing capabilities are almost unlimited.

Some synthesizers and keyboards have built-in hardware sequencers. The built-in sequencer allows you to do many of the same things that sequencer software allows. However, a hardware sequencer would not have the capabilities of a computer.

Sequencer software such as Cakewalk will let you record in real time as an instrument is being played. You can also use the step-entry mode and enter one note at a time. The notes can be entered from a computer keyboard or a piano-type MIDI keyboard that is connected to the computer.

The software is intelligent enough to take step-entry notes and combine them with the proper staff notation and timing. Some software will even add the proper chords to the step entry.

Some Windows sequencer software programs are Cakewalk Professional, Cadenza, Master Tracks Pro, and Midisoft for Windows. Many of the music software programs will also print out music scores.

When you consider the modern technology that allows the editing and re-editing of a song until the cut is perfect, you just have to admire the works of some of the early recording artists. They usually didn't get the opportunity to go back and change a mistake or to improve a lick here and there.

## Piano keyboards

It is possible to use a computer keyboard to edit or create music; however, it is a lot easier to work with an electronic piano keyboard. Many of the electronic keyboards have built-in synthesizers and MIDI connections.

If you are interested in music, one of the magazines that you should subscribe to is the *Electronic Musician* (800-843-4086). They have excellent articles about music and new devices. This magazine is of interest to professional musicians as well as amateurs and anyone who enjoys music. They also publish an annual *Digital Piano Buyer's Guide* that is available from the Mix Bookshelf (800-233-9604). The Mix Bookshelf specializes in books for musicians. One book that they carry is *The Musical PC*. It is an excellent book for anyone who wants to learn more about music and computers. Another book they carry is *Making Music With Your Computer*. It would be very helpful to anyone just getting into music. There are also articles in the book that would be of interest to the old pro.

Another magazine for musicians and anyone interested in music is called *Musician* (800-347-6969). It is published primarily for the professional musician, but it is of interest to anyone who enjoys music and wants to keep up with what is happening in the music and entertainment field.

# Music software and hardware

There are several software packages that you can use with your Pentium Pro to make music. This section lists just a few.

The Cakewalk Company (800-234-1171) has some of the most comprehensive music software in the business. They also have Cakewalk Pro Audio, which is a MIDI sequencer. Call them for information and a Demo Pack.

The Kurzweil Company (800-421-9846) also has an extensive line of music products.

Pro Tools III from Digidesign (800-333-2137) lets you record, edit, process, mix, and master your music.

Jammer from Soundtrek (800-778-6859) allows you to enter a few chords then choose from over 200 band styles to create professional sounding songs.

The EMAGIC Company (916-477-1051) has several software packages. Call them for a brochure.

The Free Play Company (310-459-8614) has World Music Menu that can help you create music similar to that of countries from around the world.

The PG Music Company (800-268-6272) has Band-In-A-Box that lets you type in a few chords, and it will supply the rest. It will automatically generate professional quality accompaniment instruments. PG Music also offers several other music software programs.

There are many other companies that offer software that can let you make beautiful music with your Pentium Pro. To find out more about these companies, subscribe to the *Electronic Musician* and the other music magazines and catalogs listed earlier.

# Catalogs

You will need music software for your PC. The Soundware Catalog (800-333-4554) lists hundreds of music software programs. They have a comprehensive and detailed description of each program listed. Even if you don't intend to order the program, the descriptions in the catalog can give you a good idea of what is available. Call them for a catalog.

The Musician's Friend Catalog (800-776-5173), the American Musical Supply Catalog (800-458-4076), and Manny's Mailbox Music (800-448-8478) all have hundreds of musical instruments, supplies, videotapes for training, and books. Call them for catalogs.

# Musician trade shows

Partly due to the success of the COMDEX shows, there are now a lot of trade shows. Here are a couple that you might be interested in.

The National Association of Music Merchants (NAMM) has two large shows each year, usually one near Los Angeles in the winter and one in Nashville during the summer. There are usually hundreds of exhibitors at these shows. You will find just about every imaginable musical product at these shows. They have dozens of rooms where they demonstrate amplifiers and loudspeakers. There will be hundreds of electronic keyboards on the floor; everything from the small toys up to the very expensive grand pianos. They will also have several old fashioned nonelectronic pianos all the way from the spinet up to the concert grand. If you are at all interested in music, this is the place to see all that is available.

To find out when and where the next NAMM show will be held, you can call 619-438-8001.

The Consumer Electronics Show (CES) also presents two large shows each year: a winter show held in Las Vegas during the first week in January and a summer show held in Chicago during the first week in June. This show also has several music and musical instrument exhibitors. To find out more about this show, call 202-457-8700.

If you are interested in multimedia, you can order my book *Build Your Own Multimedia System and Save a Bundle* from McGraw-Hill (800-822-8158). It is also available at most bookstores.

# 15
# Some applications

There are many applications and ways to use your computer. I can't possibly list them all, but this chapter covers just a few uses.

## For the kids

One of the better reasons to have a home computer is if you have children. If you don't have a computer for the kids, then you should be ashamed of yourself. You are depriving them of one of the greatest learning tools of all time.

There is a lot of software for the kids. One of the better magazines that offers and reviews this type of software is *KidSoft* (800-354-6150). Check other computer magazines for ads.

## Resume

There are few people who can't use a good resume. It is one of the better ways to get your foot in the door if you are looking for a job. Many of the larger companies are now using scanners to create databases of all the resumes that are sent to them. They can then have the computer search for whatever qualities they are looking for at the moment. To make sure your resume gets into their computer, you should use a good printer or typewriter with a standard font to create it. To find out what the companies are looking for, look in the want ads from major companies to see what keywords are used. List your strongest and best skills first. Don't hide them in the middle of a long list.

There are several books and software programs that can help you create a good resume. Here are a couple of books:

- *Be Your Own Headhunter Online* by Pam Dixon, published by Random House
- *Electronic Resume Revolution* by Joyce Lain, published by John Wiley & Sons

Here are a couple of resume software programs:
- ResumeMaker Deluxe CD from Individual Software (800-822-3522)
- The Perfect Resume by Davidson (800-545-7677)

According to a recent Careers edition of the Los Angeles *Times*, the top jobs at this time are for computers and technology. Here are some of the jobs:
- Computer Graphics Designers
- Computer Network Builders
- Financial Information Technologists
- Web Page Designers
- Multimedia Designers
- Internet Security

Many of these jobs require a degree in computer science. Most local colleges and universities now offer many computer courses. There are several colleges and universities that now offer home-study courses or distance learning. Some offer college credit courses over local TV channels.

# Home office

SOHO is a new acronym that has recently been created. It means *Small Office, Home Office*. Many businesses can be operated from a home office. Several advantages in having a home office are no commuting, no high office rent, possibly take care of young children at same time, and setting your own hours. More businesses are allowing their employees to work from home and telecommute. There are some jobs that can be done from home as easily as at a big office.

There are several computer programs that let you connect your home computer to an office computer. A modem and almost any communications software—such as LapLink, CrossTalk, ProComm, or QModem—will let you access another computer.

## Deducting the cost of your computer

If you have a home office for a business, you might be able to deduct part of the cost of your computer from your income taxes. You might even be able to deduct a portion of your rent, telephone bills, and other legitimate business expenses.

## Some IRS rules

I can't give you all of the IRS rules for a home office, but there are several deductions available if you use a portion of your home exclusively and regularly to operate your business. These deductions might include portions of your real estate taxes, mortgage interest, operating expenses (such as home insurance premiums and utility costs), and depreciation allocated to the area used for business. You might even be able to deduct a portion of the cost of painting the outside of your house or repairing the roof.

You should be aware that the IRS looks very closely at home office expenses. Before you deduct these expenses, I would recommend that you buy the latest tax books and consult with the IRS or a tax expert. There are many rules and regulations, and they change frequently. For more information, call the IRS and ask for publication #587, *Business Use of Your Home*. Look in your telephone directory for the local or 800 number for the IRS.

Here is another recommendation, whether you have a home office or not, keep good records. I have been rather sloppy in keeping records in the past. However, after being audited twice for a home office, I am a changed man. I now use the askSam database program to keep track of all my expenses. The askSam for Windows system is very easy to use. Information can be entered as structured data, or it can be entered much like you were using a word processor. The askSam Systems software is available from most large software companies, or you can call them at 904-584-6590.

Another excellent program for record keeping is Quicken from Intuit. The data from Quicken can be imported into TurboTax, which can help make the onerous tax time task a bit easier.

## Home office as a tax preparer

Congress and the IRS change the tax rules every year. Every year, they become more and more complicated. It is almost impossible for the ordinary person to be aware of, comprehend, and understand all of the rules and regulations. Some of the rules are even difficult for the IRS. If you call several IRS offices with complicated questions, about 50% of the answers you get will be completely opposite.

If a person works at a single job and has a single source of income, the forms are fairly simple. However, if you have several sources of income or a small business, preparing your taxes can be a nightmare. It is an impossible task for many people, and they must hire a tax preparer. Many of the tax preparers charge from $50 to over $100 dollars an hour.

Because the tax rules change so often and are so difficult for the average person to comprehend, being a tax preparer is almost like having a guaranteed income.

If you have any inclination for accounting and tax preparation, then you might consider taking a course to become a CPA or tax preparer. Many community colleges offer courses in accounting. However, the H&R Block Company is probably the best place to learn tax preparation. They conduct several classes throughout the year in various locations.

Just to give you an indication of how profitable tax preparation can be, the H&R Block Company owns CompuServe.

## Accountant

It is not absolutely necessary to be an accountant to be a tax preparer, but it helps a whole lot. Another reason to learn accounting is that many small businesses can't afford to hire full-time accountants. Many of them hire accountants on a part-time basis to keep their books and accounts in order.

There are several good software programs that can be used for accounting. The ACCPAC accounting package from Computer Associates Company (516-324-5224) is a very good accounting program for both small and larger businesses. Call them for brochures. Another low-cost accounting package is Peachtree Accounting for Windows. This program is available from most software companies or from PC Zone mail order (800-258-2088). Other accounting packages available from PC Zone are Stage-Soft Accounting for Small Business and One-Write Plus Accounting. Call them for a current catalog.

M.Y.O.B. Accounting is designed for small businesses. It has General Ledger, Sales, Inventory, Checkbook, Purchases, and Card File. It is available from Egghead (800-344-4323) or most other software stores. They also carry QuickBooks Pro from Intuit. It has several modules that are ideal for small businesses, such as Time Tracking, Estimating, Project Costing, Payroll, and Accounting.

## Tax programs

Because you have a computer, it might not be necessary for you to pay a tax preparer to do your taxes. There are several tax programs that can do the job for you. Unless you have a very complicated income, it can be done quickly and easily. In many cases, the cost of the program would probably be less than the cost of having a tax preparer do your taxes.

Besides doing your own taxes, most of these programs will allow you to set up files and do the taxes of others. Many of the software companies offer tax preparation programs for professional tax businesses, but usually at a much higher price.

All of the programs operate much like a spreadsheet in that the forms, schedules, and worksheets are linked together. When you enter data at one place, other affected data is automatically updated. Most of them have a built-in calculator so that you can do calculations before entering figures. Many of them allow "what if" calculations to show what your return would look like with various inputs. Most of the companies also have software for state income taxes. Most of them will allow you to print out IRS forms that are acceptable. The following sections contain brief reviews of just a couple of the better known programs.

### TurboTax

TurboTax is unique in that it offers modules for 41 states. It is an excellent program and is fairly easy to install and learn. It starts out with a personal interview about your financial situation for the past year. It then lists forms that you might need. Based on the present year's taxes, it can estimate what your taxes will be for next year.

ChipSoft and the Intuit Company (415-322-0573) have now merged. Quicken, from Intuit, is a financial software program that is an ideal adjunct to TurboTax. You can use Quicken to keep track of all your financial records, then at the end of the year, the records can be directly imported into the TurboTax program.

ChipSoft Inc.
5045 Shoreham Pl. #100
San Diego, CA 92122-3954
Phone: 619-453-8722

### J.K. Lasser's Your Income Tax

Your Income Tax has several state modules. It has a scratch pad, calculator, and next-year tax planner. The popular J.K. Lasser's Tax Guide is included with the package.

J.K. Lasser
1 Gulf + Western Plaza
New York, NY 10023
Phone: 800-624-0023 (800-624-0024 in New York)

### Kiplinger TaxCut

The Kiplinger TaxCut program has lots of tips from the *Kiplinger Magazine* and from H&R Block. With this low-cost program, you can file electronically. TaxCut is available from Egghead (800-344-4323) and most other software stores.

### Electronic Filing

The IRS is now accepting electronic filing from certain tax preparers and companies. Eventually you should be able to complete your taxes from one of the previously listed programs, then use your modem to send it directly to the IRS. This, of course, saves you a lot of time and will save the IRS even more. Ordinarily the IRS has to input the data from your return into their computers by hand. Can you imagine the amount of time saved if they can receive it directly into their computers. So the IRS encourages electronic filing.

Electronic filing also offers advantages to you. Here are just a few:
- Faster refund (up to three weeks faster)
- Direct deposit of the refund
- More accurate return resulting in fewer errors
- IRS acknowledges receipt of the return
- It reduces paperwork
- Saves IRS labor, therefore taxpayers money

Some people have used electronic filing to file false claims for refunds. You can be sure that from now on the IRS agents will be checking to make sure that no one is filing refund claims for their cat or dog.

There are still some limitations. For more information call 800-829-1040 and ask for the Electronic Filing Coordinator. You could also check with your local IRS office to see if electronic filing is possible in your area.

## Other tools of the trade

The following sections cover some other tools that can go very well with your computer in business uses.

### Point-of-sale terminals

Point-of-sale terminals (POS) are usually a combination of a cash drawer, a computer, and special software. They provide a fast customer checkout, credit card handling, and audit and security; reduce paperwork; and provide efficient accounting. By keying in codes for various items, the computer can keep a running inventory of everything that is sold. The store owner can immediately know when to reorder certain goods. A POS system can provide instant sales analysis data as to which items sell best, buying trends, and, of course, the cost and the profit or loss.

There are several POS systems. A simple cash drawer with a built-in 40-column receipt printer can cost as little as $500. More complex systems can cost $1500 and more. Software can cost from $175 up to $1000. However, they can replace a bookkeeper and an accountant. In most successful businesses that sell goods, a POS system can easily pay for itself.

Here are a few of the POS hardware and software companies:

| | |
|---|---|
| Alpha Data Systems | 404-499-9247 |
| CA Retail | 800-668-3767 |
| Computer Time | 800-456-1159 |
| CompuRegister | 314-365-2050 |
| Datacap Systems | 215-699-7051 |
| Indiana Cash Drawer | 317-398-6643 |
| Merit Dig. Systems | 604-985-1391 |
| NCR Corp. | 800-544-3333 |
| Printer Products | 617-254-1200 |
| Synchronics | 901-761-1166 |

### Bar codes

Bar codes are a system of black and white lines that are arranged in a system much like the Morse code of dots and dashes. By using combinations of wide and narrow bars and wide and narrow spaces, any numeral or letter of the alphabet can be represented.

Bar codes were first adopted by the grocery industry. They set up a central office that assigned a unique number, a Universal Product Code (UPC), for just about every manufactured and prepackaged product sold in grocery stores. Different sizes of the same product have a different and unique number assigned to them. The same type of products from different manufacturers will also have unique numbers. Most large grocery stores nowadays sell everything from automobile parts and accessories to drugs and medicines. Each item has its own bar code number.

When the clerk runs an item across the scanner, the dark bars absorb light and the white bars reflect the light. The scanner decodes the UPC number and sends it to the main computer. The computer then matches the input number to the number stored on its hard disk. Linked to the number on the hard disk is the price of the item, description, amount in inventory, and several other pieces of information about the item. The computer sends back the price and the description of the part to the cash register where the information is printed out. The computer then deducts that item from the overall inventory and adds the price to the overall cash received for the day.

A store might have several thousand items with different sizes and prices. Without a bar-code system, the clerk must know most of the prices, then enter them in the cash register by hand. Many errors are committed. With bar codes, the human factor is eliminated. The transactions are performed much faster and with almost total accuracy.

At the end of the day, the manager can look at the computer output and immediately know such things as how much business was done, what inventories need to be replenished, and what items were the biggest sellers. With the push of a button on the computer, he or she can change any or all of the prices of the items in the store.

Bar codes can be used in many other ways to increase productivity, keep track of time charged to a particular job, track inventory, and many other benefits. There are very few businesses, large or small, that cannot benefit from the use of bar codes.

There are several different types of bar code readers or scanners. Some are actually small portable computers that can store data, then be downloaded into a larger computer. Some systems require their own interface card, which must be plugged into one of the slots on the computer motherboard. Some companies have devised systems that can be inserted in series with the keyboard so that no slot or other interface is needed. Key Tronic has a keyboard with a bar-code reader as an integral part of the keyboard.

If you are interested in the bar code and automatic identification technology, there are two magazines that are sent free to qualified subscribers. They are:

ID Systems
174 Concord St.
Peterborough, NH 03458
Phone: 603-924-9631

Automatic I.D. News
P.O. Box 6158
Duluth, MN 55806-9858

Call or write for subscription qualification forms. Almost everyone who has any business connections can qualify.

### Bar-code printers

There are special printers that have been designed for printing bar-code labels. Labels can also be printed on the better dot matrix printers and on laser printers. There are several companies that specialize in printing up labels to your specifications.

# Networks

The term *network* can cover a lot of territory. There are some networks that are worldwide. The telephone system is a good example of a worldwide type of network. There are some computer networks that connect only two or three computers; others that have thousands tied together.

Networks are made up of two major components: hardware and software. The hardware can consist of boards, cables, hubs, routers, and bridges. There are several different companies who supply network operating software (NOS). The main ones are Novell, Microsoft, and IBM.

There are a few standards so that the hardware and software from the major companies are compatible. For example, software from either Novell or Microsoft will work on boards and systems from several different vendors and manufacturers.

There are several different types of networks, such as zero-slot, proprietary systems, peer-to-peer, local area networks (LANs), and wide area networks (WANs). A local area network is usually a system within a single building, plant, or campus. A LAN might include several different types of systems.

A zero-slot network is usually two computers tied together with a cable through their serial or parallel ports. Special software can allow access of the hard disk of each unit. Files can be viewed, copied, and transferred between computers. It is a very inexpensive way to share resources. A disadvantage is that it might be limited to a maximum of 115,000 bits per second, which is relatively slow. Another disadvantage is that the distance between the two computers might be limited to about 50 feet.

LapLink from Traveling Software (800-527-5465) is very good if you need to tie a couple of computers together in a small office.

There are some companies that have proprietary systems for small networks and peer-to-peer systems. Moses Computer (408-358-1550) has several systems that are ideal for small networks. I have a MosesALL! IV! Computer network system in my office.

For small businesses or small groups, a proprietary system might be all that you need. They are usually inexpensive, yet can have many of the utilities and functions of the large systems.

I also have two other types of network interface cards (NICs) in my office. They are both Ethernet boards. I have several software programs that these boards will work under, such as Microsoft LAN Manager, Novell's NetWare Lite, Windows for Workgroups, Windows 95, and Windows NT.

A disadvantage with using proprietary systems is that they have their own non-standard software and hardware. These proprietary systems might not work with the standard network operating software and hardware. A peer-to-peer network can be rather sophisticated. It requires a network card in each computer and requires special software. Depending on the type of system, it can operate from 1MHz up to 10MHz or more.

A peer-to-peer network is distinguished from a client/server network in that the computers on peer-to-peer networks communicate with each other rather than with a large file server. They can share and transfer files and utilize the resources of all the computers on the network.

In a file server network, one computer is usually dedicated as the server. A Pentium Pro type computer is ideal as a file server. It can have a very large hard disk that contains all of the company's files and records. The individual computers attached to the server are called *workstations*. The workstations can access the files and records and change or alter them as necessary.

A file server network offers several advantages to the company. They only have to buy software for one machine. They do have to pay for a license for each of the networked computers, but it costs much less than having to buy software for each machine.

A network can keep all of the records and data in one place. This can allow close control of the updating and revisions of the data. A network can allow communication between each of the networked computers. It might also allow the users to share a single printer, fax, modem, or other peripherals.

One disadvantage is that, if the main server goes down, the whole system is down. The data and records must also be routinely backed up. For critical data, it might be necessary to have a redundant array of inexpensive disks (RAID) that would automatically make two or more copies of all data. A less expensive system would be to use a couple of large IDE hard disks and a couple of SCSI hard disks. Because they use different interface controllers, there is less chance that both of them would fail.

For critical data, it is also necessary that the server be supplied with an uninterruptible power supply (UPS). A UPS is essential in areas where there is frequent lightning and electrical storms. It is also necessary in areas where there are wide variations in the electrical supply where there might be "brownouts".

Of course, the company will need network operating software (NOS). Novell is the leader in both software and network interface cards (NICs) hardware. The Windows NT can also be used as a NOS.

There are several companies that provide NOS and NICs for small networks. Lantastic from the Artisoft Company (602-670-7326) is one of the better known suppliers. Novell also has Novell Lite for small networks. The Microsoft Windows 95 can also be used for small networks.

There are three main methods, or topologies, of tying computers together: Ethernet, Token Ring, and Star. Each system has some advantages and disadvantages. The Ethernet system is the most popular.

If you would like to learn more about networks, you might want to order the book *Build Your Own LAN And Save A Bundle* from McGraw-Hill. I highly recommend it. It was written by the same person who wrote the book you are reading.

# Desktop publishing

If a company has to depend on outside printing for brochures, manuals, and documents, it can be quite expensive. Desktop publishing (DTP) can save the company a lot of money. There are some high-end DTP software programs, such as PageMaker and Corel Ventura, that are necessary if you expect to do a lot of DTP. For many projects, however, Word for Windows 95, WordPerfect for Windows, or any other good word processing program might be all you need.

One of the better high-end packages is Corel Ventura, which has several good graphic and drawing packages. They have clip art and just about everything else that is needed for desktop publishing.

You might also need a good laser printer and scanner for DTP. If you plan to do any color work, you will need a color printer and scanner.

DTP Direct (800-395-7778 or 800-325-5811) is a desktop publishing catalog. They list several DTP software packages. They also list several hardware DTP products. The ads in many of the computer magazines don't have much information about the product because the space is expensive. However, many of the catalogs have a fairly good summary of the various features of the products. Call them for a copy of their catalog.

There are several good books on DTP. McGraw-Hill publishes several. Call 800-822-8158 and ask for a catalog.

There are also several magazines that are devoted to DTP. Almost every computer magazine often carries DTP articles.

# Presentations

The word *presentation* as used in this chapter has several meanings. A presentation can be used for sales and promotions, training employees, and informing employees and other persons of policies, benefits, events, changes, updates, news, and many other messages.

Presentations are not only for businesses. Almost any communication is a presentation. Even a discussion with your spouse about upgrading your computer is a presentation. Every time you have a conversation with a person, you are usually presenting ideas that you want the other person to "buy." There might not be any monetary reward if a person buys your ideas, but there might be a substantial reward and sense of satisfaction to your ego. Whether we realize it or not, most of us are nearly always presenting and selling our ideas. Usually for this type of presentation, we don't need a lot of software and hardware.

However, for an old-fashioned presentation where a person stands up before a group with a projector and pointer, you might need software and hardware for text, graphics, sound, and video. A few years ago, software and hardware to accomplish all of this would have required large studios full of equipment and would have cost many thousands of dollars. Today it can be done relatively inexpensively with a desktop multimedia PC. I will talk about some of the tools that are available to help one make a better presentation.

## The need for presentations

Presentations are very important business tools for sales, contract proposals, and all of the other things listed earlier. Business presentations are also used for reports. Businesses spend billions of dollars each year on presentations trying to get their message out. However, a poor presentation can be a terrible waste of a company's valuable resources. Quite often, it is not the message that is at fault, but the messenger.

## Designing a good presentation

It is not always the presenter's fault for giving a bad presentation. He or she might not have the proper tools to make a good presentation. There are several new electronic tools, but one of the more important tools is proper training. There are a few people who are born with the charisma that makes them the perfect silver-tongued orators. They don't need to be trained. However, if you are like most of us, you might need to learn a few basic rules to become a better presenter.

The AskMe Multimedia Center (612-531-0603) has an excellent software package, Super Show & Tell, for developing presentations. Michael O'Donnel, the company president, has written a booklet called *Making Great Presentations Using Your PC*. The AskMe Company has also produced *A Guide To Multimedia On The PC*, a 52-page spiral bound book that has a wealth of information. Call them for copies of these very helpful books.

Presentations are so important that there is a magazine devoted solely to presentations. It is free to those who qualify. Almost anyone in business can qualify. For a qualification form, write to:

*Presentations*
Lakewood Building
50 South Ninth Street
Minneapolis, MN 55402-9973

Whether you ever expect to do any professional presentations or not, you should know how to give them. You should know the basic principles of public speaking. One of the best and least expensive ways to learn is through a Toastmasters group. There are usually chapters in most cities. Look in the phone book.

## Electronic notes

If you are giving a talk and need notes, put them on a laptop computer. Use a large type. Have the notes arranged so that, each time you press PgDn, new notes would roll up. Pressing PgUp would let you easily go back and review. Set the computer on the podium, then glance down now and then at your notes.

Laptops have now become very inexpensive unless you are looking for one with color and an active-matrix display. If you do much public speaking, keeping your notes on a laptop is much better than hand-written notes.

## Displaying the presentation

The slide and the overhead projectors are still the most popular and most used. Of course, there is no sound or motion on these systems.

With an LCD panel, any image that appears on a computer screen can be projected onto a wall or a large theater type screen. The output of a computer is plugged into the LCD panel, which is then placed on the bed of an overhead projector system. Whatever appears on the computer screen appears on the LCD panel, which is then projected onto the screen.

If the computer has a sound board and speakers, a complete presentation with color, sound, and motion is possible.

Some of the LCD panels can be connected to a TV, VCR, or camcorder and project the output onto a large screen. Some of the LCD panel systems can be rather expensive. They have an active-matrix screen, the same type of screen used in the more expensive notebook computers. The active-matrix means that they require a separate transistor for every pixel in the panel, which might be several hundred thousand. One reason the active-matrix panels are so expensive is that a single defective transistor makes the whole display panel defective.

There are some less expensive LCD panels that are monochrome but that can display several shades of gray. The list prices for the LCD panels start at about $1000, but the color active-matrix can cost from $4000 and go as high as $10,000 or more.

Here are a few companies who manufacture LCD panels:

| | |
|---|---|
| In Focus Systems | 800-327-7231 |
| nViwew Corp. | 800-736-6439 |
| Proxima Corp. | 800-447-7694 |
| Sayett Technology | 800-678-7469 |
| Sharp Electronics | 201-529-9636 |
| 3M Corp. | 800-328-1371 |

## Projection monitors

The NEC Company (800-632-4636) has a couple of MultiSync Projection Monitors. This system takes the output from a computer, VCR, or other video source and projects it onto a large screen. The system uses red, green, and blue projection lamps such as those used on very large screen television sets.

There are several other companies who make similar screen projection monitors.

## Large-screen TV

Several companies have developed small devices that allow the output of a computer to be plugged into a large screen TV. The Advanced Digital Systems (310-865-1432) has the VGA to TV Elite.

Consumer Technology (800-356-3983) has The Presenter and The Presenter Plus, small pocket-sized devices that can connect a computer output to a TV. These devices can be used with a desktop PC or a small laptop. You can carry your presentation with you on a laptop and display it on a large television. The devices work with standard TVs or with the S-Video TVs.

The Comedge Company (818-855-2784) has the Audio/Video Key, a device that is similar to those listed previously. It can be used to connect a computer to a TV, VCR, or camcorder. It has both standard video and S-VHS outputs.

Ordinarily there is a lot of loss and degradation when a video signal is copied. If you have ever seen a video tape copy of a copy, you can see just how much is lost. Many of the newer VCRs and television sets are now equipped with the S-VHS or Super-video option. This option separates the chrominance signals from the luminance signals of composite video. The resulting signals are much cleaner with a lot less signal loss. If you are thinking of buying a new TV or VCR, look for the S-video input and output types.

## Camcorder presentations

All three of the previous devices can also be used to record a presentation from the computer to a VCR or camcorder. If you record your presentation on an 8mm tape recorder, you can easily take it with you. The palm-sized camcorders are small and relatively inexpensive and can be connected to any TV. The 8mm tape cartridges can hold up to two hours of text, graphics, speech, or music. The cartridges are small enough to fit several in a coat pocket. The camcorders can run off a small battery, so they don't have to have an external power source.

The Gold Disk Company (800-465-3375) has VideoDirector. This software comes with cables that plug into your computer and camcorder video recorder. You can use the software and cables to edit and record clips of your tapes. It works under Windows, so it is very easy to use. The VideoDirector is ideal for editing home video tapes or for professional editing for presentations. They have both DOS PC and Macintosh versions.

A camcorder can be an excellent presentation tool. Sony and several other companies are now manufacturing digital camcorders.

Snappy is a small device that captures a single photo from a camcorder, VCR, or TV. Once the single frame is captured on disk, it can be edited, changed, or morphed. For a free demo disk and more information, call Snappy at 800-306-7529.

Several companies are now making digital still cameras. There are a lot of opportunities for business use of this type of camera. Photos taken with a digital still camera can be downloaded directly to a hard disk. The photos can then be printed out with a color printer. For some applications, even a low-cost color inkjet printer would do.

Several realty companies in my area take color photos of houses that they have listed. They then have four-color brochures printed up and mail them to potential buyers. Four-color printing can be very expensive. Besides, by the time the brochures are printed, the house might have already been sold. It would be a lot less expensive and take a lot less time if a person used a digital camera to take photos of the houses for sale, then used an inkjet printer to print up color brochures. Rather than using an inkjet printer, you might want to use one of the more expensive dye sublimation or color laser printers. Check the printers listed in chapter 12.

There are many other business uses for digital cameras. At this time, they are a bit expensive, but they will be coming down in price very soon.

Here are a few companies who make fairly inexpensive digital cameras that cost from $500 to $1000 at this time:

| | |
|---|---|
| Apple QuickTake | 800-538-9696 |
| Casio QV-10 | 800-962-2746 |
| Chinon ES-3000 | 800-441-0222 |
| Kodak DC40 | 800-235-6325 |
| Logitech FotoMan Pixtura | 800-231-7717 |
| Dycam DC-10 | 800-883-9226 |

These companies have several different models. There are several other companies that manufacture very expensive professional digital cameras that cost from $3000 up to $40,000. Here are just a few:

| | |
|---|---|
| Dicomed Digital Camera | 800-888-7979 |
| Kodak DCS 420, DCS 200 | 800-344-0006 |
| Leaf Lumina, Leaf DCB II | 508-836-5500 |
| Nikon E2 | 800-526-4566 |

We are all presenters and salespersons in almost everything we do. We can be much better salespersons if we communicate better.

# Summary

There are thousands of different applications for your Pentium Pro computer. I can't possibly list them all. It is a most versatile and fantastic tool.

# 16
# Essential software

This chapter can save you hundreds of dollars on software. You cannot operate a computer without software. It is equally as necessary as hardware. Software is merely instructions that tells the hardware what to do. Computers are dumb and will only do what the software tells them to do.

## Off-the-shelf and ready-to-use software

There are a few basic programs that you will need. I can't possibly even list all of the software that is available for the Pentium Pro. There is more software, already written and immediately available, than you can use in a lifetime. The software companies are constantly revising and updating their software. There are off-the-shelf programs that can do almost everything that you could ever want to do with a computer.

There are several categories of programs that you will need. Just a short time ago, we all needed a separate disk operating system (DOS), but Windows 95 has eliminated the need for that. Windows 95 does a lot, but we still need word processors, databases, spreadsheets, utilities, shells, communications software, and graphics programs. Depending on what you intend to use your computer for, there are hundreds of others for special needs.

### List price versus discount price

*Note:* I list prices several times in this chapter. The prices listed are for comparison only. They will be different by the time you read this, no doubt lower.

Software can be more expensive than the hardware. The prices can also vary from vendor to vendor. Quite often, software will have an inflated list price that is about twice what the discount price will be. The software vendor can say, "Look at how much you are saving. We cut the price almost in half just for you." Most people are a bit wiser now, so many of the companies have stopped listing an unreasonable price and just list a "Discount" price. If you look through the catalogs listed in this chapter, you will find that the discount price is the same, or within just a few dollars, in almost all of the catalogs. However, there are a few that have prices that are considerably lower. Order all of the catalogs, and do your own comparisons.

## Surplus Software

One of the best ways that I know of to save on software is to buy it from Surplus Software (800-753-7877). Quite often, there are quite a lot of software packages that have not been sold when a new version is released.

The software business is somewhat like the soap business. The software and soap companies have to come out with a new and improved version every year. Quite often, the new-and-improved versions don't perform much better than the old ones did, or they might do things that you have no need for. Like most people, I never use all of the capabilities of my software.

If you would like to save some money and don't mind using an older software version, call Surplus Software and ask for a copy of their free catalog. They have hundreds of surplus software packages still in their original shrinkwrap. Unfortunately, they don't have space to list them all. If you don't see a package that you need, call them and ask for it.

The Surplus Software Company also carries several hardware components.

## Software upgrades

Most of the computer and software stores, such as Egghead and CompUSA, participate in upgrade discounts. These discounts can save you a considerable amount of money. There are two different types of upgrades: live upgrade and competitive upgrade.

### Live upgrade discounts

You can buy Microsoft PowerPoint 3.0 for $18.99 from Surplus Software. This software can probably do just about all that you could ever want to do. However, if you really must have the latest, Microsoft PowerPoint for Windows 95 is advertised in a discount software catalog for $299. However, you can get it for $92 with a *live* upgrade.

A live upgrade is a previous version of the same product. So, if you buy the 3.0 version from Software Surplus, you can get the very latest Windows 95 version for a total cost of $111. You would save $188.

Another example is that you can buy Microsoft Word for Windows 2.0 for about $30. You can use it as a live upgrade to buy Microsoft Word 7.0 for Windows 95 for $92. Without the live upgrade, Microsoft Word 7.0 will cost $299. If you have or buy an older copy of Microsoft Excel, PowerPoint, or Word, you can trade it in for a copy of Microsoft Office for Windows 95 for a cost of only $184. Without an upgrade, Microsoft Office for Windows 95 costs $457.

### Competitive upgrade discounts

You can get an even better deal if you trade in an older copy of one of Microsoft Word's competitors, such as WordPerfect, AMI Pro, or even WordStar. The Software Surplus catalog offers earlier versions of most of these packages.

Microsoft is not the only one who plays this game. You can trade in any previous version of WordPerfect or a competitor for WordPerfect 6.1 for Windows 95. One catalog lists it for $279, but with a trade-in, you can get it for only $89.

Many other companies will also accept competitive trade-ins for upgrades.

### Proof of purchase for upgrade discount

Before you buy a major software product, you might call the software company and ask what would qualify for a competitive package to trade in for what you want to buy. There is usually quite a bit of latitude.

Often they will ask for the title page from the original manual for proof of purchase. The software companies have no use for the older used copies. It would just clutter up their stores. You can keep the old software and the rest of the manual.

The proof of purchase varies among the different software publishers. You might be required to provide one or more of four general types of proof of purchase or ownership:

- The title page of the user manual
- A copy of a sales receipt or invoice
- The serial number of the software program
- A photocopy of the original program disk

Most of the larger software vendors, such as Egghead, CompUSA and others, participate in these programs. If you are buying through mail order, you can mail or fax a copy of the required items. Call the companies, and ask what their requirements are. Call the catalog companies, and ask for a copy of their catalogs.

## CD-ROM discs and multimedia

The Surplus Software Company also lists hundreds of low-cost CD-ROM discs. The discs have hundreds of different kinds of software for business, graphics, education, science, games, entertainment, and other subjects. If you like beer, they even offer a CD that tells you how you can brew your own.

They list several multimedia kits with CD-ROM drives, sound boards, and titles for very low prices. The kits might have double-speed CD-ROM drives; however, if you used the low-cost d-Time[10] CD-ROM drive accelerator software from Ballard Synergy (206-656-8070), it would provide about the same benefit that a more expensive quad-speed drive would give you. The d-Time[10] uses your hard disk to cache data from the CD-ROM disc. Access and transfer rate then becomes essentially whatever the speed of your hard disk is.

# Shareware and public-domain software

Also remember that there are excellent free public-domain programs that can do almost everything that the high-cost commercial programs can do. Check your local bulletin board, user group, or the ads for public-domain software in most computer magazines. There are also some excellent shareware programs that can be registered for a nominal sum.

## Try before you buy

The Software Dispatch Company (800-289-8383) can send you a CD-ROM disc that has several software programs on it. You can look at them and try them. If you find one that you would like to buy, just give them a call. Have your credit card ready. They will give you a password that you can use to unlock that particular program and download it to your hard disk. It has just about all the software that a person in a small office or home office (SOHO) would ever need.

## Software catalogs

There are several direct-mail discount software companies. If you are undecided about what you need, call the companies for a catalog, then decide. Many of the companies that send out catalogs sell both software and hardware. They usually have very good descriptions of the software and hardware along with prices. In a book like this, I just don't have the available space to describe the software and hardware like the catalogs do. The catalogs are an excellent way to get the basic facts about software.

You should be aware that some of the companies are not exactly discount houses. You might find better prices at your local store or in some of the computer magazines.

You should also note that some of the catalogs do not have a date on them. They usually have some sort of unintelligible code near the mailing address. If you order from one of the catalogs, they will ask you for the code. They will then charge you the price listed in that particular catalog. Prices of software and hardware change almost overnight. So, if you don't have the latest catalog and you order, you might not be paying the latest price.

Here are just a few of the companies who will send you their software catalogs:

| | |
|---|---|
| Computer Discount Warehouse (CDW) | 800-330-4239 |
| DellWare | 800-847-4051 |
| Egghead | 800-344-4323 |
| Desktop Publishing (DTP Direct) | 800-325-5811 |
| Elek-Tek | 800-395-1000 |
| Global Software & Hardware | 800-845-6225 |
| J&R Computer World | 800-221-8180 |
| JDR Microdevices | 800-538-5000 |
| Insight CD-ROM | 800-488-0002 |
| MicroWarehouse | 800-367-7080 |
| PC Connections | 800-800-5555 |
| The PC Zone | 800-258-2088 |
| PowerUp! Direct | 800-851-2917 |
| Shareware Express | 800-346-2842 |
| Software Spectrum | 800-787-1166 |
| Tiger Software | 800-888-4437 |

J&R Computer World supplies mostly Macintosh software.

# Essential software needed

I can't possibly list all of the thousands of software packages available. The computer magazines listed in chapter 17 often have detailed reviews of software. Of course, they usually have many advertisements for software in every issue. The following sections briefly cover some of the essential software packages that you will need.

## Operating systems software

DOS to a computer is like gasoline is to an automobile. Without it, it won't operate. DOS is an acronym for *disk operating system*. However, it does much more than just operate the disks. In recognition of this, OS/2 has dropped the D.

If you are new to computers, DOS should be the first thing that you learn. DOS has over 50 commands, but the chances are that you will never need to know more than 15 or 20 of the commands. DOS 6.2 has a very poor manual, but it has very good on-disk help. At the prompt, just type HELP command_name or HELP ?.

### MS-DOS

You won't need DOS with Windows 95, but Windows 95 can only be used on 386DX systems and up. There are millions of people with older XTs, 286s, and 386SXs that will still need DOS. There are many people who will not move up to Windows 95, so Microsoft will continue to offer MS-DOS. However, it is doubtful that they will update it as often as in the past.

### IBM PC-DOS

IBM claims that their PC-DOS 7.0 is smaller and faster and has several features not found in MS-DOS 6.22. PC-DOS 7.0 can be loaded on top of any DOS that you might already have. It will automatically update and replace those files and commands that have the same name. Some of the files in PC-DOS 7.0 have a similar function but different names, such as RAMBOOST, which is better than MEMMAKER at providing free memory. Like Microsoft, IBM went to outside companies and licensed some of the features, such as the Stacker compression software. To match MS-DOS, they also used Central Point's backup software and several other very useful utilities.

PC-DOS 7.0 also has support for the PCMCIA technology, PenDOS, CD-ROM support, and much more.

### OS/2 Warp

OS/2 Warp breaks the 640K barrier and can seamlessly address over 4GB of RAM. It can do true multitasking and run several programs at the same time. If one program crashes, it does not affect the other programs. It can run all DOS software and any of the software that has been developed for Windows.

OS/2 also has Adobe Type Manager (ATM), which allows scalable fonts for Windows and printing. It has several other excellent utilities and goodies. Version 3 has a BonusPak that allows Internet connection and includes fax software, multimedia, and much more. They even include a few games, such as solitaire and chess, if you have nothing else to do.

OS/2 Warp is a 32-bit system. It can be run on 16-bit 286 systems, but they recommend a 386SX or higher. They also recommend at least 4MB of RAM; it would be better to have 8MB or more.

OS/2 Warp is very easy to install and comes with an on-disk tutorial for easy learning.

At the time of this writing, there is speculation that IBM is working on an OS/2 version 4 that will meet or exceed all of the features found in Windows 95.

### Windows 95

One of the problems with DOS is that you often had to type in arcane commands. Many of the commands were difficult to remember. One reason for the success of the Macintosh is that you only had to point to a command with a mouse and click.

Windows 95 is now very much like the Mac in that respect. It does everything that DOS and Windows 3.1 did and more. Windows 3.1 could be run on the 16-bit 286 and 386SX, but some of Windows 95 is 32-bit software, so it will require a 386DX as a minimum. It will run with only 4MB of RAM, but 8MB is recommended; it would be better yet to have at least 16MB.

Windows 95 will go a long way toward making Plug-and-Play a reality. Programs that carry the Windows 95 logo are supposed to meet the Plug-and-Play specifications set out by Microsoft.

### Windows NT

At the time this is being written, Microsoft is doing a revision of Windows NT. There are many things in Windows 95 that will be in the new Windows NT. However, this is high-end software that will be used primarily on servers and large systems. Many of the high-end RISC systems use Windows NT. The new version should be available by the time you read this.

## Word processors

The most used of all software is word processing. There are literally dozens of word processor packages, each one slightly different than the others. It amazes me that they can find so many different ways to do the same thing. All of the major word processor programs come with a spelling checker and a thesaurus, which can be very handy. They usually also include several other utilities, such as a calculator, communications programs for your modem, outlines, desktop publishing, print merging, and many others.

### WordPerfect

WordPerfect has the ability to select fonts by a proper name and has simplified printer installation and the ability to do most desktop publishing functions, including columns, import graphics, and many other useful functions and utilities.

WordPerfect also has several other software products such as WordPerfect Presentations; WordPerfect Office for e-mail, scheduling, and calendaring; DataPerfect, a database; and WordPerfect Works, an integrated software package.

Novell has recently sold WordPerfect to the Corel Corporation. This should make it a bit easier for them to compete with Microsoft Word.

### Microsoft Word 7.0 for Windows 95

Microsoft Word for Windows lets you take advantage of all the features and utilities of Windows. If you have previously learned a different word processor, such as WordPerfect, Word for Windows can let you use the WordPerfect commands. Besides an excellent word processor, Word for Windows does just about everything that is needed for such things as desktop publishing, generating reports, and making charts, drawings, and presentations. It does columns, imports graphics, and can import data from databases, spreadsheets, and other files. It even has a corrector for people like me who constantly type "teh" instead of "the." It has many more features than I would ever use, even if I could learn them all.

### Lotus Word Pro 96

Lotus Word Pro 96 has all the tools you need to create professionally looking documents. It has several preformatted templates and intuitive tools, such as Revision Marking, Highlighter, and Comment Notes.

There are several other very good word processor programs.

## Grammar checkers

You might be the most intelligent person alive, but you might not be able to write a simple intelligible sentence. There are several grammar checking programs that can work with most of the word processors. They can analyze your writing and suggest ways to improve it. Here are just a couple of them:

Right Writer    Que Corp.            800-992-0244
Grammatik       Reference Software   800-872-9933

## Database programs

Database packages are very useful for business purposes. They allow you to manage large amounts of information. Most programs allow one to store information, search it, sort it, do calculations, make up reports, and use several other very useful features.

At the present time, there are almost as many database programs as there are word processors. Some of them will allow the interchange of data from one program to another.

The average price for the better known database packages is almost twice that of word processors.

### dBASE

dBASE II was one of the first database programs for the personal computer. It has gone through several revisions and improvements. It is a very powerful program and has hundreds of features.

Previous versions were highly structured and could be a bit difficult to learn. The new Windows version is very easy to use; in many cases, you just point and click or click and drag. You can create forms or design reports very quickly and easily. It has excellent built-in help and tutorials. dBASE is downward compatible, so the 7 million users who have databases generated by the older versions can still use their old data.

It is now possible to buy Visual dBASE 5.5 and Visual dBASE Compiler bundled together so that you can easily create and distribute database applications.

### Paradox

Paradox is fairly easy to learn and use and is fast and powerful. It is designed for both beginners and expert users. It is a powerful full-featured relational database that can be used on Windows 95 or Windows NT, on a single PC or on a network.

The query by example is very helpful for beginners and experts alike. Paradox has a very powerful programming language, PAL. Experienced programmers can easily design special applications.

You can contact Borland International at 408-438-5300.

### askSam

The funny looking name is an acronym for *Access Knowledge via Stored Access Method*. It is a free form, text-oriented database management system. It is very much like a word processor. In fact, if you can use a word processor, you will have no trouble using askSam. Data can be typed in randomly, then sorted and accessed. Data can also be entered in a structured format for greater organization.

It is not quite as powerful as dBASE 5 or Paradox, but it is much easier to learn and use. It is also much less expensive. It is ideal for most business database needs. It is also great for personal records needs, such as for expenses. I have been audited twice by the IRS because of my home office. I now put all of my tax records in askSam. It will save me a lot of time and trouble the next time they audit me.

The Windows version even has a spell checker and hyperlink. A hyperlink in a document can link up with other parts of a document, open a new document or report, and perform several other useful functions.

They also have discount programs for students. Students can get a very good discount when they buy the program when the order is placed by an instructor. Any instructor who places an order for 10 or more copies will get a free copy. They also have a very low price to upgrade from a previous version.

You can contact Seaside Software at 800-800-1997.

### ACT! for Windows

ACT! for Windows from Symantec (408-253-9600) is a business contact database program that lets you store names, addresses, phone numbers, notes, and other information about your customers and accounts. It has a history log that automatically records all completed activities for each contact. The information and records can be easily accessed in seconds.

### High-end database programs

There are several high-end database programs, such as Oracle and Sybase SQL, for networks and network servers. Most of these databases are 32-bit programs that will suit the Pentium Pro very well.

## Spreadsheets

Spreadsheets are primarily number crunchers. They have a matrix of cells in which data can be entered. Data in a particular cell can be acted on by formulas and mathematical equations. If the data in the cell that is acted on affects other cells, recalculations are done on them.

Several of the tax software programs use a simple form of spreadsheet. The income and all of the deductions can be entered. If an additional deduction is discovered, it can be entered and all the calculations will be done over automatically.

In business, spreadsheets are essential for inventory, expenses, accounting purposes, forecasting, making charts, and dozens of other vital business uses.

There are a large number of spreadsheet programs. The following sections cover just a few.

### Lotus 1-2-3

Lotus was one of the first spreadsheets. The current version for Windows is a spreadsheet, database, and graphics package all in one. It is still one of the most powerful and popular spreadsheets.

The discount price listed in several catalogs is $309.95. The upgrade price is $95.95. Any previous version of 1-2-3 can be used for a live upgrade.

Competitive spreadsheets—such as Excel, Quattro, Quattro Pro, or Super-Calc—can qualify for a competitive upgrade. Prices listed are for comparison only and will probably be different by the time you read this.

Check through any of the catalogs listed earlier or call Lotus Development (617-577-8500). Lotus is now a division of IBM.

### Microsoft Excel

Microsoft Excel is a very powerful spreadsheet program with pull-down menus, windows, and dozens of features. It can even perform as a database. It has a long list of other features. Excel is one of the products that makes up Microsoft Office.

Several catalogs have a discount price for Excel of $299.95. A live upgrade is only $89.95, and the competitive upgrade is $119.95.

### Quattro Pro

The Quattro Pro spreadsheet looks very much like Lotus 1-2-3. In fact, Lotus sued Borland because it has the "look and feel" of 1-2-3. After dragging through the courts for several years and costing hundreds of thousands of dollars, a judge has ruled against Lotus.

Quattro Pro has better graphics capabilities for charts, calculates faster, has pull-down menus, can print sideways, and has several features not found in Lotus 1-2-3. It is fully compatible with Lotus 1-2-3 spreadsheet files. It is very easy to learn and has Object Help, Interactive Tutors, and Experts.

Like most of the other major software packages, earlier versions of Quattro is available from Surplus Software for a very low price.

The Quattro division is now a part of Novell. They have recently updated and revised the program.

There are many other spreadsheet programs. Check the ads and reviews in computer magazines.

## Suites

Several companies are now bundling several software packages together as a suite. The suites usually have a word processor, database, and spreadsheet and perhaps one or two other packages. The software in the suite packages is integrated so that the programs will all work together. A suite usually costs much less than buying each package separately.

The following sections cover just a few of the more popular suites.

### Microsoft Office

Microsoft Office has several different versions. One version includes Microsoft Word 6.0 for word processing, Excel 5.0 for spreadsheets, PowerPoint for presentations, and Mail for e-mail and fax systems. Another version includes all of these plus Access 2.0, for database.

### Microsoft Home and Small Business Value Pack

Another version of Microsoft Office, the Microsoft Home and Small Business Value Pack has Microsoft Word, Microsoft Excel, Microsoft Publisher, and Microsoft Bookshelf.

### PerfectOffice

The PerfectOffice Suite includes six major software packages. They are WordPerfect 6.1, Quattro Pro 6.0, Presentations 3.0, InfoCentral 1.1, Envoy 1.0, and GroupWise 4.1. The packages work together so that data from any one program can be moved back and forth to any other one.

WordPerfect, of course, is about the most popular word processor in the world, Quattro Pro is one of the better spreadsheets, Presentations is one of the better programs for designing your own presentations, Envoy is an electronic document publisher and lets you view documents that might have been created in fonts that you don't have, and GroupWise is an integrated package for e-mail, calendaring, scheduling, and task management.

PerfectOffice works on almost all networks, such as NetWare, Windows for Workgroups, Windows NT, Banyan Vines, and others.

### Lotus SmartSuite 96

Lotus SmartSuite includes Word Pro 96 for word processing, Lotus 1-2-3 for Windows for spreadsheets, Lotus Approach 96 for a database, Lotus Organizer for managing personal information, and Freelance Graphics 96 for creating presentations.

### Microsoft Works

Microsoft Works could be called a poor man's suite. It has a word processor, spreadsheet, database, and communications, charting, and drawing software all in one package. It also includes Microsoft Bookshelf. A discount house is offering this software package for $73. The same discount house offers other suites for prices from $279 up to $559. So you know that the Microsoft Works package cannot be nearly as powerful or have as many goodies as the full-featured suites. However, depending on what you want to do, the Microsoft Works might be all you need.

## Utilities

Utilities are essential tools that can unerase a file, detect bad sectors on a hard disk, diagnose, unfragment, sort, and do many other things. Norton Utilities was the first, and is still foremost, in the utility department.

### WINCheckIt 4.0

WINCheckIt from Touchstone (800-531-0450) has several very helpful utility modules plus four complete books. Test It checks your modem's configuration, speed, and line connection. The motherboard serial and parallel ports, hard drive, and floppy drive are also tested. Rate It tests and rates CD-ROM drives, determines their capabilities, and displays details. Uninstall It can find and uninstall application files that are duplicates or that are no longer being used. Tune It can defragment memory, provide CD-ROM and video Benchmarks and rate the overall system. Clean It can compress and manage seldom used files. Find It is a four-volume technical library on CD-ROM from McGraw-Hill. The four books included on the CD-ROM are *Windows 95 Made Easy*, *Windows 3.1 Made Easy*, *DOS Made Easy*, and *Upgrade or Repair Your PC And Save A Bundle, 4th Revision*. I am the proud author of the *Upgrade or Repair Your PC* book. Every word and photo of my 440-page book is on the CD-ROM. The cover prices of the four books is over $95. The street price of WINCheckIt is about $39 at this time. This is a fantastic bargain for a fantastic product.

### Norton Utilities

Norton Utilities is a package that everybody should have. It has several excellent utilities that can save you time and money. The Norton Disk Doctor (NDD) file can automatically repair disk problems, both hard and floppy. The Norton Disk Editor will let you explore and repair sectors of a hard disk. File Fix lets you repair data files. The Unerase command is great for recovering accidentally erased files.

The latest version of the Norton Utilities for Windows 95 improves many of the old standard features and adds several new ones. It has added several new utilities that can help in diagnosing, troubleshooting, and repairing.

Norton can automatically check all of your hard drives for crosslinked files, will fix any corrupted files, and ask if you want to make out a report. It will then make a mirror image of the FAT and store it in a second location. If the primary FAT is damaged, you will still be able to access your data from the second FAT.

Norton AntiVirus is a simple and easy-to-use package that detects, destroys, and prevents virus infections.

To find out more about Norton and other Symantec products call their FaxBack number at 800-554-4403. Ask for their catalog directory to determine which numbers to order.

### SpinRite 4.0

The current version SpinRite has several new features that were not in the original versions. It performs the most rigorous hard disk tests of any other software. It can detect any marginal areas and move the data to a safe area. SpinRite can maximize hard disk performance and prevent hard disk problems before they happen.

You can contact Gibson Research at 714-348-7100.

### Disk Technician Gold

Disk Technician (619-274-5000) does essentially the same type of tests that SpinRite does, but not quite as rigorous. Disk Technician also has several automatic features and can now detect most viruses. It can be installed and will work in the background to detect any errors as they happen when writing to a hard disk.

# Directory and disk-management programs

There are dozens of disk-management programs that help you keep track of, find, rename, view, sort, copy, and delete your files and data on your hard disk and perform many other useful utilities. They can save an enormous amount of time and make life a lot simpler.

### XTree for Windows

XTree was one of the first and still one of the best disk-management programs available. I use it to view my files then delete unnecessary ones. I also use it to copy and backup files from one disk or directory to another. It will also let you order the files by date or alphabetically. I often look at the date stamp so that I know which files are the latest. It has many other excellent features. I don't know how anyone can get along without XTree.

XTree is a part of the Symantec Companies. Symantec has a large number of excellent software products. If you have a fax machine, you can call their automated fax system at 800-554-4403 and have them fax you information about any of their products.

### CleanSweep

CleanSweep can find and give you the option of removing duplicate and unwanted files. When a program is installed, it might have several files. Some of them might even be hidden. If you decide later to delete one of these programs, it might leave several files on your disk just taking up space. CleanSweep can find these files and let you delete them or archive them.

# Computer-aided design (CAD) programs

Most CAD programs are high-end programs that require very good high-resolution monitors and powerful computers. The Pentium Pro is an ideal computer for computer-aided design.

### AutoCAD

AutoCAD from the Autodesk Company is a high-end, high-cost design program. It is quite complex with an abundance of capabilities and functions. However, it is also rather expensive at about $3000.

Autodesk is the IBM of the CAD world and has more or less established the standard for the many clones that have followed.

You can contact Autodesk, Inc. at 415-332-2344.

### Generic CADD

Autodesk has several modules and other programs that cost less than the full-blown AutoCAD. One of them is Generic CADD 6.0. For more information, call Autodesk at 800-228-3601, Ext. 803.

### Home Series

Autodesk has a set of five low-cost programs they call the Home Series. These programs are HOME, KITCHEN, BATHROOM, DECK, and LANDSCAPE. You don't have to be an architect to design your dream home; design an up-to-date kitchen, bathroom, or deck; or plan your landscape. Each of the five programs have a list price of $59.95. The programs come with a library of professional symbols—such as doors, outlets, furniture, fixtures, and appliances—that you can import and place in your drawing. The program tracks the materials specified in your drawing and automatically creates a shopping list.

### 3D PLAN

Autodesk recently added 3D PLAN, a program that will let you look at any of the plans that were created in the HOME, KITCHEN, BATHROOM, DECK, OR LANDSCAPE programs in three dimensions. Surfaces are shaded to add a realistic appearance.

I would recommend these programs for anyone who plans to design their own home or do any remodeling on an older home. They can save you hours of time and lots of money.

You can contact Autodesk at 800-228-3601.

### DesignCAD 2D and DesignCAD 3D

These CAD programs will do just about everything that AutoCAD will do at a lesser cost. DesignCAD 3D allows you to make three-dimensional drawings.

You can contact American Small Business Computers at 918-825-4844.

There are several other companies that offer CAD software. Check the computer magazines.

## Miscellaneous software programs

There are many programs for things such as accounting, statistics, finance, graphics, and many other applications. Some are very expensive; some are very reasonable.

### CorelDRAW

CorelDRAW can be used for such things as drawing, illustration, page layout, charting, animation, desktop publishing, and presentations. It has word processing, OCR, over 5000 drag-and-drop symbols and shapes, over 18,000 clipart images, over 750 fonts, and many other features and utilities.

This is all in CorelDRAW version 3. It comes on a 600MB CD-ROM disc. They have also added more fonts, features, and functions to CorelDRAW and released it as CorelDRAW 4. It comes on two CD-ROM discs. Both releases are available.

Corel has several other excellent software packages. Call them at 613-728-3733 for a brochure.

### CorelSCSI

CorelSCSI is a program that has software and several SCSI drivers that work with most major SCSI host adapters, such as Always, DPT, Ultrastor, and Adaptec. It also has SitBACK (a software program for unattended backup) and Corel Tape Backup software. It also has several other programs and utilities.

You can contact Corel Corp. at 613-728-3733.

### Uninstaller for Windows

When a program for Windows is installed on your computer, it copies pieces and portions into several different areas. If you decide later that you don't want that application, you can use DOS to delete the program. However, it will not delete all references to the program. Every time you load Windows, it might hunt for that program, then tell you that it can't find it.

Even some demo programs load themselves into several areas that are difficult to clean out. Use the DOS EDITOR and look at the WIN.INI sometime. You might find references there to programs that you erased months ago. These leftover bits and pieces can clutter up your disk considerably.

The Uninstaller from MicroHelp can track down all the different parts of a Windows program and delete them. Even if you are a Windows pro, the Uninstaller can save you time.

You can contact MicroHelp, Inc. at 770-516-0899.

### CleanSweep 95

CleanSweep 95 checks can check all of the files on your hard disks. If it finds two or more files with the same name in different directories, it will display them. It will also show the date the file was created, the number of bytes in the file, and how often the file has been accessed. You then have the opportunity of backing up or archiving one or both of the files. You are also given the option of moving the file and all of its associated components to another directory or to a network. It also will let you delete one or more files and its associated components.

You can order CleanSweep 95 from Quarterdeck (310-309-3700).

### StreetSmart

StreetSmart from Charles Schwab Company (800-334-4455) lets you use your computer and modem to trade stocks, options, mutual funds, and bonds. It lets you research Dow Jones News and Dow Jones databases; use MarketScope for S&P database and news, stock ratings, and buy/sell recommendations; and use Company Reports to do comprehensive research on earnings and financials. You can create your own performance graphs, import and export critical financial data, and customize your portfolio reports. If you have any interest in the stock market, then you should have a copy of StreetSmart.

### Money Counts

This is a very inexpensive program that can be used at home or in a small business. With it, you can set up a budget, keep track of all your expenses, balance your checkbook, and several other functions. Money Counts is available at a very low cost.

You can contact Parsons Technology at 800-223-6925.

### It's Legal

It's Legal helps you create wills, leases, promissory notes, and other legal documents.

Contact Parsons Technology at 800-223-6925.

### WillMaker

WillMaker from Nolo Press (510-549-1976) is a low-cost program that can help you create a will. Everyone should have a will, no matter what age you are or how much you own. Many people put it off because they don't want to take the time or they don't want to pay a lawyer a large fee. This inexpensive software can help you easily create a will that can prevent many family problems.

We don't like to think about this sort of thing, but it happens to everyone, sooner or later.

### Living Trust Maker

Living Trust Maker from Nolo Press (510-549-1976) is a program that every family should have. Even if you have a will, it is possible that it could end up in probate court. You might have heard some of the horror stories about how probate can take several years to settle and the costs can completely eat up all of a large estate. A living trust can avoid probate and its lengthy and costly processes.

Ordinarily, a living trust requires a lawyer and can be relatively expensive. With the Nolo Press Living Trust Maker, you can create your own living trust without a lawyer. The program allows you to fashion the trust to your unique needs. The software guides you through the process, but it comes with a large user guide and legal manual that can explain and answer most of your questions. Nolo Press has free technical support if you have any problems.

### Software for kids

One of the big reasons to have a home computer is for the kids. If you have children and you don't have a computer, then they are being handicapped. In today's society, a child needs all of the help he or she can get to make it as an adult. A computer is absolutely essential to help in the very important early training. There are thousands of software programs—commercial, shareware, and public domain—that have been developed for children. Most of the software catalogs listed in this chapter have children software listings.

A good example of a children's educational program is the Smithsonian Institution Dinosaur Museum from the Software Marketing Corporation (602-893-2042). Many of the programs such as this come on CD-ROMs. This one comes on five 1.44MB floppies. The program is in 3D, so a pair of plastic 3D video glasses comes with it.

The *KidSoft Magazine* (800-354-6150) has reviews of dozens of reviews of software for kids.

### Software training

Most software manuals are very poorly written. You can usually tell how bad the manuals are by the number of books written telling you how to use the software. Microsoft is the largest software publisher in the world. They also have a very large book publishing house: Microsoft Press. They publish hundreds of books each year to help people learn to use the software they publish. A cynical person might suspect that Microsoft publishes poor manuals so that they can sell more books.

There are also several companies that conduct training classes and seminars for learning some of the most popular software. These seminars can cost several hundred dollars for a one- or two-day session. I can't learn enough in one or two days to justify the cost of some of the seminars. If you pay $500 or $600 for a software package, you shouldn't have to spend another $500 or $600 to learn how to use it.

One of the better ways to learn software is by using video tapes. The ViaGrafix Company (800-842-4723) has about 200 different video tape courses. They have tapes on all of the most popular software and even some that is not so popular. You should be able to find a tape for almost any program imaginable. They even have instructional tapes on networking, telecommunications, programming, and much more. You can view the tapes at your leisure and learn at your own pace. Call them for a catalog.

ViaGrafix now has several training programs on CD-ROM, which are even better than a video tape.

### LapLink for Windows

If you do any traveling, it is almost essential that you have a laptop computer. If you work in an office, it is very convenient to copy data from a desktop PC to a laptop to bring work home. However, it is sometimes a problem transferring files and data from the PC to the laptop then back to the PC.

For many years, Traveling Software (800-343-8080) has been foremost in providing software and cables specifically for this purpose. They have now developed several new utilities that make the file transfer faster and easier. You can now use it with a modem to tie into the office PC or a network so that you can work at home, update your files, or access your e-mail while traveling.

The cables use the LPT1 parallel printer ports or COM serial ports or can be used by modem or wireless devices or over a network, such as Novell NetWare. Using the cables and software, two computers can be tied together in a very low-cost network. If you own a laptop or work in an office with two or more computers, you could probably save a lot of time with LapLink for Windows.

# Summary

I can't possibly mention all of the fantastic software that is available. There are thousands of ready-made software programs that will allow you to do almost anything with your computer. Look through any computer magazine for the reviews and ads. You should be able to find programs for almost any application.

# 17
# Component sources

How much you save by assembling your own Pentium Pro will depend on what components you buy and who you buy them from. You will have to shop wisely and be fairly knowledgeable about the components to take advantage of good bargains. It is very difficult to keep up and know what is going on in this ever-changing industry. One of the best ways to do this is to subscribe to some of the many computer magazines. You can look through the magazines and do price comparisons of the various components and systems.

Another good way to keep up is to attend the many computer shows and swap meets.

## Computer shows and swap meets

I have done a lot of my buying at computer shows and swap meets. There is a computer show or swap almost every weekend in the larger cities. Sometimes there are two or three in the Los Angeles area on the weekends. If you live in or near a large city, check your newspaper for ads.

To set up a computer swap, an organizer will usually rent a large building, such as a convention center or a large hall. Booth spaces are then rented out to the various local vendors. Most of the booths will have good reputable local business people. Most of the shows have a circus-like atmosphere about them, and I often go just because of this.

One of the best features of the swap meets is that almost all of the components that you will need are there in one place on display. Several different booths will have similar components for sale. I usually take a pencil and pad with me to the shows. I walk around and write down the prices of the items that I want to buy and compare prices at the various booths. There can be quite a wide variation in the prices. I bought a good printer at one show. One dealer was asking $995 for it in one booth. About 50 feet away, another dealer was offering the same printer for $695.

You can also haggle with most of the dealers at the shows. Especially when it gets near closing time. Rather than pack up the material and lug it back to their stores, many will sell it for a lower price.

The Softbank Company (617-433-1500) sponsors the Computer Dealers Exposition (COMDEX). They put on the two biggest annual computer shows in the country. The spring show is usually held in Atlanta or sometimes in Chicago. Then a much bigger fall COMDEX is held during November in Las Vegas. The attendance goes up every year. When I first started attending in 1984, they only had about 60,000 people at Las Vegas. They now attract over 200,000. Every hotel room in Las Vegas is usually sold out six months before the show. They have now started a New Media Expo which, will be held in Los Angeles in the spring. The Interface Company also puts on international shows in several foreign countries.

# Your local store

Most of the vendors at the swaps are local business people. They want your business and will not risk losing you as a customer. However, there might be a few vendors from other parts of the country. If you buy something from a vendor who does not have a local store, be sure to get a name and address. Most components are reliable. However, there is always a chance that something might not work. You might need to exchange it or get it repaired, or you might need to ask some questions or need some support to get it working.

Again, computers are very easy to assemble. Once you have bought all of the components, it will take less than an hour to assemble your computer. However, it is possible to make a mistake. Most components are now fairly reliable. However, there is a possibility that a new part that you buy and install could be defective. Most of the dealers will give you a warranty of some kind and will replace defective parts. If there is something in the system that prevents it from operating, you might not be able to determine just which component is defective. Besides that, it can sometimes take a considerable amount of time to remove a component like a motherboard and return it to someone across town or, even worse, someone across the country. So, if at all possible, try to deal with a knowledgeable vendor who will support you and help you if you have any problems.

# Magazines and mail-order

Every computer magazine carries pages and pages of ads for compatible components and systems that can be sent to you through the mail. If you live in an area where there are no computer stores, or shows, you can buy by mail.

One of the biggest magazines in size and circulation is the *Computer Shopper*. It usually has over 1000 tabloid-sized pages. About 90% of the magazine is made up of full page ads for computer components and systems. They do manage to get a few articles in among the ads. For subscription information, call 800-274-6384.

The *Computer Shopper* and some of the other magazines have a categorized list of all the products advertised in the magazine and what page the product is on. This makes it very easy to find what you are looking for. Sometimes they will have several vendors offering the same product. This makes it easy to determine which one offers the better price.

Another reason to use mail order is because it can be less expensive than the local vendors. The local vendors usually have their stores in a fairly high-rent district; the mail-order people might be working out of their back bedroom. Most local vendors have to buy their stock from a distributor. The distributor usually buys it from the manufacturer or a wholesaler. By the time you get the product, it might have passed through several companies who each have made some profit. Most of the direct marketers who advertise by mail have cut out the middlemen and passed their profit on to you.

Still another reason why I do a lot shopping by mail is because of state taxes. In California, the state sales tax is 8.0% to as much as 8.5%. If I buy a computer system in California for $1000, it will cost me over $80 just for sales taxes. Even if I have to pay shipping charges for mail order, it is usually much less than the sales tax. The states have tried several times to eliminate this loophole and make you pay taxes no matter where you buy, but so far they have been unsuccessful.

Without computer magazines, there would be no mail-order and without mail-order, there would be no computer magazines. Ads are the lifeblood of magazines. The subscription price of a magazine doesn't even come close to paying for the mailing costs, so they must have ads to exist.

Most mail-order vendors are honest, but a few bad advertisers can ruin a magazine. *PC World* has a regular Consumer Watch column. If you have a problem with a mail-order vendor that you can't resolve, write to them. They can usually get it resolved. For *PC World* subscription information, call 800-234-3498.

The magazines have formed the Microcomputer Marketing Council (MMC) of the Direct Marketing Association. They police the advertisers fairly closely. They have an action line at 212-297-1393, or you can write to them at the following address:

Direct Marketing Association
6 East 43rd St.
New York, NY 10017

You should be sure of what you need and what you are ordering. Some of the ads aren't written very well and might not tell the whole story. Ads are expensive, so they might abbreviate or leave out a lot of important information. If possible, call them up and make sure. Ask what their return policy is for defective merchandise. Also ask how long before the item will be shipped, and ask for the current price. The ads are usually placed about two months before the magazines are delivered or hit the stands. The way prices are coming down, there could be quite a change in cost at the time you place your order. Of course, if you send them the advertised price, I am sure that they will not refuse it. A $2 or $3 phone call could save you a lot of time, trouble, grief, and maybe even some money.

## Ten rules for ordering by mail

The following sections provide some brief rules that you should follow when ordering by mail.

### Rule 1: Look for a street address

Make sure the advertiser has a street address. In some ads, they give only a phone number. If you decide to buy from this vendor, call and verify that there is a live person on the other end with a street number. However, before you send any money, do a bit more investigation. If possible, look through past issues of the same magazine for previous ads. If the company has been advertising for several months, then they are probably okay.

### Rule 2: Compare other vendor prices

Check through the magazines for other vendors' prices for this product. The prices should be fairly close. If it appears to be a bargain that is too good to be true, then . . . You know the rest.

### Rule 3: Buy from MMC members

Buy from a vendor who is a member of the Microcomputer Marketing Council (MMC) of the Direct Marketing Association (DMA) or another recognized association. There are now about 10,000 members who belong to marketing associations. They have agreed to abide by the ethical guidelines and rules of the associations. Except for friendly persuasion and the threat of expulsion, the associations have little power over the members. However, most of the vendors realize what is at stake and put a great value on their membership. Most who advertise in the major computer magazines are members.

The post office, the Federal Trade Commission, the magazines, and the legitimate businessmen who advertise have taken steps to try to stop the fraud and scams.

### Rule 4: Do your homework

Read the ads carefully. Advertising space is very expensive. Many ads use abbreviations. Many ads might not be entirely clear. If in doubt, call and ask. Know exactly what you want, and state precisely the model, make, size, component, and any other pertinent information. Tell them which ad you are ordering from, and ask them if the price is the same, if the item is in stock, and when you can expect delivery. If the item is not in stock, indicate whether you will accept a substitute or want your money refunded. Ask for an invoice or order number. Ask the person's name.

Write down all of the information, the time, the date, the company's address and phone number, a description of the item, and the promised delivery date. Write down and save any telephone conversations, including the time, date, and person's name. Save any and all correspondence.

### Rule 5: Ask questions

Ask if the advertised item comes with all of the necessary cables, parts, accessories, software, etc. Ask what the warranties are. Ask what the seller's return and refund policies are. Find out with whom should you correspond if there is a problem.

### Rule 6: Don't send cash

If you send cash, you will have no record of your purchase. If possible, use a credit card. If you have a problem, you can possibly have the bank refuse to pay the amount. A personal check can cause a delay of three to four weeks while the vendor waits for it to clear. A money order or credit card order should be filled and shipped immediately. Keep a copy of the money order.

### Rule 7: Ask for a delivery date

If you have not received your order by the promised delivery date notify the seller.

### Rule 8: Try the item out as soon as you receive it

If you have a problem, notify the seller immediately by phone, then in writing. Give all of the details. Don't return the merchandise unless the dealer gives you a return material authorization (RMA). Make sure to keep a copy of the shipper's receipt or packing slip or some evidence that the material was returned.

### Rule 9: What to do if it is defective

If you believe the product is defective or you have a problem, reread your warranties and guarantees. Reread the manual and any documentation. It is very easy to make an error or misunderstand how an item operates if you are unfamiliar with it. Before you go to a lot of trouble, try to get some help from someone else. At least get someone to verify that you do have a problem. There are many times when a problem will disappear and the vendor will not be able to duplicate it. If possible, when you call, try to have the item in your computer and be at the computer so you can describe the problem as it happens.

### Rule 10: Try to work out your problem with the vendor

If you cannot, then write to the consumer complaint agency in the seller's state. You should also write to the magazine and to the DMA.

## Federal Trade Commission rules

The following sections provide a brief summary of the FTC rules.

### Rule 1: Must ship within 30 days

The seller must ship your order within 30 days unless the ad clearly states that it will take longer.

### Rule 2: Right to cancel

If it appears that the seller cannot ship when promised, he must notify you and give a new date. He must give you the opportunity to cancel the order and refund your money if you desire.

### Rule 3: Must notify if order can't be filled

If the seller notifies you that he cannot fill your order on time, he must include a stamped self-addressed envelope or card so that you can respond to his notice. If you do not respond, he can assume that you agree to the delay. He still must ship within 30 days of the end of the original 30 days or cancel your order and refund your money.

### Rule 4: Right to cancel if delayed

Even if you consent to a delay, you still have the right to cancel at any time.

### Rule 5: Must refund money if canceled

If you cancel an order that has been paid for by check or money order, he must refund the money. If you paid by credit card, your account must be credited within one billing cycle. Store credits or vouchers in place of a refund are not acceptable.

### Rule 6: No substitutions

If the item you ordered is not available, the seller cannot send you a substitute without your express consent.

# Sources of knowledge

There are several good magazines that can help you gain the knowledge needed to make sensible purchases and to learn more about computers. These magazines usually carry interesting, timely, and informative articles and reviews of software and hardware. They also have many ads for computers, components, and software.

Some of the better magazines that you should subscribe to are the *Computer Shopper*, *Byte*, *PC Computing*, *PC World*, and *PC Magazine*. Most of these magazines are available on local magazine racks, but you will save money with a yearly subscription. Besides they will be delivered to your door.

If you need a source of components, you only have to look in any of these magazines to find hundreds of them. If you live near a large city, there will no doubt be several vendors who advertise in your local paper.

Another source of computer information can be found in the several good computer books published by McGraw-Hill.

There are hundreds of computer and computer-related magazines. If you read every one of them, you still will not be able to keep up with the flood of computer information.

## Recommended computer magazines

Here are just a few of the magazines that will help you keep abreast to some degree:

*AUDIO-FORUM*
96 Broad St.
Guilford, CT 06437

*Black Box Corporation*
P.O. Box 12800
Pittsburgh, PA 15241

*Byte Magazine*
P.O. Box 558
Hightstown, NJ 08520

*CD-I World*
P.O. Box 1358
Camden, ME 04843-1358

*CD-ROM Multimedia*
P.O. Box 2946
Plattsburgh, NY 12901-9863

*CD-ROM Professional*
462 Danbury Rd.
Wilton, CT 06897-2126

*CD-ROM Today*
Subscription Department
P.O. Box 51478
Boulder, CO 8032-1478

*Compute!*
P.O. Box 3245
Harlan, IA 51593-2424

*Computer Currents*
5720 Hollis St.
Emeryville, CA 94608

*Computer Graphics World*
P.O. Box 122
Tulsa, OK 74101-9966

*Computer Life*
P.O. Box 55880
Boulder, CO 80323-5880

*Computer Pictures*
Knowledge Industry Publications
701 Westchester Ave.
White Plains, NY 10604

*Computer Shopper*
P.O. Box 51020
Boulder, CO 80321-1020

*Computer World*
P.O. Box 2044
Marion, OH 43306-2144

*ComputerCraft*
76 North Broadway
Hicksville, NY 11801-9962

*Desktop Video World*
P.O. Box 594
Mt. Morris, IL 61054-7902

*Digital Imaging Micro Publishing*
21150 Hawthorne Bld. #104
Torrance, CA 90503

*Electronic Musician*
P.O. Box 41525
Nashville, TN 37204-9829

*High Color*
P.O. Box 1347
Camden, ME 04843-9956

*HOME & STUDIO RECORDING*
Music Maker Publications, Inc.
7318 Topanga Canyon Blvd.
Suite 200
Canoga Park, CA 91303

*Home Office Computing*
P.O. Box 51344
Boulder, CO 80321-1344

*Imaging Magazine*
1265 Industrial Highway
Southampton, PA 18966
800-677-3435

*Insight Direct Inc.*
800-796-1111

*International Spectrum*
10675 Treena St.
Suite 103
San Diego, CA 92131

*Internet*
P.O. Box 713
Mt. Morris, IL 61054-9965

*KidSoft Magazine*
718 University Ave. #112
Los Gatos, CA 95030-9958
800-354-6150

*LAN Magazine*
P.O. Box 50047
Boulder, CO 80321-0047

*MicroComputer Journal*
Classified Dept. 76
N. Broadway
Hicksville, NY 11801

*MicroTimes Magazine*
5951 Canning St.
Oakland, CA 94609

*MUSICIAN'S Friend*
P.O. Box 4520
Medford, OR 97501

*National Association of Desktop Publishers*
P.O. Box 11668
Riverton, NJ 08076-7268

*Nuts & Volts*
430 Princeland Ct.
Corona, CA 91719-1343

*Open Computing*
P.O. Box 570
Hightstown, NJ 08520-9328

*PC Computing*
P.O. Box 50253
Boulder, CO 80321-0253

*PC Magazine*
P.O. Box 51524
Boulder, CO 80321-1524

*PC Novice*
P.O. Box 85380
Lincoln, NE 68501-9807

*PC Today*
P.O. Box 85380
Lincoln, NE 68501-5380

*PC World Magazine*
P.O. Box 51833
Boulder, CO 80321-1833

*PRE-*
8340 Mission Rd. #106
Prairie Village, KS 66206

*Publish!*
P.O. Box 51966
Boulder, CO 80321-1966

*Repair, Service & Remarketing News*
P.O. Box 670
Joplin, MO 64802-0670
417-781-9317 (voice)
417-781-0427 (fax)

*Video Magazine*
Box 56293
Boulder, CO 80322-6293
800-365-1008

*Videomaker Magazine*
P.O. Box 469026
Escondido, CA 92046
800-334-8152

*Virtual City*
P.O. Box 3007
Livingston, NJ 07039-9922

*Virtual Reality*
P.O. Box 7703
San Francisco, CA 94120
415-905-2563

*Voice Processing Magazine*
P.O. Box 6016
Duluth, MN 55806-9797

*Windows Magazine*
P.O. Box 58649
Boulder, CO 80322-8649

## Free magazines to qualified subscribers

The magazines listed in this section as being free are sent only to qualified subscribers. The subscription price of a magazine usually does not come anywhere near
covering the costs of publication, mailing, distribution, and other costs. Most magazines depend almost entirely on advertisers for their existence. The more subscribers that a magazine has, the more it can charge for its ads. Naturally they can
attract a lot more subscribers if the magazine is free.

*PC Week* and *InfoWorld* are excellent magazines. They are so popular that the
publishers have to limit the number of subscribers. They cannot possibly accommo-
date all of the people who have applied. They have set standards that have to be met
in order to qualify. They do not publish the standards, so even if you answer all of the
questions on the application, you still might not qualify.

To get a free subscription, you must write to the magazine for a qualifying application form. The form will ask several questions, such as how you are involved with
computers, the company you work for, whether you have any influence in purchas-
ing the computer products listed in the magazines, and several other questions that
give them a very good profile of their readers.

One way to qualify for most of these free magazines is to become a consultant.
There are very few rules and regulations as to who can call themselves a consultant.
(You should be particularly aware of this fact if you decide to hire a consultant.)

The following list of magazines is not nearly complete. There are hundreds of trade magazines that are sent free to qualified subscribers. The Cahners Company alone publishes 32 different trade magazines. Many of the trade magazines are highly technical and narrowly specialized.

*Advanced Imaging*
445 Broad Hollow Rd.
Melville, NY 11747-4722

*Automatic I.D. News*
P.O. Box 6158
Duluth, MN 55806-9870

*AV Video Production
& Presentation Tech.*
701 Westchester Ave.
White Plains, NY 10604
(914) 328-9157

*Beyond Computing, An IBM
Magazine*
1133 Westchester Ave.
White Plains, NY 10604

*California Business*
P.O. Box 70735
Pasadena, CA 91117-9947

*CD-ROM News Extra*
462 Danbury Road
Wilton, CT 06897-2126

*Client/Server Computing*
Sentry Publishing Company
1900 West Park Dr.
Westborough, MA 01581-3907

*Communications News*
2504 Tamiami Trail North
Nokomis, FL 34275
813-966-9521

*Communications Week*
P.O. Box 2070
Manhasset, NY 11030

*Computer Design*
Box 3466
Tulsa, OK 74101-3466

*Computer Products*
P.O. Box 14000
Dover, NJ 07801-9990

*Computer Reseller News*
P.O. Box 2040
Manhasset, NY 11030

*Computer Systems News*
600 Community Dr.
Manhasset, NY 11030

*Computer Tech. Review*
924 Westwood Blvd. #65
Los Angeles, CA 90024

*Computer Telephony*
P.O. Box 40706
Nashville, TN 37204-9919
800-677-3435

*Data Communications*
P.O. Box 477
Hightstown, NJ 08520-9362

*Datamation*
P.O. Box 7530
Highlands Ranch, CO 80163-9130

*Designfax*
P.O. Box 1151
Skokie, IL 60076-9917

*Document Management & Windows
Imaging*
8711 E. Pinnacle Peak Rd., #249
Scottsdale, AZ 85255

*EE Product News*
P.O. Box 12982
Overland Park, KS 66212

*Elect. Publish & Print*
650 S. Clark St.
Chicago, IL 60605-9960

*Electronic Design*
P.O. Box 985007
Cleveland, OH 44198-5007

*Electronic Manufacturing*
P.O. Box 159
Libertyville, IL 60048

*Electronic Publishing*
P.O. Box 3493
Tulsa, OK 74101-9640

*Electronics*
P.O. Box 985061
Cleveland, OH 44198

*Enterprise Systems Journal*
P.O. Box 3051
Northbrook, IL 60065-3051

*Federal Computer Week*
P.O. Box 602
Winchester, MA 01890

*ID Systems*
P.O. Box 874
Peterborough, NH 03458

*Identification Journal*
2640 N. Halsted St.
Chicago, IL 60614-9962

*Imaging Business*
P.O. Box 5360
Pittsfield, MA 01203-9788

*InfoText, Interactive Telephone
Applications*
Advanstar Communications
P.O. Box 6490
Duluth, MN 55806-6490

*InfoWorld*
P.O. Box 1172
Skokie, IL 60076

*InterActivity Media Magazine*
P.O. Box 1174
Skokie, IL 60076-8174

*Lan Times*
122 East, 1700 South
Provo, UT 84606

*Lasers & Optronics*
301 Gibraltar Dr.
Morris Plains, NJ 07950

*Machine Design*
P.O. Box 985015
Cleveland, OH 44198-5015

*Managing Office Technology*
1100 Superior Ave.
Cleveland, OH 44197-8092

*Manufacturing Systems*
P.O. Box 3008
Wheaton, IL 60189-9972

*Medical Equip. Designer*
29100 Aurora Rd., #200
Cleveland, OH 44139

*Micro Publishing News*
21150 Hawthorne Blvd. #104
Torrance, CA 90503

*Mini-Micro Systems*
P.O. Box 5051
Denver, CO 80217-9872

*Mobile Office*
Subscription Department
P.O. Box 57268
Boulder, CO 80323-7268

*Modern Office Technology*
1100 Superior Ave.
Cleveland, OH 44197-8032

*MrCDRom*
MAXMEDIA DISTRIBUTING, INC.
P.O. Box 1087
Winter Garden, FL 34787

*Multimedia Merchandising*
P.O. Box 99400
Collingswood, NJ 08108-9972
609-488-6188 (fax)

*Network Computing*
P.O. Box 1095
Skokie, IL 60076-9662

*Network World*
161 Worcester Rd.
Framingham, MA 01701
508-875-6400

*New Media Magazine*
P.O. Box 1771
Riverton, NJ 08077-7331
415-573-5170

*NewMedia*
P.O. Box 10639
Riverton, NJ 08076-0639

*Office Systems*
P.O. Box 3116
Woburn, MA 01888-9878

*Office Systems Dealer*
P.O. Box 2281
Woburn, MA 01888-9873

*PC Week*
P.O. Box 1770
Riverton, NJ 08077-7370

*Photo Business*
1515 Broadway
New York, NY 10036

*Photo Lab Management*
P.O. Box 1700
Santa Monica, CA 90406-1700

*Quality*
P.O. Box 3002
Wheaton, IL 60189-9929

*Reseller Management*
Box 601
Morris Plains, NJ 07950

*Robotics World*
6255 Barfield Rd.
Atlanta, GA 30328-9988

*Scientific Computing*
301 Gibraltar Dr.
Morris Plains, NJ 07950

*Software Magazine*
Westborough Office Park

1900 West Park Dr.
Westborough, MA 01581-3907

*Speech Technology Magazine*
CI Publishing
43 Danbury Rd.
Wilton, CT 06897-9729
203-834-1430

*STACKS*
P.O. Box 5031
Brentwood, TN 37024-5031

*Sun Expert*
P.O. Box 5274
Pittsfield, MA 01203-9479

*Surface Mount Technology*
P.O. Box 159
Libertyville, IL 60048

*Telecommunications*
P.O. Box 850949
Braintree, MA 02185

*The Network Journal*
600 Harrison St.
San Francisco, CA 94107
1-800-950-0523

*The Programmer's Shop*
5 Pond Park Rd.
Hingham, MA 02043-9845

## Component and software catalogs

Several companies publish special catalogs for components and software through direct mail. Even IBM has got into the act. You should be aware that most of these companies charge a bit more than those who advertise in the major magazines. However, ads cost a lot of money, so there usually isn't too much information about an advertised product in the major magazines. The direct mail-order companies usually have room in their catalogs to give a fairly good description and lots of information about the product. The catalogs are free. Here are just a few:

MAILER'S Software
970 Calle Negocio
San Clemente, CA 92673

Arlington Computer Products
800-548-5105

Bull Express
800-343-6665

CompuClassics
P.O. Box 10598
Canoga Park, CA 91309

Compute Ability
P.O. Box 17882
Milwaukee, WI 53217

Computers & Music
647 Mission St.
San Francisco, CA 94105

DAMARK
800-729-9000

Data Cal Corp.
800-842-2835

Data Comm Warehouse
800-328-2261

DataCom Mall
800-898-3282

Dell Network & Communications
800-509-3355

DellWare
800-449-3355

Digi-key Corporation
701 Brooks Ave. South
P.O. Box 677
Thief River Falls, MN 56701-0677

Digital PCs Catalog
800-642-4532

DTP direct
800-890-9030

Edmund Scientific Company
101 E. Gloucester Pike
Barrington, NJ 08007-1380

Edutainment Catalog
(Mostly kids software)
800-338-3844

Egghead Software
800-344-4323

ELEK-TEK
800-395-1000

GLOBAL COMPUTER SUPPLIES
2318 East Del Amo Blvd.
Dept. 64
Compton, CA 90220
800-845-6225

Global DataCom
800-440-4832

Global Industrial Equipment
800-645-1232

Hello Direct
(Telephone products)
800-444-3556

IBM PC Direct
800-426-2968

Image Club Graphics
800-387-9193

JDR Microdevices
2233 Samaritan Dr.
San Jose, CA 95124

KidSoft Software Catalog
800-354-6150

MEI/Micro Center
800-634-3478

MicroWarehouse
1720 Oak Street
P.O. Box 3014
Lakewood, NJ 08701-3014

MOMENTUM GRAPHICS, INC.
16290 Shoemaker
Cerritos, CA 90701-2243

Mr. CD-ROM
800-444-6723

Multimedia World
P.O. Box 58690
Boulder, CO 80323-8690

One Network Place
4711 Golf Rd.
Skokie, IL 60076

Paper Catalog
205 Chubb Ave.
Lyndhurst, NJ 07071

Pasternack Enterprises
P.O. 16759
Irvine, CA 92713

PC Connection
6 Mill St.
Marlow, NH 03456

PC Mall
800-555-6255

PCs Compleat
800-385-4522

Personal Computing Tools
90 Industrial Park Rd.
Hingham, MA 02043

Power Up!
800-851-2917

PrePress
11 Mt. Pleasant Ave.
East Hanover, NJ 07936-9925

Presentations
Lakewood Building
50 South Ninth St.
Minneapolis, MN 55402-9973

Processor
800-334-7443

PROJECTIONS
P.O. Business Park Dr.
Branford, CT 06405

QUEBLO
1000 Florida Avenue
Hagerstown, Maryland 21741

Software Labs
100 Corporate Pointe #195
Culver City, CA 90230-7616

Software Spectrum
800-787-1166

Soundware
200 Menlo Oaks Dr.
Melo Park, CA 94025

SOUTH HILLS DATACOMM
760 Beechnut Dr.
Pittsburgh, PA 15205

System ID Warehouse
Barcode Catalog
800-397-9783

T2 Tech Squared
800-890-9375

TENEX Computer Express
56800 Magnetic Drive
Mishawaka, IN 46545

TigerSoftware
800-888-4437

Tools for Exploration
4460 Redwood Highway, Suite 2
San Rafael, CA 4903

United Video & Computer
800-448-3738

UNIXREVIEW
P.O. Box 420035
Palm Coast, FL 32142-0035

## Public-domain and shareware software

There are several companies who provide public-domain, shareware, and low-cost software. They also publish catalogs listing their software. Some might charge a small fee for the catalog.

Computer Discount Warehouse
800-330-4CDW

Computers International
619-630-0055

Industrial Computer Source
800-523-2320

International Software Library
800-992-1992

J&R Computer World
800-221-8180

Jameco Electonic Components
415-592-8097

Micro Star
800-443-6103

MicroCom Systems
408-737-9000

MMI Corporation
800-221-4283

National PD Library
619-941-0925

Numeridex
800-323-7737

PC Plus Consulting
818-891-7930

PC-Sig 1030D
800-245-6717

PrePress Direct
800-443-6600

PsL News (cost $24 year)
800-242-4775

Public Brand Software
800-426-3475

Selective Software
800-423-3556

Shareware Express
800-346-2842

Software Express/Direct
800-331-8192

Softwarehouse
408-748-0461

The Computer Room
703-832-3341

The PC Zone
800-258-2088

Zenith Data Systems
800-952-3099

## Computer books

There are several companies that publish computer books. One of the larger companies is Mc-Graw-Hill. Send orders to McGraw-Hill, Inc., Customer Services, P.O. Box 545, Blacklick, OH 43004-0545 (phone 1-800-722-4726, fax 1-614-755-5645). Another good source for computer books is Osborne/McGraw-Hill (800-227-0900). Call them for a current catalog listing of the many books that they publish. I admit that I am a bit prejudiced, but I recommend them highly.

# 18
# Troubleshooting and repairing your PC

This is one of the longest chapters in this book, but I must tell you that you might not be able to find the answer to your problems in this chapter. There are 1001 things that can go wrong in a computer, in both hardware and software. This chapter could be 10 times as long and still not cover every possible problem. However, this chapter will cover most of the major problems that you might experience.

When speaking of troubleshooting, most people think of hardware problems. However, I have had far more trouble with software problems than with hardware. Software problems can be even more difficult to solve than hardware problems.

Windows 95 can help solve some problems. When I built my 200MHz Pentium Pro, rather than buy all new components, I just upgraded my old 60MHz Pentium. I had two hard disks in the unit: a Maxtor 540MB IDE and a 1.05GB Seagate SCSI. When I attached all of the components to the Pentium Pro motherboard on the bench top, they all worked perfectly. However, when I installed the components in the case and tried to boot up, the Windows 95 screen came up and froze.

I rechecked all of my cable connections, made sure that the boards were seated, then tried again to boot up. Again, it got as far as the Windows 95 screen, then froze. I turned off the power and, this time, pressed F8 as it was booting up. Out of the options that came up, I chose number 5, Step-by-step confirmation. This displays each line of the CONFIG.SYS and asks whether you want to load it or not. When it got to the line that loaded my SCSI driver, the system hung up again. So I knew that it must be either my Toshiba CD-ROM or my Seagate hard drive.

I disconnected them both and the system booted perfectly. I then reconnected the CD-ROM and it booted perfectly. I then switched the connector from the CD-ROM to the hard disk, and it hung again. So evidently, something happened to the hard disk during the time I disconnected it on the bench and installed it in the case.

Of course I was disappointed. I had paid over $700 for this SCSI drive a couple of years ago. I wasn't too concerned about the data on the drive because I had it all backed up on the Maxtor IDE drive. That is the beauty of having at least two large hard drives.

I called the Seagate customer service center at 800-468-3472 and was pleasantly surprised to learn that I had a 5-year guarantee on this drive. All I had to do was send it in, and they would either repair or replace it. A couple of weeks later, they sent me a new drive. Of course, because it was a different drive, none of my data was on it. There was no note or indication as to what the problem had been.

Finding the cause of the problem is the first step in fixing it. There are several hardware and software diagnostic tools available that can help you find and fix the problems. A few of them will be discussed.

# Computer basics

Troubleshooting will be a little easier if you know just a little of the electronic basics. Computers are possible because of electricity. Under the control of software and hardware, small electric on/off signal voltages are formed when we type from the keyboard or when data is read from a disk or other means of input. This voltage is used to turn transistors on and off to perform various tasks.

An electric charge is formed when there is an imbalance or an excess amount of electrons at one pole. The excess electrons will flow through whatever path they can find to get to the other pole. It is much like water flowing downhill to find its level.

Most electric or electronic paths have varying amounts of resistance so that work or heat is created when the electrons pass through them. For example, if a flashlight is turned on, electrons will pass through the bulb, which has a resistive filament. The heat generated by the electrons passing through the bulb will cause the filament to glow white hot and create light. If the light is left on for a period of time, the excess electrons from the negative pole of the battery will pass through the bulb to the positive pole of the battery. Electrons will continue to flow until the amount of electrons at the negative and positive poles are equal. At this time, there will be a perfect balance and the battery will be dead.

A computer is made up of circuits and boards that have resistors, capacitors, inductors, transistors, motors, and many other components. These components perform a useful function when electricity passes through them. The circuits are designed so that the paths of the electric currents are divided, controlled, and shunted to do the work that we want done. The transistors and other components can force the electrons to go to the memory, a disk drive, the printer, or wherever the software and hardware directs it to go.

If an electronic circuit is designed properly, it should last several lifetimes. Unlike an electron tube, which has filaments that burn out, there is nothing in a semiconductor or transistor to wear out. Occasionally, however, too many electrons might find their way through a weakened component and cause it to heat up and burn out. Also, for some reason, the electrons might be shunted through a path or component where it shouldn't go. This might cause an intermittent, partial, or complete failure.

# Electrostatic voltage

Before you touch any electronic component or handle them, you should ground yourself and discharge any electrostatic voltage that might have built up on your body. It is possible for a person to build up a charge of 4000 volts or more of electrostatic voltage. If you walk across a carpet and then touch a brass doorknob you may see a spark fly and get a painful shock.

If you should touch a fragile electronic component, this high voltage can be discharged through the component. It might weaken the component or possibly ruin it. Most electronic assembly lines have the workers wear a ground strap whenever they are working with any electrostatic discharge sensitive components. You can discharge yourself by touching an unpainted metal part of the case of a computer or other device that is plugged into a wall socket. The computer or other grounding device does not have to be turned on for you to discharge yourself.

# Document the problem, write it down

The chances are that, if a computer is going to break down, it will do it so at the most inopportune time. This is one of the basic tenets of Murphy's immutable and inflexible laws.

If your computer breaks down, try not to panic. Ranting, cussing, or crying might make you feel better, but it won't solve the problem. Instead, get out a pad and pencil and write down everything as it happens. It is very easy to forget. Write down all the particulars, how the cables were plugged in, the software that was running, and anything that might be pertinent. You might get error messages on your screen. Use the PrtSc (for Print Screen) key to try to print out the messages.

If you can't solve the problem, you might have to call someone or your vendor for help. If you have all the written information before you, it will help. Try to call while at your computer, if possible, as it is acting up. If it is a software problem, have your serial number handy. Most organizations ask for that before anything else.

# Instruments and tools

For high levels of troubleshooting, a person would need some sophisticated tools and expensive instruments to do a thorough analysis of a system. You would need a good high-frequency oscilloscope, a digital analyzer, a logic probe, and several other expensive pieces of gear. You would also need a test bench with a spare power supply, disk drives, and plug-in boards.

It would be very helpful to have a diagnostic card, such as the POST-PROBE or the Ultra-X, and several of the diagnostic and utility software programs such as those discussed later in this chapter.

It would be helpful to have a known good computer with some empty slots so that you could plug in suspect boards and test them.

You would also need a voltohmmeter, some clip leads, a pair of side cutter dikes, a pair of long-nose pliers, various screwdrivers, nut drivers, a soldering iron, and solder.

You would need a good workbench with plenty of light over the bench and a flashlight or a small light to light up the dark places in the computer case.

Besides the expensive tools and instruments needed for high-level troubleshooting and repair, you would need quite a lot of training and experience.

Fortunately, we don't need the expensive and sophisticated tools and instruments for most of our computer problems. Just a few simple tools and a little common sense are all that is needed for the majority of the problems. Here are some tools that you should have around. It is good to have these tools even if you never have any computer problems:

- You should have a pad and pen near your computer so that you can write down all of the things that happen if you have a problem.
- You should have several sizes and types of screwdrivers. A couple of them should be magnetic for picking up and starting small screws. You can buy magnetic screwdrivers, or you can make one yourself. Just take a strong magnet and rub it on the blade of the screwdriver a few times. The magnets on cabinet doors will do, or you can use the voice coil magnet of a loudspeaker. Be very careful with any magnet around your floppy diskettes. It can erase them.
- You should also have a small screwdriver with a bent tip that can be used to pry up ICs. Some of the larger ICs are very difficult to remove. One of the blank fillers for the slots on the back panel of the computer also makes a good prying tool.
- You should have a couple pairs of pliers. You should have at least one pair of long-nose pliers.
- You should have a set of nutdrivers. Many of the screws have slotted heads for screwdrivers as well as hexagonal heads for nutdrivers. Using a nutdriver is usually much easier to use than a screwdriver.
- You might need a pair of side cutter dikes for clipping leads of components and cutting wire. You might buy a pair of cutters that also have wire strippers.
- By all means, buy a voltohmmeter. There are dozens of uses for a voltohmmeter. They can be used to check for the wiring continuity in your cables, phone lines, switches, etc. You can also use a voltohmmeter to check for the proper voltages in your computer. There are only two voltages to check for: 12 volts and 5 volts. The newer DX4 and Pentium 90, 100, and 120MHz CPUs require 3.3 volts, but usually a voltage regulator on the motherboard or on the CPU socket reduces the 5 volt supply to the required 3.3 volts. You can buy a relatively inexpensive voltohmmeter at any of the Radio Shack stores or at an electronic store.
- You will need a soldering iron and some solder. You shouldn't have to do much soldering, but you never know when you might need to repair a cable or do some other minor job.
- You should also have several clip leads. Clip leads are insulated wires with alligator clips on each end. You can use them to extend a cable, for shorting out two pins, or for hundreds of other uses. You can buy them at the local Radio Shack or electronic store.
- You need a flashlight for looking into the dark places inside the computer or at the cable connections behind the computer.

The chances are very slim that you will ever need these tools unless you are in the repair business. Even then, there will be very few times when you will have to use some of them, especially if you are working on a Pentium Pro system. Still it is nice to have them available if you ever do need them.

# Solving common problems

For many of the common problems, you won't need a lot of test gear. Often a problem can be solved by using your five senses: sight, hearing, smell, touch, and taste. Actually we won't be using our taste very often.

*Eyes*—If we look closely, we can see a cable that is not plugged in properly, a board that is not completely seated, a switch or jumper that is not set properly, and many other obvious things, such as smoke.

*Ears*—We can use our ears for any unusual sounds. Ordinarily, those little electrons don't make any noise as they move through your computer at about two thirds the speed of light. The only sound from your computer should be the noise of your drive motors and the fan in the power supply.

*Smell*—If you have ever smelled a burned resistor or a capacitor, you will never forget it. If you smell something very unusual, try to locate where it is coming from.

*Touch*—If you touch the components and some seem to be unusually hot, it could be the cause of your problem. Except for the insides of your power supply, there should not be any voltage above 12 volts in your computer, so it should be safe to touch the components, even when the power is on. Before touching a component, be sure that you have discharged yourself of any electrostatic voltage.

# The number one cause of problems

If you have added something to your computer or done some sort of repair and the computer doesn't work, something might not have been plugged in correctly or some minor error was made in the installations. If you have added a component, remove it to see if the computer works without it. Never install more than one item at a time. Install an item, then check to see if it works, then install the next one.

By far, the greatest problem in assembling a unit, adding something to a computer, or installing software is not following the instructions. Quite often, it is not necessarily the fault of the person trying to follow the instructions. I am a member of Mensa and have worked in the electronic industry for over 30 years. However, sometimes, I have great difficulty in trying to decipher and follow the instructions in some manuals. Sometimes a very critical instruction, or piece of information, might be inconspicuously buried in the middle of a 500-page manual.

# The importance of documentation

You should have some sort of documentation or manuals for all of your computer components and peripherals. You should have a written record of the switch and jumper settings of each of your boards. It is also very important that you have the drive type and the CMOS information of your hard disk drives written down with your records or on a special floppy disk. If, for some reason, your system fails, you might not be able to access your hard drive and its data if you don't know the drive type listed in your CMOS configuration. You should know what components are inside your computer and how they are configured. The Plug-and-Play components now make it a lot easier, but there are still a lot of items that do not conform to the PnP specifications.

Norton Utilities lets you make a Rescue disk that has a copy of your CMOS, boot record, partition tables, AUTOEXEC.BAT, and CONFIG.SYS. This disk is bootable, so it can be used any time that you might lose your CMOS or any of the other vital information. PC Tools will also let you make an Emergency disk similar to the Norton Rescue disk.

# What to do if it is completely dead

There are several software diagnostic programs. They are great in many cases; however, if the computer is completely dead, the software won't do you any good.

If your computer is completely dead, the first thing to do is to check the power outlet. If you don't have a voltmeter, plug a lamp into the same socket and see if it lights. Check your power cord. Check the switch on the computer. Check the fan in the power supply. Is it turning? The power supply is one of the major components that frequently becomes defective. If the fan is not turning, the power supply might be defective. However, the fan might be operating, even though the power supply is defective. Do any of the panel lights come on when you try to boot up? Does the hard disk motor spin up?

If there is a short anywhere in the system, the power supply will not come on. The fan won't turn, and none of the drives will come on. The power supply has built-in short circuit protection that shuts everything down when the output is shorted. The power supply has four or more cables for the various drives. Unplug the drives one at a time and try the system. If the system works after a drive is unplugged, then you have found the problem. (I hate to say this, but I am pretty sure that one of Murphy's laws dictates that a problem will never be this easy to solve.)

If a SIMM or memory chip is not completely seated, the computer might not boot up. You might not get any kind of error message or warning.

You can check any of the cables from the power supply with a voltohmmeter. The power supply will not work unless it has a load, so have at least one disk drive plugged in. There should be +12 V between the yellow and black wires and +5 V between the red and black. If there is no voltage, then you probably have a defective power supply.

If you hear the fan motor and the panel lights come on but the monitor is dark, check the monitor's power cord, the adapter cable, and the adapter. The monitor also has fuses, but they are usually inside the monitor case. Check the documentation that came with your monitor. You should also check the monitor's brightness and contrast controls. If you have just installed the monitor, check the motherboard or adapter for any switches or jumpers that should be set. Check the documentation of your adapter board. You should also check your CMOS setup to make sure that the BIOS knows what type of monitor you have.

Remove all of the boards except for the monitor adapter and disk controller. Also disconnect all peripherals. If the system works, then add the boards back until it stops. Be sure to turn off the power each time you add or remove a board or any cable. If you have spare boards, swap them out with suspected boards in your system.

# CONFIG.SYS and AUTOEXEC.BAT

In the DOS era, you could see your AUTOEXEC.BAT working during bootup. In Windows 95, it is now usually hidden, but it is still working just as it did before. If you have just added a new piece of software and your system doesn't work or it doesn't work the way it should, check your AUTOEXEC.BAT and CONFIG.SYS files. Many programs change these files as they are being installed. These files might have commands and statements that conflict with your new software or system. I try out a lot of different software and systems. I have had problems where a statement or command was left in the AUTOEXEC.BAT or CONFIG.SYS file from a system no longer being used. It might ask the computer to perform a command that is not there. It will go off in never-never land and keep trying to find the command or file. You will usually have to reboot to get out.

You might get an error message that says, Unrecognized command in CONFIG.SYS. It might then have an additional message: Bad or missing file, driver, or path. You could have a misspelled word in the CONFIG.SYS file, or you might have left out a back slash or forward slash. It is quite easy to type in the wrong slash, such as a / instead of a \. The structure of CONFIG.SYS is rather strict and doesn't provide much room for error. You can use the EDIT command to change, add to, or delete portions of your AUTOEXEC.BAT or CONFIG.SYS files. Whenever you make a change to them, always keep the old one as a backup. You can rename them with the DOS REN command. You can call the old files, CONFIG.OLD, AUTOEXEC.1, or whatever. If your new AUTOEXEC.BAT or CONFIG.SYS doesn't work, you can always go back and rename the old files back to their original names.

If you have a long AUTOEXEC.BAT file that doesn't work, you might try editing out parts of it, then rebooting and retrying it. (Use the DOS EDIT command, which uses ASCII text. Don't use a word processor because it adds symbols and characters that will confuse the system.) You can temporarily change lines in your AUTOEXEC.BAT or CONFIG.SYS files by adding a REM (for *remark*) at the beginning of a line that you don't want to be executed.

By pressing F8 while booting up, DOS 6.2, PC-DOS 7.0, and Windows 95 will let you look at each line of the AUTOEXEC.BAT and CONFIG.SYS files and will ask if you want to load it: yes or no. If you say no to a certain line and the system then works, you have found the problem.

You should always have a "clean" boot disk that has a very lean AUTOEXEC.BAT and CONFIG.SYS on it. There might be times when you don't want any TSRs or anything in your 640K to run a special program. If you have a lot of TSRs or other things in your 640K of memory, you might not be able to run some programs. Use the DOS MEM-MAKER or the IBM PC-DOS 7.0 RAMBOOST program to create more free memory.

# Beep error codes

Every time a computer is turned on, or booted up, it does a power on self test (POST). It checks the RAM, floppy drives, hard disk drives, monitor, printer, keyboard, and other peripherals that you have installed. If everything is okay, it gives a short beep then boots up.

If it does not find a unit or if the unit is not functioning correctly, it will beep and display an error code. It might beep two or more times depending on the error. If the power supply, motherboard, CPU, or possibly some other critical IC is defective it might not beep at all.

You can check the beep system by holding a key down while the system is booting up. You might hear a continuous beep. After the boot is complete, the system might give two short beeps and display the message, Keyboard error. Press F1 to continue.

There are several other beep error codes that are in the system BIOS. Each BIOS manufacturer might use slightly different codes for some of the errors it finds. Some of the beep codes are for fatal errors that cause the system to hang up completely. The beeps will be arranged so that you might get a beep, a pause, another beep, then three beeps close together, or 1-1-3. This code would indicate that there was a failure in the CMOS setup system. One long and two short beeps, accompanied by a POST code of 400, 500, 2400, or 7400, could mean that there is an error in the CMOS RAM, a motherboard switch setting, or defective video card. A 1-1-4 would indicate that there was an error in the BIOS itself. A continuous beep or repeating short beeps could indicate that the power supply or the motherboard had a fault.

# POST codes

The POST codes start with 100 and can go up to 20,000. Ordinarily the codes will not be displayed if there is no problem. If there is a problem, the last two digits of the code will be something other than 00s. The BIOS manufacturers develop their own codes, so there are some slight differences, but most of them are similar to those listed in Table 18-1.

Several companies have developed diagnostic cards or boards that can be plugged into a slot on the motherboard to display the POST codes. If there is a failure in the system, it can tell you immediately what is wrong.

If you have eliminated the possibility of a defective plug-in board or a peripheral, then the problem is probably in your motherboard. If the power supply is okay, you could use a diagnostic card, such as the POST-PROBE from Micro 2000 (818-547-0125), the R.A.C.E.R. II from Ultra-X (800-722-3789), or the RACER II from Microdata (800-539-0123). These three cards are quite similar in the tests that they perform. They can be plugged into a computer that is completely dead except for the power supply, and they will check every chip and component on the motherboard.

Each card has a small digital display that lights up a code for the condition of each component. These cards will work on any ISA or EISA machine, XT, 286, 386, 486, or Pentium.

R.A.C.E.R. is an acronym for *Real-time AT/XT Computer Equipment Repair*. There are several other POST cards on the market, but some of them are not very sophisticated. The Ultra-X R.A.C.E.R. II has several ROMs that can run over 70 diagnostic tests. Besides displaying the test codes on the plug-in board, the progress of the tests can be displayed on a monitor. If there is a failure in one of the tests, a fault tree will be displayed that lists in order which chips might be at fault. In a computer where several chips interact, it is often difficult to determine exactly which chip might be at fault. The Ultra-X can narrow it down to a very few. At the end of the test, a report can be printed out.

**Table 18-1.  The POST codes.**

| Code | Meaning |
|------|---------|
| 101 | Motherboard failure. |
| 109 | Direct Memory Access test error. |
| 121 | Unexpected hardware interrupt occurred. |
| 163 | Time and date not set. |
| 199 | User indicated configuration not correct. |
| 201 | Memory test failure. |
| 301 | Keyboard test failure or a stuck key. |
| 401 | Monochrome display and/or adapter test failure. |
| 432 | Parallel printer not turned on. |
| 501 | Color graphics display and/or adapter test failure. |
| 601 | Diskette drives and/or adapter test failure. |
| 701 | Math coprocessor test error. |
| 901 | Parallel printer adapter test failure. |
| 1101 | Asynchronous communications adapter test failure. |
| 1301 | Game control adapter test failure. |
| 1302 | Joystick test failure. |
| 1401 | Printer test failure. |
| 1701 | Fixed disk drive and/or adapter test failure. |
| 2401 | Enhanced Graphics display and/or adapter test failure. |
| 2501 | Enhanced Graphics display and/or adapter test failure. |

Businesses can lose a lot of money when a computer is down. These diagnostic cards are tools that every professional repair shop and every computer maintenance department should have. It might also be well worth the money for an individual to buy one. If you have to take your computer to a repair shop, at $50 to $100 an hour, the repair could be rather expensive. You will also have to give up some of your time and some trouble just to take the computer in to the shop. If the shop is busy, it might be some time before you get your computer back.

# Diagnostic and utility software

There are several excellent diagnostic software programs available. Some of the utilities and tests are quite similar in some of the programs. Most of them test and report on your system configuration and your system memory. Many of them do a test on your hard drives. Some of them, such as SpinRite and Disk Technician, are primarily designed for hard disk tests and preventive maintenance.

Most BIOS chips have many diagnostic routines and other utilities built-in. These routines allow you to set the time and date, tell the computer what type of hard drive and floppies that are installed, the amount of memory, the wait states, and several other functions. The AMI and DTK BIOS chips have a very comprehensive set of built-in diagnostics. They can allow hard and floppy disk formatting, check speed of rotation of disk drives, do performance testing of hard drives, and perform several other tests.

## MSD command

If you own a copy of MS-DOS 6.0 or later, you have a MSD (Microsoft Diagnostics) command. This utility can be used to search for files or subjects, and it will also give you a wealth of information about your computer. It can show you the IRQs, the memory usage, your AUTOEXEC.BAT and CONFIG.SYS, and many other useful bits of information. You can view the information or have it printed out. Depending on what you have in your computer, it might take up to 20 pages to print it all out.

## Norton Utilities

Norton Utilities from Symantec Corp. (408-253-9600) includes several diagnostic and test programs and essential utilities. One of the programs is Norton Diagnostics (NDIAGS). This tests the memory, CPU, DMA controllers, the real time clock, CMOS, and serial and parallel ports.

Software cannot recognize and test the serial and parallel ports unless you have a loopback plug installed. These are 9- and 25-pin connectors that plug into the serial and parallel sockets. Some of the pins in these connectors are shorted out so that the software can recognize them. Figure 18-1 shows some loopback plugs. A couple of them are shown with the cover removed so that you can see the wire that shorts out a set of pins.

Of course, Norton Utilities has all of the standard utilities, most of which are periodically updated and improved with new releases. Some of the standard utilities are Unerase, Disk Doctor, Disk Test, Format Recover, Directory Sort, System Information, and many others.

**Fig. 18-1** Some loopback plugs for testing serial and parallel ports.

## PC Tools

PC Tools (503-690-8090) from Central Point Software has even more utilities than the Norton Utilities. PC Tools can diagnose and repair disk partitions, boot records, FATs, lost clusters, and other disk problems. It also lets you create an Emergency Disk, which is similar to the Norton Rescue disk. It has a utility that can recover data from a disk that has been erased or reformatted. It has several other data recovery and DOS utilities. It can also be used for hard disk backup. It can also detect well over 1000 different viruses. PC Tools has now been merged with Symantec.

## MicroScope

MicroScope from Micro 2000 (818-547-0125) is an excellent diagnostic software tool. It can test the CPU, IRQs, DMAs, memory, hard disk drives, floppy drives, video adapters, and much more. It can search for network cards and display their I/O and node addresses. It shows IRQ and I/O address. It tests memory and displays available memory space. It displays CMOS contents and will let you run CMOS setup. It can run video tests for memory and character sets. It can do a read, write, and random seek test of the hard drives. It will even allow you to edit sectors of the hard drive. It can be set up to run any or all of the tests continuously. It can be set to halt on an error or to log the error and continue.

## QAPlus/FE

QAPlus/FE from DiagSoft (408-438-8247) is a very sophisticated software program. Among its many functions is the ability to diagnose problems on the disk systems, memory, video, IDE and SCSI drives and interfaces, interrupts, BIOS, and serial and parallel ports. To test the serial and parallel ports, you need loopback plugs. The loopback plugs come free with QAPlus/FE diagnostic software.

If a semiconductor or system is going to fail, it will usually do so within the first 72 hours of use. Many vendors do a burn-in on their products to find any such systems before they are shipped. However, many vendors might not have the time nor the software to properly exercise the units. The QAPlus/FE can perform rigorous and continuous tests on systems for burn-in. If you buy an expensive system or component, it might be well worth the cost of buying a copy of QAPlus/FE just for the burn-in capability. If you find a defective component early, it can usually be sent back to the dealer or replaced at no cost.

## WINCheckIt and CheckIt PRO:Analyst

WINCheckIt from TouchStone (800-531-0450) was discussed in chapter 16 as an essential piece of utility software. It is also very useful as an essential piece of diagnostic software.

TouchStone has been developing diagnostic and utility software for some time. Their first product, CheckIt, was developed several years ago. They then improved it and called it CheckIt PRO. They improved it again, added several new features, and called it CheckIt PRO:Analyst for Windows. It is a comprehensive analysis tool that can be used by ordinary users as well as advanced users. It can collect configuration and performance data, test hardware integrity, evaluate a system to compare performance with other systems, determine upgrade needs, and assess compatibility of hardware and software.

They are constantly improving their products and should have a new one on the market by the time you read this. Call them for the latest version.

## The Troubleshooter

The Troubleshooter from AllMicro (800-653-4933) has its own self-booting operating system that bypasses DOS. It can test the motherboard, run memory tests, test the hard disks and floppy disk drives, check and test the serial and parallel ports, and test the video adapter, keyboard, and mouse. It can identify the system hardware and print out a report. It is a good low-cost software tool.

## WinSleuth Gold Plus

WinSleuth Gold Plus from Dariana Software (714-236-1380) is another good low-cost diagnostic software tool. Dariana has a BBS number for technical support. WinSleuth Gold Plus can check hardware configuration, give you BIOS information and CMOS settings, and perform CPU tests, keyboard tests, and many more tests. It is a very good tool to have in your library.

## WINProbe

WINProbe is now a part of the Quarterdeck Company (800-683-6696). The PC Certify program that comes with WINProbe can save a lot of time and trouble. PC Certify can also be used to test all types of hard drives and floppy drives and the controllers.

Besides the drives, PC Certify does complete diagnostic tests on the whole computer. It tests the memory, serial and parallel ports, BIOS, video adapter, monitor, keyboard, and printer. The tests can be run continuously for as many times as you desire. These tests are ideal for burning in a computer. The PC Certify program will even print out a form for a technician to fill out. The form shows what tests were run and has a space for the technician to verify and sign.

The WINProbe portion also has the following diagnostic utilities:
- Audio for sound tests
- Communications for serial ports
- Floppy Drive RPM test
- Floppy Drive Surface Analysis
- Hard Drive Surface Analysis
- Keyboard tests
- Math Coprocessor and Motherboard CPU function tests
- Mouse driver tests
- Printer cable test
- RAM chip test
- Video mode tests

## First Aid for Windows Users and PC 911

First Aid for Windows Users from CyberMedia (800-721-7824) is a low-cost program that can spot problems, diagnose them, then fix most of them automatically.

For those that it can't fix automatically, it can help you fix them manually. It fixes problems with printing, multimedia, bad INI files, path problems, missing application components, networks, and many others. The software is optimized for several of the well-known brand-name programs, such as Microsoft Office, Word, Excel, Corel Draw, Quicken, Paradox, and many others. In addition, they offer free upgrades to the program that can be downloaded from CompuServe.

PC 911 is a low-cost companion program to First Aid for Windows from Cyber-Media. PC 911 keeps track of all changes made to your PC's set up files. Several times in the past, I have installed programs that automatically changed my AUTOEXEC. BAT and CONFIG.SYS files to where my system would no longer operate. Recently, a program changed my files so that I was not able to use my word processors. It took me a couple of hours to find the problem. PC 911 could have saved me that time. PC 911 can also help you with conflicts in IRQs, DMAs, and other problems when installing multimedia and other cards.

First Aid and PC 911 can be bought separately or you can save about one-third by buying them as a bundle. They are well worth it.

### Which one should you buy

If I could only afford one program, I would be hard pressed to choose one. All of them are good tools. Many of them have a few similar utilities, but there are also different utility features in every one of them. I can't possibly list all of the features of the products here. I suggest that you call each company and ask for literature on their products.

I can't even list all of the diagnostic products that are available. New ones are being developed daily. Check computer magazines for ads and reviews.

# Spares

One of the easiest ways to check a part is to have a good spare handy. If you suspect a board, it is very easy to plug in a known good one. If your computer is critical to your business and you cannot afford any down time, then you should have a few spares handy. I would suggest that you have a spare floppy disk drive, floppy disk controller board, monitor adapter, and spare keyboard. These items are all fairly inexpensive. Depending on how critical your business is and how important your computer is to it, you might even want to have spares of all your components, such as a motherboard, power supply, and all of your plug-in boards.

You might have some very expensive video adapters, VL Bus IDE, PCI bus interfaces, or other boards that can cost hundreds of dollars. However, there are usually some equivalent inexpensive boards for all of the boards in your system. For example, a good PCI IDE interface with caching can cost from $150 to $200 or more. You can buy a simple ISA IDE interface for less than $10. A good high-resolution PCI graphics monitor adapter can cost as much as $500, but you can buy an ISA adapter that doesn't have all of the goodies for about $30. A low-cost board can help pinpoint the problem. If your monitor doesn't light up but it works with a replacement adapter, then you know the probable cause of the problem.

# DOS error messages

Even with Windows 95, you will still have DOS running in the background for many programs. DOS has several error messages if you try to make the computer do something it can't do. However, many of the messages are not very clear. Don't bother looking in the MS-DOS manual for error messages, they are not there. If you are using the IBM PC-DOS and you get an error message, just type HELP *N*, where *N* is the first letter of the error message, and an explanation will pop up.

I have dozens of books on DOS, but few of them make any reference to the DOS error messages. One of the better books I have is *DOS, The New Complete Reference* by Kris Jamsa, published by Osborne-McGraw-Hill (800-227-0900). Another book by Jamsa, *DOS Secrets, Solutions, and Shortcuts*, explains the DOS commands in great detail and the DOS error commands and what to do about them. These reference books should be in your library.

The following sections cover some of the more common DOS error messages.

## Access denied

You might have tried to write on or erase a file that was protected. The file might have been hidden or protected by an *ATTRIB* command. Use the ATTRIB command to change it.

## Bad command or file name or File not found

You might have made a mistake in typing in the command, or the command or file does not reside in the current directory.

## CHKDSK errors

You should run CHKDSK often. Some people put CHKDSK /F in their AUTOEXEC.BAT so that it is run every time the system is booted up. (Disk Technician can do it for you.)

The CHKDSK command might give you an error that says *nnn* lost clusters found in n chains. Convert lost chains to files Y/N. Reinvoke CHKDSK with the /F (for fix) parameter, and the lost clusters will be converted to FILE000*n*.CHK files. These are usually incomplete files. When you delete a file, sometimes portions of it might be left in a sector, or something might have caused an error in the FAT and caused portions of two different files to be written in a single sector or cluster. The files created by CHKDSK /F are usually incomplete. In most cases, they can be deleted. MS-DOS 6.22 and Windows 95 still have CHKDSK, but they also have ScanDisk, which does a better job than CHKDSK.

## General failure reading or writing drive n:, Abort, Retry, Fail

The disk might not be formatted. It is also possible that track 0 on the disk, which stores the FAT, has become defective. It might be possible to restore the disk by using Norton's Disk Doctor (NDD) utility on it.

## Invalid directory

If you do a CD (change directory) command from the root directory, all you have to type is CD NORTON, or any directory you want to change to, and it will change immediately. If you happen to be in the WordPerfect directory and you type CD NOR-TON, it will say that it is an invalid directory. If you are in any directory except the root directory, you have to type CD \NORTON, or whatever directory. If you type CD /NORTON, using the forward slash instead of the back slash, you will get the same error message.

### Non-system disk or disk error.
### Replace and strike any key when ready

You had a nonbootable disk in drive A:.

### Not ready error reading drive A. Abort, Retry, Fail

You might have asked the computer to go to drive A:, and it was not ready or there was no disk in the drive.

## Software error messages

Most software packages have their own error messages. In many cases, the manual will not tell you what the error message means. You will probably have to call the software company to get an answer.

## Glitches

There are times when something might go wrong for no apparent reason and the computer might hang up. Glitches can happen when you are running almost any kind of program. Sometimes you can get out of them with a warm boot (pressing Ctrl, Alt, and Del simultaneously). Other times, you might have to turn off the computer, wait a few seconds, then turn it back on.

You should remember that anything that you are working on is in memory. If you are working on a file that is on your disk, then you still have a copy on the disk; however, if it is something that you have just typed in, when you turn off the computer or reboot, anything in memory is gone forever. It is a good idea to save your data to disk every so often while you are working on it. By all means, try to save your work before rebooting; however, quite often, if the computer hangs up, there is nothing you can do except to grit your teeth and reboot.

## Power supply

The power supply is one of the most frequent causes of problems. Most of the components in your computer are fairly low power and low voltage. The only high voltage in your system is in the power supply, and it is pretty well enclosed. So there is no danger of shock if you open your computer and put your hand inside it. However, you should *never ever* connect or disconnect a board or cable while the power is on. Fragile semiconductors might be destroyed if you do so.

Semiconductors have no moving parts. If the circuits were designed properly, the semiconductors should last indefinitely. Heat is an enemy and can cause semiconductor failure. The fan in the power supply should provide adequate cooling. All of the openings on the back panel that correspond to the slots on the motherboard should have blank fillers. Even the holes on the bottom of the chassis should be covered with tape. This forces the fan to draw air in from the front of the computer, pull it over the boards, and exhaust it through the opening in the power supply case. Nothing should be placed in front of or behind the computer that would restrict air flow.

If you don't hear the fan when you turn on a computer or if the fan isn't running, then the power supply could be defective.

Table 18-2 lists the pin connections and wire colors from the power supply.

### Table 18-2.  Power supply connections.

| Pin | Color | Function |
|-----|-------|----------|
| *Disk drive power supply connections* | | |
| 1 | Yellow | +12 VDC |
| 2 | Black | Ground |
| 3 | Black | Ground |
| 4 | Red | +5 VDC |
| *Power supply connections to the motherboard (P8)* | | |
| 1 | White | Power good |
| 2 | No connection | |
| 3 | Yellow | +12 VDC |
| 4 | Brown | –12 VDC |
| 5 | Black | Ground |
| 6 | Black | Ground |
| *Power supply connections to the motherboard (P9)* | | |
| 1 | Black | Ground |
| 2 | Black | Ground |
| 3 | Blue | –5 VDC |
| 4 | Red | +5 VDC |
| 5 | Red | +5 VDC |
| 6 | Red | +5 VDC |

The 8-bit slotted connectors on the motherboard have 62 contacts: 31 on the A side and 31 on the B side. The black ground wires connect to B1 of each of the eight slots. B3 and B29 have +5 VDC, B5 has –5 VDC, B7 has –12 VDC, and B9 has +12 VDC. These voltages go to the listed pins on each of the eight plug-in slots.

Most of the other contacts on the plug-in slots are for address lines and data input/output lines. They are not often involved in problems.

# Intermittent problems

Intermittent problems can be most frustrating and maddening. They can be very difficult to find.

If you suspect a cable or a connector, try wiggling it to see if the problem goes away or gets worse. I once spent several hours trying to find the cause of a floppy disk problem. It turned out to be a loose wire in the connector. It was just barely touching the contact. A slight vibration could cause the disk drive to become erratic. A wire or cable can be broken and still make contact until it is moved.

You might also try unplugging a cable or a board and plugging it back in. Sometimes the pins might be slightly corroded or not seated properly. Recently I turned on one of my computers that hadn't been used for about a month. I got a message that the FDC (floppy disk controller) had an error. This board also controls my hard disks, so I was a bit concerned. I unplugged the controller board, cleaned the contacts, and plugged the card back in. (The copper contacts on a plug-in board can become corroded. You can clean them with an ordinary pencil eraser.) However, I still got the FDC error message.

I got out another FDC and prepared to plug it in. However, I had to change the setting of a shorting bar on the controller board. On a hunch, I slipped the shorting bar on and off my original controller a few times, then tried the board again. The floppy drives worked perfectly. The shorting bar on the jumper pins had become corroded during the time it was not used.

The contacts of the edge connectors on floppy drives and plug-in boards can also become corroded. Sometimes just unplugging and plugging them back in several times can wipe away the corrosion.

Before unplugging a cable, you might put a stripe on the connector and cable with a marking pen or nail polish so that you can easily see how they should be plugged back in.

You might even have a problem in the contacts of a DIP switch. You might try turning it on and off a few times.

*Caution!!* Again, always write down the positions before touching any switch. Make a diagram of the wires, cables, and switch settings before you disturb them. It is easy to forget how they were plugged in or set before you moved them. You could end up making things worse. Make a pencil mark before turning a knob, variable coil, or capacitor so that it can be returned to the same setting when you find out that it didn't help. Better yet, resist the temptation to reset these types of components. Most were set up using highly sophisticated instruments. They don't usually change enough to cause a problem.

If too much current flows through a chip, it can get hot and fail. It might only fail at certain times when you are running a particular program. If you suspect a chip and it seems to be warmer than it should be, you might try using a hair dryer to heat it up. If it fails due to the extra heat, then you have found the problem. Be careful that you do not heat up a good chip and cause it to fail.

If a component seemed to be too hot, at one time, we could spray a coolant on it, such as Freon. Because of environmental concerns, you might no longer be able to buy Freon. You might try using ice water in a plastic baggie. This will cool it. If the component then works properly, you have found your defect.

Some of the diagnostic software will run a system in an endless loop to try to force the system to fail.

# Serial ports

Conflicts in setting up serial port devices can cause a lot of problems. Like the parallel ports, pins for the serial ports are available on any of the bus plug-in slots.

The serial ports might be available as a group of 10 pins on the motherboard or on a multifunction plug-in board. The serial port can be a male DB25 connector with pins or a male DB9 connector. The original RS232 specification called for 25 lines. However, most systems only use four or five lines, so the DB9 connector with 9 pins is more than sufficient. Many of the mice sold today have the DB9 connector.

The serial ports are most often used for a mouse or other pointing device, modems, fax boards, plotters, scanners, and several other devices. DOS supports four serial ports: COM1, COM2, COM3, and COM4. However, DOS only has two Interrupt Request (IRQ) lines for the serial ports: IRQ4 for COM1 and IRQ3 for COM2. So COM3 and COM4 must share the IRQ lines with COM1 and COM2. You will need special software to permit sharing. They can share because it is not likely that all four IRQ lines would be used at the same time.

If two devices are set for the same COM port, it will cause a serious conflict. Neither device will operate properly. When installing a mouse, modem or fax board, the interface plug-in boards must be configured so that none of the devices use the same port. If you have devices already installed on your system, you might not know which port they are set for.

There are several programs that can help you determine which ports are being used. One of the better ones is a low-cost shareware program called Port Finder. It is available from James McDaniel of mcTRONic Systems (713-462-7687).

# Software problems

I have had a lot of problems with software. Quite often, it is my fault for not taking the time to completely read the manuals and instructions. However, I don't usually have the time to read and study every page in the manual when I install a program.

Many of the programs are getting easier to run. Plug-and-Play will eliminate a lot of problems. However, there will still be lots of software problems that you will probably run into. Many vendors have support programs for their products. If something goes wrong, you can call them.

Some companies charge for their support. Some have installed a 900 telephone number. You are charged a certain fee for the amount of time on the phone. It can cost a lot of money to maintain a support staff.

If you have a software problem, document, or write down, everything that happens. Before you call, try to duplicate the problem, or make it happen again. Carefully read the manual. When you call, it is best to be in front of your computer with it turned on and with the problem on the screen if possible. Before you call, have the serial number of your program handy. The first things they will probably ask for are your name and serial number. If you have bought and registered the program, it will be in their computer.

Most software programs are reasonably bug-free. However, a lot of things can go wrong if the exact instructions and procedures are not followed. In many cases, the exact instructions and procedures are not very explicit. It seems that most software manuals are written by people who know the software very well, but they seem to forget that the person using it for the first time does not know it.

For every major program, there are dozens of books written to help you learn how to use it. Many training programs have been developed to teach people how to use "user friendly" software.

# User groups

There is no way to list all of the possible software or hardware problems. Computers are dumb and very unforgiving. It is very easy to plug a cable in backwards or forget to set a switch. There are thousands of things that can go wrong. Sometimes it can be a combination of both software and hardware. Often there is only one way to do something the right way, but 10,000 ways to do it wrong. Sometimes it is difficult to determine if it is a hardware problem caused by software or vice versa. There is no way that every problem can be addressed.

One of the best ways to find answers is to ask someone who has had the same problem. One of the best places to find those people is at a user group. If at all possible, join one and become friendly with all of the members. They can be one of your best sources of troubleshooting. Most of them have had similar problems and are glad to help. Many local computer magazines list user groups in their area. The nationally distributed *Computer Shopper* alternates with a listing of bulletin boards one month and user groups the next.

Thank you for buying my book. I wish you all the best. I hope all your problems are easy ones.

# Glossary

**access time**—The amount of time it takes to find and read data from a disk or from memory. The average access time for a hard disk is based on the time it takes the head to seek and find the specified track, to lock on to it, and to spin around until the desired sector is beneath the head.

**active partition**—The partition on a hard disk that contains the boot and operating system. A single hard disk can be partitioned into several logical disks, such as drive C:, drive D:, and drive E:. This can be done at the initial formatting of the disk. Only one partition, usually drive C:, can contain the active partition.

**adapter boards or cards**—The plug-in boards needed to drive monitors.

**address**—The numerical value, usually in hexadecimal format, of a particular location in a computer's random-access memory (RAM).

**algorithm**—A step-by-step procedure, scheme, formula, or method used to solve a problem or accomplish a task. It can be a subroutine in a software program.

**aliasing**—The undesirable jagged stair-stepped appearance of lines in some computer graphics. (*See also* antialiasing.)

**allocation units**—DOS takes one or more sectors of a disk and calls it a cluster. It might take one or more clusters and call them an allocation unit.

**alphanumeric**—Data that has both numerals and letters.

**analog**—A term describing a circuit, device, or system that responds to continuously variable parameters. Generated by hardware rather than by software.

**analog-to-digital converter**—A circuit that periodically samples a continuously variable voltage and generates a digital representation of its value, also called an ADC, A-to-D, or A/D converter.

**analyst**—A person who determines the computer needs to accomplish a given task. The job of an analyst is similar to that of a consultant. Note that there are no standard qualifications requirements for either of these jobs. Anyone can call themselves an analyst or a consultant. They should be experts in their field, but might not be.

**ANSI**—An abbreviation for the American National Standards institute. A standard adopted by MS-DOS for cursor positioning. It is used in the ANSI.SYS file for Device drivers. ANSI, in the Windows context, refers to the ANSI character set that Microsoft uses for Windows.

**antialiasing**—Some computer graphics have lines that have jagged or a stair-step edges. Some software and hardware can automatically smooth out or reduce those defects.

**API**—An abbreviation for Application Programming Interface. Generically, a method of accessing or modifying the operating system for a program. In Windows, the API refers to the functions provided to allow applications to open and close windows, read the keyboard, interpret mouse movements, and so on. Programmers call these functions hooks to the operating systems.

**ASCII**—American Standard Code for Information Interchange. Binary numbers from 0 to 127 that represent the upper- and lowercase letters of the alphabet, the numbers 0 to 9, and the several symbols found on a keyboard. A block of eight 0s and 1s is used to represent all of these characters. The first 32 characters, 0 to 31, are reserved for the noncharacter functions of a keyboard, modem, printer, or other device. Number 32, or 0010 0000, represents the space, which is a character. The numeral 1 is represented by the binary number for 49, which is 0011 0001. Text written in ASCII is displayed on the computer screen as standard text. Text written in other systems, such as WordStar, has several other characters added and is very difficult to read. Another 128 character representations was added to the original 128 for graphics and programming purposes.

**ASIC**—An acronym for Application Specific Integrated Circuit.

**assembly language**—A low-level machine language, made up of 0s and 1s.

**asynchronous**—A serial type of communication where one bit is transmitted at a time. The bits are usually sent in blocks of eight.

**AT systems**—AT is Advanced Technology. The 286, 386SX, 386DX, and 486 are all based on the original IBM AT 16-bit bus. Even the mighty Pentium Pro is based on the AT.

**ATM**—Asynchronous Transfer Mode. A high-end, high-speed method of data transfer.

**AUTOEXEC.BAT**—If present, this file is run automatically by DOS after the computer boots up. It is a file that you can configure to suit your own needs. It can load and run certain programs or configure your system.

**AVI**—An abbreviation for Audio Video Interleaved. The Microsoft Application Programming Interface (API) designed to compete with Apple's QuickTime methodology. AVI techniques provide a software synchronization and compression standard for audio and video signals competing with DVI.

**.BAK files**—Any time that you edit or change a file in some of the word processors and other software programs, they will save the original file as a backup and append the extension .BAK to it.

**BASIC**—Beginners All-Purpose Symbolic Instruction Code. A high-level language that was once very popular. There are still many programs and games that use it. BASIC programs usually have a .BAS extension.

**batch**—The batch command can be used to link commands and run them automatically. The batch commands can be made up easily by the user. They all have the extension .BAT.

**baud**—A measurement of the speed or data transfer rate of a communications line between the computer and printer, modem, or another computer.

**benchmark**—A standard type program against which similar programs can be compared.

**bidirectional**—Both directions. Most printers print in both directions, thereby saving the time it takes to return to the other end of a line.

**binary**—Binary numbers are 0s and 1s.

**BIOS**—An acronym for Basic Input Output System. The BIOS is responsible for handling the input output operations.

**BitBlt**—An abbreviation for Bit Block Transfer. An assembly-level function used for copying graphic images in Windows applications from a source to a destination graphic context.

**bitmapped**—The representation of a video image stored in the computer memory. Fonts for alphanumeric characters are usually stored as bitmaps. When the letter *A* is typed, the computer goes to its library and pulls out a preformed *A* and sends it to the monitor. If a different size *A*, or font, is needed, it will require another bitmap set. Graphic images can also be bitmapped. They consume an enormous amount of memory. Newer techniques allow different size and type of fonts to be scaled rather than bitmapped. (*See* typeface.)

**bits**—A contraction of *binary digits*.

**boot or bootstrap**—When a computer is turned on, all of the memory and other internal operators have to be set or configured. A small amount of the program to do this is stored in ROM. Using this, the computer pulls itself up by its bootstraps. A warm boot is sometimes necessary to get the computer out of an endless loop or if it is hung-up for some reason. A warm boot can be done by pressing Ctrl, Alt, and Del simultaneously.

**buffer**—A buffer is usually some discrete amount of memory that is used to hold data. A computer can send data thousands of times faster than a printer or modem can utilize it. The data can be input to a buffer, which can then feed the data into the printer as needed. The computer is then freed to do other tasks.

**bug, debug**—The early computers were made with high-voltage vacuum tubes. It took rooms full of hot tubes to do less than a credit card calculator can do today. One of the large systems went down one day. After several hours of troubleshooting, the technicians found a large bug that had crawled into the high-voltage wiring. It had been electrocuted but had shorted out the whole system. Since that time, any type of trouble in a piece of software or hardware is called a *bug*. To debug is to try to find all of the errors or defects.

**bulletin board system**—Usually a computer with a hard disk that can be accessed by a modem. Software and programs can be uploaded or left on the bulletin board by a caller, or a caller can scan the software that has been left there by others and download any that he or she likes. The BBSs often have help and message services. They are a great source of help for a beginner.

**burst mode**—The bus is taken over and a packet of data is sent as a single unit. During this time, the bus cannot be accessed by other requests until the burst operation is completed. This allows as much as 33MB per second or more to be transmitted over the bus.

**bus**—Wires or circuits that connect a number of devices together. It can also be a system. The configuration of the circuits that connect the 62 pins of the 8 slots together on the motherboard is a bus.

**byte**—Eight bits, or a block of eight 0s and 1s. These 8 bits can be arranged in 256 different ways. This is $2^8$. Therefore, one byte can be made to represent any one of the 256 characters in the ASCII character set.

**cache**—A close-by area of memory that stores frequently used data. Software often uses the same data repeatedly. If the data is stored in a local memory cache, it can save much processing time. The 486 and Pentium have a level 1, or L1, cache built into the CPU. The motherboards also have a level 2, or L2, cache. The Pentium Pro has two 8K L1 caches in the CPU and a very fast nearby L2 cache in the same package, so it doesn't need cache on the motherboard.

**camcorder**—A contraction of *camera* and *recorder*. The term describes a video camera and videocassette recorder combined into a single, handheld unit.

**carriage width**—The width of a typewriter or printer. The two standard widths are 80 and 132 columns.

**CAV**—An abbreviation for Constant Angular Velocity devices, such as computer-hard disks. The hard disk spins at a constant speed no matter which track is being accessed. (*See also* CLV.)

**CCD**—An abbreviation for Charge-Coupled Devices. An integrated circuit consisting of a linear array of semiconductor photoreceptor elements. CCDs are used to create a bitmapped image. Each photoreceptor creates an electrical signal representing the luminance of one pixel. CCDs are primarily used in scanners, color xerographic printers, and video cameras.

**CD**—An abbreviation for *compact disc*. CDs are the original format for distributing compact optical disks for audio reproduction (CDAudio). This early format was jointly developed by Phillips N.V. and Sony Corporation and is described in Phillips N.V.'s Yellow Book. Control of Yellow Book CD-ROMs, such as starting and stopping the drive and file selection with your computer, requires Microsoft's MSCDEX.DRV driver.

**CD-DA**—An abbreviation for Compact Disc-Digital Audio, also called Red Book audio. CD-A requires compatibility with MPC specification 1.0. It enables interleaving of audio with other types of data, so recorded sound can accompany images. The CD-DA format is defined in the International Electrotechnical Commissions' (IEC) Standard BNNI-5-83-095.

**CD+Graphics**—A format in which the subchannel of an audio CD contain graphic images that can be displayed on a computer or a television set.

**CD-I**—An abbreviation for Compact Disc-Interactive. CD-I refers to a class of CDs primarily designed to be viewed on conventional television sets by means of a CD-I player. CD-I players incorporate at least 1MB of memory (RAM), special pointing devices, and remote-control systems. CD-I players also can be used for training and other commercial and industrial applications. CD-I formats are covered by Phillips N.V.'s Green Book specification.

**CD+MIDI**—A format in which the subchannel of an audio CD contains data in standard MIDI file format that can be routed to a MIDI OUT connector and played on external MIDI synthesizers or internally by audio-adapter cards.

**CD-MO**—An abbreviation for Compact-Disc Magneto-Optical. Magneto-optical CDs and CD-ROMs are capable of multiple use because they can be erased and rerecorded. The standards for CD-MOs are incorporated in Phillips N.V.'s Orange Book 1 specification.

**CD-R**—A recordable CD-ROM system.

**CD-ROM**—An acronym for Compact Disc Read-Only Memory. CD-ROMs can incorporate both audio and graphic images as well as text files. Phillips N.V.'s documentation for this standard has a yellow binding, hence the term Yellow Book audio. MPC Specification 1.0 requires multimedia PCs to include a CD-ROM.

**CD-ROM XA**—An abbreviation for CD-ROM Extended Architecture, which was jointly developed by Philip's N.V., Sony Corporation, and Microsoft Corporation in 1989. CD-ROM XA provides storage for audio and other types of data interleaved on a CD-ROM, enabling access simultaneously.

**cell**—A place for a single unit of data in memory, or an address in a spread sheet.

**Centronics parallel port**—A system of 8-bit parallel transmission first used by the Centronics Company. It has become a standard and is the default method of printer output on the IBM.

**character**—A letter, number, or 8-bit piece of data.

**chip**—An integrated circuit, usually made from a silicon wafer. It can be microscopically etched and have thousands of transistors and semiconductors in a very small area.

**CISC**—An acronym for complex instruction set computing. This is the standard type of computer design as opposed to the RISC, or reduced instruction set computers, used in larger systems. It might require as many as six steps for a CISC system to carry out a command. The RISC system might need only two steps to perform a similar function.

**clock**—The operations of a computer are based on very critical timing, so computers use a quartz crystal oscillator to control their internal clocks. The standard frequency for the PC and XT is 4.77 million cycles per second, or million Hertz. The 486 CPUs can operate from 16 to 99MHz.

**cluster**—Each track of a disk is divided into sectors. Two or more sectors can be called a cluster. This term has been replaced by the term allocation units. An allocation unit can be one or more sectors. (*See also* allocation unit.)

**CLV**—Constant Linear Velocity, such as the technology used in CD-ROM drives. The spindle motor speeds up or slows down depending on area of disc that is being read. A portion of a track at a 2" diameter of the disc is much shorter than one at 3". So an inner track would go by much quicker than the outer track. Complex electronics constantly controls the speed of the motor so that all portions of the track is read at the same speed.

**COLD**—An acronym for Computer Output to Laser Disk. A system using recordable CD-ROM or other optical disk technology that stores and indexes data on CD-ROM discs, optical disks, or other media as an alternative to paper printouts for archiving and backup.

**COM**—Usually refers to serial ports COM1 or COM2. These ports are used for serial printers, modems, a mouse, plotters, and other serial devices.

**.COM**— A .COM or .EXE extension on the end of a filename indicates that it is a program that can run commands to execute programs.

**COMMAND.COM**—An essential file that must be present to boot and start the computer.

**COMDEX**—Computer Dealers Exposition, the nation's largest computer exposition and show, usually held once in the spring in Atlanta and in the fall in Las Vegas.

**console**—In the early days, a monitor and keyboard were usually set up at a desk-like console. The term has stuck. A console is a computer. The command COPY CON allows you to use the keyboard as a typewriter. Type COPY CON PRN or COPY CON LPT1 and everything you type will be sent to the printer. At the end of your file, or letter, press Ctrl–Z or F6 to stop sending.

**consultant**—Someone who is supposed to be an expert who can advise and help you determine what your computer needs are. Similar to an analyst. There are no standard requirements or qualifications that must be met. Anyone can call themselves an analyst or consultant.

**conventional memory**—Also called *real memory*. The first 640K of RAM memory, the memory that DOS handles. The memory actually consists of 1MB, but the 384K above the 640K is reserved for system use.

**CPS**—When referring to a printer, the speed that it can print characters per second.

**CPU**—Central Processing Unit, such as the Intel Pentium Pro. The CPU is the brains of the computer system.

**CRT**—A cathode ray tube. The large tube that is the screen of computer monitors and TVs.

**CTI**—Computer Telephone Integration.

**current directory**—The directory of files that is in use at the time.

**cursor**—The blinking spot on the screen that indicates where the next character will be input.

**daisy chain**—The connection of several devices on a SCSI controller. Also a network in which data flows from one receiving device's MIDI Thru port to another receiving device's MIDI In port.

**DAT**—An acronym for Digital Audio Tape. DAT is a process of recording sound in helical bands on a tape cartridge. This process is similar to recording video signals.

**database**—A collection of data, usually related in some way.

**DATE command**—The date will be displayed anytime DATE is typed at the prompt sign.

**daughterboard**—An additional board, such as a modem or extra memory, that is plugged into a board that is plugged into a motherboard.

**default**—A parameter value that exists when hardware is turned on or an application is run.

**digital-to-analog converter**—A circuit that generates a continuously variable representation of a digital signal; also called a DAC or D/A converter.

**DIMM**—An acronym for Dual In-line Memory Module.

**DIN**—An acronym for Deutches Institute fur Normalization. DIN is an organization similar to ANSI that establishes and coordinates standards for Germany. It has become the de facto standards bureau for Europe.

**DIP**—An acronym for dual inline pins that refers to the two rows of pins on the sides of most integrated circuit chips.

**DMA**—Direct Memory Access. Some parts of the computer, such as the disk drives, can exchange data directly with the RAM without having to go through the CPU.

**documentation**—Manuals, instructions, or specifications for a system, hardware, or software.

**dot matrix**—A type of printer that uses a matrix of thin wires or pins to make up the print head. Electronic solenoids push the pins out to form letters out of dots. The dots are made when the pins are pushed against the ribbon and paper.

**double density**—The 5.25" 360K and 3.5" 720K disks are double sided, double density. The 1.2MB and 1.44MB are high density.

**drag-and-drop**—A Windows process whereby an icon representing an object, such as a file, can be moved (dragged) by the mouse to another location, such as a different directory, and placed (dropped) in that location. Visual Basic provides drag-and-drop capabilities for control objects.

**DRAM**—Dynamic Random Access Memory. This is the usual type of memory found in personal computers. It is the least expensive of memory types.

**DSP**—An abbreviation for Digital Signal Processing. Although all synthesized sound involves DSP, the term is usually applied to the creation of electronic, acoustic effects such as reverberation, chorusing, flanging, and panning.

**DSVD**—Digital Simultaneous Voice and Data, a utility on some of the newer modems.

**DTP**—Desktop publishing. A rather loose term that can be applied to a small personal computer and a printer as well as to high-powered sophisticated systems.

**DTV**—The abbreviation for desktop video. The term describing the production of videotape presentations using the multimedia capabilities of personal computers. DTV implies the capability to edit video tapes by using the playback and record functions of VCRs that can be remotely controlled by a computer.

**duplex**—A characteristic of a communications channel that enables data to be transmitted in both directions. Full duplex allows the information to be transmitted in both directions simultaneously. In half duplex, it can be transmitted in both directions, but not at the same time.

**DVI**—An abbreviation for Intel's Digital-Video Interactive standard. DVI simultaneously displays compressed video images and sound files. IBM has adopted the DVI standard for its Ultimedia product line. Microsoft adds DVI capability through its DVMCI extensions.

**echo**—A command that can cause information to be displayed on the screen from a .BAT or other file. Echo can be turned on or off.

**ECP**—Enhanced capability ports. High-speed UART serial ports.

**EDO memory**—Enhanced Data Output memory. DRAM memory that is much faster in the way it processes reads and writes. It is used in most high-speed motherboards.

**EIDE**—Enhanced Integrated Disk Electronics. An interface for connecting hard disks, CD-ROMs, and other devices to the computer.

**EISA**—An abbreviation for Extended Industry Standard Architecture. A bus specification used to interconnect adapter cards employing 32-bit memory addresses or providing multiprocessor capabilities. The EISA standard was declared by a group of PC-compatible hardware suppliers to compete with IBMs Micro Channel Architecture.

**EPP**—Enhanced Parallel Port. A faster parallel port that can be used for external drives or backup devices.

**ergonomics**—The study and science of how the human body can be the most productive in working with machinery. This would include the study of the effects of things like the type of monitor, the type of chair, lighting, and other environmental and physical factors.

**Error Correction Code (ECC)**—A coding system that, in conjunction with an Error Detection Coding scheme, can reconstruct erroneous data to its original value.

**Error Detection Code (EDC)**—A coding system that detect errors in a single byte or in blocks of data. Single-byte errors are caught by parity checkers such as the ones employed in the PC's memory system. Errors in blocks of data are commonly determined by using techniques such as the Cyclic Redundancy Codes (CRC), which is used for data transfer by modem. More sophisticated EDC methods are employed when error correction is required, such as with CD-ROMs.

**.EXE**—A file with this extension indicates that it is an executable file that can run and execute the program. It is similar to the .COM files.

**expansion boards**—Boards that can be plugged into one of the eight slots on the motherboard to add memory or other functions.

**extended memory**—Any RAM memory added to a computer over and above the 640K.

**FAT**—An acronym for the File Allocation Table. This is a table on the disk that DOS uses to keep track of all the parts of a file. A file might be placed in sector 3 of track 1, sectors 5 and 6 of track 10, and sector 4 of track 20. The File Allocation Table keeps track of where they are located and directs the read/record head to those areas when requested to do so.

**field**—In video terminology, one half of a television image. A field consists of either the even or odd lines of a frame. When used in conjunction with computer databases, a field is a single, distinct element of a complete database record.

**firewall**—A method to prevent unauthorized access to a network from an internet. It is a safeguard usually implemented by software.

**fonts**—The different types of print characters, such as Gothic, Courier, Roman, Italic, and others. Each is a collection of unique characters and symbols. A typeface becomes a font when associated with a specific size.

**format**—The process of preparing a disk so that it can have data recorded on it. The format process lays down tracks and sectors so that data can be written anywhere on the disk and recovered easily.

**fragmentation**—If a disk has records that have been changed several times, there are bits of the files on several different tracks and sectors. This slows down writing and reading of the files because the head has to move back and forth to the various tracks. DOS has a DEFRAG command that makes all of the files contiguous. Several of the utility programs, such as Norton Utilities, PC Tools, and others can also do defragmention. It can speed up your disk access time considerably.

**frame rate**—In film or video, the frequency at which single frames are shown, usually equal to 24, 25, or 30 frames per second.

**frequency**—The rate of oscillation, which determines pitch, measured in cycles per second, or Hertz.

**fundamental frequency**—A sound's primary frequency; the first harmonic.

**game port**—An Input/Output (I/O) port for joysticks, trackballs, paddles, and other devices.

**genlock**—A process for synchronizing the video display of a computer to the frame synchronization signal of NTSC, PAL, or SECAM video. This process allows computer-generated graphics to be viewed on a television set or recorded with a

VCR. Genlock capability is required to add computer-generated titling to video productions.

**GIF**—An acronym for Graphic Interchange Format. GIF is the file format (and extension) storing most graphic images in the CompuServe forum libraries.

**gigabyte**—One billion bytes. This will be a common size memory in a very short time.

**glitch**—An unexpected electrical spike or static disturbance that can cause loss of data.

**global**—A character or something that appears throughout an entire document or program. Pertaining to a computer program as a whole. Global variables and constants are accessible to, and can be modified by, program code at the module and procedure level.

**googool**—A very large figure, 1 followed by 100 zeros.

**grayscale**—A description for monochrome (black-and-white) images displayed in various intensities of black. The most common format is an 8-bit grayscale providing 256 shades of gray. Four-bit grayscale images with 64 shades are also used.

**GUI**—An acronym for graphical user interface. It usually makes use of a mouse, icons, and windows such as those used by the Macintosh.

**handshaking**—A protocol or routine between systems, usually the printer and the computer or two modems, to indicate readiness to communicate with each other.

**hardware**—The physical parts that make up a computer system, such as disk drives, keyboards, monitors, etc.

**Hayes-compatible**—Hayes was one of the first modem manufacturers. Like IBM, they created a set of standards that most others have adopted.

**hexadecimal**—A system that uses the base 16. Our binary system is based on 2, and our decimal is based on 10. The hexadecimal goes from 00, 01, 02, 03, 04, 05, 06, 07, 08, 09, 0A, 0B, 0C, 0D, 0E, and 0F. 10 would be 16 decimal, and it starts over so that 20 would be 32 in decimal. Most of the computer's memory locations are in hexadecimal notation.

**hidden files**—The files that do not show up in a normal directory display, such as the DOS files that are necessary to boot a computer. They are hidden so that they will not be accidentally erased. You can use the ATTRIB command to see them.

**high-level language**—A language, such as BASIC, Pascal, or C. These program languages are fairly easy to read and understand.

**HTML**—HyperText Markup Language, a language used on the Internet. It is similar to SGML and is used to code ASCII documents as the format of text and headers.

**Hz**—An abbreviation for Hertz, the fundamental unit of frequency of audio and radio waves. Hertz was previously called cycles per second (cps).

**IC**—Integrated Circuit. The first integrated circuit was the placing of two transistors in a single can early in the 1960s. Then ways were found to put several semiconductors in a package. It was called SSI, or Small Scale Integration. Then came LSI (Large-Scale Integration), then VLSI (Very Large-Scale Integration). Today we have VHSIC (Very High-Scale Integrated Circuits). We have almost run out of descriptive adjectives.

**icon**—In Windows, a small graphic image, usually in color. An icon identifies the application in the Program Manager window when the application is minimized and in other locations in the application chosen by the programmer.

**IDE**—An acronym for Integrated Disk Electronics. A hard disk system with most of the control electronics on the disk. It also includes an interface to connect the hard disk to the computer. IDE is somewhat similar to SCSI.

**interface**—A piece of hardware or a set of rules that allows communications between two systems.

**interlaced**—The method of displaying television signals on conventional TV sets and computer images on video display units. Alternative fields of images, consisting of the even or odd horizontal lines comprising the image, are displayed in succession.

**interleaved**—A method for containing sound and video information in a single file but in separate chunks, so digital images and audio signals can be transferred from a file to the computer's memory without delays incurred by CD-ROM seek operations.

**internal commands**—Those commands that are loaded into memory when DOS boots up.

**interpreter**—A program that translates a high-level language into machine-readable code.

**ISA**—An abbreviation for Industry Standard Architecture. The specification of the connections to plug-in adapter cards with 16-bit memory addressing capability. ISA is the bus structure used in original IBM-compatible computers.

**ISDN**—Integrated Services Network. A standard for telephone communications for digital transmission of voice, data, and images.

**IVR**—Interactive Voice Response used in many automated telephone systems.

**JPEG**—Joint Photographic Experts Group. A specification system for compression of photos and graphics images.

**.JPG**—The file extension for graphic image files stored with JPEG compression.

**jumper**—A small, plastic-enclosed spring clip making an electrical connection between two adjacent square metal pins, usually in the form of a header. Jumpers are used to set device addresses, interrupt levels, and select other optional features of adapter cards. They are also found on motherboards.

**kilobyte**—1000 bytes, or 1K. More exactly, it is 1024 bytes. This is $2^{10}$.

**LAN**—An acronym for Local Area Network where several computers might be tied together or to a central server.

**laser printer**—A type of printer that uses the same type of "engine" used in copy machines. An electronically controlled laser beam sweeps across a drum. The beam leaves a static charge on the drum with an image of the letters or graphics that is to be printed. The charged areas of the drum then pick up toner particles and deposit them on the page. The page is routed through a heat process that fuses the toner particles to the page.

**low-level language**—A machine-level language. Usually in binary digits that would be very difficult for the ordinary person to understand.

**macro**—A series of keystrokes that can be recorded, somewhat like a batch file, then be typed back when one or more keys is pressed. For example, I can type my entire return address with just two keystrokes.

**mainframe**—A large computer that can serve several users. Also called "big iron."

**megabyte**—1,000,000 bytes, or 1MB. More precisely, it is $2^{20}$, or 1,048,576 bytes. It takes a minimum of 20 data lines to address 1MB, a minimum of 24 lines ($2^{24}$) to address 16MB, and a minimum of 25 lines ($2^{25}$) to address 32MB.

**menu**—A list of choices or options. A menu-driven system makes it very easy for beginners to choose what they want to run or do.

**MHz**—Megahertz. A million cycles per second. Older technicians still call it CPS. A few years ago, a committee decided to honor Heinrich Rudolf Hertz (1857-1894) for his early work in electromagnetism. So they changed the cycles per second, CPS, to Hertz or Hz.

**MIDI**—Musical Instrument Digital Interface. A means of communicating musical information among computers and microprocessor-based devices.

**modem**—An acronym for *modulator-demodulator*. A device that allows data to be sent over telephone lines. A modem changes the digital voltages, or modulates them, to an analog voltage while it is being transmitted over the telephone lines. The receiving modem demodulates the signals back to a digital form.

**MPEG**—Motion Pictures Expert Group. A specification system for compression of motion pictures and graphics.

**MTBF**—An acronym for Mean Time Between Failures. An average of the time between failures, often used in describing a hard disk or other component specification.

**multitasking**—The ability of the computer to perform more than one task at a time. Many computers have this capability when used with the proper software.

**multiuser**—A computer that is capable of providing service to more than one user, such as a server for a local area network (LAN).

**nanosecond**—One billionth of a second, abbreviated *ns*. The speed of memory chips is measured in nanoseconds, usually ranging from about 30 to 100. Faster computer clock speeds require memory chips with lower nanosecond response times.

**noninterlaced**—The preferred method of displaying computer images, usually on a multisynchronous video display unit, in which the image is created by displaying consecutive rather than alternate scanning lines.

**NTSC**—National Television Standards Committee of Federal Communications Commission. This is the standard used in the U.S. and a few other countries.

**null modem cable**—A cable with certain pairs of wires crossed over. If the computer sends data from pin 2, the modem can receive it on pin 3. The modem would send data back to the computer from its pin 2 and be received by the computer on pin 3. Several other wires would also be crossed.

**OCR**—Optical Character Recognition. Software that allows scanners to recognize printed characters and convert them to digital characters for computer input.

**oscillator**—Computers must have very accurate timing pulses. They use crystal oscillators to create the precise clock timing signals. They have quartz crystals that vibrate at accurate frequencies when a voltage is applied.

**PAL**—An acronym for Phase-Alternative Line system. PAL is the television transmission standard of Western Europe (except France). PAL displays 625 lines per frame at a rate of 25 frames per second.

**palette**—A Windows data structure defining the colors of a bitmapped image in RGB format.

**parallel**—A system that uses 8 lines to send 8 bits at a time, or one whole byte.

**parity checking**—In the computer memory system, it is an error-detection technique that verifies the integrity of the RAM memory contents. This is the function of the ninth chip in a memory bank. Parity checking systems are also used in other areas, such as verifying the integrity of data transmitted by a modem.

**PCI**—An acronym for Peripheral Component Interconnect. A bus system developed by Intel Corp.

**PCMCIA**—Personal Computer Memory Card International Association. A specification that was originally developed for laptop computers. Most laptops have slots that will accept a large number of available cards.

**Photo CD**—A trademark of the Eastman-Kodak Company for its technology and CDs that provide copies of photographic color images in a format compatible with CD-I and CD-ROM XA drives. Photo CDs are produced from 35-mm film images by licensed photo-finishing facilities. These facilities have equipment that can write to the special Photo CD media.

**plotter**—An X-Y writing device that can be used for charts, graphics, and many other functions that most printers can't do.

**Plug-and-Play (PnP)**—If the system has a BIOS that supports PnP, a board or other device that has been manufactured to the PnP specifications can be attached to the computer, and it will automatically be configured to operate without having to set jumpers for the IRQ or DMA.

**POTS**—An acronym for Plain Old Telephone Service, such as that used by us peons who can't afford ISDN, PBXs, voice mail, and other new telephony technology.

**PowerPC**—An IBM acronym that means Performance Optimization With Enhanced RISC architecture Personal Computer.

**prompt**—The greater-than sign that shows that DOS is waiting for an entry. The PROMPT command can be programmed to display almost anything you want it to. If you place the command PROMPT $P$G in your AUTOEXEC.BAT file it will cause the current drive letter and current directory to be displayed.

**protocol**—The rules and methods by which computers and modems can communicate with each other.

**QIC**—Quarter-Inch Cartridge tape. A width of tape used in tape backup systems.

**RAM**—An acronym for Random Access Memory. This is computer memory that is used to temporarily hold files and data as they are being worked on, changed, or altered. It can be written to and read from. It is volatile memory. Any data stored in it is lost when the power is turned off.

**RGB**—Red, Green, and Blue, the three primary colors that are used in color monitors and TVs. Each color has its own electron gun that shoots streams of electrons to the back of the monitor display and causes it to light up the various colors.

**RISC**—An acronym for Reduced Instruction Set Computing. A design that allows a computer to operate with fewer instructions, which allows it to run much faster.

**ROM**—Read Only Memory. It does not change when the power is turned off. The primary use of ROM is in the system BIOS and on some plug-in boards.

**scalable typeface**—Unlike bitmapped systems where each font has one size and characteristic, scalable systems allows typeface to be shrunk or enlarged to different sizes to meet specific needs. This allows much more flexibility and uses less memory. There are also scalable graphic systems.

**SCSI**—An acronym for small computer system interface, pronounced *scuzzy*. A fast parallel hard disk and interface system developed by Shugart Associates and adopted by the American National Standards Institute (ANSI). The SCSI system allows multiple drives to be connected.

**SECAM**—An acronym for Systeme Couleur avec Memoire. SECAM is the French standard for television transmission (819 horizontal lines per frame displayed at 25 frames per second). SECAM is the standard for most of Eastern Europe, including the former USSR and in African countries where French is the most common second language.

**sector**—A section of a track on a disk or diskette. A sector ordinarily holds 512 bytes. A 360K diskette has 40 tracks per side. Each track is divided into 9 sectors.

**seek**—To locate a specific byte, sector, cluster, record, or chunk within a disk file.

**serial interface**—A connection between devices that transfers information one bit after another.

**Shadow RAM**—A technology provided on some motherboards that allows the option to copy system ROM BIOS into unused portions of high memory. Because RAM is faster than ROM, it can speed up the system somewhat.

**SGML**—Standard Generalized Markup Language. Used on the Internet as a way of coding ASCII documents.

**SIMM**—An acronym for Single Inline Memory Module.

**SMP**—Symmetrical Multiprocessing. The use of two or more CPUs on a motherboard; often used in high-end servers. The Pentium Pro lends itself well to this type of operation.

**source diskette**—When using the command DISKCOPY, the original diskette to be copied from.

**SRAM**—Static RAM. A type of RAM that can be much faster than DRAM. SRAM is made up of actual transistors that are turned on or off and will maintain their state without constant refreshing, such as is needed in DRAM. SRAM is considerably more expensive and requires more space than DRAM.

**SSA**—Serial Storage Architecture. A proposed standard for a high-end, high-speed interface for storage devices.

**streaming**—The technique used to transfer information from a file structure, such as on a disk or CD drive, to the computer's memory. Streaming takes place in groups of bytes less than the entire file's length, usually processed in memory as a background activity.

**superscalar microprocessor**—A microprocessor that is capable or executing more than one instruction per clock cycle. The Pentium and RISC CPUs use superscalar technology to speed up processing.

**SVGA**—A Super Video Graphics Array adapter that can display a resolution of 800 × 600 pixels.

**swapfile**—An area set aside on a hard disk by Windows. If you are running a large program and it happens to point to an address that is not in memory, it will go to the hard disk for it. It will then remove a *page* that is in memory and swap it to the hard disk and bring in to RAM the address that is needed.

**sync**—An abbreviation for synchronization.

**TAPI**—An acronym for Telephone Application Programming Interface.

**target diskette**—When using the DISKCOPY command, the diskette to be copied to.

**technolust**—The desire for ever bigger, faster, and more powerful computers. Some people think it should be classified as a sin and added to the 726 that are presently classified.

**technophobia**—The fear of computers and any new technology. Though similar in some respects, it should not be confused with agoraphobia, claustrophobia, or xenophobia.

**.TGA**—The file extension identifying files created in the format used by Truevision's TARGA series of graphic adapter cards.

**.TIF**—An acronym for Tagged Image Format. TIF is a format for storing black-and-white, grayscale, and color bitmapped images developed by Aldus Corporation.

**time code**—A method of identifying the time an event (such as a single motion picture or video frame) occurs in a format that can be understood by a computer.

**time stamp**—The date and time data attributes applied to a disk file when created or edited. In MIDI files, a time stamp identifies the time that MIDI events (such as Note On or Note Off) should occur, so the correct tempo is maintained.

**TSR**—A acronym for Terminate and Stay Resident. When a program, such as Sidekick, is loaded in memory, it will normally stay there until the computer is booted up again. If several TSR programs are loaded in memory, there might not be enough left to run some programs.

**TTS**—Text to speech. Software and hardware using OCR and artificial speech.

**TUI**—Telephone User Interface.

**TWAIN**—This is an acronym for Technology Without An Interesting Name. TWAIN is the standard for scanners.

**twip**—Window's smallest unit of graphic measurement. A twip is a $20^{th}$ of a point or $1/1440^{th}$ of an inch.

**typeface**—Print or display type of a single design. Typeface is often confused with the term *font*, which means a particular size of a typeface. A typeface might be a member of a typeface or type family, including related designs with attributes such as bold, Roman (regular), italic, compressed, or extended.

**UART**—Universal asynchronous receiver/transmitter. Most data in a computer is an 8-bit parallel form. A UART is an integrated circuit that transforms the parallel data into a serial form for such items as a mouse, modem, plotters, and some printers.

**UMA**—Universal Memory Architecture. A standard for memory.

**UMB**—Upper Memory Block. Refers to the 384K of memory above the first 640K. Sometimes a program will not run if there is not enough free memory in the 640K area. The MEMMAKER command can free up more space in the lower 640K.

**user friendly**—Usually means bigger and more expensive. It should make using the computer easier. Memory is now less expensive, so large programs are being developed to use more memory than ever before.

**user groups**—Usually a club or a group of people who use computers. Often the club will be devoted to users of a certain type of computer. However, in most clubs, anyone is welcome to join.

**vaporware**—Products that are announced, usually with great fanfare, but are not yet ready for market.

**VDT**—Video Display Terminal, or monitor.

**VESA**—An acronym for the Video Electronic Standards Association. VESA is a group of manufacturers and software developers who create standards for graphic and video display adapter cards.

**virtual**—Something that might be essentially present, but not in actual fact. If you have a single disk drive, it will be drive A:, but you also have a virtual drive B:. If you wanted to copy a file from one floppy disk to another on your single drive, you could use the command COPY A:*filename* B:*filename* (*filename* would be the name of the file you wanted to copy).

**virus**—Destructive code that is placed or embedded in a computer program. The virus is usually self-replicating and will often copy itself onto other programs. It might lie dormant for some time, then completely erase a person's hard disk.

**VGA**—A monitor resolution standard of 640 × 480 pixels.

**VLB**—An acronym for VESA Local Bus. A system adopted by the Video Electronics Standards Association.

**volatile**—Refers to memory units such as RAM that lose stored information when power is removed. Nonvolatile memory would be similar to that of ROM or a hard disk.

**VRAM**—Video RAM. A type of special RAM used on video or monitor adapters. The better adapters have more memory so that they can retain full-screen high-resolution images.

**VRML**—Virtual Reality Modeling Language. A language for creating 3D objects.

**wildcard**—A character that substitutes for and allows a match by any character or set of characters in its place, such as the ? and *.

**WORM**—An acronym for Write-Once Read-Many. The WORM system uses a laser to write on a special optical disc. CD-WO (the Write-Once CD standard) is a special type of WORM format.

**WRAM**—Samsung's Window RAM.

**write-back cache**—In the write-back type, upon a cache hit, the cache is updated and the main memory is not affected. Upon a cache miss, the main memory is updated.

**write-through cache**—Upon a cache hit, the cache and the main memory are updated. Upon a cache miss, only the main memory is updated.

**YC**—An encoding method used in S-Video. In YC, the luminance (Y) and chrominance (C) signals are separated. The chrominance signal incorporates both hue and saturation information.

**zoom**—To magnify an image on a video display.

# Index

Illustrations are in **boldface**.

# About the author

Aubrey Pilgrim has been twice listed by *MicroTimes* magazine as one of the most influential leaders in the computer industry due, in large part, to his highly successful series of "Build Your Own . . . and Save a Bundle" books, which have sold more than 200,000 copies. *PC World* has dubbed him the "preeminent guru on the inner workings of computers" for his ability to present technical material in a no-nonsense, accessible fashion the average computer owner can understand. His other books include *Build Your Own Pentium Processor PC, Build Your Own 486/486DX™, Upgrade or Repair Your PC, Build Your Own Multimedia PC,* and *Build Your Own LAN*. You may contact Pilgrim on Prodigy at TJJC38A or on CompuServe at 73740,2561.